In The
FOOTSTEPS

OF

GEORGE

WASHINGTON

A GUIDE TO SITES COMMEMORATING OUR FIRST PRESIDENT

William G. Clotworthy

With a Foreword by

Jack D. Warren, Jr.

The McDonald & Woodward Publishing Company

Blacksburg, Virginia

The McDonald & Woodward Publishing Company
Blacksburg, Virginia 24062

In the Footsteps of George Washington
A Guide to Sites Commemorating Our First President

A McDonald & Woodward Guide to the American Landscape

Printed in the United States of America
By McNaughton & Gunn, Inc., Saline, MI

10 09 08 07 06 05 04 03 02 02   10 9 8 7 6 5 4 3 2 1

First Printing July 2002

Library of Congress Cataloging-in-Publication Data

Clotworthy, William G., 1926-
In the Footsteps of George Washington : a Guide to Sites Commemorating our First President / William G. Clotworthy ; with a foreword by
Jack D. Warren, Jr.
p. cm.
Includes bibliographical references and index.
ISBN 0-939923-79-3 (alk. paper)
1. Washington, George, 1732-1799—Homes and haunts—Guidebooks.
2. Washington, George, 1732-1799—Monuments—Guidebooks. 3. Historic sites—East (U.S.)—Guidebooks. 4. East (U.S.)—Guidebooks. I.
Title.
E312.5 .C58 2002
973.4'1'092—dc21

                                                          2001052149

Contents

For JoAnn

A heart that's true, there are such things
A dream for two, there are such things
Someone to whisper, "Darling, you're my guiding star"
Not caring what you own, but just what you are.

— Song Lyric

Acknowledgments

For assistance in writing and editing this book, I must single out my friend Jack Warren for special thanks. Jack is the author of *The Presidency of George Washington*, published in 2000 by the Mount Vernon Ladies' Association, and has written numerous articles about George Washington, the colonial period, and the founding of the republic. Jack is a dedicated preservationist who secured National Historic Landmark status for George Washingtons Boyhood Home at Ferry Farm and currently serves as a consultant to the George Washington Birthplace National Monument and the George Washington House Project in Barbados. He works frequently with Mount Vernon as well. I'm profoundly grateful to Jack for writing the gracious and informative foreword to this book and for sharing his knowledge of George Washington with me. I could not have asked for a more qualified person to review the book that is, without question, richer for his contribution.

As I have conducted research on books about presidents, I have always appreciated and valued the assistance I have received from the hundreds of devoted park rangers, historians, archivists, docents, senior citizen volunteers and staffers who dedicate their careers to the preservation of presidential homes and sites, thus perpetuating this important part of our heritage. Their knowledge, unfailing courtesy, and cooperation have helped me immeasurably. It has been a privilege to meet and work with these fine Americans and I am honored to salute them for their important and often under-appreciated work.

Thanks to: Ranger Michael Allen, Snee Farm; Reverend Allen, Michael Cresap Museum; Taryn Amkney, Fort Ligonier; Kathryn Anderson, Governor Stephen Hopkins House; Suzy Anderson, Pennsylvania Hospital; Susan Anthon, Carlyle House; Ginger Astle, Perryville, Maryland; Carrie Athay, Tudor Place; Barbara Austen, Fairfield Historical Society; Larry Bacon, John Brown House; Historian Thomas Baker, Guilford Courthouse National Military Park; Joanne Ball, Drake House Museum;

Jan Ballard, Moravian Museum of Bethlehem; Nancy Barksdale, Historic Kenmore; Sally Barley, Maryland Studies Center; Barbara Barton, Gadsbys Tavern Museum; Cricket Bauer, Gadsbys Tavern Museum; Bill Beck, Historic Fredericksburg Foundation; Cary Behrends, The Presidential Museum; Kathy Belanger, Yorktown Victory Center; Gregory Bell, Betsy Ross House; Linda Bishop, John Rutledge House Inn; Elizabeth Bittle, Peter Wentz Farmhouse; Superintendent Paul Blandford, Longfellow National Historic Site; Erica Blumenfeld, Dutchess County Historical Society; David Blythe, Martinsburg-Berkeley County Convention and Visitors Bureau; Dawn Bonner, Mount Vernon; Susan Borchardt, Gunston Hall; George Boudreau, Philadelphia Society for the Preservation of Landmarks; Historian Lee Boyle, Valley Forge National Historical Park; Gail Braxton, The Association for the Preservation of Virginia Antiquities; Susan Brody, Red Lion Inn and Quaker Meeting House; Father Bull, Christ Church, Durham Parish; Margo Burnet, Stenton; Lucy Burns, Historic Morrisville Society; David Byrnes, The Square House; Ray S. Campbell, Jr., Clerk, Caroline County, Virginia; Ranger Vance Campbell, Morristown National Historical Park; Peggy Carlsen, Rockingham State Historic Site; Helle Carter, Shirley Plantation; Nancy Ceperly, Johnson Ferry House; Reverend Gary Charles, Old Presbyterian Meeting House; Sue Chen, Edward McCradys Tavern; Geraldine Chillas, The Questers; Ann Claire, Thomas Jefferson Visitor Center; Superintendent Jane Clark, Fort Necessity National Battlefield; Herbert R. Collins, Curator Emeritus, Smithsonian Institutions; Toni Collins, Brandywine Battlefield Park; Superintendent Sheilah Cooke-Kayser, Boston National Historical Park; Laura Correa, Van Cortlandt House Museum; Ranger Joe Craig, Saratoga National Historical Park; Katherine Craig, Boxwood Hall; Mickey Crowell, Gunston Hall; Bruce Dalleo, New Castle Historic Society; Maxine Dalsemer, Philadelphia Visitors Information; Charlene Daniels, Historical Society of Pawling; Zina Davis, Museum of American Political Life; Ranger Lee Dickinson, Independence National Historical Park; Michael L. Dixon, The Historical Society of Cecil County; Gail Donahue, Woodlawn Plantation; Superintendent John Donahue, Washingtons Birthplace National Monument; Pat Doyle, Georgetown, South Carolina, Historical Society; Ann Marie Duffy, Cliveden; Arlene Duvall, Rising Sun Inn; Landis Eaton, Joseph Stout House; Judy Edelhoff, The National Archives; Fran Eldred, Mrs. Coxe's Tavern; Kim Ellis, Rappahannock Historical Society; Nancy Fastabend, Historic Kenmore; Sylvia Evans, Wilton Museum House; Jean Federico, Office of Historic Alexandria;

Acknowledgments

Historian Paula Felder, Fredericksburg, Virginia; Ranger Kelly Felner, Longfellow National Historic Site; Kristin Ferrante, Bucks County Chamber of Commerce; Sue Fischer-Seeger, Christ Church, Cambridge, Massachusetts; Mrs. Bruce Fisher, Westover; Frank Fisher, The Betsy Ross House; James W. Fletcher, III, Thornton Hill; Betty Fowler, Point Pleasant Battle Monument State Park; Christopher Fox, Fort Ticonderoga; Ned Freer, Bedford County, Pennsylvania; Stacy Freeman, George Washingtons Grist Mill Historical State Park; Melvin Fulton, Saint Pauls Chapel; Ranger Grant Gates, Great Falls Park; Becky Graves, George Washingtons Office Museum; Ranger Peggy Gaul, Colonial National Historical Park; Ranger Jerry Gauman, National Capitol Region; Murrie Gayman, Historic Moland Park; Jack Giblin, Point State Park; Tracy Gillespie, Loudoun Museum; Mary Alice Glover, National Park Service; John Gott, Fauquier County Heritage Society; Andrea Gottschalk, Fairmount Park Commission; Dave Graham, George Washington Masonic National Memorial; Superintendent Robert Grau, Independence National Historic Park; Glen Griffith, Schuyler Mansion; Julie Grimes, Commonwealth of Virginia; Kathy Grosfils, Colonial Williamsburg; Nadja Gutowski, Virginia Historical Society; John and Jan Haitis, The Blue Bell Inn; Charles Hall, Old Exchange and Provost Prison Museum; William Hammack, Museum of American Presidents; John Harrington, Purdy House; Peggy Hartwick, Uwchlan Conservation Trust; Jeremy Harvie, Alexandria, Virginia; Lynne Hastings, Hampton National Historic Site; Historian Richard Hatcher, Fort Sumter National Monument; Elaine Hayes, Mount Gulian; Karen Hedelt, Historic Fredericksburg, Virginia; Kirk Heflin, Chatham; Susan Helman, State of Maryland; Lura Hill, Historic Fredericksburg, Virginia; Tom Hillman, Betsy Ross House; Matthew Hiott, Old Exchange Building and Provost Dungeon; Marilyn Hochmuth, Weems-Botts Museum; Pat Honeyset, Maryland State House; Mayor Al Hopkins, Annapolis, Maryland; Tom Hughes, Washingtons Headquarters, Newburgh; Hazel Hutcherson, Saint Johns Church; Billy Hutson, Old Exchange Building and Provost Dungeon; Stephanie Jackal, Historic Savannah Foundation; Jennifer Jacobs, Litchfield Historic Society; Judy Johnson, Connecticut Historical Society; Connie Jones, DeWint House; Roy Jorgensen, Van Wyck Homestead; Sue Keenan, Buccleuch Mansion; Louise Kelly, Carters Grove Plantation; Jean Kelsey, Connecticut Daughters of the American Revolution; Ellyn Kern, *The President's Journal;* Kathleen Kleinsmith, Mount Vernon; Albert Klyberg, Rhode Island Historical Society; Joyce Knabb, Old Salem; Les Kozerowitz, Norwalk

Public Library; Historian Bob Krick, Chatham; Jim Kurzenberger, Old Dutch Parsonage, Wallace House; Superintendent John Kwiatowski, Springfield Armory; Dr. Joseph D. Kyle, Hanover Tavern; Ranger Steve Lane, Federal Hall National Memorial; Ranger James Laray, George Washington National Memorial; Flo Lehotsky, Sun Inn; Sandy LeMieux, John Brown House; Susan Leppert, Fort Bedford Museum; Bert Lippincott, Newport Historical Society; J. Rodney Little, State of Maryland; Morris Loflin, The Charleston Museum; Don Loprieno, Stony Point Battlefield; Albert R. Lounsbury, Saratoga Springs; Joan E. Lyons, George Washingtons Grist Mill Park; Karen MacInnis, Marblehead Historical Society; Lorraine MacAuley, Madam Brett Homestead; Antoinette Maciolek, Philadelphia Zoo; Jacob Mahaffey, Historian; Ranger Sue Malone, Faneuil Hall; Superintendent John Manson, Boston National Historical Park; Jeffrey Marshall, Heritage Conservancy; Donna McDermott, Valley Forge National Historical Park; Babs Melton, Museum of American Presidents; Barbara Mitchell, Amstel House; JoAnne Mitchell, Alexandria, Virginia Convention and Visitors Association; Ranger Robert Mitchell, Hampton National Historic Site; Sally McDonough, Mount Vernon; Reverend Brian McGurk, Saint Peters Parish Church; Patricia McGurk, Fishkill Historic Society; Stephanie McLellan, River Farm; Dr. Barbara McMillan, Mount Vernon; Dolly McMullan, Kershaw County Chamber of Commerce; Denning McTague, Denning House; Mrs. William R. Miller, National Society of Colonial Dames of America; Superintendent John Mills, Princeton Battlefield State Park; Julia Mosley, Mount Vernon; Jeanne Mozier, Berkeley Springs, West Virginia; Thomas Murphy, Washington, DC Convention and Visitors Association; Jane Murray, Historic Morrisville Society; Richard Muscarello, Putnam County History Department; Donna Nedderman, Touro Synagogue; Barbara Olsen, Dey Mansion; Deborah Olsen, Historic Bartrams Garden; Eric Olsen, Morristown National Historical Park; Joan and Don Panaro, Deshler-Morris House; Alecia Parker, Historic Annapolis Foundation; Pat Patrizio, Washington Crossing Historic Park; Tricia Pearsall, James River Canal; Karen Pena, Knoxs Headquarters; Robert Perry, Mandeville House; Ranger Barbara Perdew, Great Falls Park; Roger Perry, Charles Town Historical Society; Karen Peters, Mount Vernon; Margaret Peters, Virginia Department of Historic Resources; Ranger Don Pfanz, Chatham; Tim Phelps, Peter Wentz Farmhouse; Nancy Piwowar, Drake House Museum; Gail Potter, Webb-Deane-Stevens Museum; Bert Prol, Ringwood State Park; Ann Puckett, Hampton Plantation; Michael Quinn, Mount Vernon; Tammy Radcliff, Berkeley

Acknowledgments

Plantation; Michelle Rashoon, Tryon Palace; Dan Reibel, Old Barracks Museum; Historian Karen Rehm, Colonial National Historical Park; Lynn Reilley, Delaware State Museum; Peter A. Rerig, South Carolina Historical Society; Rector Spencer Rice, Saint Johns Church; William W. Richardson, III, Chelsea Plantation; Diane Rofini, Chester County Historical Society; Richard Romanski, Pennsylvania Historical Society; Leslie Rose, Woodbury Historical Society; Ed Russell, The Old Mansion; John Ryan, Bethlehem, Pennsylvania; David Sala, Artist/ Historian; Patrick Saylor, Colonial Williamsburg; Jennifer Schwav, Great Dismal Swamp; Bob Seabury, Warren Tavern; Katherine Schweriner, Pennypacker Mills; Ellen Scott, Old Fort House Museum; Caroline See, Fort Ashby; George Seghers, George Washington Masonic National Memorial; Ranger Phil Sheridan, Independence National Historical Park; Alice Sheriff, Shaw Mansion; Ranger Lou Sideris, Minute Man National Historical Park; Roseanne Shuttleworth, Fort Cumberland; Reverend Norman Siefferman, Saint Pauls Church; Jessica Silver, Saint Pauls Chapel; Alice Smith, Montgomery County Historical Society; Ida Smith, Hale-Byrnes House; Ken Snodgrass, Morris-Jumel Mansion; Dan Snydacker, Newport Historical Society; Shirley Stalker, Governor Jonathan Trumbull House; Marsha Starkey, Harpers Ferry National Historical Park; Historian Bob Stober, Snee Farm; Pam Stoddard, Kingston Free Library; Gary Stone, Monmouth Battlefield State Park; Martha Stonequist, Saratoga Springs; Robert Storms, Norwich Historic Society; Jeanne Straughan, Washingtons Birthplace National Monument; Bob Study, Pottsgrove Mansion; Harry Kels Swan, Washington Crossing State Park; Stacey A. Swigart, Valley Forge Historical Society; Mary Thompson, Mount Vernon; Ellan Thorson, Ann Arundel Chapter, DAR; Doris Thumm, Colonial Williamsburg; Dennis Tice, Bedford County; Ben Tinsdale, Hope Lodge; Ann Tom, Lee-Fendall House; Christine Townley, Mary Ball Washington Museum; Jane Townsend, New Windsor Cantonment; Ranger Bill Troppman, Valley Forge National Historical Park; DeVonne Trockaya, Pohick Church; Ranger Larry Trombello, Washingtons Birthplace National Monument; Robert Trombetta, Point State Park; Kay Tyler, Sherwood Forest; Greta Tyrrel, Georgia Trust for Historic Preservation; David Vecchioli, Archivist, Morristown National Historical Park; Nina Vogel, Charles Town Historical Society; Priscilla Waggoner, Historic Yellow Springs; Ann Wagner, Montpelier; Betty Warden, Falls Church; Steve Wartenberg, *The Intelligencer-Record;* Shirley Weisburg, Allegany County Visitors Bureau; Jan Westfall, Chatham, New Jersey, Preservation Commission; Tom

Whalen, General Wayne Inn; Frank Wheeler, Georgia Historical Society; John Wright, Washingtons Headquarters, White Plains; Kevin Wright, Steuben House; Ursula Wright, Governor John Langdon House; Kelly Youles, Historic Kenmore; Claire Young, Holcombe-Jimison Farmhouse; Molly Zink, Henry Ford Museum.

The following individuals, agencies, businesses, and institutions kindly provided color photographs and allowed them to be reproduced as plates in this book. For this, I thank Philip Beaurline: 3; Colonial Williamsburg Foundation: 6; Jim Holcomb, National Park Service: 9; Marblehead Historical Society: 13; National Park Service: 1, 10, 12; Natural Bridge of Virginia: 5; The Old Exchange and Provost Dungeon: 14; Barbara Porter, National Park Service: 11; John Rutledge House: 15. The photographs used in plates 2, 4, 7, 8, and 16 were taken by the author. I have provided credits for black and white photographs in the captions to those photographs.

For assistance with editing the manuscript and for completing the maps that make up such an important part of this book, I thank members of the support staff at McDonald & Woodward Publishing Company, especially Carol Boone and Jay McDonald for assistance with the maps and Judy Moore for her extensive and good humored editorial guidance.

Thanks, everyone!

All of the people named above have provided great help in bringing this project to completion, but decisions about the scope and content of the book, and responsibility for the accuracy of information provided here are, I'm afraid, all mine.

Every effort has been made to ensure the accuracy of the information in the book. However, some information — visiting hours, admission fees, area codes or facilities for the disabled — is subject to change. When planning a visit to any of the sites, it would be prudent to call or write the site to obtain up-to-date information.

Foreword

Jack D. Warren, Jr.

In the spring of 1892, workmen at a construction site in Augusta, Georgia, made a curious discovery. Digging on the site of an old stable, they uncovered a marble tombstone and beneath, a small brick burial vault enclosing the remains of a dog. The tombstone had been placed in 1798, although the dog, a greyhound, had died in the summer of 1791. His name was Cornwallis.

Cornwallis — named for the British general who surrendered at Yorktown — was George Washington's canine companion on his 1791 presidential tour of the South. It's not clear whether Cornwallis rode in Washington's carriage or trotted alongside down the thousand miles of rutted dirt roads between Mount Vernon and Augusta. If he went on foot most of the way, as I imagine, he probably died of exhaustion. His master set a terrific pace.

Like many of the stories told about George Washington, there is a touch of fable to this one. The newspaper account of the workmen's discovery was published on April 1, leading some Augustans to regard the whole thing as a hoax. But like the story of the little hatchet and the cherry tree, it embodies a fundamental truth about Washington. The hundreds of places Washington is supposed to have slept actually testify to his inexhaustible energy. To sleep in all of those places — scattered between Maine and Georgia — he had to get to them first. This was no mean feat before turnpikes, railroads, and steamboats revolutionized transportation. And Washington visited more of his own country while in office than any president before the twentieth century. He certainly drove himself hard enough to run a dog to death. Even a greyhound.

Washington left Mount Vernon on his tour of the South on the morning of April 7, 1791. A few miles from home, while he was crossing the Occoquan River on a ferry, his lead horse was startled and went overboard, dragging the rest of the team into deep water. A dozen people jumped in to get the tangled harnesses off and save the horses from drowning. Cornwallis, I imagine, stood on the side of the ferry and barked. Washington slept that night in Dumfries, pressed on early the next morning, stopped for breakfast in Stafford, and reached Fredericksburg — just forty miles from Mount Vernon — at one o'clock.

In the days and weeks that followed, Washington and Cornwallis pushed south to Richmond, Petersburg, and New Bern, North Carolina. President and dog rode down South Carolina's "Long Beach" (now Myrtle Beach) and on to Charleston. They moved on to Savannah, then west to Augusta, where Cornwallis breathed his last. Washington pushed on without him, north through the Carolina backcountry to Virginia. Everywhere he went he was met by cheering crowds and an unprecedented outpouring of patriotic sentiment.

Washington reached Mount Vernon on June 12. His horses, he reported, were "much worn down." He said nothing about himself. He had covered 1,887 miles in sixty-seven days. In doing so he had made the distant federal government — a tiny institution in a great land — seem real to thousands of ordinary Americans. He also set a precedent that the federal government should concern itself with the needs of ordinary citizens in every part of the country. He left behind a deeper attachment to the United States, and scattered reminders — like the curious grave of the faithful Cornwallis — of the personal loyalty he excited in Americans wherever he went.

That loyalty lives on in Bill Clotworthy, who has scoured the eastern United States for sites associated with the life of our first great national hero. This book is the product of those labors. He has found scores of sites, ranging from the great plantation houses of Virginia, the battlefields of the French and Indian War and the Revolution, to the dozens of other places where Washington attended church, spent the night, or held a council of war. He has found places where Washington is said to have planted a tree and even taken a bath. He is carrying on a long tradition. Pilgrims have been making their way to some of those places since the earliest days of the republic. In 1777, pioneering American historian Ebenezer Hazard went out of his way to visit Ferry Farm, the plantation near Fredericksburg, Virginia, where Washington grew up. Although the Revolutionary War was still underway — and its outcome uncertain — Washington had already become the heroic symbol of the American cause and the embodiment of the revolutionary ideal of republican virtue.

Foreword

The patriotic impulse that led Hazard to Washington's childhood home has inspired millions of Americans in the last two centuries. In the first years of the republic, the former British colonies that made up the new nation had little common history and few shared symbols. Washington was the chief symbol of American nationhood. Nearly every site associated with him became a place of veneration.

That so many of these sites are still preserved and accessible to the public is a testament to Washington's enduring historical reputation. Mount Vernon, acquired for the American people in 1858 by the Mount Vernon Ladies' Association, remains one of the most popular historical attractions in the United States. George Washington Birthplace National Monument, the first historic site incorporated into the National Park System, has welcomed visitors since 1932. And as recently as 1996, patriotic Americans joined ranks to prevent commercial development from swallowing up the site of Washington's childhood home, which was recently designated a National Historic Landmark.

Bill Clotworthy has done a remarkably thorough job documenting these and dozens of other places. He has done it the old-fashioned way, by visiting them personally. Yet in the end, he confesses, he cannot document all of the sites associated with the Great Man. There always seems to be one more to discover. Washington leaves him, like the unfortunate Cornwallis, panting beside the road. But historic travelers and armchair tourists could not find a better guidebook or a friendlier, more enthusiastic guide.

Introduction

In today's world of historical revisionism, there are those occasional voices who represent George Washington as an aristocratic figurehead of no particular importance, a second-rate general with bad teeth whose early life and character are represented by apocryphal stories of cherry-tree-chopping and dollar-tossing across the Rappahannock River. In other contemporary accounts, however, a more positive picture emerges. Richard Brookhiser's brilliant *Founding Father: Rediscovering George Washington,* for example, portrays him as a complex, intelligent, audacious leader whose career as farmer, soldier, founder, politician, and statesman — all of which covered forty-five years of embattled decision-making that has been unparalleled in our history — was remarkable. Throughout his decades of service, Washington viewed himself as a simple farmer who, like Cincinnatus, wanted only to return home after fulfilling his duty, disdaining all offers of personal power and aggrandizement (figures 1, 2). In fact, however, he was called to public service time and again and spent most of his life as a military officer, politician, and statesman.

George Washington was, of course, a real person, not merely an image on a dollar bill, the subject of an unfinished portrait hanging on school-room walls across the country, or Abraham Lincoln's partner in selling mattresses or used cars on Presidents' Day (Brookhiser says, "In democracies, vulgarity is a form of honor").[1] After the passage of two centuries we shall never really know him, but a familiarity with the places where he was nurtured, the homes where he lived, the battlefields where he fought, and the buildings where he ate, slept, conferred, and governed may help us to understand him a bit better than otherwise would be possible. The purpose of this book is to identify and briefly describe those places that were a part of Washington's life and that are still extant so that all of us may, if we wish, experience many of the places where

Figure 1. George Washington's place in American history is unique. Here he is shown taking the oath of office as the first President of the United States at Federal Hall, New York City, on April 30, 1789. (Image courtesy of Mount Vernon Ladies' Association)

Figure 2. Mount Vernon was home to George Washington for most of his life, and was the one place with which he identified most strongly and consistently. (Photograph courtesy of Mount Vernon Ladies' Association)

this remarkable life unfolded and where substantial parts of our national character were formed (figures 3, 4).

Fortunately, the American people have come to realize the importance of presidential history, perhaps most obviously expressed through the construction of modern presidential libraries that are stocked with millions of important — and sometimes not-so-important — papers along with museum exhibits and shops selling presidential mementos and educational resources. It was not always so, however. Mount Vernon, the first of our historic presidential homes to be preserved, had fallen into decline by the mid-1800s. Dangerously close to bankruptcy, the property was saved from probable destruction only by the quick action of the Mount Vernon Ladies' Association, organized in 1858. The Ladies' Association bought and refurbished Mount Vernon and continues to administer and maintain the property in all of its colonial glory as one of the premier examples of the preservation of a presidential property, its value as an historical asset, and its use as an educational resource.

There are, of course, many extant sites associated with George Washington — more, in fact, than for any other president — and each of these sites has its own story. As I was working on my earlier book *Homes and Libraries of the Presidents,* my publisher, Jerry McDonald, suggested the idea of *In the Footsteps of George Washington,* a project which would help make it possible to follow Washington's life both chronologically and geographically, a sort of biographical travelogue fleshed out with expanded descriptions of extant sites associated with our first president. It seemed a daunting task, a typical writer's block, but once I forced myself to begin work on the project I found myself involved in a labor of love, respect, and admiration. This book describes some 300 places that are affiliated with Washington's busy and full life — places ranging from his birthplace at Popes Creek, Virginia, through his life as surveyor, military officer, farmer, and politician, to the site of his death and burial at his beloved Mount Vernon. Many of the most hallowed places in our nation's history are included among the sites described in this book, but there are also some little-known places, such as George Washington's Bathtub in Berkeley Springs, West Virginia, where residents with perfectly straight faces tell visitors that a certain indentation in one of the rocks is absolutely, positively the very spot where Washington enjoyed the spring's warm, soothing therapeutic waters.

France

Great
Britain

Weak and
Contested
Claims

Great
Britain

Spain

1732

United States

Organized States

Spain

1799

Figure 3. The geopolitical transformation of eastern North America during the lifetime of George Washington was extensive and profound, and nobody was more central
to this transformation than George Washington – surveyor, explorer, businessman,
economic expansionist, military leader, and politician.

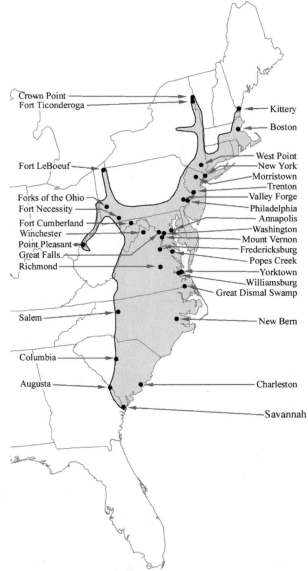

Figure 4. George Washington's earlier life as surveyor, explorer, businessman, and military leader took him to many parts of what was then British North America, and as President of the United States he made a point of visiting most of the states that at the time were parts of the new nation over which he presided. Shown here is that part of what is now the United States through which George Washington traveled, including representative sites that he actually visited.

Introduction

Thanks to the efforts of dedicated historians, preservationists, civic leaders, and politicians, many buildings and even entire towns of Washington's time have been preserved, reconstructed, or replicated. All of these places strive to recreate elements of the ambience of the colonial and early national days when George Washington and his contemporaries lived and worked in these very places. At Popes Creek Plantation, Fredericksburg, Mount Vernon, Alexandria, Valley Forge, Independence Hall, Fraunces Tavern, Williamsburg, and the others, we can almost feel Washington's presence. Standing on the veranda of Mount Vernon, one can picture George and Martha relaxing at the end of the day, gazing across the broad Potomac to the fertile Maryland shore. Visiting the rolling hills of Valley Forge with its rude huts, one senses the deprivation and hardship of the men and women who gave so much two centuries ago so that we might enjoy freedom today. The Capitol Building and Raleigh Tavern in Williamsburg seem to resound with the tempered dialogue and perhaps more assertive arguments of George Washington and other patriots who discussed the serious issues of the day — pleading and persuading as they made political decisions that helped pave the long road to American freedom. In Philadelphia's Independence Hall one cannot help but be moved by the thought that in this very building some of the most fateful decisions in the history of our nation were made by men of vision, character, and courage, all of whom looked to George Washington as one of their most important leaders. Washington not only assumed command of the Continental Army, and went on to win the war for American freedom, but by sheer force of personality and strength of principle he then assumed the central role in molding and cementing our form of self-government, all the while setting unmatched standards of personal propriety.

As the first president, Washington's every official action — every gesture, every decision, every order, every foreign treaty — was precedent setting. A thousand and one first-time decisions were his, whether they dealt with selecting "President" as the title of office, approving the method of introducing the president at public gatherings, choosing a site for the national capital, making appointments to office, or setting agendas for domestic and foreign policy. Each president who has followed Washington's shining example has given something of himself to the creation and perpetuation of our heritage. Each has made difficult decisions. Each has made positive contributions to our way of life, building on the solid foundation laid by George Washington.

History tells us that a healthy and deferential relationship with Congress may be Washington's greatest legacy as president. He was under pressure, especially during the Revolutionary War, to don the mantle of king, emperor, or dictator — yet he had an unwavering belief in the separation of military power and the civilian control of government. Often frustrated by Congress's inability or refusal to provide enough money, men, and materiel to support the Continental Army, he nonetheless continued to inform and consult with Congress, a practice entailing persuasion and compromise that continued through his presidency. Another president, 150 years later, would say, "My definition of a leader. . . is a man who can persuade people to do what they don't want to do, or do what they're too lazy to do, and like it."[2] Harry Truman, meet George Washington.

A visit to any presidential site is rewarding. The host personnel, whether park rangers, program specialists, curators, docents, or other volunteers, are friendly, knowledgeable, and anxious to enhance every visitor's enjoyment of the facility. In particular, they want visitors to leave with a deeper awareness of the men who have led our nation through two centuries to its current position of preeminence in the world. Thus visits to the places where George Washington lived, worked, fought, governed, and relaxed can provide poignant, emotional, and inspiring insight into the places and processes that molded, and were molded by, our first president. Such visits will refresh the spirit and deepen the appreciation of one who has gone before — one ever deserving of "Light Horse Harry" Lee's eulogy tribute, "To the memory of the Man, first in war, first in peace, and first in the hearts of his countrymen."[3]

~

This book is divided into three sections. Section I presents a brief outline of George Washington's life. Section II identifies and describes more than 150 extant publicly accessible sites that commemorate the life of George Washington and provides additional sources of information about the life and legacy of Washington, including museums with Washington-related exhibits, monuments, and memorials. Section III describes privately owned sites with historic ties to the man, and contains a bibliography of Washington-related publications.

Introduction

In the narrative and site descriptions that follow I have used some political, military, and architectural terms that deserve explanation. The Colonial period is used to describe that part of American history when the thirteen separate colonies that eventually became the nucleus of the United States were still possessions of Great Britain. The Revolutionary period incorporates the years between the First Continental Convention of 1774 and the Peace Treaty signed in Paris in 1783. From that time on, the thirteen newly formed states were loosely governed under the Articles of Confederation until the Constitution of the United States was written and ratified in 1789. We have chosen to call those years the Federal period.

For consistency and clarity, the term Continental Army is used throughout to describe Washington's command during the Revolutionary War. In fact, the regular army was not pieced together until after Washington took command in 1775; then, it was recruited from the ranks of the militia and other provincials holding the hills around Boston. It was not until late in 1777 that Congress authorized the raising of eighty-eight regiments for a Continental Army. After all, there was not an effective national government, merely a Congress of thirteen disparate colonies, each with its own militia with differing lengths of service commitments and more informal recruiting and training methods. Every able-bodied man was officially part of a militia, subject to call-up in an emergency. However, these men were required to serve only for certain lengths of time as determined by the government of the colony — and in some cases they were restricted to service within the borders of their own colony. The militia augmented the regulars (who had signed up for the duration of the conflict) in a haphazard, inconsistent manner, and failure of the colonies to provide adequate personnel and supplies plagued the commanding general throughout the conflict. It is a mark of George Washington's organizational genius and moral stature that he was able to not only maintain the fighting force under such conditions, but lead it to victory against what was arguably the most powerful military establishment of its day.

Each colony could also raise its own regular army. For example, troops George Washington led to protect the western frontier in 1754 were not militia, but an army Virginia raised for that specific purpose. The lessons he learned then, and later during the French and Indian War, were to bear fruit, for it was at that time that he learned to assume responsibility, how to deal with subordinates, and gain the good will and confidence of troops. He learned that transport and supply meant planning ahead plus attention to detail. He learned that shortages were inevitable and learned of the frustration of working with a sometimes passive and oftimes negative government. Most important, he learned patience, how to deal with adversity, to learn from his own mistakes, and to hate war. These lessons helped carry Washington through the most horrific periods of the Revolutionary War — and the most trying periods of his presidency.

The French and British each had long had a military presence in North America, their conflicting economic interests in Canada and the Ohio Valley culminating in the Seven Year's War, known in British North America as the French and Indian War. Both sides consisted of regular army troops augmented by Indian allies, although the British were wary of Indian loyalty and used the Indians with reluctance. During the Revolutionary War, however, with an over-extended military attending to world-wide commitments, the British hired thousands of German mercenaries, who were professional soldiers called Hessians, named for the German province of Hesse where most were recruited. Some scholars have opined that the British army, filled with a great many regulars who had been impressed into service, weakened with less than inspired foreign troops, long supply lines, and a command structure far away in London, was not a major fighting force. Whatever the case, George Washington took brilliant advantage of existing circumstances.

Although this book is not an architectural treatise, it describes over 150 houses that have providentially survived centuries of use, and some that have been reconstructed or replicated. There are simple stone farmhouses or clapboard homes built in secular styles, whereas others are magnificent homes and buildings representative of more formal architectural norms. For clarification, the term Georgian describes a house style brought from England during the eighteenth century and named for the four kings George who ruled from 1714 to 1830. Georgian styling is marked by symmetry in both the interior floor plan and the exterior façade, with gabled roofs and a central chimney. Georgian was also influenced by the Italian architect Palladio who emphasized connections between nature and architecture, as manifested by the splendid gardens and sweeping lawns found at many Georgian homes. Adams-style, named for the Scottish-English architect Robert Adams, refers to interiors of great delicacy — ceilings, porticos, tiny moldings, and fireplaces — most common in Georgian houses.

The earliest homes incorporating a distinctly American architectural style, called Colonial, were utilitarian in design, their construction influenced by weather conditions and familiarity with construction methods rather than artistry. In New England, Colonial homes were characterized by a box-like appearance wherein two stories of small rooms were situated around a central chimney, with a steeply-pitched roof and exterior siding of clapboard or shingles. In the Hudson Valley of New York, Dutch settlers had their own variations of Colonial. There, the houses were built of Dutch bricks, with a steeper sloping roof and Dutch fillips in the tile work. In Virginia, Colonial more often meant brick houses of a story and a half, with two end chimneys and a sloped roof.

Whatever the style, all of the houses described in this book are connected to George Washington, and visits to them serve to inspire us by his presence. Take with you the thought that you are somewhere George Washington slept or walked, dined or conferred, fought or governed — and that each, to some degree, bears the imprint of our nation's preeminent guiding spirit.

SECTION I

A SHORT BIOGRAPHY OF GEORGE WASHINGTON

A Short Biography of George Washington

. . . a country where heaven and earth never agreed better to frame a place for man's habitation — a fruitful and delightsome land. . . .

— Captain John Smith, 1608 [4]

The Northern Neck of Virginia, just an hour southeast of Washington, DC, is bounded on the north by the Potomac River, on the south by the Rappahannock River, and on the east by Chesapeake Bay. Three-hundred-fifty years after its settlement by Europeans it remains agricultural, a land of rolling countryside with no malls and few fast-food restaurants. It is traversed by neither interstate highway nor rail line. Historical markers abound, in part because the Northern Neck was the birthplace of presidents George Washington, James Madison, and James Monroe as well as Confederate General Robert E. Lee.

Today, paved roads cross the Northern Neck in place of the horse trails and carriage tracks of an earlier time. Commercial river traffic has given way to recreational boating. "Ordinaries" have been replaced by motor inns and once-large plantations have been divided into wineries, family farms, and retirement communities. On the other hand, there is still the charm of country life with its county fairs and market days. Crabbers unload fresh Chesapeake Bay crabs each morning as they have done for generations, and worship services are held each Sunday at Saint Pauls in King George and Christ Church in Irvington as they have been for more than 250 years.

In the early days of the Virginia Colony, its economic lifeblood was carried by its rivers — the James, the mighty Potomac, the placid Rappahannock, and the York. Ships bound for England departed with cargoes of agricultural products that included the most profitable of all — tobacco.

15

In 1657, a young Englishman from Northumberland arrived on the shores of the Northern Neck near present-day Colonial Beach as mate of the ketch *Sea Horse*. Being readied for its return to England with a full load of tobacco, the ship foundered on a shoal and a violent winter storm sent her to the bottom. The crew successfully re-floated the ship, but the tiny vessel needed time for refurbishing and reloading before it could begin the return voyage. During the delay, Nathaniel Pope, a prosperous landowner-planter with a marriageable daughter, Anne, befriended the young sailor. For both romantic reasons and other more practical considerations, the young man decided to remain in Virginia. By virtue of his fortuitous marriage — father-in-law Pope gave the newlyweds a fertile 700-acre farm on Mattox Creek as a wedding present — personal ambition, hard work, and shrewd land speculation, the young entrepreneur became owner of thousands of productive agricultural acres. He also served as Coroner, Trustee of Estates and Justice of the County Courts, vestryman of Appomattox Parish, and Colonel of Militia — an impressive legacy of diligence, responsibility, and public service that would be handed down to his descendants. The young man was John Washington.

John and Anne Washington's eldest son, Lawrence, was born in 1659 on a second Washington farm on Bridges Creek, four miles from the Mattox Creek property that Nathaniel Pope had presented to John and Anne the year before. The family's good fortune enabled Lawrence to be educated in England, but he returned to Virginia upon his father's death. Destined to continue the family's tradition of public service, he became an attorney, a justice of the peace before the age of twenty-one, a burgess by the age of twenty-five, and eventually the sheriff of his home county. His interest in farming and land speculation, however, was never strong, and the Washington landholdings remained static during his lifetime.

Lawrence married well. Mildred Warner was the daughter of a Speaker of the House of Burgesses who was a member of its ruling council. She bore Lawrence three children, including Augustine, George Washington's father. After Lawrence's life was cut short in 1698, Mildred remarried and moved to England with her new husband and her three children. Upon her death in 1700 or 1701, Augustine returned to Virginia and spent the rest of his childhood and adolescence with a relative, John Washington, of Chotank, part of what is now King George County. At his majority, Augustine claimed his inheritance, the rich farmland along Bridges Creek. Augustine, described as a sturdy, vigorous man, was a natural son of the soil who expanded the family land holdings and extended personal interests into ownership of an iron mine and foundry. He, too, demonstrated his sense of public responsibility by serving as a vestryman, county justice, military officer, and sheriff.

In 1718, Augustine purchased 150 acres on Popes Creek where it feeds into the Potomac River, and constructed the house where he lived with his first wife until her death, and then with his second wife, Mary Ball. Mary was the daughter of Colonel Joseph Ball of Epping Forest, near Lancaster, almost at the eastern end of the Northern Neck. Mary had married widower Augustine shortly after his first wife had passed away, and assumed responsibility for Augustine's household and his three children, Lawrence, Augustine, Jr., and Jane. Augustine and Mary's first child was George, born in 1732 in the house Augustine had built on the Popes Creek property.

The plantation at Popes Creek was typical of a prosperous lower gentry family. The master's house was the center of family life and the farm was tended by indentured servants from England or slaves, many of them imported from Africa or the West Indies. The Washington family remained at Popes Creek only three and one half years, then when George was still a toddler they moved to Little Hunting Creek Plantation, another of Augustine's properties farther up the Potomac. The Little Hunting Creek Plantation, later to be memorialized as Mount Vernon, had been patented by John Washington, handed down to Lawrence, then willed by him to his daughter Mildred who then transferred title to her brother Augustine. Augustine's family did not remain at Little Hunting Creek very long, as he had invested in a mining and foundry venture in the Accokeek area of Stafford County. This enterprise involved time-consuming, on-site management that required Augustine to live closer to the mine. When an estate of 260 acres on the north bank of the Rappahannock River, across from Fredericksburg, became available, Augustine purchased the property and added more acreage until he owned 600 acres. The house, as far as can be determined, was comfortable but not elaborate; the farm was not large but it was maintained by slaves and was largely self-sufficient. There were cattle, poultry, and other animals to provide food, hides, and other necessities for the growing family that, by this time, included seven children.

Ferry Farm, as this property has been known since the nineteenth century, was where George Washington grew into manhood and began to assume adult responsibilities when Augustine unexpectedly died in 1743. George was eleven. In the primogeniture atmosphere of the day, eldest son Lawrence inherited Little Hunting Creek Plantation, second son Augustine, Jr., was willed the property at Popes Creek, and George was left Ferry Farm and several small lots in Fredericksburg held in trust by his mother. Widowed and left to run the farm and rear the children alone, Mary Washington faced a difficult future that required no little amount of courage and determination.

Lawrence and Augustine, Jr. took up residence at their newly acquired properties while George, the younger son with more limited prospects, remained with his mother at Ferry Farm. Over the next few years at Ferry Farm, Fredericksburg, and Lawrence's home at Little Hunting Creek, George developed his ambition and acquired his surveying skills.

Little is known of George Washington's adolescence. We do know his education was brief and mostly informal, yet consistent with the station in life assigned to him by his patrimony. Stepbrothers Lawrence and Augustine, Jr. were educated in England whereas Mary's children, possibly because of financial constraints, remained in Virginia. In fact, John Adams would eventually look down on Washington for being uneducated, but what he lacked in formal training was more than made up for by his orderly mind, dedication, personal ambition, and innate qualities of leadership.

From George Washington's genealogy, we know that his forebears were hard working, ambitious, and driven to succeed. His ancestors had membership in the planter aristocracy, that group of landowners in colonial Virginia whose social, political, and economic attitudes and influence derived from those of the English gentry. They believed in participating in the civil and military affairs of the colony and performing their duties without complaint, even though such service might entail the sacrifice of individual comfort and welfare. That selfless philosophy may explain much about George Washington's willingness to serve the cause of liberty, to participate in the building and operation of the government, and to become the nation's first chief executive.

Washington remained close to the land and the natural world throughout his life, and he always professed to be just a farmer. Even as he prepared to leave the presidency, he wrote to Dr. James Anderson on December 24, 1795, "No pursuit is more congenial with my nature and gratification, than that of agriculture; nor none I so pant after as again to become a tiller of the earth."[5] We must assume that this affinity for the farming life also developed out of positive experiences of Washington's youth — at Popes Creek, Little Hunting Creek, and Ferry Farm.

〜

The thirteen British colonies that later joined together to form the United States contained no more than two million inhabitants in the middle of the eighteenth century, and Virginia at that time had less than 250,000 citizens. The thirteen colonies were compressed into a narrow sliver of land along the Atlantic coast, where they were threatened by the Spaniards to the South and the French to the North while being hemmed in to the West by forbidding terrain of rugged mountains, inhospitable forests, unnavigable rivers, and unfriendly Indians.

These thirteen British colonies manifested three distinct personalities. The New England colonies, refuges from religious persecution in Europe, were historically Puritan. Farmers carved out a hardscrabble existence from the thin, rocky soil, attempts were made to tame rivers that would provide power for manufacturing, merchants centered their activities in the small settlements and port cities, and well-educated men turned to teaching and the ministry.

The middle colonies — New York, New Jersey and Pennsylvania — were home to an unusual mix of people and cultures. English settlers predominated, but a variety of minority groups — the Dutch in New York, the Scots and Germans in Pennsylvania, and a scattering of Frenchmen, Swedes, African Americans, and others — made these colonies the prototype of the American "melting pot." Although large estates were to be found in New York, modest farms dominated the region while the ports of Philadelphia and New York City became increasingly important centers of wealth and influence.

The southern colonies were primarily agricultural, and their population was scattered across numerous small and large rural landholdings. Virginia, for example, reflected a rigid social structure, recognizing in descending order gentlemen, yeomen, servants, and slaves. In Virginia there was a place for every man and every man had his place.

Most colonial Virginians had few close neighbors. Royal Governor Spotswood had reported in 1710:

> *At the first settlement of the country . . . people seated them-selves along the bank of the great river and knew very little of the inland parts beyond their own private plantations, being kept in awe by the Indians from vent'ring farther; neither had they any correspondence than only by water.*[6]

It may be that George Washington never saw a town until 1738 when his family moved to Ferry Farm near Fredericksburg. In 1750, ordinary folk could buy goods from small shops, but for the planters and storekeepers, manufactured goods had to be imported from England, sight unseen, and there were few communities that might be considered "towns" in the entire colony. Towns were almost superfluous since the economy was based almost exclusively on tobacco and dominated by large, self-contained estates. Those plantations in the Tidewater had private docks big enough to receive ocean-going ships which would unload supplies from England, reload with casks of tobacco, and set sail for home without ever docking at a town.

Yet, by the 1740s, settlers had begun to move westward into the wilderness, away from the Tidewater. Those brave souls had to be served with shipping points and markets, thus upriver port towns like Fredericksburg and Dumfries, at or near the fall line — the head of navigation for ocean-going vessels — were founded to meet their needs. Westward expansion also meant that land needed to be explored, bounded, and surveyed. Tradition holds that young George Washington discovered his father's set of surveyor's instruments in a shed and took to them as a duck takes to water. By the time he was fifteen, he was proficient enough to run simple lines and earn a little money surveying for friends and neighbors. During those adolescent years, he frequently visited Lawrence at Mount Vernon where the adult talk was of land being opened in the west and of grand designs that would push the boundaries of Virginia far beyond the Blue Ridge. While at Mount Vernon, George met Lawrence's neighbor at nearby Belvoir Plantation, Colonel William Fairfax, cousin of the Proprietor, Lord Fairfax. Colonel Fairfax's son, George William, was to become one of Washington's closest friends, and George William's wife, Sally, was the woman some historians believe was the endearing and unrequited love of George Washington's life.

George's relationship with his half-brother Lawrence was an important one. Lawrence, fourteen years older than George, was an influence on the younger man, though perhaps not an inspiration. One of Lawrence's career recommendations nearly changed the course of history. Lawrence had briefly served in the military and urged young George to join the British Navy, a recommendation rejected by Mary Washington who refused to grant her permission. Thus history was spared the possibility of a British Admiral Sir George Washington. Lawrence's most important contribution to George's welfare was to introduce him to society, particularly the Fairfaxes and their influential circle of associates. George's relationship with the Fairfaxes fueled the ambition of the hardworking, able young man.

In 1748, the Fairfaxes planned a trip to explore their extensive land holdings in the Shenandoah Valley, and young George was invited to accompany the party as assistant surveyor. Go with them he did, and on the journey he endured the physical hardships of traveling long distances on horseback, sleeping outdoors in all kinds of weather, eating food cooked over open fires, fighting rugged terrain and wilderness, confronting Indians, and meeting strange white settlers who lived much like the Indians and spoke Dutch or German. This journey was an important step in George's maturation, one that helped prepare the impressionable sixteen-year-old for what would come to be difficult and dangerous years ahead.

For the next few years, Washington moved between Ferry Farm and Mount Vernon while he worked as a surveyor. One of his jobs was to assist John West lay out the boundaries and building lots of Alexandria, Virginia. Most of his work during this time, however, was in the Shenandoah Valley and other areas of western Virginia. He was even appointed head surveyor for Culpeper County, quite a responsibility for a young man not yet twenty years of age! Surveying in those days was arduous, physically demanding, and oftimes dangerous. The crews had to endure the rigors of working in swamps and dense woods, climbing rugged, inhospitable mountains, and crossing or canoeing down cold and rushing rivers. The rugged life served Washington well as he not only gained financial rewards and valuable leadership experience, but he also matured physically. Already taller than the average man, he was beginning to look like a leader. It has often been reported that George Washington had a great physical presence.

Washington and his surveying crews worked in the area generally bounded by Frederick Town (now Winchester, Virginia), Bath (now Berkeley Springs, West Virginia), and Wills Creek (now Cumberland, Maryland), areas within a radius of about fifty miles from the confluence of the Shenandoah and Potomac rivers. Travel was by horseback or on foot over poorly marked roads, little more than trails that had been hacked out by frontier woodsmen, farmers, or trappers who lived in rude shelters many miles apart. Today, Winchester is reached by modern roads that cut through forests and mountain passes. In 1750, however, Washington's party had to cross the Occoquan River at Woodbridge, follow the river northwestward past Bull Creek and Mountain (now Manassas), to Ashbys Gap north of what is today Upperville, then cross the Blue Ridge to Frederick Town — a tiny group of shacks and an "ordinary," its population perhaps a few hundred residents.

In 1751, a family emergency took precedence in Washington's life. Brother Lawrence had never been physically strong, and it is suspected that he suffered from tuberculosis. George accompanied him to Bath in search of some relief in the spa's therapeutic waters. The trips failed, so the brothers decided to sail to Barbados in hopes that the warmer climate would restore Lawrence's health. That, too, proved fruitless, and Lawrence passed away shortly after returning to Mount Vernon in 1752. One positive result of the adventure was, ironically, another illness. While in Barbados, George contracted smallpox which, after a few agonizing weeks, subsided, leaving him immune from the disease that took so many lives and would later ravage his army.

Lawrence left Mount Vernon to his infant daughter, Sarah. In the event of her death before she had children, the estate was to pass to George. However, it was also specified that Lawrence's widow, Anne, should possess the property while she lived. Sadly, infant Sarah died in 1754. Later that year George leased Mount Vernon from Anne, who had remarried and moved to Maryland. Upon her death in 1761, George Washington became the outright owner of Mount Vernon.

At the time of Lawrence's death, however, George's head was filled only with youthful thoughts of fame and fortune in the west. Earlier, he had purchased several thousand acres of prime land on Bullskin Creek in the Shenandoah Valley, so that by the age of nineteen he was already a landowner and a successful businessman with grandiose dreams of further land development, financial wealth, and improved social position.

Early in the 1750s, however, there were fateful and dangerous developments taking place in the Ohio Valley and beyond, and provocative reactions to these events occurred in Virginia's capital of Williamsburg that would change Washington's life — and the course of history. George Washington was destined to become an indispensable man.

When Washington returned from Barbados in 1752, he had carried a greeting from its governor to Lieutenant Governor Robert Dinwiddie of the Virginia colony, a man who would play an intimate and important part in George Washington's life. The royal governorship of the colony was a sinecure held by a well-connected absentee in England so that Dinwiddie, as lieutenant governor, was the de facto representative of the crown in Virginia. His appointment, too, was political in nature, and it had important commercial ramifications as Dinwiddie was also a merchant with a vested interest in the Ohio Company, a venture aimed at developing land west of the Alleghenies. Dinwiddie was outraged to learn that France had mounted an expedition that was traveling through the wilderness burying markers stating France's claim to all the land drained by the Ohio River — including the land that the Ohio Company intended to develop.

France and England had been in conflict for many years, each attempting to become the most powerful nation in Europe, both militarily and economically. The French, determined to prevent their enemies from stealing a march on the American continent, were systematically establishing their territorial claims and, in 1753, began to fortify a route between Lake Erie and the Ohio River. Three forts were erected in what is now Pennsylvania, and indications were that even more would be built farther south, as far as the Forks of the Ohio.

Dinwiddie wrote to London, indignantly complaining of the French expansion into the Ohio Valley. King George II replied that Virginia should also build forts on the Ohio, but only after sending an emissary to determine if the French were indeed on English soil. If so, the emissary should persuade them to depart, and if they should refuse to leave, the crown instructed, "We do strictly command and charge you to drive them out by force of arms."[7]

George Washington, meanwhile, had been named one of four adjutants of the Virginia militia. He was assigned initially to the southern military district, which held no interest for him. He wished instead for a command in the more prestigious and glamorous northern district, a post to which he was transferred in 1753. His duties, not onerous, were to "instruct the officers and soldiers in the use and exercise of arms."[8] There is no record that militia meetings were much more than social gatherings with little military training, especially since Washington and the other adjutants had precious little military knowledge to impart.

After Washington learned of Dinwiddie's dilemma in the west, he immediately volunteered to act as the government's emissary to the French. To Dinwiddie, Washington, in spite of his youth, seemed a sensible choice; he was not an outsider who might use the venture for personal gain, he had a military title, some knowledge of the terrain, experience in frontier living, and, above all, ambition and courage. A leading London magazine later would comment on the appointment, stating, "He was used to the woods — a youth of great sobriety, diligence and fidelity."[9] Author James Thomas Flexner added, "Thus was a mission of world-shaking implications given to an obscure youth in a provincial corner of the earth."[10] Washington himself remembered years later that the appointment "was deemed by some an extraordinary circumstance that so young and inexperienced a person should have been employed on a negotiation with which subjects of the greatest importance were involved."[11]

Washington's first hurdle was going to be hard enough. Merely finding the French in the Ohio Valley wilderness was not going to be an easy task, especially as winter was closing in, the snow was beginning to fall, and the rivers were wide, fast, and cold. Extra provisions and warm clothing were packed for what promised to be an arduous journey through an unfamiliar land fraught with danger, some natural and some man-made. Unfriendly Indians roamed the forest, and every step would bring Washington closer to a European enemy that would not welcome the intrusion. Washington knew neither the Indian language nor French, so he hired an interpreter, a Dutchman who, unfortunately, spoke bad English along with bad French. Sensibly, he hired an experienced guide, Christopher Gist, who would prove to be invaluable in dealing with the Indians, the wilderness, and the elements.

Bearing a letter from Governor Dinwiddie to the French, Washington's group began its adventure in mid-November in Winchester and proceeded to Wills Creek before turning to the northwest and crossing Laurel Hill. A few days later the party reached the Youghiogheny River and followed it to its confluence with the Monongahela, from where they followed the eastern bank of the Monongahela to its junction with the Allegheny. After fording the Allegheny, the group continued for another dozen miles to the Indian village of Logtown. Throughout the trip, the inexperienced leader found it necessary to meet, negotiate, and trade with the Indians his party encountered, some of whom were more friendly to the French than to the English. Washington's physical presence, native intelligence, and bravado undoubtedly placed him in good stead through the many tight spots he probably encountered on this journey.

After acquiring some Indians as guides, Washington's band of Virginians headed north to Venango (now Franklin) where French Creek empties into the Allegheny River. There, Washington met with a small group of Frenchmen who were living in a fortified house, but to his dismay the commandant to whom Dinwiddie's letter was addressed was stationed at Fort LeBoeuf, another sixty miles up French Creek. Moving onward, Washington and his men encountered excessive rains, snows, and bad traveling through many mires and swamps during the next four and a half days. They finally reached Fort LeBoeuf where they were received cordially, if without warmth. Perhaps the garrison was impressed by the fact that the Virginians were there at all, considering the bad weather and unpleasant travel conditions they had experienced.

While the commandant, Legardeur de St. Pierre, drafted a reply to Dinwiddie, Washington had full access to the fort and, proving to be an expert observer, took surreptitious notes regarding its construction and location. When St. Pierre's reply was ready, Washington prepared for a return journey that would prove to be even more difficult and dangerous than the trek north. The weather had further deteriorated, rivers had frozen, and the temperature had continued to drop. After a trip he later described in his official report "as fatiguing a journey as it was possible to conceive,"[12] he delivered St. Pierre's reply to Dinwiddie late in January, 1754 — the letter still in miraculously good condition after having been exposed to such challenging conditions.

The French reply and Washington's verbal report confirmed Dinwiddie's worst fears regarding France's intentions. Washington was instructed to prepare a full written report for the King's Privy Council. Skipping over his more lurid and sensational personal adventures, including a ducking, near-death in a river, and an attack by an Indian, one cannot help but be impressed by the young man's courage, determination, and brashness. One senses he was master of any situation and that he was moving forward toward a goal with energy and purpose. On this assignment, Washington got to where he was supposed to go, delivered his message, and returned home safely after encountering and overcoming extremely difficult hardships.

According to the Journal of the House of Burgesses, Washington's monetary reward from the assembly for several months of danger, discomfort, and discouragement was £50 "to testify approbation of his proceedings on the journey to the Ohio."[13] He was offended by their parsimony, although it was not the last time Washington would have financial problems with politicians and bureaucrats. Nonetheless, with the publication of his written report, he found himself with favorable personal notoriety. In response to his pronouncements and opinions, arguments were voiced within the assembly and throughout Virginia for and against military action in the west.

In response to the French presence in the upper Ohio Valley, Governor Dinwiddie authorized a 300-man army and enlisted assistance from other colonies with vested interests in the Ohio region. Joshua Fry, a mathematics professor at the College of William and Mary, was named army commander with newly promoted Lieutenant Colonel George Washington as his second in command. Before Fry could even begin to get organized, reports filtered in from the northwest, indicating that a large French army was on the move south, immediately endangering a small Virginia task force of frontiersmen who had begun to construct a tiny fort at the Forks of the Ohio. In response, Dinwiddie ordered Washington to the Ohio with whatever troops were ready, with Commander Fry to follow. Washington's orders were for him to be primarily defensive, although it was made clear that any attempt by the French to interfere with Britain's settlements were to be resisted by force.

Washington hastened to Wills Creek in March, 1754, and discovered problems not unlike those he would experience throughout his military career. First, he had to get men to enlist, then he had to obtain an appropriation to pay for the uniforms and salaries. Food and military hardware were difficult to secure, and wagons and horses had to be procured by purchase or by expropriation from reluctant farmers. By force of personality, by gentle and sometimes not-so-gentle persuasion, Washington managed to scrape up supplies and to recruit and train a small force. On April 18, he led 159 men with some baggage and a few cannon out of Wills Creek and headed for the Forks of the Ohio almost 200 miles away. There was merely a narrow trail heading west, so the little army had to chop out a wider track for the wheeled vehicles — a time-consuming, tedious, and physically demanding process. Part way to its objective, Washington's force met Ensign Edward Ward, commander of the garrison from the Forks, who reported that he and thirty-three soldiers had surrendered their little fort to a superior force of almost a thousand French soldiers.

Washington's own army was no match for such overwhelming numbers, yet at the same time he was faced with a difficult political dilemma. Indians who had indicated a willingness to defy the French were waiting to see if a substantial English army was en route to assist them if they should decide to attack the French. Washington reasoned that maintaining Virginia's good relations with the Indians required a show of strength, and he made an ill-fated decision — he would move toward the French by pressing on to the Monongahela River, then he would wait there for the orders and reinforcements that he presumed were on the way.

The road ahead was even more imposing than that over which they had already traveled, progress was even slower, and they were delayed at one point by the flooding Youghiogheny River. While waiting to cross, a courier arrived with a letter reporting that Fry was indeed on the way. The prudent thing to do would have been to establish camp and wait for the promised reinforcements, but youth is often impetuous. As soon as the river was passable, Washington forged ahead and within a few days he reached a field named the Great Meadow where, using wagons and brush, he set up a weakly fortified defensive position on a poorly situated site in the middle of the open meadow. Receiving word that a small party of French was camped nearby, and never content to remain idle, Washington organized a small raiding party made up of some of his own men and some Indian allies under Chief Half-King. In a coordinated maneuver, the Virginians and the Indians surrounded the unsuspecting French and opened fire. Washington's ambush was a success; several Frenchmen, including their leader, the Sieur de Jumonville, were killed and all of the others, save one, were captured.

Correctly assuming that the French would retaliate, Washington strengthened his fortified site at the Great Meadow, which he called Fort Necessity. Within days, a troop of one hundred Virginia regulars arrived under the command of Captain James Mackay. More confident with these additional troops on hand, Washington led a small reconnaissance group forward to Gist's trading station on the Redstone River where he was informed that a major French force was advancing in his direction. Washington backtracked to Fort Necessity to await the expected attack. The French professionals and their Indian allies had no difficulty in surrounding the tiny fort, firing at will, and killing all the animals and many of the fort's defenders. The defense of Fort Necessity had become even more difficult when a torrential rain flooded the fort and made the gunpowder unusable. The battle had become a disaster for the Virginians; the floodwater ran red with the blood of the defenders. With rain pouring down, the French called for a parley, the result of which was the surrender of the abject garrison. Exhibiting uncharacteristic mercy, the French allowed Washington and what remained of his troops to retreat with their wounded, their weapons, and their tattered military honor. Needless to say, the battle at Fort Necessity was not George Washington's finest military hour.

The effects of the debacle at and near the Great Meadow were far-reaching. The French claimed that de Jumonville had been leading a diplomatic delegation to the British when he was attacked by Washington. The terms of Washington's surrender at Fort Necessity, a product of sloppy translation, defined the death of de Jumonville as an "assassination," a gaffe used by the French as propaganda to discredit the English. The battle of Fort Necessity, a mere skirmish in a remote meadow in the American wilderness, was later described as the first shots fired in the French and Indian War — a war that raged for seven years in North America and essentially ended French expansion on the continent. Voltaire wrote, "Such was the complication of political interests that a [cannon] shot fired in America could give the signal that set Europe in a blaze."[14]

Militarily, the clash at Fort Necessity had been a failure for the Virginians, a result of miscalculation by a raw and inexperienced military leader. Washington had also failed in his efforts to assure the Indians that the British could effectively stand up to the French; his amateurish military decisions and behavior had clouded any chance of an Indian-British alliance. On the world stage, Washington's action prejudiced the moral position of Great Britain on the eve of a global war, and while he was given high marks for personal bravery, most military professionals agreed with Lord Albemarle, titular Governor of Virginia and British Ambassador to France, who wrote to the Duke of Newcastle on September 11, 1754, "Washington and many such may have courage and resolution, but they have no knowledge or experience in our profession. Consequently, there can be no dependence on them."[15]

Ironically, Washington's fellow Virginians, ignorant of the niceties of military science, were wont to believe that their little army and its commander had fought bravely and well against a superior number of professional fighters. Washington had become a hero along the American frontier despite the loss of Fort Necessity. His name was being mentioned as a symbol of English resistance to French imperial expansion.

Washington returned to Williamsburg in July but received a cool reception from Governor Dinwiddie, who by then considered the energetic young officer a political and economic liability. Washington returned to his regiment, then almost immediately was ordered by Dinwiddie to march back across the Blue Ridge to join a British force that was preparing yet another foray across the Alleghenies. To Washington, the proposed effort seemed disconcertingly similar to the Forks of the Ohio campaign. Chastened by the experience of Fort Necessity, he considered the Virginia army to be too small, inexperienced, ill-equipped, and underfunded to conduct war. Washington's complaints about these deficiencies fell on deaf ears. Dinwiddie was unable to obtain needed assistance from other colonies, so the ill-advised campaign was aborted and the French were left in sole possession and control of the Ohio Valley.

Washington returned to Williamsburg again in October to observe the regular session of the Virginia Assembly. He voiced his wish to the assembly that his militia regiment might be incorporated into the British army, thus fulfilling his long-stated ambition to become an officer in the regular army. The British government, however, in an effort to remove any nascent conflict between regulars and colonials, divided the Virginia militia regiment into smaller companies with their commanding officers ranked no higher than captain. Outraged by a proposed demotion from colonel to captain, Washington resigned his commission.

At this same time, Ann Washington, Lawrence's widow, remarried and moved away from Mount Vernon, leaving the plantation available to George to lease. He moved in, fully prepared, physically and emotionally, to be a full-time gentleman farmer, and as it turned out, Mount Vernon would remain forever after his permanent home and anchor.

Meanwhile, the governors of Virginia, Maryland and North Carolina had recognized the danger in the west and approved an attack on Fort Duquesne, the major French fort at the Forks of the Ohio. The commander of the army was to be Governor Horatio Sharpe of Maryland, a veteran of the British army who had little respect for George Washington's military skills. As a realist, however, he knew that Washington's wilderness experience was invaluable and proffered an "honorary" rank of colonel, an offer Washington found insulting and easy to refuse. This military venture, too, proved impossible to organize and was quickly abandoned.

Barely two months later, fate stepped in when a British man-of-war carrying Major General Edward Braddock sailed into Hampton Roads, Virginia. Braddock's orders were to assault and capture Fort Duquesne with a mixed force of British regulars and colonials. The British veteran was informed that ex-Colonel George Washington was the best, albeit the only, colonial military officer who had knowledge of the terrain and understood the problems that would be encountered in the land that was about to be invaded. Witnessing the massing of troops and the dramatic incursion of a British fleet into the Potomac, Washington's love of the military and his personal ambition rose to the surface. After several personal meetings with Braddock, he accepted an offer to join the general's staff.

Washington joined the British army in Frederick, Maryland, in May, 1755. The sight of a large, disciplined, orderly encampment must have been a revelation to the young militia officer who, up to this time, had led only ragtag bands of poorly equipped and undisciplined volunteers. The army moved on to Wills Creek, the designated jumping-off spot for the march to Fort Duquesne — a journey that turned out to be more than daunting. A road wide enough to accommodate wagons, artillery, pack horses, beef cattle, and other supplies for 2000 soldiers had to be cleared by hacking through dense woods, up steep grades, over rivers and streams, and through meadows and swamps. Progress was slow, and sometimes the army moved as little as two miles a day. Frustrated by the agonizing pace, Braddock divided his force — 1200 troops with minimum artillery moved quickly forward while the slow-moving wagons and heavy baggage crept forward in their wake.

Aide-de-camp and advisor Washington, struck down by a vicious attack of the flux, was restricted to camp and unable to accompany the faster-moving group. He endured three weeks of agony before being able to mount his horse, but determined not to miss the attack on Fort Duquesne, he tied pillows to his saddle and rejoined the army a mere twelve miles from its objective. An advance party forded the Monongahela, signaled that all was secure, and moved ahead; Braddock, Washington, and the main force followed.

Suddenly there was the sound of heavy musket fire. The lead party had been ambushed by a large force of hostile, French-led Indians. The British soldiers, crowded into a narrow defile, were helpless against an invisible enemy hidden behind trees and rocks high above them. The panic-stricken redcoats retreated, running pell-mell into the main body of troops and causing further confusion. Braddock, Washington and other officers attempted without success to stop the terrified men. The classic British tactic of fighting in tight formations with massed troops in open settings was proving useless against this unseen foe, and officers and men fell by the score. Washington had two horses shot from under him and bullets pierced his clothing and hat as he tried desperately to form his colonials to fight Indian style, even while being ordered by a stubborn British officer into the center of the defile — and certain death. Sensing total annihilation, Braddock ordered a withdrawal and then fell, mortally wounded. Washington was sent forty miles to the rear to meet the second division with orders to cover the retreat of the first. The demoralized army divisions finally merged to begin a sad, slow retreat east. Washington made his way back to Mount Vernon. Devastated, discouraged, and weak, he entered the house, made his way upstairs, and threw himself on the bed in complete exhaustion. He was home.

Thirty years later, in notes he compiled for use in his biography, Washington vividly recalled the massacre, deaths, cries of the wounded, and the journey to the rear while traumatized and ailing:

*In a manner wholly unfit for the execution of the duty. . . . the
shocking scenes which presented themselves in this night march*

*are not to be described. The dead, the dying, the groans, lamenta-
tions, and cries along the road of the wounded for help . . . were
enough to pierce the heart of adamant, the gloom and horror of
which was not a little increased by the impervious darkness occa-
sioned by the close shade of thick woods.[16]*

The official inquiry into the Braddock debacle laid some blame on
the colonials, but knowledgeable observers gave high marks to George
Washington and his militiamen for their bravery and military deportment.
Braddock's ignominious defeat in the wilderness shocked the world, and
in particular prompted changes in Britain's overall military policy. The
British strategy in North America was modified, and they turned their
attention northward, away from the Ohio Valley, and concentrated on
Louisburg, France's naval base on Cape Breton Island; the Saint Lawrence
River; and the Mohawk River, a natural route leading eastward to Albany,
New York, and the Hudson River. England had experienced quite enough
of Virginia. What remained of Braddock's army marched off to Philadelphia and left Virginia to defend herself.

The defense of Virginia's western frontier became necessary almost immediately. With the British army out of the colony, Indians, backed
by the French, began a series of raids on settlers in the Shenandoah
Valley. Terrified farmers fled eastward, relating horror stories of neighbors killed and scalped. In response, the Virginia Assembly voted to raise
an army of 1200 rangers and named George Washington Commander-
in-Chief of the Virginia Militia with orders to act defensively or offen-
sively as he thought best.

Washington set up headquarters at Fort Cumberland (now
Cumberland, Maryland), undertook an inspection tour of his command,
and then rode south through the Shenandoah Valley as far as Fort Dinwiddie
in Augusta (now Bath) County, some 120 miles through country still at
times harboring hostile Indians. He returned north to Winchester where
he faced the difficult task of recruiting and supplying an army, an effort
made even more challenging by the Indian raids and the ensuing flight of
panic-stricken settlers. For some time, he was even cut off from Fort
Cumberland. He eventually reached it only to find an encampment of
Marylanders led by Captain John Dagworthy. Dagworthy purported to
outrank Washington by virtue of a paper showing him to be in the royal
service. Washington, furious at the apparent usurpation of his command,

rushed to Williamsburg to complain vociferously about Dagworthy's presence. Governor Dinwiddie wrote to Governor Shirley of Massachusetts who had succeeded Braddock as commander of all British forces in North America, gently pleading Washington's case. Shirley's noncommittal reply was so unsatisfactory that Washington asked for permission to plead his case to Shirley personally. Dinwiddie approved, but just as Washington was preparing to leave for Boston, Shirley reconsidered and ordered Dagworthy not to assume command of any Virginia troops. Washington decided to travel north anyway, with the intention of pleading his case for permanent, regular army commissions for himself and his staff. And so it was, that early in 1756, twenty-four-year-old Colonel George Washington, Commander-in-Chief of the Virginia Militia, left Williamsburg for his first trip through the middle and northern colonies of British North America.

Our study of history sometimes overlooks the fact that George Washington came from a provincial background. Except for forays into the wilderness of western Maryland and Pennsylvania and a trip to Barbados, he had never been out of Virginia. The colonial capital, Williamsburg, contained only 200 homes and a population of 1000 residents; when the assembly was in session, the population doubled. The Capitol Building and the College of William and Mary anchored either end of Duke of Gloucester Street, and the Governor's Palace and Bruton Parish Church were the only other prominent buildings — although there was a disproportionate number of taverns and ordinaries to accommodate politicians and others who attended the legislative sessions. Washington's hometown, Fredericksburg, had but a few square blocks of businesses and homes. So it was truly an adventure as Washington and a small party of aides crossed the Potomac River, rode to Annapolis, turned north across the Patapsco River via the Gunpowder and Susquehanna ferries, then picked up an easily traveled road from Elk River to Brandywine Ferry to Chester, and crossed the Schuylkill River to Philadelphia.

Philadelphia was by far the largest city in the British colonies, its 3000 houses and shops crowded together with vehicles plodding through the narrow dirt or cobblestone streets filled with pedestrians and horse droppings. In glittering uniform, a head taller than the crowds, and with a reputation celebrated throughout the colonies, Washington stood out. Even in defeat, Virginians were proud of the leader who had fought courageously against superior odds, always on their behalf. He must have attracted attention, yet the only existing record of his visit lies in shop records that show purchases for clothing and leather goods. No one at this time, of course, could anticipate the momentous events that would occur later in Philadelphia and affect the lives of both the young Virginian and the emerging nation that he would lead.

After a few days in Philadelphia, the group crossed the Delaware River at Burlington, New Jersey, and proceeded via Allentown and Cranberry Brook to Perth Amboy, where a small barge transported them across the Narrows to Flat Bush (now Brooklyn) and into Manhattan. They spent five days in New York where George inspected the city, attended parties, and spent time at dinners and the theater. Back on the road, they traveled through Westchester to New London, Connecticut, where they boarded a ship and sailed to Newport, Rhode Island. At Newport, they boarded a larger vessel that carried them to Boston.

Washington found Governor Shirley hospitable. The governor confirmed his restructured orders regarding Captain Dagworthy's responsibilities at Cumberland, but Washington was chagrined to learn that while he was traveling and out of touch, Governor Horatio Sharpe of Maryland had been appointed commander of the militia forces being raised in Maryland, Pennsylvania, South Carolina and Virginia. The commission that Washington had long dreamed about would have to wait for another day.

Washington's first visit to Boston was brief and unproductive. On the way home to Virginia, he stopped in Annapolis to confer with Governor Sharpe. Sharpe had softened his negative attitude about Washington, but he, too, gave no satisfaction regarding a permanent commission. Disappointed, Washington made up his mind to resign and become a fulltime farmer. Back in Williamsburg, however, he received bleak news from the frontier; Indian hostilities were continuing unabated. With his experience required now more than ever, Washington was persuaded not to resign but to volunteer as Sharpe's second in command. Sharpe's all-inclusive army never materialized, so the Virginia Assembly voted that their militia, which had been called up for local defense, would have no further connection with Sharpe or any other outsider. George Washington would remain in sole command of Virginia's fighting forces.

Washington knew that the way to bring an end to the Indian attacks was to force the French from Fort Duquesne, their headquarters in the upper Ohio Valley and the place from which they supported Indian incursions into the Ohio Valley and the western Virginia frontier. Under the existing circumstances, however, forcing the French to vacate Fort Duquesne was unrealistic, so Washington devised a plan to construct a wall of protection along the Virginia frontier — his militia would build a chain of defensive forts from Fort Cumberland to the border of North Carolina, each a day's march apart and garrisoned by 80 to 100 men. Of course, the young colonel faced the same frustrations as he had in the past. Recruitment was almost impossible, supplies and payrolls were not forthcoming, refugees streaming in from the frontier clogged the tiny settlements, and disputes arose between militia officers and the gentlemen officers Washington had appointed. The assembly and governor were quick to criticize his decisions and actions, yet they were unwilling or unable to solve his problems. Despite these difficulties, Washington initiated his plan of multiple forts by building the first at Winchester, and then suggested that Winchester become headquarters for the regiment since Fort Cumberland was prone to isolation when hostile Indians were in the area. Governor Dinwiddie vetoed the idea, reasoning that Fort Cumberland, which had been built by General Braddock, was a royal fort that could not be abandoned.

Washington made another inspection of the frontier in October, this one extending several hundred miles south through the Shenandoah Valley and beyond to the North Carolina border. For much of the time he rode helter-skelter on a narrow lane through forests occupied with unfriendly Indians, but he seemed impervious to harm. Later reports, for example, told of two northbound travelers who had been ambushed and killed shortly after Washington had passed them on the road.

Upon his return to Winchester, Washington wrote to the authorities in Williamsburg and reiterated his familiar litany of complaints to which he added a particularly scathing report about the lack of supplies and the general poor treatment of his army. The assembly, tired of his complaints, responded by ordering the recalcitrant colonel to abandon his little forts and move the garrisons to Fort Cumberland. He did so, though not without protest. He even defied authority by bypassing Governor Dinwiddie and sending a long and passionate letter to John Campbell, Earl of Loudoun, newly appointed as Britain's military commander and honorary Governor of Virginia. Washington wrote emotionally of his troubled heart and soul, and blamed Dinwiddie and the assembly for causing the present situation, mainly by ignoring his advice and requests. He carried on about the inadequacy of the militia, the difficulties caused by the poorly framed Draft Act, the problems with supplies and payments, and many others. Loudoun replied politely but with a lack of encouragement — the sort of non-reply that frustrated Washington so much that he became determined to call on Loudoun personally. Discovering that Loudoun was scheduled to confer with a group of colonial governors in Philadelphia, Washington begged Dinwiddie for permission to attend, which Dinwiddie reluctantly granted.

Washington might have been better served by staying at home. Loudoun kept him waiting for six weeks, then dismissed him peremptorily with orders to report back to Winchester since Fort Cumberland would henceforth be garrisoned by troops from Maryland. He was also told to provide 400 troops to South Carolina for that colony's protection and was handed a list of five frontier forts to be held by Virginia. As for Washington's other grievances, they were rejected out of hand. The country bumpkin had been treated to the cold, calculating, impersonal personality of a true aristocrat. It was a bitter lesson he would long remember.

Rejected and insulted by the authority he had turned to for help, Washington, who had given so much of himself for Virginia, was devastated by Loudoun's cavalier snobbery. He wrote to Dinwiddie of his disappointment in achieving none of his goals for Virginia's military and the protection of its people. In a bitter postscript he added, "We can't conceive that being Americans should deprive us of the benefits of British subjects,"[17] a prophetic sentiment that would soon express itself in very different ways.

Washington returned to Winchester and was greeted with rare good news. Negotiations with the southern Indians had produced results favorable to the British, and many needed warriors had joined Washington's forces. Meanwhile, the overall political and military situation was growing worse, and Washington's differences with Dinwiddie were becoming acrimonious. But the governor, gravely ill and forced to return home, was replaced by the Baron de Botetourt. Washington himself was felled by a serious recurrence of bloody flux that sent him back to Mount Vernon where he suffered for months, during which time his concerns undoubtedly drifted to brother Lawrence and the possibility of his own early death. In desperation, he made a painful journey to Williamsburg for a consultation with Virginia's leading doctor, John Amson, who assured Washington he had nothing to fear; the illness had run its course. After arriving in Williamsburg as an invalid, he left town with a fresh attitude and a new lease on life. Now, his thoughts turned not to Winchester and war, but to peace and, perhaps, matrimony.

It is likely that George Washington first met Mrs. Martha Dandridge Custis at a ball or other social event in Williamsburg. She was a fun-loving, pleasingly plump matron who lived with her husband Daniel and their two small children on a lush plantation on the Pamunkey River near its confluence with the York. In July, 1757, Daniel Custis died, leaving twenty-six–year-old Martha as one of the wealthiest widows in Virginia. Whether Washington had thought of the rich widow during his illness and gloomy meditation is not known, but upon his reprieve from Dr. Amson, he called at her plantation home, intriguingly named White House Plantation. She obviously encouraged him as he returned a week later, and sometime over the next few months, they became engaged.

At the same time, important developments were taking place in London. William Pitt, a true global visionary, was named Prime Minister and he proceeded to revolutionize Great Britain's lagging war efforts. He recalled the incompetent Loudoun and ordered three separate but intertwined colonial campaigns against the French: an attack on Louisburg on Cape Breton Island, action against Fort Ticonderoga above Lake Champlain, and the capture of Fort Duquesne at the Forks of the Ohio.

Virginia, bloodied by its failures in the wilderness and the continual incursions by hostile Indians, was in a mood to cooperate with the British government. The assembly voted to fund additional militia to garrison the frontier forts and participate in the advance on Fort Duquesne. Washington's regiment was brought to full strength and ordered to join 1200 British regulars and 2700 Pennsylvania militiamen under the command of British Brigadier General John Forbes. Washington reported to Winchester in April, moved his troops to Fort Cumberland, and waited for General Forbes to arrive.

To his surprise as well as that of the Virginia Assembly, Washington discovered that General Forbes's intent was to build a new road to Duquesne west from Philadelphia rather than to revise and improve the old Braddock road. The Virginians were outraged over this plan. Once hostilities ceased, the assembly reasoned, improvement of the Braddock road would draw commerce from the Ohio Valley to Virginia rather than Pennsylvania. Situated as it was near the head of navigation on the Potomac, Alexandria, for example, would surely become a great and important city.

Washington disputed the choice of roads with Forbes's engineer, Colonel Henry Bouquet, but no amount of persuasion, argument, or displays of bad temper could change the decision. To Virginia's disappointment, Raystown (now Bedford), Pennsylvania, became the staging point for the march to Fort Duquesne. Washington loyally accepted Forbes's decision publicly, yet continued to complain privately in letters to friends and sympathizers. Perhaps he was becoming more political, as he had recently been elected to represent the Winchester area in the Virginia House of Burgesses. In any event, road building continued across Laurel Ridge, then on to Loyal Hannon at the foot of Chestnut Ridge.

Concerned about the season, General Forbes called a parley of his officers in October to determine if they should continue westward or merely hold the area already occupied until the following spring. They decided to continue, but the army had not begun to move before Washington experienced another of his death-defying adventures. Rumors of a large enemy force in the area motivated Washington to send his second-in-command, Colonel Mercer, to investigate. Sporadic firing was heard from the forest; Mercer had found and engaged the French. An anxious Colonel Washington led a relief force into the gloom. Spotting shadowy figures ahead, his troops attacked, but Washington heard familiar voices shouting orders and realized with horror that his men were battling their fellow Virginians, members of Mercer's regiment. According to Washington's own notes, he leapt "between two fires, knocking up with his sword the presented pieces."[18] Fourteen militiamen had been killed and twenty-six were wounded, but Washington — courageously, if not foolishly, in the direct line of fire from both sides — remained untouched.

During his fight with the French, Mercer had captured three prisoners who testified that the French garrison at Duquesne was small and ill supplied. Armed with that intelligence, Forbes decided to attack and, because of his experience in the wilderness, chose Washington to lead a mobile party of 2500 soldiers. They climbed Chestnut Ridge, the last major natural obstacle before Duquesne, and entered an unblazed forest. Security was doubled as Bouquet's road builders and Washington's fighters neared the site of the Braddock massacre, but they saw no human activity until a lone Indian entered their camp to report thick smoke emanating from the Fort Duquesne area. So it was on Christmas morning that a shocked George Washington stood on a bluff and looked down upon the smoldering remains of Fort Duquesne and the burnt shells of thirty houses. The French had abandoned and torched the area before departing by canoe down the Ohio.

It must have been agonizing for Washington to witness the death of a place he had worked to eradicate for four years, especially since the victory had taken place in spite of his advice and lack of confidence in the British plan. The abandonment and destruction of Fort Duquesne energized him to make good on the threat he had made so many times — to retire. After five years as Virginia's most prominent military leader, he was about to return to private life, albeit with little satisfaction. Bitter and resentful of perceived injustices from his superiors in the field, in Williamsburg and in London, and burdened by a sense of failure, Washington returned to Mount Vernon and a frenetic but less dangerous life.

On January 6, 1759, George Washington and Martha Custis were married, probably at her home but perhaps at her nearby parish church, Saint Peters, in New Kent, Virginia. There is no record of a honeymoon trip, only that Martha attended a session of the Burgesses in Williamsburg where her new husband received the approbation and official thanks of the assembly for his military service to the crown and colony.

For the next sixteen years, George Washington was the master of what became a major agricultural enterprise that required constant attention and hard work. Thousands of acres were under cultivation; overseers and slaves needed to be fed, clothed, and tended. There were cattle and hogs to raise and fish to catch and salt. There were horses to breed and wagons and carriages to maintain. There was grain to mill and wells to dig. There were quitrents and taxes to collect and pay, and accounts to keep. Mount Vernon, to be profitable, had to be self-sustaining.

Martha had brought considerable wealth to the marriage. As the law provided at the time, a third of her late husband's fortune came to her as the widow. The rest, divided by her two minor children, was placed under George Washington's supervision, not an uncommon procedure in those days when there were neither trust officers nor bankers. The practice sometimes led to abuses, although George, reputable and loving, handled the Custis estate with care and honesty.

Martha's responsibilities at Mount Vernon were varied, although confined to the smokehouse, kitchen, wash house, spinning house, and manor house. The medical needs, training, and supervision of the household servants was her most important task; a large staff was required to cook, serve, manufacture clothing, launder, and clean, and nannies were needed for the children. Of course, she was ever the gracious hostess and constant helpmate for her husband. History has made it clear that Washington, in his marriage to Martha, fulfilled the hopes expressed in his own words that were written in 1759: "I am now, I believe, fixed at this seat with an agreeable consort for life, and hope to find more happiness in retirement than I ever experienced amidst a wide and bustling world."[19]

During these years, Washington became an inventive and visionary farmer. He gradually switched from raising tobacco to producing corn and wheat as cash crops, and by 1766 Mount Vernon was producing 7000 bushels of wheat, 10,000 bushels of corn, over 6000 pounds of pork, barrels of salted fish, and hundreds of pounds of fruits and vegetables annually. He constructed his own grinding mill, dug drainage ditches, built fences, and continually experimented with grafting, soil study, and fertilization techniques.

Yet it was hard to make ends meet. Virginia did not have its own currency, so buying and selling was by barter. Manufactured goods were available only from England, thus American suppliers and consumers were at the mercy of unknown, often unscrupulous factors in London who doubled as agents for the sale of crops and the purchase of goods for the colonists. Such buying and selling by third parties was often unsatisfactory and always frustrating.

Life at Mount Vernon was not, however, all work. The Washingtons entertained frequently and unexpected visitors graced Mount Vernon's dinner table almost every evening. There were trips to Annapolis for the races and yearly sessions of the assembly in Williamsburg. Washington, a superb horseman, indulged in fox hunting and had other interests that included cockfighting, dancing, and cards. As he became more content in retirement from the military, he participated increasingly in local civic affairs; he served as a vestryman of Truro Parish, as a trustee of Alexandria, and as a justice of the county court. A Custis house in Williamsburg was sold to accommodate the purchase of a townhouse in Alexandria, which was then used as an office and lodging for the overflow of guests at Mount Vernon.

Along with his farming and entertaining, Washington continued as a land speculator and developer. As early as 1763, he became interested in a project designed to drain the Great Dismal Swamp in southeastern Virginia bordering northeastern North Carolina. It was envisioned that the swamp might be converted into a rich agricultural region, and he made several trips to the area to evaluate such a possibility. Encouraged, he joined a group of investors interested in the project. At the same time he became a shareholder in a company formed to solicit a royal grant of thousands of acres on the Mississippi River. He remained vitally interested in the Potomac River, drawing up plans in 1769 for a privately financed system of canal locks from Georgetown to Cumberland.

In 1770, Washington learned of a government plan to give land in the west to veterans of the Fort Necessity campaign and the French and Indian War. Entitled due to his participation in the campaigns, Washington and his friend Dr. James Craik departed for the Ohio Valley to select, survey, and lay claim to their land. At Fort Pitt, the two departed by canoe down the Ohio to its junction with the Great Kanawha River, the location of present-day Point Pleasant, West Virginia, where Washington laid claim to nearly 3000 acres of prime bottomland.

Although Washington's life seemed tranquil after his return from the Ohio Valley, there were personal problems within the Washington family. In 1772, Mary Washington reluctantly moved from Ferry Farm to a pleasant home that George had purchased for her in Fredericksburg. Then, in 1773, Patsy Custis, Washington's sixteen-year-old stepdaughter, victimized by epilepsy, had a seizure and died within two minutes. George and Martha had spoiled the children, and both were devastated by the child's death.

Stepson Jacky Custis was not only spoiled rotten, he was in danger of becoming a true wastrel. The Washingtons had tried valiantly to straighten out his priorities with private tutoring, but finally decided to send him to King's College (now Columbia University) in New York. Jacky resisted mightily as, unbeknownst to George and Martha, he had become engaged. Paterfamilias George refused to approve of the match until the young man completed his education, so he personally accompanied the reluctant lover to New York.

Washington was received with great honor wherever he traveled, and was entertained by Lieutenant Governor Richard Penn in Philadelphia and by Governor William Penn in Burlington, New Jersey. He and Jacky spent one evening at the home of Lord Stirling in Basking Ridge, New Jersey, before they embarked for New York where Jacky was enrolled in school. While in New York, Washington met with old friends including Thomas Gage, a veteran of the Braddock campaign and now Lieutenant General Gage, commander of British forces in America. They would meet again.

Jacky was not happy in New York and his fiancee, Eleanor Calvert, visited Mount Vernon in an effort to persuade Martha to intervene on behalf of the young couple. George found himself portrayed as the sole impediment to true love, so in an effort to promote domestic harmony, he reluctantly granted approval for the match. Nineteen year-old Jacky left school, the marriage took place, and the groom, predictably, went on to become a rich idler.

Some modern historians have remarked on Washington's failure to have children. Martha was obviously fertile, so it is likely that, despite his physical bearing and prowess, George was sterile, perhaps as a result of smallpox. Relevant to the subject is the old saying, "Providence kept George Washington from having children of his own so that he could better be the father of his country."[20]

Momentous events affecting the colonies were taking place as the British Parliament enacted increasingly repressive laws and resistance to them sharpened. Louis Rubin, in his book *Virginia, A Bicentennial History,* summarized this period as follows:

> *The American Revolution came about because by the 1750s almost all the thirteen colonies, and Virginia perhaps most of all, were strong, prosperous, increasingly self-sustaining political and social units, grown accustomed to governing themselves and ever more insistent upon doing so. Virginia, with its population of 550,000, was ready for self-government and had, in fact, all but enjoyed just that in the 1730s and 1740s, and was not willing finally to accept royal government that did not offer it what in*

effect was the status of a self-governing dominion. . . . What Virginia had to offer Americans as they moved toward their independence was not only a matchless set of able, vigorous leaders, but — by the standards of the time — a thoroughgoing commitment to representative government. The very fact that of all the colonies, Virginia was closest to England in outlook and temper meant that it was most prepared to demand liberty.[21]

Along with all other colonials, George Washington the planter and farmer was affected by these new and repressive regulations emanating from Parliament. Although a member of the House of Burgesses, he remained relatively passive, his interests reflected mainly on the local level. Perhaps then, as today, all politics are local. At least Washington thought so. In 1764, Parliament forbade the printing of paper money in Virginia which meant that hardly anyone in the colony could pay their debts. In the next year, Parliament passed the Stamp Act, objectionable to the colonists as a tax legislated abroad and collected by the crown — but without consultation. Virginia was particularly vociferous as it had enjoyed a modest form of home rule through its assembly. The Stamp Act proved so unpopular that it was soon repealed, except for a duty on tea. Parliament did not cease and desist from other attempts to make life difficult and expensive for the colonists, as in 1767, for example, when the Townshend Acts ordered that import duties collected in America on glass, lead, paint, paper, and tea were to be used to make royal officials independent of colonial appropriations.

In 1769, Washington received reports from Philadelphia and Annapolis, the capitals of the Pennsylvania and Maryland colonies, that proposed active resistance to the onerous provisions of the Townshend Acts. He forwarded the reports to his neighbor George Mason at Gunston Hall without realizing that Mason had helped write the articles of resistance. Mason, a leading scholar-politician of the time, had been instrumental in developing and nurturing Washington's political thoughts. Mason, for example, had drafted the Virginia Bill of Rights that later became the inspiration for the Declaration of Independence.

Washington and Mason met to make a list of goods to be proscribed, a list they took to Williamsburg for presentation to the House of Burgesses just as the burgesses were pleading with King George III to abandon the Townshend Acts. Governor Botetourt, on behalf of the crown, responded to their demands by dissolving the assembly. Infuriated, the leaders repaired to Raleigh Tavern where Burgess Washington presented the non-importation agreement he and Mason had drafted. The rump assembly accepted it, but the agreement proved unenforceable. Even so, Parliament had received the colonists' message loud and clear, and eventually the dreaded act was repealed.

Relations between the colonists and the mother country continued to deteriorate, especially when Lord North began an ill-fated term as Prime Minister. That was 1770, the year of the Boston Massacre in which British regulars clashed with a mob of unruly citizens and five colonials were killed. Oddly, that confrontation is not mentioned in any of Washington's extant correspondence. Then, on June 10, 1772, another incident served to further ignite dissatisfaction with the crown. A British revenue cutter, the HMS *Gaspee,* had run aground in Narragansett Bay while chasing an American smuggler and thereafter was assaulted and burned by a band of Rhode Island Sons of Liberty. The British Court of Inquiry investigating the matter claimed the power to send any person even suspected of complicity to England for trial. That threat prompted Washington and others to form a Committee of Correspondence to expedite the exchange of information among the colonies; to keep all colonies informed of what was threatened against any one of them, in the interest of mutual self-defense.

The following year, a group of colonials, protesting a punitive tax on tea, dressed themselves as Indians, boarded three British vessels in Boston harbor, and threw their cargoes of tea into the water, an event known as the Boston Tea Party. Washington considered it to have been a lawless act and disapproved of the behavior. On the other hand, he was infuriated by the harsh British reaction to the event — punitive cancellation of the Massachusetts charter and the arrival of additional British troops in the colonies. His anger further intensified when the British Secretary of State, Lord Hillsborough, denied his and other veterans' claims to thousands of acres in the west based on their service during the French and Indian War. Hillsborough ruled that the land grants were available only to veterans who had served in the regular army, not to colonials. Then the implementation of the Quebec Act, which transferred jurisdiction over the area between the Mississippi and the Ohio rivers — land for which Washington had fought for on behalf of Virginia and Britain — to

Catholic Quebec, was an additional insult that strengthened the dissatisfaction of Washington and others with the existing British government.

Virginia sent seven representatives to the First Continental Congress, held in Philadelphia in 1774: George Washington, Peyton Randolph, Richard Henry Lee, Richard Bland, Benjamin Harrison, Edmund Pendleton, and Patrick Henry. There is no record that Washington made any significant contribution to the Congress; his impact was subtle as he met leaders from other colonies and exchanged views on a one-on-one basis. The record does reflect that his military bearing, his forthright thoughtful views, and his youthful vigor impressed the delegates. The Congress, showing no willingness to compromise with the crown, adjourned after scheduling another session for the following spring.

While in attendance at the Congress, Virginia's militia companies elected Washington as their field officer. This meant that in the event of hostilities, he would be called to command, a disagreeable outlook at best. He had already witnessed war, and like most other military commanders, dreaded it. And from a personal standpoint, he had a great deal to lose. Everything he owned and worked for, including Mount Vernon, would be lost if the colonials should go to war with Britain and be defeated.

Washington's already gloomy mood did not brighten when he learned that there had been fighting at Lexington and Concord in Massachusetts between British soldiers and colonials in April, 1775. It was becoming more and more likely that more serious hostilities were imminent. With a heavy heart, Colonel George Washington left Mount Vernon on May 4 to attend the Second Continental Congress in Philadelphia and unknowingly assume his unique place in history. Washington hoped that war would not come but, in case it should, he had packed his military uniform and sword.

In response to the events that had taken place in Lexington and Concord, an informal army of 20,000 militiamen and other New Englanders assembled near Boston, resolved to resist any attempts by the British to leave the city. It was clear to the colonials that Massachusetts could not stand alone against the British; any effective resistance would require the organized cooperation of the other colonies. John Adams of Massachusetts led an effort to select George Washington as commander-in-chief of a new Continental Army, reasoning that Washington was, first of all, an experienced military leader known to be brave, modest, sober, and temperate. And, the cause of unity among the colonies required the highly visible participation of somebody from outside of New England. And, as author John Ferling has written, "Finally, by chance not only was [Washington] healthy in 1775, he looked as men thought a soldier should — big, strong, robust, agile, hard."[22] The fact that Washington wore his uniform to the congressional sessions obviously had not hurt his chances of being selected to command the new army.

As he prepared to leave to assume command of his army, he paused to write Martha, bidding farewell with uncharacteristic emotion:

My Dearest:

I am now set down to write to you on a subject that fills me with inexpressible concern, and this concern is greatly aggravated and increased when I reflect upon the uneasiness I know it will cause you. It has been determined in Congress that the whole army raised for the defense of the American cause shall be put under my care, and that it is necessary for me to proceed immediately to Boston to take upon me the command of it.

You may believe me, my dear Patsy, when I assure you, in the most solemn manner, that, so far from seeking this appointment, I have used every endeavor in my power to avoid it, not only from my unwillingness to part from you and the family, but from a consciousness of its being a trust too great for my capacity, and that I should enjoy more real happiness in one month with you at home than I have the most distant prospect of finding abroad, if my stay were to be seven times seven years. But it has been kind of a destiny that has thrown me upon this service, I shall hope that my undertaking it is designed to answer some good purpose. You might and, I suppose, did perceive from the tenor of my letters that I was apprehensive I could not avoid this appointment, as I did not pretend to intimate when I should return. That was the case. It was utterly out of my power to refuse this appointment, without exposing my character to such censures as would have reflected dishonor on myself and given pain to my friends. This, I am sure, could not, and ought not, to be pleasing to you, and must have lessened me considerably in my own esteem. I shall rely, therefore, confidently on that Providence which has heretofore preserved and been bountiful to me, not doubting but that I shall return safe to you in the fall.[23]

It would be eight long years before Washington would again call Mount Vernon home.

Only a day before his departure from Philadelphia, news was received of the misnamed Battle of Bunker Hill, just north of Boston. The courier proclaimed a major victory by the colonials, a message that made Washington even more anxious to reach Massachusetts as quickly as possible. Early on the morning of June 15, 1775, accompanied by personal assistants Joseph Reed and Thomas Mifflin and generals Philip Schuyler and Charles Lee, General Washington bade farewell to Philadelphia and embarked on a great adventure. What must have gone through the minds of these men as they set out for Boston where Washington was to take command of a Continental Army? The men were fully committed to the cause before them and unable to turn back — their homes, their families, and their very lives now in jeopardy.

The route to Boston took the men through the New Jersey towns of Trenton, New Brunswick, Newark and Hoboken, and then on, by ferry, to New York City where they were greeted by an enthusiastic crowd of civic leaders and well-wishers. The general spent only twenty-four hours in the city, almost the entire time in conference with General Schuyler and other officers who discussed New York City's defenses and the likelihood of a British invasion from Canada. He spoke briefly to the New York Provincial Congress in a building located near the present New York City Hall. The speech was important for in it he pledged never to forget the supremacy of civilian rule, perhaps the most important element in George Washington's legacy to the nation. Throughout the Revolutionary War, which was by this time, in fact, underway, there was often pressure for Washington to assume the mantle of military dictator, yet he resisted every such overture, as he consistently kept Congress informed of his actions and deferred to their judgements even when frustrated by their inaction or inability to provide adequate men, money, and materiel.

On June 26th, Washington and his party left New York, crossed the Harlem River at Kings Bridge on "the road to Eastchester," and rode on to New Rochelle, New York. They traveled north on the Boston Post

Road to Fairfield, Connecticut, where the general was entertained at the home of Thaddeus Burr. The next day's ride took them to New Haven where Washington spoke to a group of Yale University student army volunteers. From New Haven they rode north to Hartford, probably staying at the home of patriot Silas Deane in Wethersfield before heading to Springfield, Massachusetts, where they refreshed themselves at the tavern of Zena Parsons on the corner of Main and Elm, the site of present-day Court Square. On July 1st, they lunched at the tavern of Major Aaron Graves in Palmer before heading east to Brookfield and Worcester where they over-nighted at Stearns Tavern. The next day, they sped through Marlborough and Watertown before reaching their destination in Cambridge, thus bringing an exhausting and dusty ten-day trip to an end.

At Cambridge, Washington was appalled by the conditions and took immediate steps to rectify numerous problems. New sanitary facilities were built, regular drilling begun, discipline enforced, shelters constructed, a separate officer's corps formed, and improvements were made to the encampment's defenses. Even though the encounter at Bunker Hill, more properly Breeds Hill, had technically been a British victory, the carnage and heavy loss of life had forced the redcoats back into Boston where they were besieged by Americans who were holding the hills that surrounded the city. Washington settled in for a prolonged siege, although he expected that British Commander Lord Howe would attempt a breakout. Congress, miles away, forced Washington's hand by ordering him to attack Howe's forces. Washington, however, deliberated at length and decided his first move would be to occupy and fortify Dorchester Heights overlooking Boston. In a masterful feat of military engineering, the Americans prefabricated fascines and parapets and, under cover of darkness, fortified Dorchester Heights in one incredible night of labor. Looking up at fortified positions armed with artillery brought in from Fort Ticonderoga by Colonel Henry Knox, the British faced a choice of either attacking the colonials or suffering a prolonged and unanswerable shelling. They prudently chose a third alternative, retreat, and evacuated Boston by sea on March 17th. Washington's ragged colonials had captured Boston with a brilliantly executed offensive maneuver. On March 18, 1776, Washington wrote to the Continental Congress:

It is with the greatest pleasure I inform you that . . . the Ministerial Army evacuated the Town of Boston, and that the Forces of the United Colonies are now in actual possession therof.[24]

Even though the colonials were in control of Boston and the British army had taken flight, grave problems remained. A double-pronged foray against the British in Quebec by generals Richard Montgomery and Benedict Arnold had failed. There was a shortage of basic supplies including clothing, shoes, food, blankets, arms, gunpowder, and money. The American troops, raw and undisciplined, were decimated by disease. With no strong central government, there was a lack of cooperation from the Continental Congress. Jealousy among officers was rampant and Tory sympathizers were everywhere. Most important, however, was the uncertainty among the American military of the whereabouts and destination of Lord Howe's army and fleet. It seemed logical to Washington that Howe might attempt to unite with General John Burgoyne's army that was thought to be moving south from Canada along the Lake Champlain-Hudson River route to Albany. If the two British armies were able to link up along the Hudson Valley, New England would be isolated from the colonies to its south and the ability of the colonies to act as a united group would be greatly reduced. In an effort to prevent Howe from gaining control of the Hudson River, if indeed that was his goal, Washington began to move his forces from Boston to New York on April 4, 1776.

The colonials took the fastest route to New York, traveling via Providence, Rhode Island, and the coast of Connecticut along Long Island Sound, through Westchester into New York City. The movement of any army in 1776 was a monstrous undertaking — a line of thousands of marching men could stretch for miles, and the baggage train could be even longer. Author John Ferling described one scene as follows:

Three hundred wagons, each drawn by a team of four horses, were assembled at the Commons at Cambridge, this to transport just the ammunition and stores of the regiment of artillery; nor could these items be loaded haphazardly, for thought had to be given to placing the most essential objects in the forward vehicles. More wagons were required for hospital supplies . . . and the commander placed responsibility for the deliverance of each van's contents upon the shoulders of its teamster, and he appointed an overseer, or 'conductor' as he called him, for every thirty wagons.[25]

The officers traveled by horseback while the men walked. Advance quartermaster units moved ahead of the main army, searching for both signs of the enemy and proper sites for each night's bivouac. The army trudged behind: the cavalry leading, followed by infantry companies, more cavalry, wagons carrying supplies for each night's encampment, transports of weaponry, baggage wagons, the artillery train, and at last the rear guard. The army was normally made up of six-man squads, each carrying its own tent and cooking pot. The soldiers rose before dawn and were on the road before daylight. The march continued until late in the afternoon, then camp was made early enough for latrines to be dug and firewood to be gathered for that night's use.

Washington accompanied the army for only part of the journey. He rode ahead to Providence where he headquartered in the home of Rhode Island's governor for a few days, and then rejoined the troops in Norwich, Connecticut, before he raced ahead again to arrive in New York on April 13, to await the arrival of the British fleet. His first headquarters was at a house on Pearl Street at Cedar, then he moved to the Mortier House, later known as Richmond Hill, at the southeast corner of Varick and Charlton streets. He faced a complex and daunting task. First, he ordered every able-bodied soldier and workman to work building and digging defenses for an anticipated British attack. Street barricades were built in lower Manhattan, Brooklyn, and at Kings Bridge to the north; gun emplacements were set on Governors Island and fortifications constructed in the Bronx. Except for a short trip to Philadelphia to report to Congress, the commander-in-chief was everywhere — urging, cajoling, persuading, and supervising. In late June, the first ships of the British fleet arrived and anchored off Sandy Hook. The wait was over.

In Philadelphia, meanwhile, Congress approved the Declaration of Independence and had sent a copy to General Washington. On July 9th, Washington ordered the army to form on the green at New York's City Hall, located at Chambers Street and Broadway, where officers read the document to the assembled troops who greeted it with tumultuous cheers. In remarks following the reading, Washington said, in part:

The General hopes that this important event will serve as a fresh incentive to every officer and soldier to act with fidelity and courage, as knowing now the peace and safety of his country depend, under God, solely on the success of our arms: and that he

*is now in the service of a state possessed of sufficient power to
reward his merit, and advance him to the Highest Honors of a free
country.*[26]

By this time, the British fleet had anchored in Gravesend Bay south
of Brooklyn, waiting for reinforcements of Hessian mercenaries hired by
the crown. On August 22, 1776, 400 transport ships and thirty-seven
men-of-war began to discharge thousands of troops on the south shore
of Long Island. The battle for New York City was about to begin.

The Battle of Long Island, most of which was fought in Brooklyn,
would not be General Washington's finest hour, nor his army's. While
the defensive line of the Continental Army — a string of interconnected
forts on heights six miles inland (at present-day Prospect Park) — was
strong, the Americans failed to protect many of the roads that radiated
from the hills to the beach. Washington's Intelligence Corps had failed
him as well, as the British had landed twice the number of troops that
were expected. The numerical advantage of the British enabled Lord Howe
to conduct a flanking movement around the American left, a tactic that
sent the Americans reeling. Almost totally surrounded, they were saved
from destruction only by the valiant stand of a group of Marylanders, the
onset of darkness, and by Howe's lack of a killer instinct. As night fell,
the vulnerable Americans were locked into a single redoubt, but Howe
decided to conduct a siege rather than storm the heavily armed fort.
Many students of the Revolutionary War feel that Howe's reluctance to
take the fort was a direct result of his fear of another catastrophe similar
to that at Bunker Hill where the British suffered heavy losses. In any
event, he hesitated, a decision exacerbated by bad weather that precluded
any aggressive action. The delay gave General Washington time to decide that the American position on Long Island was indefensible and
must be abandoned.

In any war there are turning points. The successful evacuation of
Long Island by 12,000 men under the nose of a superior British force
was one of the most dramatic and important actions of the Revolutionary
War. Under cover of darkness and providential fog, the Americans assembled and marched silently to the beach (now Empire-Fulton Ferry
State Park) where they embarked for Manhattan in flatboats skippered
by crews of Massachusetts fishermen. A story told about this evacuation is that General Israel Putnam had Indians in his detachment wail and

yell war chants; their terrifying noises not only scared the British but set every dog and cat on Long Island yowling, screeching, and barking, the cacophony serving to cover the sounds of the American retreat. Thanks to a combination of nerve, good fortune, and bad weather, the evacuation went smoothly, with the rear guard gaining the river as daylight broke. In *George Washington's War,* author Robert Leckie wrote:

> *Out on the water a young Connecticut lieutenant named Benjamin Tallmadge peered through the swirling mists of the fog and saw the last man step down the slippery steps of the landing into a boat. He was very tall and wore a blue sash across his breast.*[27]

It must have been a furious Lord Howe who awoke the next morning to discover that his enemy had slipped from his grasp. The colonials, however, were now bottled up on another island, Manhattan, and were still vulnerable. The British fleet controlled the waterways, and the only escape route for the Americans was across Kings Bridge at the northern end of the island. Numerous military and civilian conferences were held to discuss the tricky question of whether New York City should be defended. Washington's first impulse was to burn and then evacuate the city to prevent its use by the British as winter quarters. Upon reconsideration, however, he sensed that abandonment would "dispirit the Troops and enfeeble our Cause."[28] It was decided to defend the city by setting up a line at Harlem Heights.

On September 15th, Howe attacked the colonials at Kips Bay on the east side of Manhattan where a small band of green, shell-shocked defenders was routed by heavy naval shelling and an amphibious assault. Washington raced down from his headquarters in a futile attempt to stem the tide of frightened men. The general rode among the men waving his sword — shouting, imploring and ordering them to stand fast and fight. In his preoccupation with stopping the rout he failed to notice the enemy approaching. An aide grabbed the reins of his horse and hurried the commander-in-chief to a safer place just in the nick of time. As had occurred several times before — on the road from Fort LeBoeuf, during the debacle at Fort Necessity, at the ambush of Braddock, on the rides through the Shenandoah Valley, and in the evacuation of Long Island — George Washington escaped injury during the heat of truly dangerous situations. He seemed to lead a charmed life, impervious to danger and bullets, and throughout the war he would continue to defy death and to lead by courageous example.

Washington was an inspiring leader, always fighting alongside his men and always fighting the Continental Congress on their behalf. He was loyal; he never took a furlough or leave throughout the entire eight years of the war. Even during the most bitter periods — at Morristown, Valley Forge, and other winter encampments — he remained in the field with the army. While it is true that his winter lodgings and headquarters were more often than not comfortable homes and that Martha was with him on many occasions, he shared the army's discomfort, ever ready to fight for their well-being, whether for basic supplies of food, better equipment, or money. The old canard about "George Washington slept here" doesn't take into account that the commanding general had his own tent and folding camp bed when on the road. He ate army food and shared army hardships. While he slept in many places, quite a few were in the field and not all of them were comfortable.

At Harlem Heights on northern Manhattan, the Americans waited for Howe's next move. It soon came as a tepid attack that was repulsed in a sharp firefight in a buckwheat field (now the site of Barnard College on Broadway, between 116th and 120th streets). The skirmish was indecisive, yet Washington was heartened when his troops stood and fought, a promising sign after the rout at Kips Bay a few days earlier. Howe then ordered an ill-advised landing at Throgs Neck at the American rear, but consistent with his character, he moved too slowly to trap the colonials. They managed to retreat to White Plains, which left Fort Washington (just north of the George Washington Bridge, between 183rd and 185th streets) as the only remaining colonial defensive position in New York City. Howe's formidable army, apparently unaware of the location of the disorganized rebels, did nothing to stop them, and by the time the Americans were found, Washington had fortified the high ground near the present-day junction of the Cross-Westchester and Taconic parkways.

At White Plains, Howe succeeded, with a bitterly fought frontal attack, in dislodging the Americans from the two hills upon which the colonial defenses were situated. Washington moved his troops to the rear in good order, expecting to battle on the same field the next day, but the British did not press the attack. After several days of inactivity, the British army began to move into their winter quarters in New York, planning to assault Fort Washington on their way back into the city.

Washington repaired to Fort Lee in New Jersey, directly across the Hudson River from Fort Washington, and waited for Howe's next move. There, Washington and his counselors debated the fate of Fort Washington — whether to abandon or defend the structure which some felt was impregnable. Washington vacillated on the issue for several days, then decided to make a personal inspection of the fort before reaching his decision. But he was too late. As he was crossing the river, the British struck, and within a single day had forced the surrender of 2000 defenders and captured quantities of valuable arms and supplies.

With the loss of Fort Washington, Washington abandoned Fort Lee and headed south to escape the pursuit of the rejuvenated and aggressive British army. General Lord Cornwallis was dispatched to cross the Hudson to capture Fort Lee, and then follow and harass Washington's army as it retreated across New Jersey. Washington crossed the Hackensack and Passaic rivers, then moved southward through Newark, Brunswick, Burlington, and Trenton before finally crossing the Delaware River into Pennsylvania, north of Philadelphia. The retreat of the Continental Army must have been difficult as the weather was cold and wet, the roads were rivers of mud and ice, clothing and shelter were inadequate, food was scarce, and a well-supplied enemy continued to nip at its heels. Somehow the ragged band persevered and reached safety in Pennsylvania.

At that point, the British occupied all of New Jersey; their forces were spread across the state in a series of seven encampments that stretched from Fort Lee to Trenton. General Howe remained in winter quarters in New York City, warm and comfortable. His opponent and an ill-supplied band of raw, inexperienced militiamen and regulars were camped in freezing discomfort in Bucks County, Pennsylvania, from where they kept a wary eye on the eastern shore of the Delaware River. Discouraged, demoralized, and near defeat, Washington had reached what was to be the lowest point of his command. "I think the game is pretty near up," he wrote to his nephew John Augustine Washington on December 17.[29] Civilian and army morale was low, and the Continental Congress, restless and fearful, prudently fled Philadelphia for Baltimore in mid-December. Even one signer of the Declaration of Independence had given up and defected to the British. Faced with almost certain defeat, what was one to do? Well, if that one was George Washington, there was only one answer. Attack!

In the depths of personal despair, George Washington initiated what would be perhaps his finest military hour — the American assault on the Hessian barracks at Trenton, New Jersey, on Christmas Night, 1776. The story is well documented — the dangerous crossing of the ice-filled Delaware River, the nine-mile midnight march in beating sleet to Trenton, and the attack on the surprised, sleepy, hung-over Hessians — an assault performed with courage, intelligence, and vision. It was a bold, inventive maneuver of real genius; not only a military success but more importantly, a brilliant political stroke, a major victory when one was desperately needed to keep alive the ongoing fight for freedom.

Washington, leading his victorious army and over 900 prisoners, returned to the encampment in Pennsylvania. Flushed with victory, he hoped to take advantage of intelligence reports that two other Hessian regiments had broken camp and moved north, a circumstance which would have left much of southern New Jersey open for occupation by the Continental Army. With many enlistments due to expire, Washington knew that it was essential to immediately fight again, and win. With the promise of bonuses, he persuaded many soldiers to reenlist for at least six weeks, and on December 29th, the rejuvenated army once again crossed the Delaware River to New Jersey.

Washington established headquarters in Trenton and deployed the army in a poor defensive position on the south side of the Assunpink River, with their backs to the Delaware. They waited nervously for the British response to their audacity at Trenton. The response was not long in coming. On January 2, 1777, Lord Cornwallis, at the head of 8000 men, reached the Assunpink after a miserable march over wet, boggy roads, constantly harassed by colonial guerillas and riflemen. As a result of the delaying tactics, Cornwallis was unable to attack until dusk. After two or three sharp exchanges he opted to wait for daylight to unleash his next assault. His men were exhausted and hungry, and he was sure he could easily crush the half-starved colonial rabble the next day.

At dawn, Cornwallis found nothing. Washington, catlike, had escaped again. Under cover of darkness, the Americans had skirted wide around the left flank of the sleeping redcoats and moved farther to the north, intending to strike Cornwallis from the rear. Washington's audacious plan had three objectives. Another victory, however small, would assist in recruitment. A major victory might serve to discourage the British from continuing their occupation of New Jersey, or it might even discourage them from continuing the war. And the British supply depot at New Brunswick was an enticing target, a source of always-needed materiel.

Washington's first objective was Princeton, where a sharp firefight ensued. A small British rearguard routed one group of Americans with a bayonet charge, but General Washington, in another of his death-defying acts, rode up and down the front to rally his troops who responded by sending the British reeling into retreat. After collecting supplies and destroying what couldn't be taken from Princeton, a village of fifty-four homes, the American army headed farther north with Cornwallis in pursuit. Washington realized that his exhausted army was not fit to fight again soon, so he marched his weary but jubilant troops through the rolling hills of western New Jersey into winter quarters at Morristown.

Washington did not achieve all of his military objectives with his offensive thrusts, but his victories at Trenton and Princeton had accomplished something more significant — they had earned the recognition and respect of several European leaders. Washington was hailed as a military genius by Frederick the Great of Prussia, who extolled, "The achievements of Washington and his little band of compatriots . . . were the most brilliant of any recorded in the history of military achievements."[30]

Of more importance in the long run, it was the positive reaction of the French that helped turn the tide of the war. After Princeton, the French, tacitly neutral, switched from secret ally to outspoken and practical friend to the Americans. A stream of French arms and munitions began to flow into the colonies, followed by a flood of European military professionals and soldiers-of-fortune anxious to join the revolutionary cause — among them Baron von Steuben, Thaddeus Koscziusko, Casimir Pulaski, Baron von Kalb, and the Marquis de Lafayette.

The five months that Washington's army spent at Morristown was a period of intense activity. Housing was constructed, defenses were dug, and Washington moved into a long frame tavern where he was joined by Martha in the spring. As enlistments expired, new recruits were needed and they had to be trained. Intelligence was analyzed and plans laid. Decisions were made regarding other theaters of operation. Raids were conducted to disrupt Lord Howe's supply lines so as to limit the ability of the British to move about and fight effectively later in the year. Ferling, commenting on just how important these raiding parties were, has written:

> *The victualing requirements of an eighteenth-century army were enormous. The British soldier was supposed to have a daily ration of one pound of bread and either one pound of beef or nine ounces of pork; in addition, oatmeal, cheese, peas, rice, butter, molasses, rum and porter were supposed to be a regular part of his diet, and all this might be supplemented by vinegar, sauerkraut, or various fresh vegetables when available. Multiply these per capita requirements by an army that normally exceeded twenty thousand men, and it became obvious that Britain's logistical problems would have been considerable even if the American forces had not attempted to impede its operation. While Washington's harassing activity did not immediately end the war, it did make the redcoats dependent on London for the barest necessities. Thereafter Britain would have to ship 20 million pounds of bread, flour and rice to America each year, as well as 2 million pounds of salt beef and 10 million pounds of salt pork, plus still more incredible quantities of additional staples. And that was just to feed the men. About 28 million pounds of hay and 12 million pounds of oats per year were required for the horses. Then there were munitions and weapons, uniforms and tents, cooking utensils and medical supplies, skilled artisans and replacements for dead and wounded soldiers and the equine corps. Even coal and wood had to be shipped across the Atlantic, and all this had to compete for space on the British ships that plied the trade lanes of the Empire.[31]*

Lord Howe spent the winter formulating, then discarding, plan after plan of his own. It was not until mid-June that his army left on a meandering campaign through New Jersey. His first target was the small town of Somerset Court House, after which he went on to Princeton and Trenton in an attempt to flush the Americans from their lair at Morristown. American intelligence had anticipated Howe's maneuver, so Washington had moved to Middlebrook (now Bound Brook), about seven miles from the major British outpost at New Brunswick. From Middlebrook, small mobile forces attacked and harassed the British foraging parties. The harassment, combined with the possibility of having to engage the main colonial army head on, forced Howe to fall back to Amboy. After heavy fighting and inconsequential skirmishing, Howe embarked to New York while Washington headed back to Middlebrook, bringing to an end one of the most pointless British military ventures in the entire war.

At about that time, Washington received the distressing news that on July 6, 1777, Fort Ticonderoga had fallen to the forces of General John Burgoyne moving south from Canada. The commander-in-chief started north to assist in the defense of the critical Hudson River lifeline when, to his consternation and bewilderment, Howe and the British army sailed from Staten Island in 260 ships. Washington surmised that Howe was sailing north to join forces with Burgoyne, yet intelligence filtered in that Howe's fleet was headed south, in which case his presumed objective was Philadelphia. Uncertainty became the order of the day as an assault on Philadelphia by the British was certainly not as important strategically as a union of Howe's and Burgoyne's forces on the Hudson. Hence the sail south might have been a feint. Even more improbable was the possibility that Howe might be sailing to the Carolinas, perhaps to Charleston. Eventually, the British fleet was sighted sailing north on Chesapeake Bay! On August 25th, British troops began to disembark at Head of Elk (Elkton) in Maryland. Apparently the British were planning to attack Philadelphia from the south.

It was unlikely that Howe would have passed up the chance to join forces with Burgoyne, but Washington decided to believe his intelligence and marched his army through Philadelphia and set up a line of defense south of the city at Brandywine Creek. A famous sidebar to the story of the American army's march was its colorful parade through Philadelphia — a patently obvious public relations spectacle aimed at boosting civilian morale. General Washington on his prancing steed cut a heroic figure leading the parade, and the army looked almost military. Clothes and uniforms had been washed, sprigs of greenery were attached to caps, horses were curried, and leather and brass were polished. The only concession was that female camp followers did not take part in the march, but were allowed to rejoin the army only as it exited on the other side of town.

The Continental and British armies clashed at Brandywine Creek on

September 11, 1777, and the Americans were defeated. Howe out-ma-neuvered Washington again by performing a classic flanking movement behind the American right, just as he had done at Long Island. The fighting had been fierce, and although the British won the field, the Americans had fought with valor and discipline, and retreated in good order northwestward to Chester and thence west beyond Germantown. Lord Howe occupied the capital city of Philadelphia, greeted as a conquering hero by the city considered the "Land of the Tories." After deploying part of his army to Germantown to keep an eye on the ever dangerous and elusive George Washington, Howe established his headquarters in Philadelphia.

After Brandywine, the American army bivouacked at Pottstown, Pennsylvania, where the troops rested, waited for reinforcements, and recovered from their wounds. Little could they imagine that their commander, stung by the recent defeat, was considering another dramatic response. During a series of meetings at various locations in Bucks and Montgomery counties, Washington planned an attack on the British outpost at Germantown and scheduled the assault for October 4, 1777. Success depended on precise timing, but poor coordination among the American forces, bad weather conditions, and a fierce holding action by British regulars defending Cliveden Mansion, turned the tide of the battle. The inspired defense of the British slowed the American advance just long enough to turn victory into defeat. The improving American army had fought well, however, and for the fifth time Howe failed to destroy Washington's army. After the battle, the American forces withdrew to Whitemarsh, Pennsylvania, for rest before moving to their permanent winter quarters. About this episode, Robert Leckie has written:

> *The fact that less than a month after losing one army at Brandywine, Washington was able to march with another right up to the brink of victory against the flower of Europe, led by one of the most successful tacticians of the age, could not have failed to impress France and Spain, already agreeably surprised by what the Americans were doing to the British army at Saratoga, under General Burgoyne.*[32]

What the Americans had accomplished at Saratoga, New York, in September and October was nothing short of a military miracle — the abject surrender of Burgoyne's army to the Americans led by General

Horatio Gates. News of the magnificent American victory raised morale throughout the colonies, especially at Whitemarsh. Increased confidence in their leaders and a belief in their cause would be sorely needed as the army moved to the camp that was to be their home for the next five months, a place in the foothills of Pennsylvania called Valley Forge.

Valley Forge. Mere mention of the name conjures up thoughts of cold, hunger, disease, deprivation, and loneliness — a legacy of that tortuous winter of 1777–1778 when 12,000 ill-clad, starving colonial soldiers encamped in eastern Pennsylvania. Preoccupation with the suffering that took place at Valley Forge, however, often distracts from the accomplishments that took place there. During this encampment, Washington reconstructed the officer's corps, reorganized and trained soldiers and, not incidentally, thwarted a political and military cabal that had formed against his leadership. The most important achievement, however, was the basic military training instituted by Baron von Steuben, a recent arrival from Prussia. Half professional soldier, half charlatan, von Steuben proved to be just what Washington's army needed — a disciplinarian who believed in drill, drill, and more drill, designed to instill personal pride and the importance of cooperation among soldiers and their units in battle. Von Steuben's teachings would quickly bear fruit.

As winter released its grip, news was received that France had officially recognized the independence of the United States by signing the Franco-American Treaty in Paris on February 6, 1778. The message gave cause for celebration throughout the colonies and General Washington declared May 6 to be a day of exultation. The troops celebrated with parades, reviews, and artillery displays; the officers with the same, along with feasting and drinking.

The treaty also brought France into the war on the side of the American colonies, an action that forced Britain, whose military was already spread thin around the world, to relax its naval blockade of America so that more of the fleet could be used to protect the home island. Too, the British foreign ministry had to send additional forces to the Caribbean to protect British holdings against French incursions. Thus, it became impossible for Britain to hold New York, Philadelphia, and portions of Rhode Island simultaneously. Since New York was the most easily defended of the three, British troops in Philadelphia were ordered to New York. General Henry Clinton, who had relieved Lord Howe, led the British army north from Philadelphia; the train of troops, wagons, artillery, and camp followers extended over twelve miles. Two days later, on June 21, 1778, Washington was in pursuit.

Swinging northward, Washington crossed the Delaware River forty miles above Philadelphia and then angled eastward across New Jersey. Advance units were already at work attacking and harassing Clinton's army with its huge, unwieldy baggage train. Slogging through ankle-deep mud, the British were bedeviled by heat, thunderstorms, guerilla action, a shortage of forage, and a lack of civilian cooperation. As anxious as he was to reach Sandy Hook and the safety of the British fleet, Clinton was forced to rest his troops fifteen miles short of this goal at the tiny town of Monmouth Court House (now Freehold). It was here that George Washington's revitalized Continental Army — fit, trained, supplied, and ready to fight — caught up with him. The armies clashed, American leadership failed, and the Battle of Monmouth resulted in a draw at best. Washington had placed his senior officer, General Charles Lee, in charge of the attack. A former English officer turned rebel and an otherwise bizarre character, Lee had foolishly allowed himself to be captured by the British early in the war. Even after repatriation and rehabilitation, he was wont to criticize his superiors, especially Washington. He even questioned the decision to attack Monmouth Court House, the very assault he was asked to lead! History has questioned Washington's decision to assign the job to Lee who performed poorly, especially when he ordered a retreat that infuriated Washington who, in character, personally had to step in and prevent another rout. Lafayette, who witnessed this battle, wrote:

> *Never was General Washington greater than in this action. His presence stopped the retreat; his dispositions fixed the victory [there wasn't one]; his fine appearance on horseback, his calm courage roused to animation by the vexations of the morning, gave him the air best calculated to excite enthusiasm. . . . I thought then as now that never had I beheld so superb a man.[33]*

Strongly chastised in the heat of battle by Washington, Lee's actions were later criticized by his military peers. Ever a severe critic of his commander-in-chief, he demanded a court martial in an effort to clear his sullied reputation. His wish was granted; the court found him guilty of dereliction of duty and he left the service in disgrace. The Battle of Monmouth, while not a victory for the Americans, had at least set the stage for Washington to be rid of his most bothersome critic. With Lee gone, Washington was the undisputed American commander, his stature unrivalled and his authority uncontested. The battle had also proved the value of von Steuben's training, as the Americans had fought with confidence, discipline, and great courage. Ironically, when they awoke the next morning anxious to renew the fight, they discovered Clinton had slipped away under the cover of darkness. He was in Sandy Hook, safe under the protection of the British fleet.

The most famous story of courage at Monmouth was that of Mrs. Mary Ludwig Hayes, wife of an American artilleryman. The latter stage of the battle was fought in debilitating heat near one hundred degrees. Mrs. Hayes endeared herself to her husband and his comrades by rushing back and forth from a stream with buckets of cool water, her heroic action forever earning her the sobriquet, "Molly Pitcher." It may be apocryphal, but when her husband collapsed at his cannon, she was said to have taken his place among the artillery crew firing it.

With Clinton safe in New York, Washington led his troops northward. After crossing the Raritan River, they tarried in New Brunswick, then marched to Paterson. Crossing the Hudson, they joined General Gates at White Plains, where they established a strong defensive position and waited to find out just what Clinton would do. During this encampment, Washington wrote, "It is not a little pleasing, nor less wonderful to contemplate that after two years of maneuvering . . . both armies are brought back to the very point they set out from."[34] Geographically, Washington was correct, but it is astonishing to think of the more dramatic changes that had taken place. After the debacles of Long Island, Fort Washington, White Plains, and others, after being beset by every imaginable privation, and after being outgunned, outmanned, and sometimes outmaneuvered, the Americans had brought the British to a standstill. And, with the imminent arrival of a French fleet, it was the British army that was now bottled up in New York.

For the remainder of 1778, neither George Washington nor Sir Henry Clinton engaged in further military action. Washington went into winter quarters at Middlebrook, New Jersey, from where he supervised the construction of a sweeping defensive line that stretched north from

Middlebrook to West Point and Peekskill in New York and on to Danbury, Connecticut. The defenses were strong and the winter mild, so the commander should have felt confident about the future, but he was deluged with bad news from the north, west, and south. American General John Sullivan and a French fleet, in a poorly coordinated engagement with the British, had experienced a major bloodying at Newport. British regulars and Indians were ravaging the western frontier. Lieutenant Colonel Archibald Campbell, leading a force of 3500 British regulars, had captured Savannah, Georgia — an early consequence of Great Britain's newly formed southern strategy.

Author John Ferling has described the period from 1778 to 1780 as "The Forgotten Years" of the war since Washington's personal involvement in the conflict was minimal. During the summer of 1779, however, Clinton made threatening moves on the Hudson River and captured an unfinished fort at Stony Point, America's southernmost defense post on the river. Washington decided to retake the facility, and after reconnoitering the site, devised a plan that involved an attack by General "Mad Anthony" Wayne and a select force of regulars. The attack on July 16th was a complete success, and it prompted a subsequent assault at Paulus Hook (now Jersey City). While neither fort was held very long by the Americans, the minor victories served as important morale builders for the army, which was still disappointed over its failure to achieve victory at Monmouth.

One piece of good news did reach Washington. General Clinton, disappointed at having not received reinforcements, abandoned both the Newport and Hudson River fortifications, and was digging in at New York City for an expected assault by Franco-American forces from land and sea. The French fleet, however, had been ordered to sail south to the Caribbean and initiate action against the British there. Washington, unable to attack Clinton without French naval assistance, abandoned his plan to attack New York and again moved his army to its winter quarters in Morristown, a decision he would soon regret.

The winter of 1779–1780 was the coldest and most severe in the history of New Jersey. New York Harbor froze over, and severe blizzards raked Morristown, blowing away tents and creating deep, impenetrable drifts. Provisions were scarce; food, uniforms, shoes, blankets, and firewood were in short supply, and morale plummeted. General Washington, although living in relative comfort in the spacious Ford Mansion, was fully aware of the horrible conditions faced by his men, and described the winter as "the most distressing of any we have experienced since the beginning of the war."[35] Desertions were common, perhaps even understandable in light of existing conditions, but somehow Washington kept the army intact throughout the winter. Further grim news reached Washington in the spring — the British had captured Charleston, South Carolina, and almost 6000 Americans were taken prisoner. Later that year, Americans under the command of General Horatio Gates lost an engagement against Cornwallis at Camden, South Carolina.

By late spring, most of Washington's troops had left for duty at West Point when the British and Hessian forces, reinforced over the winter, left Staten Island and advanced into New Jersey. Washington ordered the remnants of his force to Springfield where, on June 21st, the enemy was turned back after a brisk fight, which allowed the remaining troops to move to West Point. With this engagement, Morristown's role in the American Revolution was over — yet, historically, Morristown is remembered as America's most severe trial of the Revolutionary War, a place where the army survived an extremely difficult period of hardship, despair, and discouragement. But how could an army not prevail when made up of soldiers such as Ebenezer Stanton who wrote home to Massachusetts, "I am in hopes the army will be kept together till we have gained the point we have so long been contending for . . . I could wish I had two lives to lose in defense of so glorious a cause."[36]

Washington, headquartered at the Theunis Dey Mansion in Wayne, New Jersey, received word that a French fleet carrying 6000 trained soldiers would be arriving soon. "Soon" turned out to be July 15th, when a French army led by the Compte de Rochambeau disembarked at Newport, Rhode Island. Washington dispatched Lafayette to coordinate with Rochambeau, with orders to press Washington's idea for the French to lay siege to New York City. Rochambeau was cool to the idea, unimpressed with Lafayette, and indicated he wanted a direct meeting with his American counterpart. Commander-in-Chief Washington instantly agreed to a conference in Connecticut, and his journey there was his first trip to New England since 1776.

The two leaders met in Wethersfield, in the home of American ambassador Silas Deane. During the session, Washington proposed several different plans for involving the French force in the war, including a siege of New York City, a joint expedition to the south, or an assault on Canada. Rochambeau reacted negatively to all of the schemes, as his orders were to move only in concert with the French fleet and he felt the fleet was inadequate to support any of the major undertakings proposed by Washington. The decision reached at Wethersfield was to defer action in 1780. Any campaigning in 1781 by the French would depend on the mood of the authorities in Versailles and the willingness of the American colonies to continue the war.

Another result of the meeting at Wethersfield — to have another meeting — was devastating to Washington and dashed his hopes for French cooperation and immediate aggressive action against the British. Discouraged, he saddled up and headed for the Hudson Highlands to inspect his defenses, primarily at West Point where he had scheduled a conference with its commander, Major General Benedict Arnold.

Rather than take the lower route to West Point through Danbury, Connecticut, Washington and his party chose to travel via Fishkill, New York, fifteen miles north of West Point on the east side of the Hudson River. After turning south at Fishkill, they chanced to meet the French ambassador, La Luzerne, on his way to Connecticut to meet Rochambeau. The ambassador suggested they return to Fishkill to dine, talk, and rest, so it was not until the next morning that Washington's party resumed its journey to General Arnold's headquarters, which was located in the home of Beverley Robinson across the Hudson from West Point. General Arnold, who had been secretly collaborating with the British, learned at this time that his British liaison, Major John André, had been captured by the Americans. Washington's delay in Fishkill allowed General Arnold enough time to escape to British lines.

Arnold's treachery reverberated throughout the nation and intensified doubts about the American cause and the likelihood that the colonies could succeed in freeing themselves from British control. The continuing military setbacks in the south, a decline in enlistments, and the absence of vigorous support for the revolutionary efforts by the citizenry characterized the times and reflected the outrage at Arnold's apostasy. Certainly the commander-in-chief was well aware of the mood of the people, yet he vented his rage and inner feelings only in private correspondence.

In the wake of Arnold's treason, Washington took immediate steps to reinforce the West Point fortifications before setting up his winter headquarters at Mount Kemble near Morristown. The winter of 1780 was, again, cruel; the men, as in earlier winters, were ill-clothed and ill-fed, and when Congress reneged on bonuses, pay packages, and other financial matters, some Pennsylvania troops mutinied and left camp to march on Philadelphia where they hoped to confront Congress with their demands. A congressional delegation met them at Princeton and persuaded them to return to camp. When a New Jersey regiment mutinied over similar problems, however, Washington's hand was forced; the men involved were dealt with harshly and their leaders were executed.

Washington considered 1781 to be a critical year — a do or die year. The American cause would be lost unless there was some positive action or victory. Some problems, especially fiscal, seemed insurmountable. From his camp in New Windsor, New York, the general had written Congress on December 22, 1780, that he needed three things: a substantial loan from another country, a guarantee that the French would establish naval superiority over the British, and thousands of additional French troops to take the field against the British. Rochambeau sympathetically dispatched his own son to Versailles to beg for money on behalf of the Americans. Meanwhile, Congress, after years of recalcitrance and political foot-dragging, ratified the Articles of Confederation. While power remained with the states, the new government created a federal department that would direct the piecemeal war effort. These moves helped, but Washington remained anxious as he awaited positive answers from France.

In October of 1780, Washington received the encouraging news that a force of colonial militiamen had routed an army of Loyalists at Kings Mountain in South Carolina, the first positive report from that beleaguered area in many months. Then he learned that an American force under Daniel Morgan's command had defeated a major British force at Cowpens, South Carolina; the British suffered over 800 casualties while Morgan lost only twelve men. Cowpens thus joined the handful of battles considered "turning points" of the Revolutionary War — Bunker Hill, Dorchester Heights, the retreat from Long Island, Trenton, Princeton, Saratoga — but none was more dramatic nor important than Cowpens. It was not the last battle of the war, nor even the last in the south, but the

extent of the British losses in manpower, combined with supply problems and lack of reinforcements, persuaded Lord Cornwallis to abandon
the Carolinas and head for Virginia where he would have the advantage
of shorter supply lines and, hopefully, the protection of the British fleet.
He would situate his forces at a river port called Yorktown.

At the moment, however, Washington was concerned about conditions in his home state, for Benedict Arnold, now a British general, had
led an invasion up the James River to capture Richmond. To counter that
thrust, Washington prepared a southern expedition that would act in concert with a French fleet that was leaving Newport, Rhode Island, for
Chesapeake Bay. He traveled to Newport to confer with Rochambeau, at
the Frenchman's Vernon House headquarters, and to finalize plans for
the Virginia campaign. By the time Washington arrived, the French fleet
had already sailed, and for weeks Washington dealt with uncertainty before he learned that the French fleet had fought only one insignificant
battle with the British before returning to Newport. The southern campaign was aborted.

For a while, nothing seemed to change. Arnold remained in Virginia
and Clinton in New York. Although the news from the Carolinas was
favorable to the Americans, Washington remained focused on New York.
He met with Rochambeau in Connecticut once again and argued for a
joint campaign against Clinton. The French General, accompanied by
Admiral de Barras, seemed sympathetic, yet urged that major action during 1781 be concentrated in the south. Washington resisted this idea and
even formulated extensive plans for a siege of New York, but its success
depended upon the cooperation of a second French fleet under the command of Admiral de Grasse. That fleet was at sea, and its destination and
intentions were unclear, so Washington's plan for the siege of New York
was put on hold as no action against New York City was possible without a strong French naval presence in New York harbor.

Fate would step forward once again. The de Grasse fleet, originally
scheduled for action in the Caribbean Sea, would be made available to the
American campaigns for the summer, but only as far north as Chesapeake Bay. Washington and Rochambeau moved quickly. The proposed
siege of New York was abandoned, and a Franco-American army marched
south in great secrecy, crossing the Hudson via Kings Ferry to Stony
Point, then under cover of the New Jersey Palisades, through Newark

and New Brunswick. They paused long enough to build a fake encampment designed to feign an attack on Staten Island, then hurried across the Delaware and headed for their final objective, Yorktown, Virginia. A parade through Philadelphia must have been particularly satisfying to the veterans of the retreat from Brandywine through Philadelphia to Pottstown four years earlier. This day they were moving in the opposite direction, accompanied by colorful and powerful French allies. There was a sense that they were on their way to victory.

Lord Cornwallis, his back to the York River, felt secure in Yorktown. While a small American force led by Lafayette had him penned in by land, Cornwallis was counting on the arrival of the British fleet to protect his rear and to remove his forces. This assumption, however, would prove to be his undoing, for the French fleet reached Chesapeake Bay ahead of the British fleet and blocked the rivers, effectively cutting off Cornwallis's retreat. Washington and Rochambeau, leading almost 15,000 men, arrived in September and joined Lafayette in facing the helpless and beleaguered Cornwallis.

The siege of Yorktown began in late September, 1781. Hemmed in by land and sea, with his supplies dwindling and American and French firepower destroying his troops at will, the army of Lord Cornwallis surrendered to General George Washington on October 19, 1781. To all intents and purposes, the Revolutionary War was over.

Washington remained at Yorktown for a week or two with plans to visit Mount Vernon, but a messenger rode in with the news that his stepson, Jacky Custis, had contracted "camp fever" on a visit to Yorktown. Washington arrived at his sister-in-law's home in Eltham just as the young man expired. Washington attended the funeral, rested at Mount Vernon for a week, then left for Philadelphia where he stayed for most of the winter, conferring with Congress and directing the strengthening of defenses throughout the colonies. Even though the British Parliament had voted early in 1782 to authorize King George to seek peace with the American colonies and peace commissioners were appointed and began to negotiate, the war was not over. Washington continued with plans for further campaigning even though the news from the peace commission pointed toward a negotiated and final peace.

Ironically, one of Washington's most vexing moments would take place during his army's final winter encampment — that of 1782–1783

— near Newburgh, New York. For years, colonial military officers had chafed at the intransigence of Congress regarding pay and pensions. With the end of the war in sight, a plot was hatched by a group of officers who threatened to resign en masse if the war continued or, even more seriously, to set up a military government by not disbanding when peace was achieved. Washington was made aware of this threat to civilian rule, and in an impassioned speech on March 5th at the headquarters building of the nearby New Windsor Cantonment, he broke the back of the actions threatened by the discontented officers. He reminded the officers of their duty and promised to fight Congress on their behalf. In one memorable moment, he brought his audience to tears as he stumbled over a passage in his written remarks, reached for his reading glasses and said, "Gentlemen, you must pardon me, I have grown grey in your service and now find myself growing blind."[37] His speech, delineating his most consistent and heartfelt principles of duty and devotion, defused the incipient rebellion and no further word about it was heard from any of the plotters.

Two months earlier, an interim peace treaty had been hammered out in Paris, but the news did not arrive in America until April. It was with a happy heart that General George Washington issued orders for a cease-fire on April 9, 1783, nearly eight years to the day that an informal band of farmer-patriots had fought a British army at Lexington and Concord in Massachusetts.

Washington stayed busy for the next few months arranging for prisoner exchanges and the dissolution of the army. He did find time for a pleasure and business trip in mid-July, when he took a three-week ride up the west bank of the Hudson to Albany, Saratoga, Ticonderoga, and Crown Point, places to which he had sent armies but had never visited. The return trip, via Schenectady, included a ride west to Fort Schuyler (near what is today Rome, New York), across the portage to Wood Creek and Lake Oneida, then on to Lake Otsego, Albany, and back to Newburgh.

Upon his return to Newburgh, Washington was summoned to meet with Congress at Princeton, New Jersey, where he and Martha set up residence at Berrien House, a country farmhouse outside of town. The general addressed Congress and met frequently with congressional committees regarding the makeup of a post-war army and other security matters. Martha left for Mount Vernon in October, but the general remained on duty waiting for word that a final, definitive peace treaty had been signed. The Treaty of Paris had in fact been signed on September 3rd, but the news did not arrive in America until three months later. The war was over.

Washington headed for West Point, and everywhere along his route was received with joy, respect, and honors. He remained at West Point for a week, then bid farewell to his officers and men. Advised that the British were finally evacuating New York, he rode south across Kings Bridge and into Harlem. At noon on November 25, 1783, the last British soldier stepped off American soil onto a waiting barge as General George Washington led a victory parade into New York City. The next week was filled with dinners, honors, fêtes, and other congratulatory affairs. His heart, however, lay far to the south in Virginia. Yet, as anxious as he was to leave New York, he was obliged to stay since General Carleton, the commander of British forces in the colonies, remained aboard ship in New York harbor, awaiting favorable weather and tides before setting sail for England.

On December 4, 1783, the British fleet weighed anchor. It was time for Washington to go home, but first he called together some of his officers for a farewell luncheon at Fraunces Tavern and when it was over — the last speech delivered, the last toast drunk, the last embrace given —he and his aide, David Humphreys, were rowed to New Jersey where they began the long, familiar trip to Trenton and Philadelphia. Pausing briefly at these places, they continued on through Baltimore before making one last stop in Annapolis, then the temporary capital of the newly independent and confederated nation. Washington submitted his meticulously kept expense account before addressing Congress on December 23rd. In the Old Senate Chamber of the Maryland State House, General George Washington stood before the Congress, a body he had fought for, and fought with, for over eight long years, and stated he was "resigning with satisfaction the Appointment I accepted with diffidence."[38] Then he was on his way out of town, anxious to keep a promise made to his wife long ago. So it was late on December 24, 1783, when former General George Washington spotted the welcoming lights of Mount Vernon. He would be home for Christmas.

Washington threw himself into the affairs of Mount Vernon with enthusiasm. Taking care of Mount Vernon had been difficult during the war; the construction of new buildings had been slow, competent help had been scarce, the soil was becoming depleted, old bills were coming due, taxes had to be paid, loans were outstanding, and now the owner constantly faced the usual problems involved with the management of a large estate. But, in spite of his rigorous daily schedule as a farmer, Washington remained an entrepreneur and speculator as well. He became interested once again in two ventures that had commanded his attention before the war — the draining of Dismal Swamp and the construction of the Patowmack Canal. He was elected president of a company formed to oversee the latter. Both projects involved traveling, whether to inspect routes and properties along the Potomac River or to Annapolis and Richmond to lobby politicians.

Never far from his mind were the thousands of acres of land in the west he had claimed before the war. With settlers now moving westward in droves, Washington felt it was important to defend the claim that had been rejected by Lord Hillsborough so many years before. So, in 1784, with a small party of friends, he set off for the west. Enroute, the party stopped to visit with George's brother Charles, who had founded a town in the lower Shenandoah Valley which he modestly named Charles Town. From Charles Town, the travelers made their way along Braddocks Road past Fort Cumberland and the Great Meadow onto Simpsons Place in southwestern Pennsylvania, a site known to the natives as Washingtons Bottom (now Perryopolis). From there, they traveled north to Millers Run on Chartiers Creek, about twenty-five miles west of Fort Pitt, where he was shocked to discover squatters on what he considered his property. He produced a deed to prove ownership, but the squatters showed little deference to the general who had just won the war that established their freedom, and they were even less impressed by a deed stamped by a royal governor back in 1770! Washington's dilemma was typical of the vexing problems faced by Americans in establishing and validating original titles to land in the west onto which they were moving. Atypically, Washington put the matter into the hands of attorneys. Two years later, the case was decided in his favor; some of the squatters on his land remained as tenants and others moved away and settled nearby. This entire tract was sold to a land agent in 1796, thereby ending a disputatious situation.

Washington returned to Mount Vernon via Morgantown, taking the opportunity to explore the wild upper reaches of the Potomac on behalf of the Patowmack Canal Company. A few months later he was in Philadelphia to meet with former officers of the enterprise, after which he traveled on to Annapolis, Richmond, and Fredericksburg to conduct other business before returning home. Except for a few short trips for board meetings in Alexandria, he did not leave Mount Vernon for another two years.

A creature of habit, Washington's routine at Mount Vernon rarely varied. He rose at 5 AM to work on correspondence and ledgers. After an hour, he shaved and dressed, then inspected the stables before returning to the main house for a light breakfast. At 7:30 AM, he rode out to check on the plantation's myriad activities, then returned shortly before 3 PM to change into more formal attire and to indulge in the day's main meal, more often than not a sumptuous repast in the company of guests. The meal was unhurried and relaxed, and featured many courses and bottles of wine. If it were still daylight when the meal was over, he might escort guests on a tour of the grounds or return to some unfinished chore. Normally he retired to the library and worked on his mail, wrote in his diary, or attended to other matters. In the early evening, he reappeared to either converse with his guests, read to his grandchildren, or eat a light supper. Precisely at 9 PM, he retired.

It would have been uncharacteristic of Washington not to follow the progress of government, and he became gravely concerned when squabbling, jealousy, and mistrust among representatives of the thirteen states appeared to jeopardize the chances to centralize power in a unified federal government. There was, in fact, no government able to effect treaties, issue currency, raise armies, collect taxes, and perform other functions needed by all of the states. It was obvious to Washington and many others that the Articles of Confederation had to be redrawn in the form of a viable national constitution.

On many occasions, George Washington had expressed the thoughts that his days were over or that history had passed him by, or that he had completed his duty. When the Constitutional Convention met in Philadelphia in 1787, however, it became apparent that Washington's thoughts were misconceptions. The general had been reluctant to attend the convention, but he was persuaded that his presence was essential to its success. Swayed to participate, he traveled from Mount Vernon to Philadelphia; he was greeted enthusiastically at every town along the way and with particular good cheer at the capital. Ever in character, he was on time, the very first delegate to arrive. Weeks later, on May 25th, the convention came to order, its first item of business to elect Washington chairman. As chairman, he was the sole delegate to attend every single session of the acrimonious and argumentative convention that lasted over four months, a period that must have seemed like a lifetime to the man in the chair. Outside the meeting hall, however, he was ensconced in the comfortable home of Robert Morris and he found time each day to ride, including several short day trips to visit old haunts at Trenton, Whitemarsh, Germantown, and Valley Forge.

By September, the delegates had completed their work of drafting a new and important document — the Constitution of the United States — which included a section describing and limiting what would be the head of state and its office, the president and the presidency. Immediately following the convention, the Constitution was sent to the states for ratification. Washington's ride home to Mount Vernon must have been bittersweet, for it was obvious that the section of the Constitution regarding the president had been drafted with only one person in mind. The new nation was about to call him to duty again.

The process of ratifying the Constitution was not quick and it was not easy; indeed, it was not until June 1788 that ratification by Virginia and New Hampshire provided the remaining votes necessary for the establishment of the new government. The next step was to elect a president through an electoral college. Whenever the presidency was mentioned in his presence, Washington demurred, unconvincingly, and it became more and more obvious that he would be the unanimous choice for president. The electors met in their state capitals on February 4, 1789, to cast their votes for president. It was no surprise to anyone when Charles Thomson, the Secretary of Congress, arrived at Mount Vernon on April 14th to officially inform the general that he had been elected president. Any doubts as to Washington's real feelings were dispelled when he made a short statement of acceptance that had been written days before.

Within forty-eight hours the president-elect was packed and off to New York City, now the capital of the new United States, for his inauguration. Accompanied by Thomson and aide David Humphreys, he made the trip in six days, his progress slowed everywhere by receptions and outpourings of genuine emotion. As described by The Commission of the Bicentennial of the United States Constitution,[39] a typical part of the journey was spent as follows:

> *20 April 1789*

> *Morning. Washington leaves Wilmington and is accompanied by his Delaware escort as far as the Pennsylvania border. There he is greeted by a military escort from Philadelphia and by state officials, war veterans, and others. Included among the officials are Thomas Mifflin and Richard Peters, two former members of the Board of War.*

> *About 7 a.m.   Washington's party reaches Chester, where it stops for about two hours to breakfast at the Washington House.*

> *9 a.m.   Leaves Chester and, ordering his carriage to the rear of the line, Washington mounts a white horse for his procession into Philadelphia. Thomson and Humphries also take individual mounts. As the procession moves towards the Schuylkill River, it increases in size; it is joined by contingents of cavalry and by a body of Philadelphia citizens, headed by General Arthur St. Clair, Governor of the Northwest Territory.*

> *About Noon.   Procession reaches Gray's Ferry Bridge on the Schuylkill, where Washington is surprised by an impressive scene: the bridge's span is decorated 'with laurel and other evergreens,' as well as the flags of the eleven states of the Union and other banners, carrying such mottoes as 'The Rising Empire,' and 'Don't Tread on Me.' All of this was accomplished by Mr. Gray and by the painter, Charles Willson Peale. At each end of the bridge is a classical arch, 'composed of laurel, emblematic of the ancient triumphal arches used by the Romans.'*

> *Thousands of spectators have come out from Philadelphia to witness the crossing. As Washington passes under one of the arches, a child lowers a crown of laurel over his head [according to some reports, the child was Angelica Peale, daughter of the painter]. At least 20,000 people line the road from Gray's Ferry Bridge into Philadelphia, and the procession swells in size as it nears the city.*

[Washington was escorted to City Tavern for a banquet where

he was entertained by band music, toasts, and artillery salutes before moving to the home of Robert Morris where he witnessed a fireworks display in his honor before retiring after a very full day. Up early the next morning, he received addresses from prominent citizens before departing for Trenton where he was greeted at the bridge across Assumpink Creek by a]:

. . . . triumphal arch with columns decorated in greenery, with a large artificial sunflower capping the arch. While crossing the bridge Washington was heralded by a group of women and girls, who sing for him an ode and strew flowers in his path.

[Similar demonstrations took place at Princeton and Woodbridge before he reached Elizabeth Town Point. The Commission describes his entry into New York]:

23 April 1789

Late Morning   About noon steps aboard a 47-foot ceremonial barge, constructed for the occasion. Rowed by 13 Masters of Vessels, dressed in white uniforms and black caps, who serve as oarsmen. The barge is festooned with an awning and red curtains. Six other barges with the Congressional delegates and other dignataries, accompany him. The flotilla departs to the salute of artillery and moves across Newark Bay, up the Mouth of the Kills and past Bedler's Island.

As the ceremonial flotilla enters New York Harbor it is joined by other vessels. 'Boat after Boat & Sloop after Sloop added to our train in all their naval ornaments,' with 'a number of Porpoises . . . playing amongst us.' Washington is saluted with odes from spectators on the adjoining ships, including one to the tune of 'God Save the King.' All the adjacent shores crowded with cheering throngs. 'The successive Motion of the hats, from the Battery to the Coffee House, was like rolling motion of the sea, or a field of grain waving with the wind.'

Washington's barge arrived at Murray's Wharf to the firing of a cannonade and wild cheering. Greeted by Governor Clinton and other dignitaries, Washington disembarked and proceeded on foot through dense crowds along Queen Street to Franklin House at #3 Cherry Street, the first residence and office of the president of the United States. From that time until Inauguration Day, April 30, President-elect Washington received visitors.

[April 30, Inauguration Day, dawned bright and clear, a hopeful augury of the future of the new nation. At sunrise the artillery at Fort George welcomed the new day and at 9 AM New York City's church bells responded by pealing their approbation and hopes].

12:30 p.m. Military escort sent to Franklin House: full ceremonial procession departs for Federal Hall via Queen (Pearl) Street, Great Dock, and Broad Streets. Colonel Morgan serves as Grand Marshall; followed by a military contingent of 500, including a troop of horse, artillery, two companies of Grenadiers, a company of light infantry, and a company of Scottish Highlanders in traditional garb.

Washington travels in a state coach, accompanied by the Senate Committee of the House, Chancellor Robert Livingston, the French and Spanish ministers, and a multitude of ordinary citizens.

At 1 PM, President-elect Washington entered the Senate Chamber where he was presented to both houses and conducted to his chair by Vice President John Adams. After a few moments he went out on the balcony to take the oath of office before a cheering crowd, then moved back into the Senate Chamber to deliver his inaugural address. Shortly thereafter the inaugural party walked up the street to Saint Pauls Chapel where a special service of thanksgiving was conducted before the new president retired to Franklin House, not to rest until the evening had ended with a special fireworks display in his honor.

Franklin House (now the site of a support for the Brooklyn Bridge) was a comfortable home on the East River that benefitted from the cool breezes that came off of the water on hot summer days and nights. New York City had a population of less than 35,000 people, and was still rebuilding from the devastation it had suffered during the years of war and from its two major fires. Roads were in bad condition; many were ankle-deep in dust that turned to mud when it rained. Hogs prowling for garbage impeded pedestrians and riders. Privately dug wells and privies pitted the entire area. But New Yorkers were, if nothing else, resilient. New streets, and even some sidewalks, were being laid out and street lamps were installed. As today, the New York City of 1788 was an exciting place with confidence in its future.

The presidency was new, and Washington fully realized that each decision he made would set a precedent. He was burdened by onerous interviews with office seekers, an important part of the process of building a government and creating a nation so it must have been a great comfort when Martha joined him four weeks after the inauguration. Shortly after her arrival, however, he was stricken by a painful and debilitating tumor in his leg that required surgical removal. It was feared that the illness might be fatal, but the president resumed normal activities following a slow, painful recovery.

Part of Washington's vision of the presidency was inclusion — to see and be seen by as many citizens as possible — to hear as many points of view as possible — thus plans were made for a presidential trip through New England. Washington's party left New York in mid-October, rode through northern Manhattan's forests to Rye, then traveled north on the Boston Post Road through Greenwich, Stamford, Fairfield, Bridgeport, Stratford, and Milford to New Haven, Connecticut. After a Sunday in New Haven where he attended two church services — one Episcopal, one Congregational — he headed north through Wallingford, Durham, and Middletown to Hartford, stopping briefly at the home of Silas Deane where he had met Rochambeau some years earlier. Then he traveled farther north to Windsor, Suffield, and Springfield before turning east to Cambridge, Massachusetts. The journey took nine days; at each town, village, hamlet, or crossroads he was greeted, serenaded, subjected to speeches, paraded, and otherwise honored. At Cambridge, Lieutenant Governor Samuel Adams and a delegation escorted him across the Charles River to Boston, where he was lodged at the widow Ingersoll's boarding house at Court and Tremont streets rather than at the residence of Governor John Hancock. Hancock, in some sort of power display, did not greet the president in person but extended him an invitation to dinner. Washington reasoned quite correctly that proper protocol provided for the governor to call on the president before the chief executive paid formal respects to a mere governor. It was a chastened John Hancock, pleading illness and on a stretcher, who called on President George Washington at Widow Ingersoll's residence the next morning.

Washington stayed in Boston only briefly, but while there he visited Harvard College and attended some state ceremonies. On the 29th of October, he was off to Marblehead to visit old compatriots before stopping in the little manufacturing towns of Lynn, Salem, and Newburyport. He then headed north and passed through the autumn glory of New Hampshire and on to a brief visit to Kittery, Maine. He had planned to cross New Hampshire and Vermont to Albany, New York enroute home, but an early snowstorm in the Green Mountains convinced him to return by an alternate route that allowed him to visit Lexington where the Revolutionary War had begun. Usually refreshed by enthusiastic greetings, the president found the return trip tedious and the lodgings often poor; he observed, for example, that Widow Collidge's house in Watertown was "indifferent" and Perkins Tavern in Pomfret, Connecticut, "by the bye is not a good one."[40] Twenty-eight days after leaving New York, he was back in the capitol, resting and working a modified schedule before Congress reconvened in January, 1790. At the same time, he and Martha were moving from Cherry Street to the Macomb House, an expensive mansion on Broadway which rented for $100 per month.

Whether to escape from Congress or to recover from the rigors of moving, Washington made a five-day trip to the "hinterlands" of Long Island in April and visited Jamaica, Brookhaven, Koram (present-day Coram), Setakit (Setauket), Huntington, Oyster Bay, Mosqueto Cove (Glen Cove), and Brooklyn before he returned to Manhattan. Today's travelers on the Long Island Expressway might be interested to know that conditions have not improved much during the past two hundred years. Washington's diary notes:

> *The first five miles of the Road [Koram to Setakit] is too poor to admit, Inhabitants or cultivation being a low scrubby Oak, not more than 2 feet high intermixed with small and ill thriven Pines . . . the whole of this days ride was over uneven ground and none of it of the first quality but intermixed with pebble stones.*[41]

In May, 1790, Washington was stricken by influenza, and medical doomsayers once again despaired for his life. After several agonizing days, however, the president, once at death's door, broke into a sweat and the crisis passed.

During the president's illness and convalescence, Congress passed the Residence Act that authorized the establishment of a permanent capital of the new nation somewhere between the eastern branch of the Potomac and the Conocheague Creek. Philadelphia, it was decided, would serve as the temporary capital for ten years until the location of the new capital was decided upon and the necessary buildings there could be prepared for service. Also, recalcitrant little Rhode Island had become the thirteenth state to ratify the Constitution, so while Congress adjourned and packed for the move to Philadelphia, President Washington made a one-week side trip to Rhode Island to acknowledge its new status as a member of the Union. Afterwards, he traveled to Mount Vernon, stopping briefly in Philadelphia to inspect and approve Robert Morris's house on Market Street as the presidential office and residence. It was the same three-story brick mansion in which he had lived during the Constitutional Convention of 1787. Considered the best house in the city, Washington ordered some modifications to make it suitable for working and entertaining before setting out for a twelve-week retreat at Mount Vernon.

During the period of relaxation at Mount Vernon, little government business crossed Washington's desk, but he did use the time to choose a spot along the Potomac River for the new "Federal City." The Residence Act of 1790 had called for a presidentially appointed committee to select the site, but Washington subverted its intent and acted unilaterally. He traveled up and down the Potomac surveying its environs for a proper location for the new capital, but it was suspected that the inspection trips were strictly for political consumption and that his mind had long been made up as to the best location for the new center of government. On January 24, 1791, the president proclaimed the Federal District would be from "just above the commencement of the Potomac River Canal" to the "lower end of Alexandria," and the Federal City itself would be constructed somewhere between the little village of Georgetown on Rock Creek and Carrollsburg, a "planned town" at the junction of the Potomac and its eastern branch.[42] Much political maneuvering and compromising, however, would take place before the president's choice of location became reality.

Washington had often expressed a desire to visit every state during his term, so following the success of his tour of New England, he made plans to travel through the southern states. He had never been to South Carolina or Georgia, and his visits to Dismal Swamp had been his only ventures into North Carolina. Riding in a new carriage, Washington left

Mount Vernon early in 1791 on a tour of the southern states. He stopped first in Fredericksburg to visit his sister, then went to Richmond to inspect the progress of the James River Canal project in which he had invested, and continued on to the area of North Carolina where generals Greene and Cornwallis had fought ten years earlier. He crossed the Roanoke River at Halifax, visited a tar-making enterprise at Greenville, was honored at a dance in New Bern, and trekked on to Wilmington on the Cape Fear River — traveling, according to his diary, "in a continued cloud of dust."[43] The dust and the tobacco lands gave way to the green rice fields of South Carolina, and he soon reached Georgetown, another war-torn hamlet struggling to recover from occupation by the British. He hurried on to the Snee Farm rice plantation of Governor Charles Pinckney and on May 2nd was rowed across the Cooper River to Charleston, where he stayed for a week.

From Charleston, President Washington headed for Savannah, the southernmost point of his journey, and by mid-May he started for home, heading inland. He stopped in Augusta, then rode back into South Carolina and lingered in Columbia before visiting Camden and the gravesite of Baron de Kalb, a European soldier-of-fortune who had fallen there while fighting for the colonial cause. From Camden, it was a short trip to Charlotte and Salisbury in North Carolina. In North Carolina he received a special welcome in the Moravian settlement of Salem where, for the first time, he was greeted with music and singing rather than artillery salutes and cannonades. From Salem, he went to Guilford Court House to honor the colonial forces and their stunning victory over Cornwallis at Cowpens and pyrrhic victory at Guilford, victories that had sent the British army back into coastal Virginia and its subsequent confinement and defeat at Yorktown.

A week later, Washington was back at Mount Vernon, refreshed at being home yet fatigued following the trip of almost 2000 miles. He was able to enjoy the plantation for only two short weeks, however, before he headed back to Philadelphia. Following a brief pause in Georgetown to confer with the commissioners of the Federal District, he rode to Frederick, Maryland, then northward to York, Pennsylvania, and thence east through Lancaster to Philadelphia.

It is interesting to note that, except for his time at Mount Vernon, George Washington spent more of his life in Philadelphia than anywhere else. In 1790, Philadelphia, the most prosperous and cosmopolitan city in the fledgling United States, had close to 45,000 residents. The downtown area stretched for ten blocks along the Delaware River and a short distance west, and a wide greenbelt extended farther west to the Schuylkill River. The city was attractive; red brick houses faced sidewalks and wide streets paved with pebbles were lined with buttonwood, willow, and poplar trees. Grand mansions of the well-to-do were being constructed to the north along the banks of the Schuylkill.

As the seat of government, Philadelphia was never dull; its drawing rooms, boarding houses, taverns, and public buildings were full of gossip, discussions, compromises, and intrigues, all of which set a pattern for democratic government thereafter. City life, however, must have been stifling for George Washington, a man of action who seemed to be always on the road. His only escapes now were periodic day trips to Valley Forge, Trenton, and other places with which he had become familiar during the war.

In 1792, Washington was unanimously re-elected to a second term of office, although he demurred even more unconvincingly than before. He was at Mount Vernon when he received the news of his re-election, and soon he was on his way to a frightened capital then in the grip of a ferocious yellow fever epidemic, one that would eventually cause the deaths of more than one in twenty Philadelphians. Because of the epidemic, the capital was temporarily moved to the more salubrious atmosphere of Germantown where Washington resided until the epidemic had passed.

Washington's second term in office was difficult. For the first time, his decisions were subjected to severe criticism. The Jay Treaty, negotiated in London by Chief Justice John Jay, was an attempt to resolve a number of differences between the two former adversaries. The treaty as submitted to Congress was very unpopular with many Americans who felt it provided no concessions to the United States. The president was also beset by the French Ambassador who attempted to influence internal affairs of the United States as a result of France's assistance during the Revolutionary War. There was quarreling between cabinet secretaries Thomas Jefferson and Alexander Hamilton, a populist uprising in New England called Shay's Rebellion, and difficult foreign policy decisions had to be made. Negotiations with Spain were initiated on matters of Florida and the Mississippi Valley, and relations with Indians in the northwest were vexatious.

Other problems arose in the summer of 1794, when a disgruntled band of farmers in western Pennsylvania objected to a federal excise tax on distilled whiskey. Their civil disobedience expanded to the point that federal tax collectors were physically assaulted, actions that prompted the federal government, after much discussion, to send troops to the area. President Washington personally led an army of regulars and Pennsylvania militia to head off "The Whiskey Rebellion." Their first night out from Philadelphia was spent in The Trappe, a German settlement near Norristown, and the next in Carlisle before they crossed over to Cumberland, Maryland, and then traveled northwestward to Bedford, Pennsylvania. At that point the president, having made a dramatic and personal speech about the responsibility, strength, and backbone of the federal government, turned his command over to others and returned to the capital. The army soon rounded up the perpetrators and squelched the rebellion almost as soon as it had begun.

Sometime in 1796, Washington made up his mind to retire at the end of his second term. With Alexander Hamilton's assistance, he wrote and issued a farewell address that contained thoughts that are as prescient today as they were when written 200 years ago. Indeed, some of these ideas have been expressed by every president since Washington — the principle that only the continuance of the Union can insure real independence, that strong national government is the "main pillar of your tranquility at home; your peace abroad; of your safety; of your prosperity; of that very Liberty which you so highly prize." Washington also emphasized that sectionalism, in his view, was the greatest danger to the unity of the new nation; that in spite of economic differences, all sections of the country had to work together to form what he called "an indissoluble community of interest as one nation."[44]

On March 4, 1797, President George Washington entered Congress Hall in Philadelphia for the last time, to be greeted by tumultuous applause. Within a few moments, Vice President-elect Thomas Jefferson entered and took a seat next to Washington. Precisely at noon, President-elect John Adams was ushered into the room and given a burst of applause. Adams then delivered a short address before taking the oath of office. The ceremony over, as the story is told, Jefferson was supposed to have gestured to Washington to proceed first from the chamber, but the ex-president, fully cognizant of protocol, would not have it. He was, after all, just an ordinary citizen now. Respectfully, he followed President Adams and Vice President Jefferson from the chamber.

Washington had culminated a public career of four decades burdened with unthinkable responsibilities, yet he had never wavered in his belief in the cause of freedom and the basic goodness of America and its democratic principles. In his first State of the Union message, he said, "The welfare of the country is the great object to which our cares and efforts ought to be directed,"[45] and that tenet had been present and remained consistent throughout his life.

George and Martha lingered in Philadelphia for a few days; they made social calls on the Adamses and other officials, shopped and were entertained at parties and dinners, and even attended a circus before they left for Mount Vernon and retirement. On the morning of March 9th, the Washingtons's carriage, unaccompanied by dragoons, congressmen, military officers, mayors, artillery regiments, pipers, or marching bands, rattled through the streets of Philadelphia into rural Pennsylvania. The Washingtons were on their way home.

Only once more would George Washington travel far from Mount Vernon. In 1798, an economic impasse with France raised fears of war with the former ally. The terrified government of the United States recommissioned Washington as commander-in-chief of the army, a post he was loath to take. Consistent with his devotion to duty, however, he accepted the commission and spent a month in Philadelphia conferring with the government and initiating the organization of an army. Fortunately, clear heads prevailed, the danger of war with France passed, and Washington returned to Mount Vernon.

Retirement for George Washington was not synonymous with inactivity. He conducted a heavy daily schedule of physical work on his plantation, continued a voluminous correspondence, entertained a constant stream of guests and curiosity seekers, disposed of his western land holdings, continued his involvement with the Patowmack Canal Company, accepted civic responsibilities in Alexandria, and pressed his concerns about progress in the development of the Federal City.

On December 13, 1799, George Washington made his usual rounds of Mount Vernon on a cold, damp day that turned to snow, then sleet. He returned home chilled to the bone, with a sore throat that developed into the edema that was destined to end his life. Doctors were called, bleeding was prescribed, plasters were applied, but to no avail. Weak and in great pain, he knew the end was near. With Martha, Doctor Craik, and his personal secretary Tobias Lear at his bedside, the great American whispered, "Tis well,"[46] before expiring at 10:30 PM on December 14, 1799.

Congress prepared a special burial crypt under the dome of the new Capitol building, but his body was not placed there. He was buried at Mount Vernon, where Martha joined him a few years later. Their final resting place, a simple family tomb overlooking their beloved Potomac, is the proper place for him to be, for Mount Vernon had ever been his rock, his strength, his solace — a representation of all that George Washington believed in and fought for. It is where he belongs.

In his message to Congress announcing Washington's death, President John Adams wrote of him:

> *Possessed of power, possessed of an extensive influence, he never used it but for the benefit of his country . . . . if we look through the whole tenor of his life, history will not produce to us a parallel.*[47]

An Outline of the Life of George Washington

Here appears a chronological outline of the full and varied life of George Washington. For brevity, we use abbreviations for George Washington (GW) and the Continental Army (CA).

1732: GW is born at Wakefield (Popes Creek Plantation), Virginia, on February 22.

1735: The Washington family moves to Little Hunting Creek Plantation (later known as Mount Vernon), Virginia.

1738: The family moves to Ferry Farm, across the Rappahannock River from Fredericksburg, Virginia.

1743: Augustine Washington, GW's father, passes away on April 12.

1748: GW moves to Mount Vernon to live with his brother, Lawrence. As an assistant surveyor for Lord Fairfax, Washington makes his first trip to the west.

1749: GW becomes the official surveyor for Culpeper County, Virginia.

1751: GW accompanies his brother Lawrence to Barbados where George contracts, and recovers from smallpox.

1752: GW meets Royal Governor Dinwiddie in Williamsburg, Virginia. Brother Lawrence passes away on July 26. GW joins the Masonic Order in Fredericksburg. The Virginia Assembly appoints GW a major in the Virginia Militia.

1753: Governor Dinwiddie appoints GW special envoy to the French who are usurping British influence in the Ohio Valley. GW makes a hazardous winter trip to deliver Dinwiddie's message to the French near Erie, Pennsylvania, and returns safely.

1754: The Virginia Assembly promotes GW to lieutenant colonel in the Virginia Militia. He suffers defeat by the French and Indians at Fort Necessity on July 3, after which he resigns his commission and returns to Mount Vernon. GW inherits Mount Vernon upon the death of Lawrence's widow.

1755: GW joins staff of British General Braddock as an aide-de-camp and participates in an abortive expedition to Fort Duquesne. In the ensuing battle, Braddock is killed and Washington withdraws the remnants of the army to Fort Cumberland. The Virginia Assembly appoints GW commander-in-chief of Virginia forces protecting the frontier.

1756: In quest of a permanent British army commission, GW travels to Boston to meet with Royal Governor Shirley but the commission is not granted.

1758: GW joins a second British expedition against Fort Duquesne, this one led by British General Forbes. After this expedition, GW resigns his commission and returns to Mount Vernon and life as a gentleman farmer. Frederick County elects GW to House of Burgesses.

1759: GW marries Martha Dandridge Custis on January 6.

1774: GW attends the Virginia Provincial Convention and is appointed a delegate to the First Continental Congress. GW attends First Continental Congress in Philadelphia, Pennsylvania, beginning September 5.

1775: GW attends the Second Continental Congress where he is named Commander-in-Chief of the CA on June 15. GW arrives in Cambridge, Massachusetts to take command of the CA on July 3.

1776: The CA occupies Boston, Massachusetts, on March 17 following a successful siege of the city. The CA loses the Battle of Long Island, New York, on August 27. The CA makes a strategic withdrawal across New Jersey and into Pennsylvania following the Battle of White Plains, New York, October 28. GW leads his army across the Delaware River and defeats the Hessians at the Battle of Trenton, New Jersey, December 25 and 26.

1777: GW defeats the British at the Battle of Princeton, New Jersey, January 3, then establishes winter encampment at Morristown, New Jersey. GW loses the battles of Brandywine, Pennsylvania, on September 11 and Germantown, Pennsylvania, on October 4, and goes into winter encampment at Valley Forge, Pennsylvania, on December 19.

1778: The CA establishes winter encampment at Middlebrook, New Jersey, on May 28, then fights the British to a military draw at the Battle of Monmouth, New Jersey, on June 28.

1779: The CA establishes second winter encampment at Morristown, New Jersey, on December 1.

1780: GW discovers Benedict Arnold's treason at West Point, New York, on September 25 and approves court martial and subsequent execution of British Major Andre on October 2.

1781: GW commands the siege of Yorktown and accepts subsequent British surrender on October 19.

1783: GW issues cease-fire order from his headquarters in Newburgh, New York, on April 13. GW issues farewell orders to the armies on November 2 and resigns his commission in Annapolis, Maryland, on December 23.

1785: Patowmack Canal Company elects GW president of the company on May 17.

1787: GW attends Constitutional Convention in Philadelphia where he is elected presiding officer on May 25.

1789: GW inaugurated as President of the United States in New York City on April 30. GW's mother passes away, August 25. GW tours New England from October 15 to November 13.

1790: GW tours Rhode Island from August 15 to 21.

1791: GW tours the southern states from April 7 to June 12.

1793: GW inaugurated as president for second term in Philadelphia on March 4. GW lays cornerstone of US Capitol Building on September 28.

1794: GW travels to western Pennsylvania to quell the "Whiskey Rebellion," September 30–October 21.

1796: GW issues his farewell address as president on September 17.

1797: GW attends the inauguration of John Adams as his successor on March 4, and then retires to Mount Vernon.

1799: GW passes away at Mount Vernon on December 14.

SECTION II

PUBLICLY ACCESSIBLE SITES IDENTIFIED WITH
GEORGE WASHINGTON

Publicly Accessible Sites
Identified with
George Washington

More than 150 publicly accessible homes, battlefields, headquarters, churches, taverns, government buildings, and other places associated with George Washington are identified and described in Section II. Each site account contains a synopsis of its historic relationship to Washington, a description of what it offers the visitor relative to Washington's legacy, access information, and sources of additional information about the site. The sites are presented generally in the chronological order in which Washington himself first experienced them. To facilitate this method of introduction, the sites have been assembled into groups that represent seven distinct phases of Washington's life.

HOME: ROOTS AND PERMANENCE IN NORTHERN VIRGINIA contains those sites on the Northern Neck of Virginia and in and near Fredericksburg and Alexandria, Virginia. These were the sites of Washington's boyhood and youth, and places to which he returned time and again when his busy life permitted.

EYES TO THE WEST includes sites from northwestern Virginia to the middle Ohio Valley that young George Washington visited as a surveyor, an officer in the Virginia militia, and a land owner. Two decades of exposure to the conflicts, and opportunities, that lay along the western frontier of Britain's middle Atlantic colonies molded Washington's personal interest in the West as well as his views of the region's national economic and geopolitical significance.

THE FARMER-POLITICIAN identifies sites that relate to the decade of Washington's life between his retirement from the Virginia militia and the first formal movements of the British colonies toward independence. During this period, Washington farmed at Mount Vernon, became involved in a number of business ventures, and served as a member of Virginia's House of Burgesses.

THE ROAD TO PHILADELPHIA focuses on those sites that Washington came to know as he traveled between Mount Vernon and Philadelphia, and while he lived in Philadelphia, when he represented Virginia at the the two Continental Congresses in 1774 and 1775.

THE REVOLUTIONARY WAR contains more sites than any other group in this section, and includes some of the most hallowed military sites in our nation's history. From the time that Washington was given command of the nascent Continental Army in 1775 until he resigned his command in 1783, he traveled widely from southern New England to Virginia as he and his army alternately pursued and evaded the opposing British military forces.

VICTORY AND THE PRESIDENCY presents sites that relate to Washington's life as a gentleman farmer and businessman following the Revolutionary War and, most importantly, as President of the United States between 1789 and 1797. While Washington was president, the nation's capital was located first in New York City and then Philadelphia, but during his tenure of office he made three important trips in an effort to strengthen the unity of the new nation — one to New England as far north as Kittery, Maine; another to Rhode Island; and a third, almost 2000 miles in length, through the southern states of North Carolina, South Carolina, and Georgia.

THE FINAL YEARS identifies some of the most important sites commemorating the last two years, but also the enduring legacy, of Washington's life. Although the years after his presidency were spent at Mount Vernon, the new national capital — whose location and configuration had been largely influenced by Washington — was taking shape nearby.

∼

HOME
ROOTS AND PERMANENCE IN NORTHERN VIRGINIA

George Washington was peripatetic at a time that travel was difficult. As surveyor, explorer, military officer, and president, he ranged from the east coast of America to the middle Ohio Valley and from the northern states of Massachusetts, New Hampshire, and the southernmost tip of Maine to the city of Savannah, Georgia, in the south. He seemed to be constantly on the move. At a time when most people rarely traveled far from their homes, Washington rarely stopped. From his home on the Northern Neck of Virginia, he left on exploration and surveying trips to the west. As he grew, he expanded his sphere of geographic familiarity by participating in military forays to the northwest. He made innumerable trips between Mount Vernon and Williamsburg as a military officer, burgess, and suitor. He endured eight years of hard travel as commander-in-chief of the Continental Army, and as president, traveled to Philadelphia, New York, New England, and the southern states.

Yet there were places to which he returned time and again — places of special importance lying in a narrow band of Virginia bounded by his birthplace at Popes Creek on the Northern Neck, Fredericksburg to the west, and Alexandria and Mount Vernon to the north. Ferry Farm, Kenmore Plantation, Gunston Hall, Pohick Church, Fredericksburg's Masonic Lodge, Chatham Manor, and others — these places were his comfort and solace, his homes and the homes of friends and family — and collectively they created the atmosphere responsible for his maturity, ambition, attitudes, and beliefs. Here he was born, and here he would die. Here he was home (Figure 5, Table 1).

Washington always professed to be just a farmer, but the tidewater culture of the time involved more than simple farming. Family plantations grew wheat, corn, and the most profitable crop, tobacco, tended by black slaves or indentured white workers. In many cases the homes of the masters were imposing mansions. There was almost a complete lack of urban life. The largest planters tended to dominate the colony by controlling vast acreages and holding the offices of authority. The gap between rich and poor grew during Washington's time and a ruling class developed, perpetuated through intermarriage and inheritance. As stifling as patrimony could be, land and education were important and the planters passed on to their children ideals of honor, dignity, and public service. The love of glory and the aggressive pursuit of fame were promoted as virtues, indicative of character that would benefit both individual and society. Washington embraced these ideals early in life — a farmer by nature, he became a public servant when called, but he always returned to northern Virginia, the land of his youth, when his service was ended.

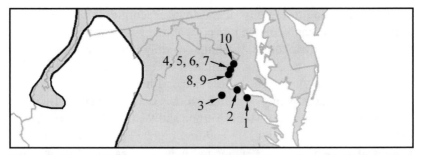

Figure 5. George Washington's early years were spent on and near the Northern Neck of Virginia. Here are identified publicly accessible sites that were important to Washington during, and often after, his childhood and youth. The names and page numbers for descriptions of the numbered sites shown here are given in Table 1.

Table 1. Publicly accessible sites identified with George Washington located on and near the Northern Neck of Virginia

MAP NUMBER	SITE NAME	PAGE NUMBER FOR SITE ACCOUNT
1.	George Washington Birthplace National Monument	95
2.	Saint Pauls Episcopal Church	98
3.	Fredericksburg area sites	99
	George Washingtons Boyhood Home	101
	Mary Washington House	105
	Hugh Mercer Apothecary Shop	106
	Rising Sun Tavern	107
	Saint James House	107
	Masonic Lodge No. 4 A. F. and A. M.	109
	Historic Kenmore	109
	Chatham	112
4.	Mount Vernon	113
5.	River Farm	119
6.	Woodlawn Plantation	120
7.	George Washingtons Grist Mill	121
8.	Gunston Hall	122
9.	Pohick Episcopal Church	125
10.	"Old Town" Alexandria sites	125
	Gadsbys Tavern Museum	127
	Stabler-Leadbeater Apothecary Shop and Museum	129
	Christ Church	130
	Carlyle House Historic Park	131
	Lee-Fendall House	132

After two hundred years we shall never really know George Washington, but several places described next are particularly important so that we can better understand the young George Washington during his formative years — Popes Creek Plantation where he was born; Fredericksburg, Virginia, where he grew to maturity; Alexandria, his second hometown; and Mount Vernon, the rock throughout much of his life. Visits to these places can bring to mind the history and lifestyles of the colonial era, and can help us understand the environment and some of the experiences that shaped the character and motivated the life of the single most influential man in the history of our nation.

1. GEORGE WASHINGTON BIRTHPLACE NATIONAL MONUMENT

WASHINGTONS BIRTHPLACE, VIRGINIA

Around 1725, Augustine Washington built a simple plantation house on land bordering Popes Creek where it feeds into the Potomac River. George Washington was born there in 1732, the first child of Augustine and his second wife, Mary Ball. The plantation at Popes Creek was not lavish but, rather, was a typical lower gentry enterprise — the master's house the center of farm life and the family served by slaves or indentured servants transported from England.

George Washington lived at Popes Creek until he was almost four and later, as an adolescent, he visited his older half-brother Augustine, Jr., who had inherited the plantation. He observed slaves working the farm and helped Augustine manage it. As the National Park Service has written in its description of Popes Creek Plantation:

> *He lived close to the natural world, his character developing to the slow rhythms of farm life, and his deep attachment to the land stayed with him until the end. We can understand these critical early influences only by taking an active role, by engaging ourselves with the past at Popes Creek. As the august symbol we know as Washington was created in the imaginations of an earlier America, we must use our own to move closer to the man.[48]*

General George Washington was in the north with the Continental Army on Christmas Day, 1779, when the plantation house at Popes Creek, then known as Wakefield, burned to the ground. Owned at the time by George's half-nephew William Augustine Washington, Wakefield was not rebuilt and its farmland was allowed to lay fallow. The property passed from the Washington family in the early part of the nineteenth century.

In 1858, the Commonwealth of Virginia acquired Wakefield to protect it as a historically significant property, but the Civil War delayed the construction of a monument. In 1882, Virginia donated the property to the federal government which erected a memorial shaft but did little else. Then, in the 1920s, a group of ladies picnicking on the grounds decried the fact that Washington's birthplace, defiled by time, elements, and human neglect, had become little more than a picnic grove. In a moment of inspiration they formed the Wakefield National Memorial Association, its purpose to reclaim the property as a site of historical importance. With significant public support and additional funding from John D. Rockefeller, Jr., the ladies purchased the land from the federal government, constructed a Memorial House and outbuildings, and planted a colonial garden. In 1930, the National Park Service agreed to assume stewardship of the site. By the next year, the Association had acquired and transferred to the government enough land to bring the holding to 394 acres. On the two-hundredth anniversary of Washington's birth, in 1932, the complex was dedicated as the George Washington Birthplace National Monument.

The Memorial House (Plate 1), surely grander than the modest Washington home, represents a typical lower gentry home of the colonial period, with four rooms and a central hallway on each floor. The bricks used for the outer walls were handmade from the clay of a nearby field and the furnishings, although not original, are representative of the period when the Washington family resided at Wakefield. Thus the Memorial House dramatically illustrates the setting into which Washington was born. Archaeological searches over the past seventy years have uncovered many Washington family artifacts as well as structural remains of the original main house, smokehouse, kitchen, and other buildings, some of which have been replicated. The birth house itself has not been reconstructed although its exact location close by the Memorial House has been outlined with oyster shells.

In 1968, a colonial living farm was established on the grounds to further enhance our understanding of the lifestyle and atmosphere of this part of colonial Virginia during the early eighteenth century. The farm features picturesque flowerbeds and a colonial herb garden — rosemary and foxglove for medicine, thyme and sage for cooking, lavender and rue for scents. Although most of the Washington farm was devoted to cash crops — tobacco, corn, and wheat — a colonial plantation had to be self-sustaining. It grew its own vegetables and grains, produced meat and hides, and fostered the growth of timber. The livestock, poultry, and crops of today's Popes Creek Plantation are old varieties and are raised using farming methods common to the colonial period. The buildings, furnishings, animals, and crops at Popes Creek offer an experience of aesthetic and historic interest whereby visitors are able to observe a way of life that has disappeared forever — that of an important river plantation active at the time the American colonies were emerging as an international commercial force.

The National Park Service Visitor Center features exhibits on the history of Wakefield and the Washington family's genealogy. A film, *A Childhood Place,* portrays life at the plantation in the early eighteenth century and is screened every thirty minutes beginning at 9:30 AM. Guided tours of the Memorial House, gardens, and farm are conducted by park rangers, and craft demonstrations are offered periodically. Well-marked hiking trails that meander through a cedar grove afford excellent views of the waterfowl of the area, and a nature trail leads to a beach and picnic area on Popes Creek.

A burying ground established by George's great-grandfather is located in the Bridges Creek section of the plantation. Thirty-two graves are found in the Washington cemetery, including that of George's father, Augustine.

DIRECTIONS: From SR 3, take SR 204 northbound 2 miles to the birthplace (Figure 6).

PUBLIC USE: Season and hours: 9 AM–5 PM daily. Closed Thanksgiving Day, Christmas Day, and New Year's Day. **Admission fee. Visitor center. Gift shop.** For people with disabilities: The visitor center is fully accessible. Transportation is provided for those unable to walk 300 yards to the Memorial House and historic area.

FOR ADDITIONAL INFORMATION: Contact: George Washington Birthplace National Monument, 1732 Popes Creek Road, Washingtons Birthplace, Virginia 22443; 804-224-1732. **Web site:** *www.nps.gov/gewa.* **Read:** Charles E. Hatch, 1979. *Popes Creek Plantation.*

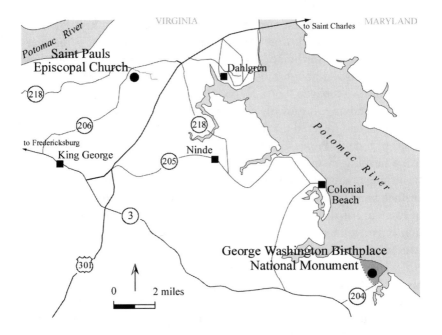

Figure 6. The location of George Washington Birthplace National Monument and Saint Pauls Episcopal Church.

2. SAINT PAULS EPISCOPAL CHURCH

KING GEORGE, VIRGINIA

George Washington spent a great deal of time in the Chotank area of King George County, roughly situated between Fredericksburg and Popes Creek. Chotank was a rolling country of rich and productive soil, perfect for tobacco cultivation. Chotank Plantation was a Washington property handed down through the distaff line of Lawrence, brother of George's great-grandfather. The Washington family was close and George visited his cousins at Chotank, especially during his formative years when social life revolved around family interaction and spiritual life focused on the parish church. The family homes at Chotank have not survived, but

Saint Pauls Episcopal Church (Plate 2) where Washington attended services, remains active. The communion silver used in Washington's time is still used on special occasions.

Chotank Parish was established in 1667 and named Saint Pauls in 1702. The brick building presently used as the church was erected in 1766 when George Washington's brother Samuel was a member of the vestry. George Washington worshipped here on several occasions. The church is sixty-two feet long with thirty-foot arms, an excellent example of colonial church architecture in the shape of a Greek cross. The walls are of locally manufactured bricks laid in Flemish bond. In 1802, Saint Pauls fell victim to the Glebe Act whereby the Commonwealth of Virginia confiscated the church building and its land. At that time the interior was dismantled and the building vandalized. It was not until 1831 that the church was reconsecrated and returned to its original function as a house of worship. Since then, Saint Pauls has not changed, nor has the quietude and lifestyle of the Chotank area.

DIRECTIONS: Saint Pauls is located about 8 miles north of SR 3 at the intersection of SR 206 and SR 218 (Figure 6).

PUBLIC USE: Worship services are held each Sunday at 9 AM.

FOR ADDITIONAL INFORMATION: Contact: Saint Pauls Episcopal Church, PO Box 134, King George, Virginia 22485; 540-663-3085.

3. FREDERICKSBURG, VIRGINIA

If George Washington had a hometown, it was certainly Fredericksburg. Washington's formative years were spent at Ferry Farm just across the Rappahannock River and later he would frequently break his journeys between Mount Vernon and Williamsburg by stopping in Fredericksburg to visit friends and family. He owned property in the town and maintained lifelong business and social connections. Several houses and other buildings from that period, including the homes of his mother, sister, and brother, remain and are open to the public.

Fredericksburg, named for Crown Prince Frederick, son of England's King George III, was founded as a tobacco trading port in

1728. Its strategic location immediately below the falls of the Rappahannock made it a successful shipping terminus serving the interior. It was a typically raw and dusty river port that grew substantially when chosen to house the county court in 1732. The court "legitimized" Fredericksburg and it soon attracted lawyers, artisans, and other "higher class" citizens. It was a young but energetic and diversified community in which George Washington grew up. From the age of six to twenty, he lived at Ferry Farm; he may have attended the Reverend James Marye's school in Fredericksburg for a term or two with his brothers and cousins. The school was very likely held at the northwest corner of Charlotte and Princess Anne streets.

Fredericksburg existed quietly during most of its first century, but during the middle of the nineteenth century its peacefulness was shattered by the Civil War. Located midway between the capital cities of Washington and Richmond, Fredericksburg changed hands seven times and four major battles — Fredericksburg, Chancellorsville, The Wilderness, and Spotsylvania — took place in the immediate vicinity. The area has been called the bloodiest land in the United States due to the fierce fighting that took the lives of 17,000 young Americans and wounded 80,000 more. Fredericksburg itself was ravaged; most of its buildings were destroyed or damaged, and scars are still visible a century later.

Following the Civil War, prosperity gradually returned, and thanks to a combination of convenient location, improved economy, and the hard work of devoted preservationists, growth was controlled and many older buildings were rebuilt, refurbished, or preserved, with Victorian dwellings rising next to colonial homes and commercial buildings. More than 350 of Fredericksburg's eighteenth- and nineteenth-century buildings form the present-day Historic District. The Civil War battlefields are maintained by the National Park Service.

Many buildings and other sites in Fredericksburg's Historic District are associated with George Washington. Among the more significant are The Mary Washington House, his mother's home, and Kenmore, his sister's magnificent mansion. Others include residences of his friends and business associates; The Charles Dick House on Caroline Street was the home of one of Washington's confidantes. Saint James House, Rising Sun Tavern, and Hugh Mercer's Apothecary Shop have been refurbished and are open for visitation. The Mary Washington Grave and

Monument is located on Washington Avenue near Kenmore Plantation and George Washingtons Horse-Chestnut Tree on Fauquier Street is the only tree left of the thirteen planted by President Washington in honor of the states in the new Union. The Historic Fredericksburg Foundation currently (2002) is restoring the 1749 Lewis Store where Mary and George Washington shopped. It is located at the corner of Caroline and Lewis streets but is not yet open for visitation.

Other important sites in Fredericksburg post-date Washington's residency and they include The National Bank Museum, Saint Georges Church, First Presbyterian Church, Rocky Lane and City Dock, The Thomas Jefferson Religious Freedom Monument, and The James Monroe Museum. All contribute important chapters to the rich history of eighteenth- and nineteenth-century Fredericksburg. Trips to Fredericksburg should begin at the Visitor Center (Site 1, Figure 7) where a video provides comprehensive information about the Fredericksburg, Stafford, and Spotsylvania areas. Numerous brochures outline various walking tours and offer recommendations for trolley and carriage tours of the Historic District. The Fredericksburg Area Museum and Cultural Center in the Historic 1816 Town Hall includes six permanent exhibit galleries that tell the story of Fredericksburg's rich and varied past.

DIRECTIONS: Fredericksburg is 50 miles south of Washington, DC, on SR 3, 3 miles east of I 95 northbound or southbound, Exit 130. Numerous directional markers on SR 3 direct visitors to Fredericksburg's Historic District (Figure 7).

FOR ADDITIONAL INFORMATION: Contact: Fredericksburg Visitor Center, 706 Caroline Street, Fredericksburg, Virginia 22401; 540-373-1776, 800-678-4748. **Web site:** *www.fredericksburgva.com.* **Read:** Paula S. Felder. 1993. *Handbook of Historic Fredericksburg, Virginia.*

3-2. GEORGE WASHINGTONS BOYHOOD HOME
STAFFORD COUNTY, VIRGINIA

George Washingtons Boyhood Home was recently the center of controversy because of a dispute between the forces of modern commerce and those of historic preservation when private owners arranged to sell the property to a major retail company that planned

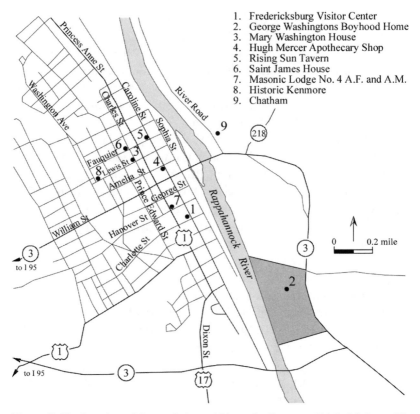

1. Fredericksburg Visitor Center
2. George Washingtons Boyhood Home
3. Mary Washington House
4. Hugh Mercer Apothecary Shop
5. Rising Sun Tavern
6. Saint James House
7. Masonic Lodge No. 4 A.F. and A.M.
8. Historic Kenmore
9. Chatham

Figure 7. The location of featured sites within and adjacent to Fredericksburg, Virginia.

to construct a shopping center on the site. Happily, reason prevailed, but only after there was public outcry, legal maneuvering, and massive fund-raising on the part of horrified but dedicated historians and preservationists. George Washingtons Boyhood Home was saved, primarily through the efforts of the non-profit Historic Fredericksburg Foundation and George Washingtons Fredericksburg Foundation. The latter bought the property and is currently conducting important archaeological studies on the site. Archaeological excavations have already turned up remains of the first Washington house that was destroyed by fire in 1740, and a large array of artifacts dating from George Washington's childhood. There is but one above-ground historic structure on the property, a small shed (Figure 8) traditionally said to be the place where young George found his father's surveying instruments and began to develop the skills that later took him west. Scholars believe this building was actually built in the nineteenth century.

George Washingtons Boyhood Home, where George lived from the time he was seven until he reached adulthood, lies directly across the Rappahannock River from what was at that time a tiny cluster of buildings known as Fredericksburg. A commercial ferry ran from the north end of the farm to the town, thus giving the property the name Ferry Farm. The Washington farmhouse was comfortable but by no means elaborate. One large room served as the living and dining room and beds were found in every room, including the parlor. The furnishings were of good quality but there were no luxuries such as books, everyday silver, or carpeting. The family's proudest possessions were two looking glasses in the hall and par-

Figure 8. The oldest surviving building on the grounds of George Washingtons Boyhood Home is this wooden shed. This building is traditionally associated with George Washington, but it might not have been built until after Washington's death in 1799. (Photograph by William G. Clotworthy)

lor. The home was short of glassware, but it was possible to set a good table and there was always enough food.

Augustine Washington died at Ferry Farm in 1743, and left the plantation to George, who inherited it in 1752. Mary Ball Washington lived there until 1771, when George Washington moved her to a cottage in town. He sold the property in 1774. The second Washington house on the plantation was torn down early in the nineteenth century.

In addition to archaeological investigations, George Washingtons Fredericksburg Foundation is formulating exciting plans for improving the basically undeveloped property. Local Boy Scouts have constructed a nature stairway and cleared a trail to the ferry terminus and there are plans to install a tourist ferry across the Rappahannock, replicating the transportation of colonial days. Historical markers on the property are helpful in understanding the history of the farm and its importance in the life and development of George Washington. A walk around George Washingtons Boyhood Home is a step back in time, especially as one stands on the banks of the Rappahannock to visualize the youthful George Washington throwing a coin across the river (it was 412 feet wide) or to stroll in the meadow to see where he (might have) chopped down his father's cherry tree.

George Washingtons Boyhood Home was unquestionably one of the most important places in Washington's life. The site was designated a National Historic Landmark in 2000. His interest in agriculture and surveying began there. What formal education he had was during the years he spent at Ferry Farm, the place where he grew to be a man of tremendous physical ability. There his character was shaped — his integrity, compassion, family devotion, and remarkable determination to succeed in the face of adversity. As historian Jack D. Warren, Jr. has said:

> *George Washington spent his formative years at Ferry Farm .... Here he developed his extraordinary character — that remarkable blend of stubborn courage, patience, and unassuming wisdom — that enabled him to lead the Continental Army to victory in the Revolution, and the new nation through its early years.*[49]

DIRECTIONS: From downtown Fredericksburg, follow SR 3 eastbound about 1 mile to the park entrance on the east side of the road (Figure 7).

PUBLIC USE: Season and hours: February 21–December 30, Monday–Saturday, 10 AM–5 PM; Sunday, 12 N–5 PM. January 2–February 20, Monday–Friday, by group reservation only; Saturday, 10 AM–4 PM; Sunday, 12 N–4 PM. **For people with disabilities:** Not accessible.

FOR ADDITIONAL INFORMATION: Contact: George Washingtons Boyhood Home, c/o Kenmore Plantation and Gardens, 1201 Washington Avenue, Fredericksburg, Virginia 22401; 540-373-3381. **Web site:** *www.kenmore.org.* **Read:** (1) David Freeman Hawke. 1988. *Everyday Life in Early America.* (2) Reed Karaim. 1996. "The Fields Where My Mother Lives." (3) Jack D. Warren, Jr. 1999. "The Childhood of George Washington."

3-3. MARY WASHINGTON HOUSE
1200 CHARLES STREET

In 1772, George Washington purchased a home for his mother where she lived for the last seventeen years of her life. Mary Washington was reported to be a demanding mother; George's relationship with her apparently was strained but dutiful, and he visited her as often as possible. The last time he called on her was as president-elect of the United States to receive her blessing. Mrs. Washington's comfortable white frame home contains some original possessions including the mirror she willed to George, the one she called her best dressing glass. Mrs. Washington's life-long hobby was gardening and the Garden Club of Virginia recently planted her vegetable and flower gardens to appear as they did in the 1780s, and her sundial still tracks the time of day. The walks are lined with boxwoods that were planted by Mrs. Washington.

In 1891, the Association for the Preservation of Virginia Antiquities saved the house from destruction, restoring it and opening it to the public. They continue their work as the proud administrator of the Mary Washington House and three other historic properties whose descriptions follow.

PUBLIC USE: Season and hours: March 1–November 30, 9 AM–5 PM daily. December–February, 10 AM–4 PM daily. Closed Thanksgiving Day, Christmas Eve, Christmas Day, New Year's Eve, and New Year's Day. **Admission fee. Gift shop. For people with disabilities:** Limited access.

FOR ADDITIONAL INFORMATION: Contact: Mary Washington House, 1200 Charles Street, Fredericksburg, Virginia 22401; 540-373-1569. **Web site:** *www.apva.org/apva/mwash.* **Read:** Frederick Bernays Wiener. 1991. "Washington and His Mother."

3-4. HUGH MERCER APOTHECARY SHOP
1020 CAROLINE STREET

Doctor Hugh Mercer practiced medicine in Fredericksburg for many years, during which time he treated Mary Washington and other prominent citizens. He joined the Revolutionary Army as a Brigadier General and lost his life at the Battle of Princeton. His office, the Hugh Mercer Apothecary Shop, is filled with authentic apothecary jars, bottles, silver-plated pills, and other nostrums. The shop has been preserved as a museum of eighteenth- and nineteenth-century medical practices where visitors are "treated" with colonial medicines and cures — leeches, lancets for bleeding, and snakeroot.

PUBLIC USE: Season and hours: March–November, 9 AM–5 PM daily. December–February, 10 AM–4 PM daily. Closed Thanksgiving Day, Christmas Eve, Christmas Day, New Year's Eve, and New Year's Day. **Admission fee. Gift shop. For people with disabilities:** Limited access.

FOR ADDITIONAL INFORMATION: Contact: Hugh Mercer Apothecary Shop, 1020 Caroline Street, Fredericksburg, Virginia 22401; 540-373-3362. **Web site:** *www.apva.org/apva/hugh.* **Read:** Susan Neiburg Terkel. 1993. *Colonial American Medicine.*

3-5. RISING SUN TAVERN
1304 CAROLINE STREET

Around 1760, George Washington's youngest brother, Charles, built a fine home in downtown Fredericksburg but soon moved west, and leased the Fredericksburg house to his son who converted it to a tavern and meeting place that catered to the finest gentlemen of the city. Named Rising Sun Tavern, it has been preserved as an eighteenth-century architectural gem evoking the atmosphere of the colonial period. Costumed "serving wenches" entertain modern visitors by serving refreshing spiced tea, which helps recreate the flavor of colonial days when the tavern was a stagecoach stop and social center of the town where George Washington, Thomas Jefferson, James Monroe, Patrick Henry, and other patriots met to dine, drink, gamble, talk — and plot the future of their homeland.

PUBLIC USE: Season and hours: March–November, 9 AM–5 PM daily. December–February, 10 AM–4 PM daily. Closed Thanksgiving Day, Christmas Eve, Christmas Day, New Year's Eve, and New Year's Day. **Admission fee. Gift shop. For people with disabilities:** Limited access.

FOR ADDITIONAL INFORMATION: Contact: Rising Sun Tavern, 1304 Caroline Street, Fredericksburg, Virginia 22401; 540-373-1569. **Web site:** *www.apva.org/apva/rising.html.*

3-6. SAINT JAMES HOUSE
1300 CHARLES STREET

Saint James House (Figure 9), a fine example of an eighteenth-century gentleman's home, was built on a lot George Washington had purchased from his brother-in-law, Fielding Lewis. Washington sold the property to James Mercer who built the small gambrel-roofed home in the 1760s. The name "Saint James" came from the street in Dublin on which Mercer's ancestral home had stood. Mercer, an active participant in civic and national affairs, was Mary

Figure 9. The Saint James House, Fredericksburg, Virginia. (Photograph by William G. Clotworthy)

Washington's attorney and a close friend of the family. In 1963, Saint James House was restored by owners William Tolerton and Daniel Breslin who filled it with priceless antiques and fine furniture, then willed the house and its contents to the Association for the Preservation of Virginia Antiquities — a generous and valuable donation to America's architectural and presidential heritage.

PUBLIC USE: Season and hours: Open only by appointment the first week in October and during Virginia Garden Week, the last full week in April. **Admission fee. For people with disabilities:** Limited access.

FOR ADDITIONAL INFORMATION: Contact: Saint James House, 1300 Charles Street, Fredericksburg, Virginia 22401; 540-373-1569. **Web site:** *www.apva.org/apva/stjames.html.*

3-7. MASONIC LODGE NO. 4 A. F. AND A. M.
803 PRINCESS ANNE STREET

In October, 1752, fourteen men formed a Masonic lodge in Charles Julian's coffee shop at the corner of Amelia and Caroline streets. Sometime during the next month, twenty-one-year-old George Washington was initiated into the lodge and became an active life-long member of the society. In the early nineteenth century, the meeting place was razed and a new lodge was built on Princess Anne Street. Today's lodge utilizes the original ceremonial paraphernalia used in Washington's initiation and a small museum area displays ledgers and minute books of his membership, a Bible used in Masonic ceremonies, and an original portrait of George Washington by Gilbert Stuart.

PUBLIC USE: Season and hours: 9 AM–4 PM. Sunday, 1 PM–4 PM. Closed Thanksgiving Day and Christmas Day. **Admission fee. For people with disabilities:** Not accessible.

FOR ADDITIONAL INFORMATION: Contact: Masonic Lodge No. 4 A. F. and A. M., 803 Princess Anne Street, Fredericksburg, Virginia 22403; 540-373-5885. **Read:** William Mosely Brown. 1952. *Washington, the Mason.*

3-8. HISTORIC KENMORE
1201 WASHINGTON AVENUE

A young entrepreneur named Fielding Lewis arrived in Fredericksburg in 1747 accompanied by his wife Catherine, George Washington's cousin. Catherine passed away three years later, and shortly thereafter Lewis courted and married Washington's only sister, seventeen-year-old Betty. It was obviously a happy union, and they had eleven children! Lewis became a major landowner in Spotsylvania and Frederick counties, held many important civic positions in Fredericksburg, and enjoyed a profitable career in commerce and manufacturing. More importantly, Lewis developed a life-long, intimate relationship with brother-in-law George, a friendship that transcended family ties. Washington's diaries record that he dined or lodged with the Lewises many times.

In 1775, Lewis initiated the construction of a magnificent mansion designed to reflect his financial and social success. The mansion he named Millwood is one of America's architectural treasures (Figure 10). An elegant and opulent grand home, it contained three of the most elaborately decorated rooms of the time, including one now called "one of the 100 most beautiful Rooms in America," which has what many consider to be the most interesting, unusual, and splendid decorative plaster ceilings in the nation (Plate 3).[50]

After his distinguished service during the Revolutionary War as manager of a gun factory, Lewis's wealth and physical health deteriorated and he passed away in 1781. Betty Washington Lewis remained at Millwood for a time but financial considerations forced her to sell, and the estate was gradually eroded by subdivision. In 1819, the mansion was purchased by Samuel Gordon, who rechristened it Kenmore.

Figure 10. Historic Kenmore, Fredericksburg, Virginia. (Photograph courtesy of Historic Kenmore)

Almost a century later, a private non-profit organization was organized to preserve Kenmore as an historically significant property, an effort that allows today's visitors to observe and enjoy an outstanding contribution to America's architectural heritage. Kenmore's gardens, in their magnificent glory, are spread over almost a city block, and visitors are charmed by the tradition of tea and gingerbread served in the kitchen dependency — a tradition dating to the day long ago when Mary Washington entertained the Marquis de Lafayette the same way.

George Washingtons Fredericksburg Foundation owns and maintains Historic Kenmore and recently purchased George Washingtons Boyhood Home at Ferry Farm. The Foundation, supported by visitors and friends from around the nation, was among the first national non-profit preservation organizations. A separate building at Kenmore houses a small museum of colonial portraiture and furniture together with displays on the Kenmore Mansion and the Lewis and Washington family genealogies.

PUBLIC USE: Season and hours: February 21–December 30, Monday–Saturday, 10 AM–5 PM; Sunday, 12 N–5 PM. January–February 20, Monday–Friday, by group reservation only; Saturday, 10 AM–4 PM; Sunday, 12 N–4 PM. Closed Thanksgiving Day, Christmas Eve, and Christmas Day. **Admission fee. Visitor center. Gift shop. For people with disabilities:** The mansion is not accessible at this time (2002) but a major renovation project scheduled for completion in 2003 includes a wheelchair lift. The Visitor Center-Museum has a videotape presentation available for those unable to visit the mansion.

FOR ADDITIONAL INFORMATION: Contact: Kenmore Plantation and Gardens, 1201 Washington Avenue, Fredericksburg, Virginia 22403; 540-373-3381. **Web site:** *www.kenmore.org.* **Read:** (1) Merrill Folsom. 1967. *More Great American Mansions.* (2) W. Vernon Edenfield and Stacia Gregory Norman. 1992. *Kenmore.* (3) Jeff Stein. 1997. "George Washington's Sister Slept Here."

3-9. CHATHAM

120 CHATHAM LANE

Chatham, a magnificent Georgian mansion built around 1770, lies across the Rappahannock River from Fredericksburg, close by George Washingtons Boyhood Home. Chatham was built on 1300 acres of prime agricultural land by William Fitzhugh, scion of a great aristocratic family that owned several plantations. Fitzhugh, an avid horse fancier, was well known for his gracious hospitality, notably to the racing set that included his friend George Washington. Fitzhugh's rich life-style eventually proved beyond his means, which forced him to move to less opulent accommodations in Alexandria, where his friendship with Washington continued.

During the Civil War, Chatham served as headquarters for Union General Ambrose Burnside and is where President Lincoln conferred with Burnside's military command. Chatham was also used as a field hospital during the Battle of Fredericksburg when both Clara Barton and Walt Whitman were members of the Union medical staff.

In 1975, Chatham's last private owner, John Pratt, donated the house, the outbuildings, and their contents to the National Park Service which now maintains the first floor of the house as a museum devoted to the history of Chatham. The upper rooms are used as administrative headquarters for the Fredericksburg and Spotsylvania National Military Park. The grounds at the rear of the house have been restored to a colonial style of landscaping.

DIRECTIONS: From downtown Fredericksburg, take SR 3 eastbound across the Rappahannock River. Turn left on White Oak Road and follow the historical signs to Chatham.

PUBLIC USE: Season and hours: 9 AM–5 PM daily. Closed Christmas Day and New Year's Day. **Admission fee. For people with disabilities:** Accessible.

FOR ADDITIONAL INFORMATION: Contact: Chatham, Fredericksburg and Spotsylvania National Military Park, 120 Chatham Lane, Fredericksburg, Virginia 22405; 540-373-4461. **Web site:** *www.nps.gov/frsp.* **Read:** Ralph Happel. 1984. *Chatham: The Life of a House.*

4. MOUNT VERNON AND ENVIRONS
MOUNT VERNON, VIRGINIA

No estate in United America is more pleasantly situated than this. It lies in a high, dry and healthy Country 300 miles by water from the Sea . . . on one of the finest Rivers in the world . . . . It is situated in a latitude between the extremes of heat and cold, and is the same distance by land and water, with good roads and the best navigation (to and) from the Federal City, Alexandria and George town; distant from the first twelve, from the second nine, and from the last sixteen miles.

— George Washington to Arthur Young, December 12, 1793 [51]

During the War for American Independence, Mount Vernon Plantation was managed in George Washington's absence by his cousin, Lund Washington. In a dramatic confrontation, a British man-of-war appeared on the Potomac River off Mount Vernon and demanded provisions. Overseer Washington acceded to the demands and the British sailed away, taking a number of slaves but sparing the house and property. Lund, who carried on detailed correspondence with General Washington regarding plantation matters, dutifully reported the incident and received a surprising reply:

I am very sorry to hear of your loss; I am a little sorry to hear of my own; but that which gives me the most concern, is, that you should go on board the enemys Vessels, and furnish them with refreshments. It would have been a less painful circumstance to me, to have heard, that in consequence of your non-compliance with their request, they had burnt my House, and laid the Plantation in ruins. You ought to have considered yourself as my representative, and should have reflected on the bad example of communicating with the enemy, and making a voluntary offer of refreshments with them with a view to prevent a conflagration.

— George Washington to Lund Washington, April 30, 1781 [52]

113

The reprimand was remarkable as Mount Vernon was the center of George Washington's life — his past and future, his solace and inspiration. It may have been a tribute to his honor, character, and single-minded devotion to principle that Mount Vernon's destruction was preferable to the service of "refreshments" to the enemy, but the rebuke seems a bit unfair to poor Lund who was faced with hostile action: cannons trained on the estate, and perhaps even pistols aimed at his person. Lund's decision may not have pleased the general, but from our modern viewpoint he was correct, otherwise we would not have the opportunity to enjoy the grandeur and inspiration of America's most respected and popular historic home, where almost a million visitors a year experience the splendor and charm of Washington's beloved and treasured estate.

Mount Vernon evolved over a period of one hundred years, from 1674 when Lord Culpeper, owner of the Northern Neck under dispensation of King Charles II, granted 5000 acres along the upper Potomac River between Dogue and Little Hunting creeks to George's great-grandfather John Washington and his partner Nicholas Spencer. The partners were required to pay rent in perpetuity and to plant the land within three years. In 1690, the tract was divided between Spencer's heirs and John's son, Lawrence Washington. During Lawrence's proprietorship, the property became known as Little Hunting Creek Plantation and it is possible, though unproven, that Lawrence built a small house. Recent archaeological findings have ascertained that the core of the present mansion was built by either Lawrence or George's father Augustine.

Lawrence willed Little Hunting Creek Plantation to his daughter, Mildred, who sold it to her brother Augustine. In 1735, Augustine moved his family, which included three-year-old George, from Popes Creek Plantation upstream to Little Hunting Creek where they stayed a few years. Augustine deeded the property to his eldest son, Lawrence, and it was he who renamed it in honor of British Admiral Edward Vernon under whom he'd served in the Caribbean. George, who idolized Lawrence, divided his formative years between Ferry Farm and Mount Vernon, and it was a tremendous emotional blow when Lawrence passed away in 1752. Under the terms of Lawrence's will, however, George was able to lease a life interest in Mount Vernon from Lawrence's widow and, when she died in 1761, he became sole owner, though he had been in residence since 1754.

At that time, the house was a modest dwelling of 1½-stories, with a central hall and four small rooms on the first floor, a typical small Virginia home, practical and perfectly comfortable for a bachelor farmer. In 1759, however, Mount Vernon was to acquire a mistress, a widow with two small children. The house was obviously inadequate so it was raised to 2½-stories and extensively redecorated.

In 1775, Washington formulated plans for significant additions to each end of the house, plus replacement of the outbuildings, the creation of service lanes, and other improvements. As the work began, however, he was chosen to represent Virginia at the Second Continental Congress in Philadelphia where he was named Commander-in-Chief of a Continental Army. He immediately left for Cambridge, Massachusetts, to take command. Except for two brief visits, he would be away from Mount Vernon for eight long years.

When General Washington returned home on Christmas Eve, 1783, most of the planned projects had been completed — the glorious piazza overlooking the Potomac was finished in 1777 and the north banquet hall in the 1780s. Additional improvements were made over the next few years, the final embellishment being a weathervane that represented, appropriately, a dove of peace.

His time at Mount Vernon would be limited. For another eight years he would reside in New York or Philadelphia; he would enjoy the ambience and curative powers of Mount Vernon only on rare occasions. It was not until 1797 that George Washington returned to Mount Vernon for good. He wrote to his friend, Dr. James Anderson, "No pursuit is more congenial with my nature and gratification, than that of agriculture; nor none that I pant after as again to become a tiller of the earth."[53]

Mount Vernon remained in the Washington family for many years after the President's death in 1799, but by the mid-1800s it had fallen into decline — agriculturally unproductive and near bankruptcy, the mansion house was in an advanced state of deterioration. An unlikely savior appeared in the person of Miss Ann Pamela Cunningham of South Carolina, a semi-invalid confined to her bed much of the time. Decrying the fact that the men of America had failed to perpetuate the glory of Washington's home, Miss Cunningham reasoned that saving Mount Vernon was urgent, important, and — yes — a noble cause in which she might lead the women of America.

From the perspective of today's instant communication it's almost impossible to grasp the enormity of Ann Pamela Cunningham's task. There was no telephone or telegraph, mail delivery was rudimentary, and personal travel by horseback or carriage was over poor or non-existent roads. Ann Pamela's only tools were her pens, but with her fervent dedication to the cause of preserving the home, memory, and heritage of George Washington she somehow organized women all over the nation. After years of emotional struggle, physical hardship, political manipulation (and remember, women did not have suffrage), fundraising, ingenious organization, and gentle and not-so-gentle persuasion, her goal was attained. In 1858, on the very eve of the Civil War, Miss Cunningham's Mount Vernon Ladies' Association took possession of Mount Vernon.

The Mount Vernon Ladies' Association was the first national historic preservation society and still functions as the caring guardian-owner of America's most cherished historic home (Figure 2). The Association's stewardship and activities in education, archaeology, and restoration have continued for over a century, and have served as models for other preservation organizations which followed its inspiring example of enlightened volunteerism.

Mount Vernon is an excellent example of colonial architecture — white, simple, and uncluttered. One of America's great architectural and emotional treasures, Mount Vernon is an evocation of eighteenth-century plantation life, meticulously restored from the paint colors on the walls to the actual furniture arrangements. The appearance of the interior during the last year of Washington's life has been replicated with great attention to detail. Bright greens and blues, handsome wood grains, and dimity and satin window hangings all reflect the ambience and history of an exciting era. Fourteen rooms are open for visitation, each filled with original pieces of furniture, paintings, silver, bric-a-brac, and each vibrant with decorated ceilings, carved mantels, and polished woodwork.

An outside exhibition area contains more than thirty acres of colorful gardens and forests that are accessible to visitors. Close by the mansion are outbuildings where the day-to-day operations of the plantation took place — where bread was baked, wool and flax were woven into cloth, laundry was washed, and meat was cured. A separate four-acre demonstration area has been designed to introduce visitors to Washington's pioneer work as a farmer, highlighting his experiments with crop rotation and other farming methods unusual for the eighteenth century. The main farm structure is Mount Vernon's newest attraction, a reproduction of Washington's unique sixteen-sided barn, built of trees cut from the estate's forests and bricks made at Mount Vernon; the finishing work was accomplished using eighteenth-century tools and methods. The barn features seasonal wheat threshing demonstrations by Mount Vernon's horses and mules and hands-on activities are scheduled from March to November.

A museum on the grounds offers an intimate glimpse of some of the Washingtons's personal possessions — clothing, military equipment, silver, porcelain, and other artifacts. The Mount Vernon Ladies' Association also sponsors a full range of special activities and educational programs — lectures, seminars, holiday fetes, anniversary celebrations, after-hours tours, and student activities that range from February's "Breakfast with George Washington" to summertime Garden and Landscape tours. A daily "Hands-On History" program for children is also conducted through the summer, and "Mount Vernon by Candlelight" is held in November and December. In 2003, ground will be broken for a 50,000-square-foot Education Center and Museum at Mount Vernon that will concentrate on Washington's early years and his military and presidential careers. Its purpose is to expand the public's insight into Washington's personal life, character, and contributions to our nation beyond the image of a farmer and entrepreneur. The Education Center is scheduled for completion in 2006.

The author Cranston Jones summed up Mount Vernon this way:

Mount Vernon has from first to last stood pre-eminent in the hearts of Americans. While it is neither the oldest, most sumptuous, nor even the most elegant of these homes that give color and high light to our national heritage, Mount Vernon at every turn testifies to the taste, planning, and dignity of General Washington himself, a Virginia gentleman who would brook no slur on his honor and could not tolerate mediocrity. No house in America so compellingly evokes the manners, concerns and delights of a great age now past. Moving through the spacious rooms that knew Washington's own measured tread, we are in an ambience of Washington's own creating, aware that for him Mount Vernon was more precious than worldly honors.[54]

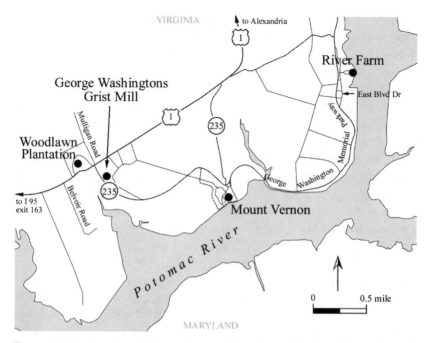

Figure 11. The location of Mount Vernon, River Farm, Woodlawn Plantation, and George Washingtons Grist Mill in northern Virginia.

DIRECTIONS: Mount Vernon is at the south end of the George Washington Memorial Parkway, 8 miles south of Alexandria, Virginia (Figure 11).

PUBLIC USE: Season and hours: April 1–August 30, 8 AM–5 PM daily. March, September, and October, 9 AM–5 PM daily. November–February, 9 AM–4 PM daily. **Admission fee. Gift shops. Food service. For people with disabilities:** A limited number of wheelchairs are available. The first floor of the mansion, restrooms, and many of the outbuildings are accessible.

FOR ADDITIONAL INFORMATION: Contact: Mount Vernon, Mount Vernon, Virginia 22121; 703-780-2000. **Web site:** *www.mountvernon.org.* **Read:** (1) Elswyth Thane. 1968. *Mount Vernon Family.* (2) Charles Cecil Law. 1985. *Mount Vernon: A Handbook.*

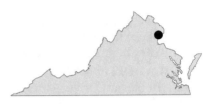

5. RIVER FARM

ALEXANDRIA, VIRGINIA

In 1653, Englishman Giles Brent obtained a royal patent on 1800 acres of prime agricultural land along the Potomac River that included the site of present-day River Farm (Plate 4). Brent sold the land to William Clifton who built a brick house in 1757 before selling the property to George Washington a few years later. Washington added River Farm to his Mount Vernon holdings and planted rye, wheat, corn, and possibly the walnut trees that still grace the property.

When Washington's personal secretary Tobias Lear married the general's niece, the couple was granted a lifetime lease on River Farm as a wedding present. The property remained in the Lear and Washington families until 1859, then knew several other owners until the American Horticultural Society purchased it in 1973. The Society's manor house headquarters stands on the foundation of the original house built by Mr. Clifton. While modern improvements have been effected over the years, the interior furnishings are a combination of antiques and reproductions reflecting the style of Washington's era. The American Horticultural Society has not only maintained but greatly enhanced the gardens in their colorful glory. An azalea garden, herb garden, rose garden, and others create an atmosphere of eighteenth-century grandeur as they border the house and sweep across the manicured lawn to the banks of the majestic Potomac River.

The oldest tree on the property is an immense Osage orange, a tree native to the western United States. It is the largest in Virginia and is believed to have been a gift to the Washington family from Thomas Jefferson. It is known that Jefferson received seedlings of the Osage orange from members of the Lewis and Clark expedition of 1804–1806.

DIRECTIONS: From the George Washington Memorial Parkway, take the Arcturus Herbert Springs Exit to East Boulevard Drive, then go north on East Boulevard Drive to River Farm, immediately ahead on the east side of the road (Figure 11).

PUBLIC USE: Season and hours: Monday–Friday, 8:30 AM–5 PM; early April through early October, Saturday, 9 AM–1 PM. **Visitor center. Gift shop. For people with disabilities:** Accessible.

FOR ADDITIONAL INFORMATION: Contact: River Farm, 7931 East Boulevard Drive, Alexandria, Virginia 22308-1300; 703-768-5700, 800-777-7931. **Web site:** *www.ahs.org.com.* **Read:** Dorothy Hunt Williams. 1975. *Historic Virginia Gardens: Preservations by the Garden Club of Virginia.*

6. WOODLAWN PLANTATION

ALEXANDRIA, VIRGINIA

On George Washington's last birthday, February 22, 1799, a gala wedding at Mount Vernon united Washington's nephew, Lawrence Lewis, and Martha's granddaughter, Eleanor "Nelly" Custis. The president's wedding gift to the couple was 2000 acres of Mount Vernon land holdings including Dogue Run Farm, a gristmill, and a distillery. Dr. William Thornton, architect of the National Capitol, designed a mansion for the newlyweds that was completed in 1805. Following Mr. Lewis's death in 1839, Nelly moved away and the house and grounds fell into neglect. In 1846, Woodlawn was offered for public sale and since that time has been a home, a working plantation, and the hub of several active communities. Its various occupants have included Quaker and Baptist settlers, a playwright, and a United States senator, all of whom have respected the history of Woodlawn by spending time and personal expense in maintaining the character and architectural integrity of the plantation.

Woodlawn became an historic property of the National Trust for Historic Preservation in 1948. The Trust's caring maintenance and administration promises the continued preservation of this important piece of America's early architectural and cultural history. As a National Trust property, Woodlawn Plantation is operated as a community preservation center working closely with other preservation groups to insure the protection and usefulness of many historic sites in and around Washington, DC.

DIRECTIONS: Woodlawn lies at the intersection of US 1 and SR 235 (figures 11, 13).

PUBLIC USE: Season and hours: March–December, 10 AM–5 PM daily. Closed January and February except for Presidents' Day; closed Thanksgiving Day, Christmas Day, and New Year's Day. **Admission fee. Gift shop. For people with disabilities:** Access to the first floor only.

FOR ADDITIONAL INFORMATION: Contact: Woodlawn Plantation, 9000 Richmond Highway, Alexandria, Virginia 22309; 703-780-4000. **Web site:** *www.nationaltrust.org.* **Read:** Chuck Lawliss. 1996. *The Early American Source Book.*

7. GEORGE WASHINGTONS GRIST MILL

ALEXANDRIA, VIRGINIA

Tobacco was the great cash crop in Tidewater Virginia but production required constant attention and it tended to deplete the soil quickly. Visionary farmer Washington successfully switched from tobacco to wheat as the principal crop at Mount Vernon and, with an increasing demand in England and local markets for flour, he found it convenient and profitable to construct his own grist mill for grinding wheat and the other cash crop, corn. The mill was a stone building of four stories with a wheel on the inside and an arch over the tailrace on Dogue Run. The mill operated two pairs of millstones, one of which ground corn into rough cornmeal. The other produced meal that was sifted into high quality flour for sale to what Washington called the "merchant trade." In the 1790s, Washington improved the mill by adding water-operated hoisting machinery that took the grain from the delivery and grinding areas on the first floor to the upper floors for storage.

The present grist mill is an accurate reconstruction, built using surviving sketches, papers, and mill records. Archaeological excavations produced additional information and confirmed locations that were instrumental in assuring accuracy. George Washingtons Grist Mill was restored by the Virginia State Department of Conservation and Recreation, which made it the centerpiece of a small state park. The grist mill reconstruction is dedicated to "The colonial builder's industry, ingenuity and craftsmanship."[55]

In April, 2002, Mount Vernon assumed responsibility for managing the grist mill. A professional miller demonstrates how the water-operated wheel grinds grain into flour and visitors learn from costumed interpreters about the slaves and millers who operated the mill and adjacent distillery over 200 years ago.

DIRECTIONS: The grist mill is on the north side of SR 235, about 0.25 mile east of US 1 (Figure 11).

PUBLIC USE: Season and hours: April–October, Tuesday–Saturday, 8 AM–5 PM. **Admission fee:** Tickets are available at Mount Vernon or at the Grist Mill. **For people with disabilities:** Not accessible.

FOR ADDITIONAL INFORMATION: Contact: George Washingtons Grist Mill, 5514 Mount Vernon Memorial Highway, Alexandria, Virginia 22309; 703-780-2000. **Web site:** *www.mountvernon.org.*

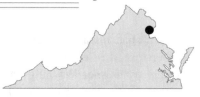

8. GUNSTON HALL

LORTON, VIRGINIA

George Mason, known as the Father of the Virginia Bill of Rights, built Gunston Hall in 1755. The manor house (Figure 12), an outstanding example of colonial Virginia architecture, centered a typical tobacco plantation that included dependencies, formal gardens, and stables. Originally an estate of 5500 acres, modern Gunston Hall is set in 550 acres of lush beauty wherein the Garden Club of Virginia has restored the gardens to their original glory, including the preservation of an unusual boxwood allee planted by Mason himself. From the end of the garden the view is across a deer park to the Mason dock on the bank of the Potomac. Many of the exterior buildings have been reconstructed or replicated to illustrate daily life in the eighteenth century and much of the manor house's interior, accurately reconstructed as a result of archaeological and architectural studies, contains a fine collection of eighteenth-century furnishings, including a few original Mason pieces. The superb woodwork, considered a masterpiece of the carver's art, was created by master

Figure 12. Gunston Hall, Mason Neck, Virginia. (Photograph courtesy of Dennis McWaters)

carver William Buckland who had been brought over from England.

Mason, statesman and political philosopher, was something of an iconoclast who rarely left Gunston Hall, his wife, and nine children. His longest absence was in 1787 when he ventured to Philadelphia to assist in writing the Constitution of the United States. His influence on Washington, Jefferson, and other patriots, however, was deep as manifested in their actions and words drawn from his teachings. Washington, his next-door neighbor, was particularly close to Mason and spent many hours with the great thinker.

Gunston Hall, along with Mount Vernon, exemplifies the finest in early colonial architecture and living standards of the northern Virginia Tidewater. Gunston Hall is owned by the Commonwealth of Virginia and is administered by the National Society of the Colonial Dames of America. The Gunston Hall Visitor Center houses a museum that features an orientation film and exhibits delineating the life of George Mason, his enormous contribution to our system of government, and the history of Gunston Hall.

DIRECTIONS: From I 95, take Exit 163 eastbound onto Lorton Road, then Armistead Road, for about 0.5 mile, then go south on US 1 0.5 mile to SR 242 (Gunston Road), then go east on SR 242 for 3.5 miles to Gunston Hall (Figure 13).

PUBLIC USE: Season and hours: 9:30 AM–5 PM daily. Closed Thanksgiving Day, Christmas Day, and New Year's Day. **Admission fee. Visitor center. Gift shop. For people with disabilities:** Call ahead for arrangements.

FOR ADDITIONAL INFORMATION: Contact: Gunston Hall, Mason Neck, Virginia 22079; 703-550-9220. **Web site:** *www.gunstonhall.org.* **Read:** (1) Rosamond Beirne and John H. Scarff. 1958. *William Buckland, 1734–1774: Architect of Virginia and Maryland.* (2) Robert Allen Rutland. 1961. *Reluctant Statesman.* (3) Peter R. Henriques. 1989. "An Uneven Friendship: The Relationship between George Washington and George Mason."

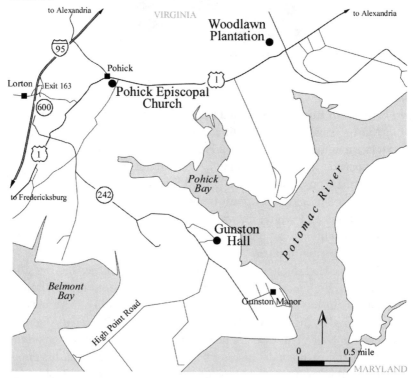

Figure 13. The location of Woodlawn Plantation, Gunston Hall, and Pohick Episcopal Church in northern Virginia.

9. POHICK EPISCOPAL CHURCH

LORTON, VIRGINIA

Pohick was the parish church for the Mount Vernon, Gunston Hall, and Belvoir areas. The building site was chosen by planter-surveyor George Washington who also designed its traditional exterior — a square brick and steepleless structure. Washington served as a Pohick vestryman for twenty-three years and a Bible he and Martha presented to the church in 1796 is proudly displayed in the nave. During the Civil War, the interior was devastated by Union troops who used the building for stables. In the early part of the twentieth century the church was reclaimed and restored, an effort that resulted in the discovery of the original baptismal font on a nearby farm where it was serving as a horse trough!

DIRECTIONS: Pohick Episcopal Church is on the south side of US 1 (Richmond Highway) on the east side of Pohick (Figure 13).

PUBLIC USE: Season and hours: 9 AM–4:30 PM daily.

FOR ADDITIONAL INFORMATION: Contact: Pohick Episcopal Church, 9301 Richmond Highway, Lorton, Virginia 22079; 703-339-6572.

10. "OLD TOWN" ALEXANDRIA, VIRGINIA

Originally known as Belhaven, Alexandria was established by the Virginia Assembly in 1749 and renamed for John Alexander, a Scotsman who had purchased the land in 1669 for "Six thousand punds of tobacco and cask"[56] which seems a more than fair bargain! By the mid-eighteenth century, Alexandria had become an important political, social, and commercial center. As a seventeen-year-old surveyor, Mount Vernon planter and neighbor George Washington had assisted in laying out the town and remained close to the community throughout his life. He maintained a Townhouse at 508 Cameron Street, was a charter stockholder in the

Bank of Alexandria at North Fairfax and Cameron streets, and served as a town Trustee. He owned a pew in Christ Church, served as an officer of the local Masonic lodge and had other personal, military, and business interests in town. Market Square at 301 King Street is thought to be the site of the nation's oldest continually operating farmer's market, and is where George Washington sent produce from Mount Vernon to be sold.

In the 1960s, Alexandria began an historic preservation and urban renewal project that focused on its contributions to America's heritage during the colonial period, the Civil War, and World Wars I and II. The historic area, "Old Town," is famous for its museums, architecture, spe-

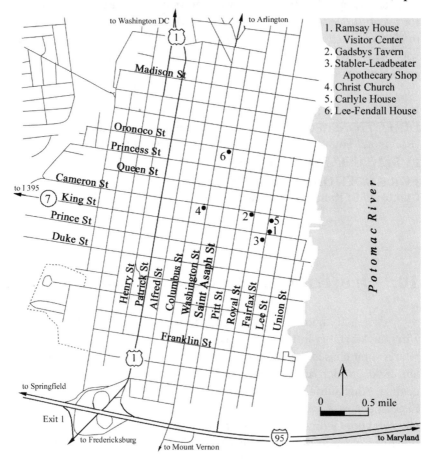

1. Ramsay House
   Visitor Center
2. Gadsbys Tavern
3. Stabler-Leadbeater
   Apothecary Shop
4. Christ Church
5. Carlyle House
6. Lee-Fendall House

Figure 14. The location of featured sites within "Old Town" Alexandria, Virginia.

cial events and fine restaurants that attract more than one million visitors each year. Visits to Alexandria begin at the Ramsay House Visitor Center (Site 1, Figure 14), staffed by friendly counselors with information on local historic attractions, accommodations, shops, and restaurants.

Ramsay House was named for one of the city's founders, William Ramsay, a Scottish merchant and confidante of George Washington. The history of Ramsay House is unclear although it may have been constructed in Dumfries around 1724, then barged to Alexandria. In any case it is undoubtedly the city's oldest house and its gambrel roof is a rare architectural fillip in the region.

A visit to Alexandria offers a unique opportunity for a hands-on experience in the study of a city that has been important to our national heritage since the colonial period. Interested educators and others searching for additional information should contact the individual sites, many of which have designed their own education programs, or the Alexandria Education Coordinator at 703-838-4399.

PUBLIC USE: *Ramsay House Visitor Center:* **Season and hours:** 9 AM–5 PM daily. Closed Thanksgiving Day, Christmas Day, and New Year's Day. **Gift shop. For people with disabilities:** Please call ahead for arrangements.

FOR ADDITIONAL INFORMATION: Contact: Alexandria Convention and Visitor Bureau, Ramsay House, 221 King Street, Alexandria, Virginia 22314; 703-838-4200. **Web site:** *www.ci.alexandria.va.us.* **Read:** William Francis Smith and T. Michael Miller. 1989. *A Seaport Saga: Portrait of Old Alexandria, Virginia.*

10-2. GADSBYS TAVERN MUSEUM

134 NORTH ROYAL STREET

Since the mid-1700s, travelers and other visitors have stopped at Gadsbys Tavern that adjoins Alexandria's Market Square. Virginia taverns in the eighteenth century were required to provide lodging for travelers before they could be licensed to sell liquor, but they were not required to provide a room, merely a place to sleep. Thus many people were accommodated by placing sleeping pallets in sleeping rooms and on the assembly room floor. Meals were communal and the tavern often served as the social and meeting hall for the community. Gadsbys was no exception, hosting social events, dancing assemblies, and meetings of local organizations. It also provided space for merchants to sell their wares and areas where traveling dentists could treat patients.

Gadsbys is actually two buildings, a 1770 Georgian tavern and a 1792 tavern-hotel, that were the center of Alexandria's political, social, and cultural life. The atmosphere of early America permeates the famed hostelry, the setting for brilliant society balls, patriot meetings, and presidential receptions, most notably the Birth Night Balls held in honor of President George Washington. No public building in Alexandria was more intimately associated with the struggle for independence than Gadsbys.

Modern visitors may tour both buildings, restored to their eighteenth-century appearance, including the sleeping rooms under the dormers and the assembly room where George Washington enjoyed dancing. Visitors are impressed with Gadsbys exquisite Georgian architecture and the ambience of the restaurant that faithfully duplicates the menu (Figure 15), serving pieces, furnishings, and server's costumes of the nation's colonial dining past.

Figure 15. A formal colonial table setting, Gadsbys Tavern Museum, Alexandria, Virginia. (Photograph courtesy of Gadsbys Tavern Museum)

PUBLIC USE: Season and hours: *Tavern:* Lunch is served from 11:30 AM–3 PM daily and dinner is served from 5:30 PM–10 PM daily. *Museum:* April 1–September 31, 10 AM–5 PM; Sunday, 1 PM–5 PM. October 1–May 31, Monday–Saturday, 11 AM–4 PM; Sunday, 1 PM–4 PM. Guided tours begin at fifteen minutes before and after each hour. **Admission fee. Gift shop. For people with disabilities:** The first floor is accessible, and a video is available to view the rest of the museum.

FOR ADDITIONAL INFORMATION: Contact: Gadsbys Tavern Museum, 134 N. Royal Street, Alexandria, Virginia 22314; 703-548-4242 (Museum), 703-548-1288 (Tavern). **Web site:** *www.ci.alexandria.va.us.* **Read:** (1) Irvin Haas. 1972. *America's Historic Inns and Taverns.* (2) Ellen K. Donald and Gretchen S. Sorin. 1980. *Gadsbys Tavern Museum: Historic Furnishing Plan.*

10-3. STABLER-LEADBEATER APOTHECARY SHOP AND MUSEUM

105-107 SOUTH FAIRFAX STREET

In 1792, Edward Stabler, a young Quaker pharmacist, opened a family business that operated continuously for the next 141 years. George Washington was among Stabler's well-known patrons, as was Washington's doctor, Elisha Dick, who ordered Glauber Salts from Stabler's when he treated Washington's terminal illness in 1799.

In 1933, the Great Depression forced the pharmacy to close, with some original herbs, potions, and labels still in their drawers. In 1935, the inventory was auctioned off. The Stabler-Leadbeater building was purchased in 1939 by the Landmarks Society which persuaded the owner of the historic drug stock to donate it to the newly-formed Stabler-Leadbeater Apothecary Museum, now a remarkable repository of herbal remedies, snakeroot, patent medicines, prescription drugs, and over 8000 pharmaceutical objects — pill rollers, drug mills, and medical glassware — a treasure trove of colonial medical history.

PUBLIC USE: Season and hours: Monday–Saturday, 10 AM–4 PM; Sunday, 1 PM–5 PM. **Admission fee. For people with disabilities:** There are two steps into the shop that is otherwise fully accessible.

FOR ADDITIONAL INFORMATION: Contact: Stabler-Leadbeater Apothecary Shop and Museum, 105–107 N. Fairfax Street, Alexandria, Virginia 22314; 703-836-3713. **Web site:** *www.apothecary.org.*

10-4. CHRIST CHURCH

118 NORTH WASHINGTON STREET

Christ Church (Episcopal) is a handsome, pristine, English country-style brick structure dating to 1767–1773. Construction costs were 820 pounds raised by a tithe on tobacco. Regular congregant George Washington purchased Pew #60 for £36.s10 and attended services until parish boundaries were redrawn that assigned Mount Vernon to Truro Parish (Pohick Church). On Christmas Day, 1783, the morning after his return home from the Revolutionary War, he worshipped at Christ Church, there to give thanks for peace.

A cut-glass chandelier represents the eighteenth century's most advanced type of lighting fixture although the wineglass pulpit and box pews are more representative of the interior styling of the period. Confederate General Robert E. Lee, who grew up in Alexandria, was confirmed in Christ Church and attended services throughout his childhood. The George Washington and Robert E. Lee pews are marked with decorative plaques.

PUBLIC USE: Season and hours: Monday–Saturday, 9 AM–4 PM; Saturday, 2 PM–4 PM.

FOR ADDITIONAL INFORMATION: Contact: Christ Church, 118 N. Washington Street, Alexandria, Virginia 22314; 703-549-1450. **Web site:** *www.historicchristchurch.org.*

10-5. CARLYLE HOUSE HISTORIC PARK

121 NORTH FAIRFAX AVENUE

Merchant John Carlyle, inspired by architectural pattern books and the stone manor houses of his native Scotland, completed Alexandria's "grandest" home around 1753. The home (Figure 16), designed in the Georgian Palladian style, provided both public spaces for entertaining and private areas for family use. Carlyle arranged the surrounding dependencies and landscaping in accordance to the needs of both his household and his business; the home signified his status as a gentleman and successful businessman. The stone foundations were originally part of a fort built around 1640 as protection against the Indians, and there are still dungeons beneath the house where Indians were held prisoner. Happily, the house itself has not been stripped over the years; the interior remains as furnished by the Carlyle family two centuries ago.

In 1755, English General Sir Edward Braddock made Carlyle House his military headquarters where he and colonial governors

Figure 16. The mansion at Carlyle House Historic Park, Alexandria, Virginia. (Photograph by Bruce Katz, Carlyle House Historic Park)

planned the campaign strategy for what would become the disastrous campaign in the French and Indian War that led to Braddock's death. At that time a youthful George Washington joined Braddock's staff and it is probable that he attended some planning sessions held in Carlyle House. Later, Washington's diaries noted that he made visits to "Col. Carlyle's" through the years. Following the Revolutionary War, Washington met at Carlyle House with the governors of Virginia and Maryland to determine the boundary between the two states.

PUBLIC USE: Season and hours: Tuesday–Saturday, 10 AM–4:30 PM; Sunday, 12 N–4:30 PM. The Carlyle House garden is a public park. **Admission fee. Gift shop. For people with disabilities:** The first floor is fully accessible, and the second floor is partially accessible.

FOR ADDITIONAL INFORMATION: Contact: Carlyle House Historic Park, 121 N. Fairfax Avenue, Alexandria, Virginia 22314; 703-549-2997. **Web site:** *www.carlylehouse.org.* **Read:** (1) Emmie Ferguson Farrar and Emilee Hines. 1971. *Old Virginia Houses Along the Fall Line.* (2) James D. Munson. 1986. *Col. John Carlyle, Gent.*

10-6. LEE-FENDALL HOUSE

614 ORONOCO STREET

In 1785, Philip Fendall, a Lee family descendant, Alexandria businessman, and active civic leader, built a gracious house where Fendall's cousin, "Light Horse Harry" Lee and his close friend George Washington visited frequently. In this house Lee wrote Alexandria's farewell address to newly-elected President Washington in 1789 and, sadly, Washington's funeral eulogy.

The large clapboard house, home to thirty-seven Lees from 1785 to 1903, is an historic house museum with many original furnishings and family records that offer an intimate study of eighteenth- and nineteenth-century family life. The Lee-Fendall House is owned and administered by the Virginia Trust for Historic Preservation that purchased it from the estate of American labor leader John L. Lewis, its owner-resident from 1937 to 1969.

PUBLIC USE: Season and hours: Tuesday–Saturday, 10 AM–3:45 PM; Sunday, 12 N–3:45 PM. **Admission fee. Gift shop. For people with disabilities:** Partially accessible.

FOR ADDITIONAL INFORMATION: Contact: Lee- Fendall House, 614 Oronoco Street, Alexandria, Virginia 22314; 703-548-1789. **Web site:** *www.ohwy.com/va/l/leefenho.htm.*

$\backsim$

EYES TO THE WEST

In 1649, King Charles II bestowed hundreds of thousands of acres on seven companions-in-exile, dividing the land "bounded by and within the heads of the Potomac and Rappahannock to give, grant or by any means sell or alienate in perpetuity..."[57] Later, in 1672, he granted the entire Northern Neck to lords Culpeper and Arlington under the same conditions. These vast land grants were called proprietaries, and every tenant farmer or other settler paid quitrents whether the proprietor lived in Virginia or resided in London. Absent proprietors employed on-site agents to manage the affairs of their proprietary. Lawrence Washington's neighbor, Colonel William Fairfax of Belvoir, was the on-site representative for his cousin, Lord Fairfax, whose father had inherited the Culpeper proprietary through marriage to Lord Culpeper's daughter. At that time, the Fairfax holdings had grown, through lawsuits and other legalities, to include what is now the Virginia counties of Northumberland, Lancaster, Richmond, Westmoreland, King George, Stafford, Prince William, Fairfax, Arlington, Loudoun, Fauquier, Culpeper, Madison, Page, Shenandoah, Rappahannock, Clarke, Warren, and Frederick, plus the West Virginia counties of Jefferson, Berkeley, Morgan, Hampshire, and Hardy.

Lawrence Washington became engaged to Colonel Fairfax's daughter, Anne, and was thus privy to Fairfax business that included plans for the redefinition of the grant's borders that would involve further expansion to an incredible five million acres by extending it west to the headwaters of the Potomac and Rappahannock rivers.

Lawrence was also president of the Ohio Company, a partnership formed in 1747 to enrich its owners through fur trading and land speculation across the Alleghenies, to an area even beyond the Fairfax Proprietary, territory claimed not only by the Virginia Colony but also by the King of France – and Indians whose ancestors had occupied the land for millennia. The shareholders were a prosperous and politically powerful cabal that included the Fairfaxes, Thomas Lee, Royal Governor Dinwiddie, and, in London, the Duke of Bedford. The group's discussions of exploration and adventure in the west surely fired the imagination of Lawrence's brother George, a teenager with proven surveying skills. When some of the Fairfax holdings were to be surveyed in 1748, the youngster was invited to join the party for an exciting trip to the western wilderness, his first adventure to an area where he would later seek his fortune and make his initial reputation as a surveyor and military figure.

It is not an exaggeration to say that George Washington was a true western visionary. Throughout his life as surveyor, explorer, landowner, military officer, and president, his eyes ever turned to the west. His sense of adventure and personal ambition for riches, social standing, and recognition motivated him, and the west is where he would prove himself — no matter how difficult, no matter what the cost.

His surveying trips, the difficult trip to Fort LeBoeuf, the embarrassment of Fort Necessity, the tragic journey with General Braddock, and the frustration of the trek with General Forbes during the French and Indian War whetted Washington's appetite for further adventures and land ownership in the west. Fort Necessity Battlefield, Washington's headquarters in Winchester, Point Pleasant Battle Monument State Park, Harpers Ferry, The George Washington Heritage Trail — even George Washington's Bathtub in Berkeley Springs, West Virginia — exist today and provide us with insight into that period in George Washington's life when so much of his attention was directed to the western frontier of the Virginia Colony (Figure 17, Table 2). It was in the west that he learned to assume responsibility for the leadership and management of groups, to deal with subordinates and the frustration of drunkenness and desertion of troops, the value of planning and attention to details, the agony of shortages of men and materiel, and to nurture his growing dissatisfaction with British colonial rule — all of which gave him valuable experience that would influence and help direct his life in the years ahead.

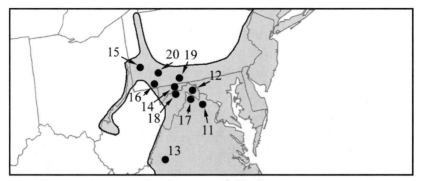

Figure 17. For much of the 1750s, George Washington's life revolved around survey-ing and military activities in the upper Potomac and Ohio river valleys. Here are identified publicly accessible sites related to Washington's interest, and presence, in the west during the decade following his first venture into that region in 1748. The names and page numbers for descriptions of the numbered sites shown here are given in Table 2.

Table 2. Publicly accessible sites identified with George Washington located in the upper James, Potomac, and Ohio river valleys.

MAP NUMBER	SITE NAME	PAGE NUMBER FOR SITE ACCOUNT
11.	Red Fox Inn	136
12.	The George Washington Heritage Trail	137
	Charles Town, West Virginia	138
	Berkeley Springs, West Virginia	139
13.	Natural Bridge	140
14.	Fort Cumberland	142
15.	Fort Pitt Museum and Point State Park	144
16.	Fort Necessity National Battlefield	146
17.	George Washingtons Office Museum	149
18.	Fort Ashby	150
19.	Fort Bedford Museum	151
20.	Fort Ligonier	153

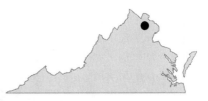

11. RED FOX INN

MIDDLEBURG, VIRGINIA

George Washington made innumerable trips between Mount Vernon and Winchester and sometimes stopped for rest and refreshment at Chinn's "ordinary," a stone structure built by Joseph Chinn in 1728 as part of the vast proprietary of Lord Fairfax. Conveniently situated midway between Alexandria and Winchester, Chinn's was very popular. The tavern has undergone several ownership and name changes yet has managed to retain its colonial charm and atmosphere. Today Chinn's is known as the Red Fox Inn.

DIRECTIONS: The Red Fox Inn is located on the north side of US 50 at the intersection with SR 626/776 (Madison Street) (Figure 18).

FOR ADDITIONAL INFORMATION: Contact: Red Fox Inn, Box 385, 2 East Washington Street, Middleburg, Virginia 22117; 703-687-6301.

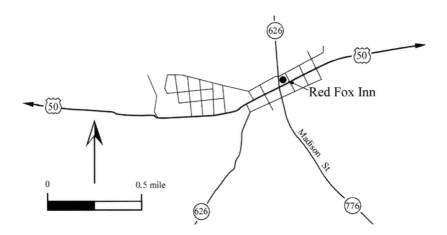

Figure 18. The location of the Red Fox Inn in Middleburg, Virginia.

12. THE GEORGE WASHINGTON HERITAGE TRAIL

WEST VIRGINIA

On November 18, 1998, the George Washington Heritage Trail (Figure 19) was dedicated at Claymont Court, a house in Charles Town, West Virginia, built around 1820 by George Washington's grandnephew, Bushrod Washington. Claymont Court was supposedly fashioned after a design created by George Washington.

The George Washington Heritage Trail is a cooperative venture of Jefferson, Berkeley, and Morgan counties as a tribute to George Washington who spent time in the area as surveyor, landowner, entrepreneur,

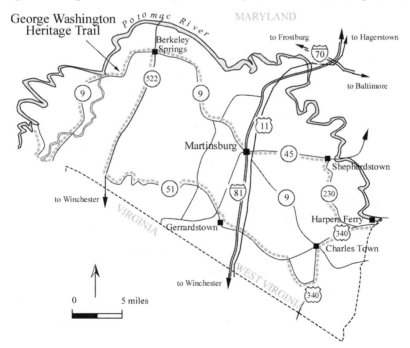

Figure 19. The location of the George Washington Heritage Trail in the eastern panhandle of West Virginia.

militia officer, and family member. Designated a West Virginia Scenic Byway, the George Washington Heritage Trail is a 112-mile scenic loop through the Eastern Gateway of West Virginia. The trail follows many of the routes traveled by Washington as it extends from Charles Town in the east, north through Shepherdstown, then west through Martinsburg to Berkeley Springs in the west, then south toward Winchester, Virginia, before turning eastward and passing through Gerrardstown on its way back to Charles Town. Interpretive centers have been established in most towns along the route with information on the various Washington sites that are available for visitation or observation.

FOR ADDITIONAL INFORMATION: Contact: Martinsburg-Berkeley County Convention and Visitor Bureau, 208 South Queen Street, Martinsburg, West Virginia 24501; 800-498-2386 *or* Travel Berkeley Springs, Inc., 304 Fairfax Street, Berkeley Springs, West Virginia 25411; 800-447-8797, 304-258-9147. **Web sites:** *www.berkeleysprings.com; www.georgewashington.org; www.travelwv.com.* **Read:** Jeanne Mozier. 1998. *Way Out in West Virginia.*

12-1. CHARLES TOWN, WEST VIRGINIA

In 1750, eighteen year-old surveyor George Washington purchased 500 acres on Bullskin Run in western Virginia where he leased part of the tract to others; the rest was farmed by an on-site overseer. A sign on Summit Point Road four miles west of Charles Town marks the location of the George Washington Farm that was later expanded to include a total of 2300 acres.

Impressed with the beauty and fertility of the land, Washington urged his half-brother Lawrence to invest in the area and Lawrence purchased thousands of acres. Upon his death and the subsequent demise of his wife, Lawrence's western property was willed to younger brothers Charles and Samuel. Charles had made a name for himself as a colonel in the Virginia militia and as a businessman in Fredericksburg, but in 1760 he decided to move to the western land he had inherited. There he laid out an entire town and named it for himself and the streets for close relatives. Thus Charles Town features Lawrence, Charles, George, Samuel, and Mildred streets. Charles Town contains several existing homes and other sites associated with the Washington family and over seventy gravestones in the Zion Episcopal Church cemetery bear the Washington name.

Legend has it that Masons in Charles Town gathered in an old cave on the outskirts of town in 1753 for a meeting presided over by Worshipful Master George Washington. Legend or fact, the cavernous underground room contains hundreds of names carved on the stone walls, among them "G. Washington." George Washingtons Masonic Cave, located on Old Cave Road, just east of the US 340 bypass, is open to the public but is not marked.

12-2. BERKELEY SPRINGS, WEST VIRGINIA

Nestled along the Potomac in the eastern Appalachians, Berkeley Springs prospers as a resort town, its warm springs used as healing, relaxing baths ever since George Washington, surveying the area for Lord Fairfax, first visited the spa which was later named Bath after the famous English resort city. For hundreds of years the mineral waters flowing at a constant seventy-four degrees have

Figure 20. George Washingtons Bathtub in Berkeley Springs State Park, Berkeley Springs, West Virginia. (Photograph by William G. Clotworthy)

139

drawn visitors seeking health and relief from the stresses of life. Washington accompanied his brother Lawrence to the springs in search of a cure for Lawrence's terminal illness and later sought relief there for stepdaughter Patsy who suffered from epileptic seizures. The entire Washington family visited on numerous occasions. The original town plat drawn in 1776 shows that George Washington owned lots 58 and 59 at Fairfax and Montgomery streets. Local historians believe that a small building at Congress and Wilkes streets, originally a tavern, hosted Washington during one visit. This building is now a law office. Washington's "bathtub" (Figure 20) is displayed in Berkeley Springs State Park and local residents, with perfectly straight faces, tell visitors that a natural indentation in the rock face of the springs was absolutely, positively George Washington's favorite spot for relaxation.

13. NATURAL BRIDGE

NATURAL BRIDGE, VIRGINIA

Natural Bridge (Plate 5), touted as one of the seven natural wonders of the world, is a 215-foot-high limestone arch beneath which flows Cedar Creek, a tributary of the James River. When surveying in the area for Lord Fairfax, George Washington reportedly found time to scale the southeast wall of the bridge and chisel his initials in the stone where they may still be seen. That story had been considered fanciful by many historians, but a surveyor's cross and a rock bearing his initials were unearthed beneath the bridge recently, lending credence to the claim that he was there.

In 1774, King George III granted the Natural Bridge to Thomas Jefferson who proclaimed it "...undoubtedly one of the sublimest curiosities in nature."[58] Natural Bridge became a retreat for Jefferson who anticipated a flood of visitors to the natural wonder. His vision was transformed into today's Natural Bridge complex with miles of hiking trails, deep caverns, a wax museum and factory, the Jefferson National Forest Visitor Center, and the Natural Bridge Inn and Conference Center. Natural Bridge features three major tourist attractions: Natural Bridge, where visitors descend into a ravine, pause below the span and wander into its shadow to wonder at its magnificence and beauty; The Wax Museum at Natural Bridge; and Natural Bridge Caverns. There is no documentation that George Washington explored the caverns, but he is memorialized in the Wax Museum devoted to the history of the Shenandoah Valley.

Natural Bridge contains spectacular caverns thirty-four-stories deep into the earth where visitors learn how the striking underground world was carved and continues to grow. Hiking trails meander along Cedar Creek that cuts through the mountainous landscape, including an interesting area where ammunition was made during the Revolutionary War, the War of 1812, and the Civil War.

DIRECTIONS: Natural Bridge is located beneath US 11 approximately 1 mile east of Exit 175, I 81 (Figure 21).

PUBLIC USE: Season and hours: *Natural Bridge:* Summer, 9 AM–9 PM daily with a special light show at 9:30 PM. Winter, 8 AM–5 PM daily with a special light show at 6 PM. *Wax Museum:* Summer, 9 AM–9 PM

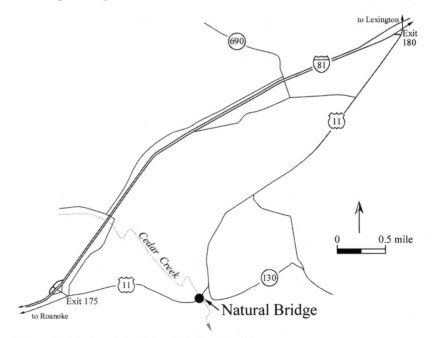

Figure 21. The location of Natural Bridge, Virginia.

daily. Winter, 10 AM–5 PM daily. *Caverns:* March–November, 10 AM–5 PM daily. **Admission fee. Visitor center. For people with disabilities:** The Natural Bridge and Wax Museum are fully accessible.

FOR ADDITIONAL INFORMATION: Contact: Natural Bridge of Virginia, Box 57, Natural Bridge, Virginia 24578; 540-291-2121, 800-533-1410. **Web site:** *www.naturalbridgeva.com.* **Read:** (1) Chester Albert Reeds. 1927. *Natural Bridge of Virginia and its Environs.* (2) Pamela Simpson. 1982. *So Beautiful an Arch: Images of the Natural Bridge, 1787–1890.*

14. FORT CUMBERLAND

CUMBERLAND, MARYLAND

Fort Cumberland played a significant role during the French and Indian War as a depot for British and colonial supplies headed for the Ohio Valley. George Washington spent a great deal of time at Cumberland where he assumed his first military command as colonel of the Virginia militia and later as an aide to British General Braddock. Their extant headquarters in a log building is merely one room that may be viewed through a picture window while listening to a recorded lecture on the history of the cabin. George Washington's headquarters is the only remaining structure left of Fort Cumberland although there are visible trenches under Emmanuel Church that was built on the site of the fort.

The headquarters building is owned by the city of Cumberland and maintained by the Cresap Chapter, Daughters of the American Revolution. The City of Cumberland has developed a self-guided walking tour of the perimeter of the remnants of Fort Cumberland that covers several city blocks. White rock markers indicate the approximate locations of the angles of the old fort and there are twenty-eight narrative plaques surrounding the fort area plus a reconstructed section of palisades and the headquarters building.

DIRECTIONS: From I 68 in Cumberland, take Exit 43 to South Mechanic Street northbound, turn west on Baltimore Street to Heritage Parklet at the corner of Canal Street, the start of the walking tour (Figure 22).

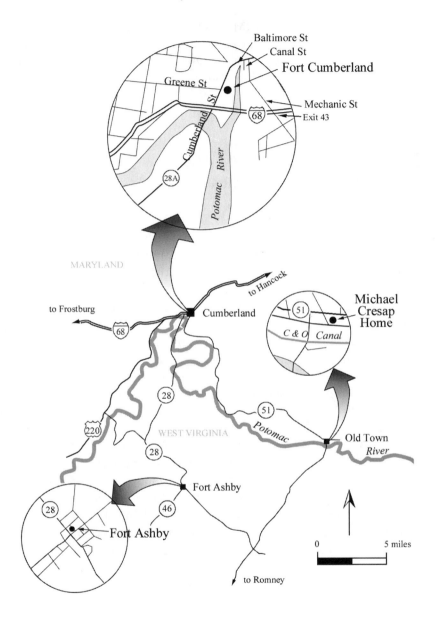

Figure 22. The location of Fort Cumberland, Fort Ashby, and the Michael Cresap Home in western Maryland and northern West Virginia.

FOR ADDITIONAL INFORMATION: Contact: Fort Cumberland, Riverside Park, Greene Street, Cumberland, Maryland 21501; 301-777-8214, 800-508-4748. **Web site:** *www.downtowncumberland.com*. **Read:** Allen Powell. 1989. *Fort Cumberland.*

15. FORT PITT MUSEUM AND POINT STATE PARK

PITTSBURGH, PENNSYLVANIA

Point State Park is a thirty-six-acre urban park that commemorates the fortress foundations upon which the City of Pittsburgh evolved. George Washington visited this site where the Allegheny and Monongahela rivers join to form the Ohio River during his journey to Fort LeBoeuf in 1753; he described it as "extremely well-situated . . . as it has the absolute command of both rivers."[59]

Washington's opinion of the site's military value was not lost on Governor Dinwiddie, who quickly ordered that a fort be built at the site as part of his efforts to insert a British presence in the region. Colonial forces thereupon set about to construct Fort Prince George. A French force and allied Indians easily overwhelmed this fort in April, 1754, and began construction of Fort Duquesne. The French remained in control of the Forks of the Ohio until November, 1758, when British General John Forbes successfully reclaimed the area for the British and renamed the fort Fort Pitt after William Pitt, then the Prime Minister of England. The strategic importance of the Forks of the Ohio was recognized by all of the contesting powers — Native, French, and British — and it was clear that whichever power controlled the site where the rivers came together would have a distinct advantage in controlling the entire Ohio Valley.

The Fort Pitt blockhouse, built in 1764, is all that remains of the original fort. A sixteen-foot well in the center of the William Pitt Memorial Hall of the Fort Pitt Museum contains a model of Fort Pitt (ten feet to the inch) that identifies the principal features of the fort and the surrounding area. Earphones are provided so that visitors may listen to a taped narration that explains the fort's history and the period when the Indians, French, and British fought for possession of the tiny fort that grew into a great city. Fort Pitt Museum focuses on the history of Pennsylvania and the French and Indian War with models, dioramas, and orientation films. The Pennsylvania Historical and Museum Commission administers the museum with the assistance of Fort Pitt Museum Associates, a volunteer organization that sponsors regularly scheduled special programs and exhibits.

In July, 2000, The Fort Pitt Museum began a major three-year building renovation project designed to transform the facility into a state-of-the-art historic site/museum. There will be 8000 square feet of additional space which will allow exhibits to be upgraded, expanded, and made interactive. Meanwhile the museum and its original exhibits remain open to the public.

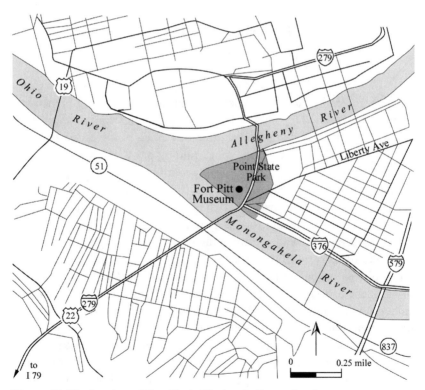

Figure 23. The location of Fort Pitt in Pittsburgh, Pennsylvania.

DIRECTIONS: Point State Park is situated in downtown Pittsburgh's "Golden Triangle," and is accessible from I 279 and I 376. Follow signs to Commonwealth Boulevard to access the Point State Park (Figure 23).

PUBLIC USE: Season and hours: Wednesday-Saturday, 10 AM-5 PM. Sunday, 12N-4:30 PM. **Admission fee. Visitor center. Gift shop. For people with disabilities:** Accessible.

FOR ADDITIONAL INFORMATION: Contact: Point State Park, 101 Commonwealth Place, Pittsburgh, Pennsylvania 15222; 412-281-9284. **Web site:** *www.fortpittmuseum.com.* **Read:** (1) Stefan Lorant. 1964. *Pittsburgh, the Story of an American City.* (2) Charles Morse Stotz. 1970. *The Model of Fort Pitt.* (3) Walter O'Meara. 1975. *Guns at the Forks.*

16. FORT NECESSITY NATIONAL BATTLEFIELD

FARMINGTON, PENNSYLVANIA

In 1754, in his first military campaign, twenty-two-year-old Colonel George Washington led a small Virginia army against the French and Indians. He reached the Great Meadow in southern Pennsylvania where he established a tiny defensive position he named Fort Necessity. Indian intelligence informed him of a French raiding party in the vicinity so he organized and perpetrated an ambush that killed several French soldiers, including their leader, Sieur de Jumonville. The French, determined to avenge de Jumonville's death, overwhelmed Washington's little band protecting Fort Necessity and forced its ignominious surrender.

The site of the battle between the forces led by Washington and the French army, is part of Fort Necessity National Battlefield, as are several other places associated with that campaign and the later Battle of Monongahela, fought nearby. Jumonville Glen is where Washington's ambush precipitated the battle and, in some opinions, the French and Indian War. Jumonville Glen is a secluded ravine evoking the isolation of the wilderness that affords a unique opportunity to understand something of the effect this type of terrain had on eighteenth-century military tactics and the difficulty George Washington and other pioneers faced in traversing and working in such conditions.

Figure 24. Reconstructed entrenchments and battlements at Fort Necessity National Battlefield, Farmington, Pennsylvania. (Photograph courtesy of National Park Service)

A reconstructed Fort Necessity, fifty-three feet in diameter with an overall perimeter of only 168 feet, occupies the site of the original fort (Figure 24). The entrenchments outside the fort are reconstructions of those built by Washington and his men in anticipation of a French attack.

British General Braddock, who died on July 13, 1755 from wounds suffered at the Battle of Monongahela, was buried in the road his men had built about one mile northwest of Fort Necessity. In 1804, a road repair crew discovered what were believed to be Braddock's remains which were re-interred on a nearby knoll, where the twelve-foot-high Braddock Monument commemorates Braddock's bravery.

The National Road, begun in 1811 as the first federally funded roadway of the United States, extended from Cumberland, Maryland to Vandalia, Illinois. It is now called US Route 40 and passes Fort Necessity. Planned during the administrations of presidents Thomas Jefferson and James Madison, it fulfilled Washington's desire for a road to unite the eastern seaboard with the land beyond the mountains. Taverns were built along the way to serve as rest stops for stagecoaches. Judge Nathaniel Ewing, owner of the Great Meadows tract upon which Fort Necessity stood, built a large house around 1827 that became Mount Washington

Tavern. The tavern stands close to the Fort Necessity Visitor Center that features an audio-visual program and exhibits that tell the story of the fort, the battle, and the archaeological studies that contributed to the fort's reconstruction.

DIRECTIONS: Fort Necessity is located on the south side of US 40 immediately west of Farmington, Pennsylvania. Braddock's Grave is also on US 40, approximately 1 mile west of Fort Necessity. Jumonville Glen is located on CR 2021 about 2 miles north of US 40 (Figure 25).

PUBLIC USE: Season and hours: 9 AM–5 PM daily. Closed Thanksgiving Day, Christmas Day, and New Year's Day. **Admission fee. Visitor center. For people with disabilities:** The visitor center, fort reconstruction, picnic area, and first floor of the Mount Washington Tavern are fully accessible.

FOR ADDITIONAL INFORMATION: Contact: Fort Necessity National Battlefield, One Washington Parkway, Farmington, Pennsylvania 15437; 724-329-5512. **Web site:** *www.nps.gov/fone.* **Read:** (1) Robert C. Alberts. 1975. *A Charming Field for an Encounter.* (2) Paul E. Kopperman. 1977. *Braddock at the Monongahela.*

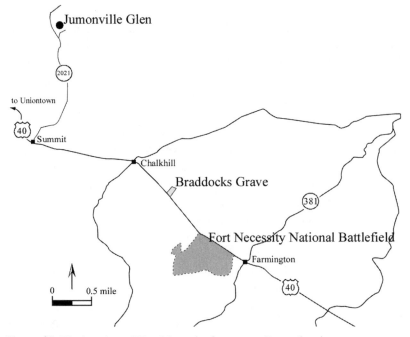

Figure 25. The location of Fort Necessity in western Pennsylvania.

17. GEORGE WASHINGTONS OFFICE MUSEUM

WINCHESTER, VIRGINIA

Early in the eighteenth century, Frederick Town was a tiny frontier crossroads village of fewer than 500 residents. As Virginia's colonists began to move west, Frederick Town, renamed Winchester in 1752, became an important commercial center where pioneers could obtain supplies for the dangerous trip farther west. Surveyor George Washington visited Frederick Town as early as 1748, and worked off and on in the area for the next four years. He returned often as a property owner, military leader, and most notably as aide-de-camp to General Braddock whose army was outfitted in Winchester preparatory to the ill-fated campaign against Fort Duquesne in the French and Indian War.

Adam Kurtz's small log home was George Washington's office when he first served as a military officer. It has been converted to a museum that displays colonial artifacts including rare surveying instruments and a model of Fort Loudoun, a fort Washington built and used as his headquarters in 1756. Fort Loudoun no longer exists.

DIRECTIONS: From I 81 northbound, take Exit 313 westbound on US 50/522 (Millwood Avenue) to Braddock Street and turn north on Braddock for 7 blocks to the corner of Cork Street and the museum. From I 81 southbound, take Exit 315 westbound on SR 7 (Berryville Avenue), go south on Pleasant Valley Road for 0.3 mile to Cork Street, then go west for 0.5 mile to the museum (Figure 26).

PUBLIC USE: Season and hours: April 1–October 31, 10 AM–4 PM daily. Sunday, 12 N–4 PM. **Admission fee. For people with disabilities:** Limited access.

FOR ADDITIONAL INFORMATION: Contact: George Washingtons Office Museum, 32 West Cork Street, Winchester, Virginia 22601; 540-662-4412. **Web site:** *www.ci.winchester.va.us.* **Read:** George Washington. 1893. *Journal of Colonel George Washington Commanding a Detachment of Virginia Troops Sent by Robert Dinwiddie, Lieutenant-Governor of Virginia.*

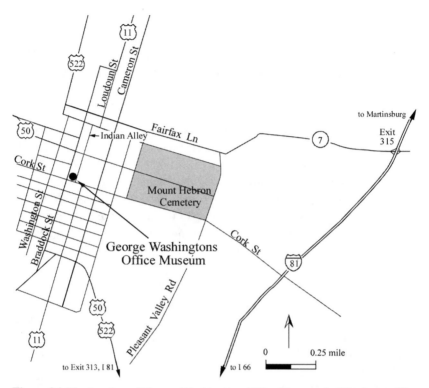

Figure 26. The location of George Washingtons Office Museum in Winchester, Virginia.

18. FORT ASHBY

FORT ASHBY, WEST VIRGINIA

Fort Ashby is the sole survivor of the sixty-nine forts built by order of Colonel George Washington to protect the western frontier of Virginia and Maryland from incursions by French and Indian raiders. In early 1756, Fort Ashby's company of rangers was defeated by a band of Indians in the only significant battle ever fought at the fort. After the raiders left, the fort was re-manned and continued to protect settlers in the region.

In the 1930s, Fort Ashby was restored by the WPA and opened as a museum of the colonial Virginia frontier. A striking feature of the main building is a huge center chimney, fourteen feet wide and four feet thick, with its original fireplace lintel, woodwork, and wrought iron. Fort Ashby is owned and maintained by the Fort Ashby Chapter, Daughters of the American Revolution.

DIRECTIONS: Fort Ashby is located in Fort Ashby at the junction of SR 28 and SR 46 (Figure 22).

PUBLIC USE: Season and hours: Open by appointment only. **For people with disabilities:** Not accessible.

FOR ADDITIONAL INFORMATION: Contact: Fort Ashby, Dans Run Road, Box 97, Fort Ashby, West Virginia 26719-0097; 304-298-3318. **Read:** Thomas Montgomery, ed. 1916. *Frontier Forts of Pennsylvania.*

19. FORT BEDFORD MUSEUM

BEDFORD, PENNSYLVANIA

Fort Bedford was a British outpost in southwestern Pennsylvania established during General John Forbes's campaign against Fort Duquesne in 1758, an undertaking in which he was accompanied by Colonel George Washington and colonial militia. Strategically located on a bluff overlooking the Juniata River, Fort Bedford controlled movement on the river and served as a supply depot for the army as it advanced over the mountains to Fort Ligonier and Fort Duquesne. The subsequent conquest of Fort Duquesne determined with finality that English-speaking people would control the Ohio Valley. Until 1770 Fort Bedford was occupied as a military outpost and refuge from Indian attacks.

The historic Fort Bedford Museum (Figure 27), located near the site of the original fort, displays Native American artifacts and thousands of household items that assist in the recreation of the atmosphere of pioneer days in western Pennsylvania. A large-scale model of the original fort is located in a reconstructed blockhouse. The Fort Bedford Museum is operated by the Pioneer Historical Society of Bedford County.

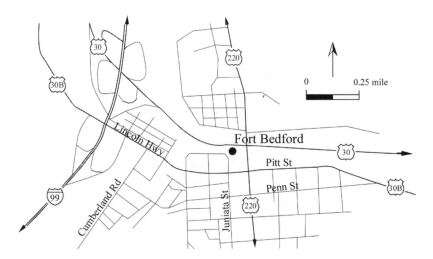

Figure 27. Reconstructed battlements at the Fort Bedford Museum, Bedford, Pennsylvania. (Photograph courtesy of Fort Bedford Museum)

Figure 28. The location of Fort Bedford Museum in Bedford, Pennsylvania.

DIRECTIONS: From the intersection of US 30 Business (Pitt Street) and US 220 in Bedford, go west on US 30 Business 1 block to Juniata Street, then go north on Juniata 1 block to the museum (Figure 28).

PUBLIC USE: Season and hours: May–October, 10 AM–5 PM daily. Closed Tuesdays in May, September, and October. Open weekends after Easter Day in April, November, and December before Christmas. **Admission fee. Gift shop. For people with disabilities:** Accessible.

FOR ADDITIONAL INFORMATION: Contact: Fort Bedford Museum, Fort Bedford Drive, Box 1758, Bedford, Pennsylvania 15522; 814-623-8891 or 800-259-4284. **Web site:** *www.bedfordcounty.net.* **Read:** Edward K. Frear. 1984. *Anarchy Trembles.*

20. FORT LIGONIER

LIGONIER, PENNSYLVANIA

The final assault on Fort Duquesne by the combined forces of General Forbes and Colonel George Washington was staged from Fort Ligonier, fifty miles southwest of the objective. The post was named in honor of Sir John Ligonier, Forbes's superior in London.

In the nineteenth century, Fort Ligonier was abandoned and began to deteriorate. In the twentieth century, a group of dedicated local citizens formed a foundation with the intention of recreating the fort and building a modern museum. Their efforts were successful as a full-scale reconstruction of Fort Ligonier has been erected on the site of the original — on a commanding hilltop in the Laurel Highlands. The fort provides an accurate and important representation of part of our colonial and revolutionary heritage and living history activities and pageantry such as battle reenactments, encampments, crafts, and archaeological digs enhance every visitor's appreciation of what was once a colonial outpost that guarded the vital land route to Fort Pitt and the unconquered west. The Fort Ligonier Museum interprets the historic site with film and exhibits. As the museum's descriptive material says:

> *Understanding is the basis for appreciation. The purpose of the museum is to give the visitor information about the global conflict of France and England, the conflict in the colonies (the French and Indian War), the French and English goals on this con-*

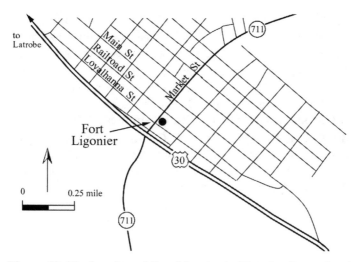

Figure 29. The location of Fort Ligonier in Ligonier, Pennsylvania.

tinent, and Fort Ligonier's role in this decisive phase of history.[60]

DIRECTIONS: Fort Ligonier is in Ligonier on SR 711 (South Market Street), 2 blocks north of US 30 (Figure 29).

PUBLIC USE: Season and hours: May 1–October 31, Monday–Saturday, 10 AM–4:30 PM; Sunday, 12 N–4:30 PM. **Admission fee. Visitor center. Gift shop. For people with disabilities:** Fully accessible.

FOR ADDITIONAL INFORMATION: Contact: Fort Ligonier, 216 S. Market Street, Ligonier, Pennsylvania 15658-1206; 412-238-9701. **Web site:** *www.fortligonier.com.* **Read:** C. Hale Sipes. 1971. *Fort Ligonier and its Times.*

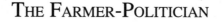

THE FARMER-POLITICIAN

During the almost-twenty-year period between the French and Indian and Revolutionary wars, George Washington spent most of his time at Mount Vernon as a gentleman farmer, but his business, political, and social affairs occasionally took him to other parts of Virginia and neighboring colonies (Figure 30, Table 3). The work was tedious and time-consuming as Mount Vernon was a major agricultural enterprise, and while Washington had often professed to be just a farmer, his farming experience at Ferry Farm and Wakefield had been limited — he now discovered that managing a plantation of 4500 acres was more than daunting.

Mount Vernon was divided into five separate farms, some of which had their own overseer, house, barns, and slave cabins. Then, in 1759, when he and Martha Custis married, he assumed responsibility for Martha's Tidewater acreage and his stepson Jacky's lands, and worried over his own hundreds of acres of leased land in the west. He realized that he would have to learn the ropes of his new vocation as he had learned his other pursuits — by observation, reading, and trial and error. In the first year, Washington planted the most profitable yet vexatious crop, tobacco. In the days before farmers practiced fertilization, tobacco quickly depleted the soil. After several years of less than abundant results, Washington realized that soil and climate conditions at Mount Vernon were not conducive for tobacco and switched his agricultural efforts to wheat and other crops around 1760. He studied and experimented with crop rotation, soil examination and fertilization techniques and was considered an inventive and progressive farmer. Washington took the business side of farming seriously. When wheat became the principal crop, he built a grist mill to grind it into flour which he offered for sale and he also charged his neighbors to grind their grain. He built a saw mill and even purchased a brigantine to expand a fishing enterprise in the Potomac.

Ever interested in land development, he explored the upper reaches of the Potomac River to the north and he visited friends among the landed gentry who lived on large plantations along the James River near Richmond. He became interested in a venture to drain parts of the Great Dismal Swamp in southeastern Virginia in the belief it could be converted to rich farmland. Accordingly, he made several trips to that region. And, in 1770, he traveled as far west as the junction of the Ohio and Kanawha rivers to claim lands promised by the crown to veterans of the French and Indian War.

The Washingtons entertained at Mount Vernon almost every evening and it is said that Washington enjoyed good conversation (along with a glass or two of Madeira), card games, backgammon, and billiards.

The Washingtons made frequent trips to Virginia's colonial capital of Williamsburg where Washington served as a burgess. There is no record that Burgess Washington took much interest in anything but local or regional matters that might have affected him personally. As author John Ferling has written:

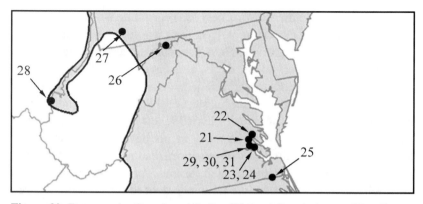

Figure 30. Between the French and Indian War and Revolutionary War, George Washington's activities were centered on Mount Vernon from where he pursued a variety of personal, social, business, and political interests. The names and page numbers for descriptions of the numbered sites shown here are given in Table 3.

Table 3. Publicly accessible sites identified with George Washington's life between the French and Indian War and Revolutionary War.

Map Number	Site Name	Page Number for Site Account
21.	Saint Peters Parish Church	157
22.	Chelsea Plantation	158
23.	Williamsburg sites	159
	George Wythe House	163
	The Capitol	164
	Peyton Randolph House	165
	College of William and Mary	165
	The Governors Palace	166
	Raleigh Tavern	166
	Bruton Parish Church	168
	Christiana Campbells Tavern	168
24.	Carters Grove Plantation	169
25.	Great Dismal Swamp National Wildlife Refuge	171
26.	Michael Cresap Home	173
27.	George Washingtons Grist Mill Park	173
28.	Point Pleasant Battle Monument State Park	175
29.	Westover	177
30.	Berkeley Plantation	178
31.	Shirley Plantation	180

Throughout the fall of 1773, a tempestuous time when actions unfolded that would shape the nation's course for years to come, George Washington, typically, had expressed no interest in the politics of the British Empire. For nearly fifteen years the management of his estate and varied business interests had been very nearly his sole concerns. Throughout that warm, pleasant Virginia autumn, he evinced no desire to alter his way of life. But sometimes the most important changes in one's life are neither planned nor anticipated.[61]

In 1775, however, Washington attended the Virginia Convention at Saint Johns Church in Richmond where he heard Patrick Henry's stirring speech in the cause of liberty. His political feelings were beginning to stir.

21. SAINT PETERS PARISH CHURCH

NEW KENT, VIRGINIA

There is some doubt as to whether George Washington and Martha Custis were married in her home — prophetically named "White House" — or journeyed to Saint Peters, her parish church, for the ceremony on January 6, 1759. In any event, they lived in her home for several months following the marriage. The house no longer stands, but the church has survived and continues to serve its community. It is a small English-style stone building with its original exterior in pristine condition and the interior lovingly restored, with glorious hand-rubbed wooden box pews and a central pulpit. Washington's diaries confirm that he attended services at Saint Peters on occasion.

DIRECTIONS: From I 64, take Exit 211 onto CR 106 northbound. 1 mile beyond the junction with SR 249, turn east onto Saint Peters Lane and follow to the church (Figure 31).

PUBLIC USE: Season and hours: By appointment only. Sunday worship services are conducted in June, July, and August at 10 AM and the rest of year at 9 AM and 11 AM.

FOR ADDITIONAL INFORMATION: Contact: Saint Peters Parish Church, 8400 Saint Peters Lane, New Kent, Virginia 23124; 804-932-4846.

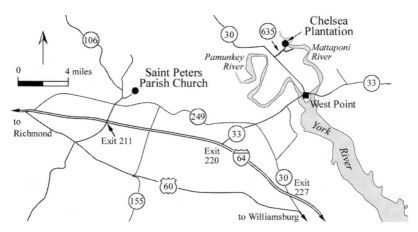

Figure 31. The location of Saint Peters Parish Church and Chelsea Plantation in southeastern Virginia.

22. CHELSEA PLANTATION

WEST POINT, VIRGINIA

Chelsea Plantation was opened for public visitation in 2000. Located on the Mattaponi River, it was within a day's ride of Martha Washington's White House and six miles from her sister's home, Eltham.

Chelsea was built in the early 1700s by Augustine Moore, a successful tobacco entrepreneur who was well connected socially and politically as evidenced by the marriage of his son, Bernard, to the daughter of Virginia's Royal Governor Alexander Spotswood. Bernard Moore was a burgess and served as one of the first three Judges of the Admiralty Court of Virginia during the early days of the Revolution. From his correspondence we know George Washington visited Bernard Moore at Chelsea on numerous occasions.

Chelsea, once the centerpiece of 8600 acres of lush farmland, is a fine example of early eighteenth-century Georgian architecture and remains fundamentally in its original form, although a wing that nearly doubled its size was added in the mid-eighteenth century. The earliest section of the building is crowned by a modillion cornice and low-hipped roof. The formal rooms are trimmed from floor to ceiling with hand-made paneling of walnut and heart of pine and the lesser rooms are wainscoted. The exterior is noted for its handsome Flemish bond articulated by glazed headers and rubbed brickwork. The grounds encompass five acres of lawn with extensive English boxwood gardens that over-look the nearly pristine Mattaponi River.

The Old Cemetery behind the mansion house contains the graves of many members of the Moore family, including Augustine, who died in 1743, and his first wife, Mary, who died at Chelsea in 1713. Chelsea is currently the residence of John Richardson III, a direct descendant of the Moore family through his father's maternal side. It is Mr. Richardson we must thank for his contribution to the study of eighteenth-century colonial plantation living by opening this architectural masterpiece for visitation.

DIRECTIONS: From I 64, take Exit 220 onto SR 33 eastbound to West Point, then go north on SR 30 approximately 4 miles to SR 635 (Chelsea Road), then go east on SR 635 1 mile to Chelsea Plantation Lane (Figure 31).

PUBLIC USE: Season and hours: Thursday–Sunday, guided tours 10 AM–4:30 PM. Group tours are available Monday–Wednesday by appointment. Closed national holidays. **Admission fee: Museum shop. Food service:** Group lunches are available by special arrangement. **For people with disabilities:** No special facilities. Call ahead for assistance.

FOR ADDITIONAL INFORMATION: Contact: Historic Chelsea Plantation, Inc., 874 Chelsea Plantation Lane, West Point, Virginia 23181; 804-843-2215. **Web site:** *www.webcentre.com/usr/chelsea.* **Read:** Edith Tunis Sale. 1927. *Interiors of Virginia Houses of Colonial Times.*

23. WILLIAMSBURG, VIRGINIA

Virginia's Historic Triangle comprises Jamestown, the first permanent English settlement in America; Williamsburg, the second colonial capital of Virginia; and Yorktown, the site of one of the most significant American victories of the Revolutionary War. Their proximity near the end of the peninsula between the York and James rivers emphasizes the commercial and political importance of colonial Virginia. Williamsburg, in particular, was witness to many important political events of the eighteenth century and the list of patriots who lived, studied, served, or visited there ranks second to none — Patrick Henry, George Washington, Thomas Jefferson, James Madison, James Monroe, Peyton Randolph, Richard Henry Lee, and George Mason are but a few of the distinguished Virginians who were active in the fight for independence.

Williamsburg was chosen by Royal Governor Francis Nicholson to replace Jamestown as the colonial capital in 1699. The College of William and Mary had been founded in Williamsburg in 1693 and it was hoped that its reputation would add sophistication to the colony's society and government, something lacking in the backwater that was Jamestown. Nicholson considered himself an urban planner and centered the town along Duke of Gloucester Street — a mile long and almost one hundred feet wide — bounded at one end by the Wren Building of the College of William and Mary and at the other by the Capitol Building. The Governors Palace was strategically set in the middle — at the head of a center mall. The three brick masterpieces were (and are) jewel-like, each in a rich setting of greenery and lush gardens.

Williamsburg was full of gaiety, pomp and circumstance for short periods in April and October when the government was in session, but was rather dull and passive the rest of the year. Virginia's colonial government hierarchy consisted of a Royal Governor (really a Lieutenant Governor appointed by the crown) served by a Governor's Council of advisors and a House of Burgesses representing property-owning male citizens. The Royal Governor, who reported directly to the crown, was the ultimate authority in the colony, but by the 1760s the House of Burgesses, with 150 years of experience and whipped by winds of change and perceived indignities from an unresponsive government far across the sea, was becoming emboldened. The burgesses began to formulate progressive ideas about their own responsibilities, prerogatives, and rights, and Williamsburg became a hotbed of political activity in America's march to freedom.

George Washington was a familiar figure in Williamsburg. One of his first trips was in 1752 to deliver greetings from the Governor of Barbados to Virginia Royal Governor Dinwiddie. For the next twenty

years he was a regular visitor as a military officer or as a burgess representing districts in western Virginia. His diaries indicate that he usually
stayed at Christiana Campbells Tavern on Waller Street when he was in
Williamsburg.

Virginia's capital was moved to Richmond during the Revolutionary War and Williamsburg began a slow decline that was not arrested
until 1926 when the Reverend W. A. R. Goodwin, rector of Bruton Parish Church, initiated the most ambitious historical restoration effort in
our nation's experience by persuading John D. Rockefeller, Jr. to purchase the entire town. Eighty-eight original buildings were restored and
400 more reconstructed, an effort that resulted in a remarkable re-creation of an important eighteenth-century urban center. Author Henry
Wiencek has written:

> *The result provides a setting for the re-creation of social life
> and political events of eighteenth-century Virginia. Costumed in-
> terpreters enact both official and mundane routines typical of the
> old colonial capital while eighteenth-century crafts and trades
> are demonstrated in reconstructed shops.*[62]

A visit to Colonial Williamsburg is a return to the time when George
Washington and his compatriots met in the forum of the House of Burgesses or in the more informal setting of Raleigh Tavern to discuss,
argue, cajole — and to act in their quest for freedom. Williamsburg is one
of America's great educational tourist attractions — a living repository
of America's rich and vibrant colonial history.

There are so many buildings of historic interest in Williamsburg
that only those most directly related to George Washington — Bruton
Church, George Wythe House, Peyton Randolph House, The Capitol,
Governors Palace, Raleigh Tavern, and The College of William and Mary
— shall be described in detail (Figure 32). Among others in the Williamsburg
re-creation are Wetherburns Tavern, James Geddy House Foundry, blacksmith and harness shops, milliners, wigmakers, cabinetmakers, the restored Public Gaol, the Pasteur and Galt Apothecary Shop, interesting
private homes, a reconstructed Public Hospital, printing office, shoe-
maker, and gunsmith shop.

The 173-acre Williamsburg re-creation is served outside the historic district by modern restaurants, hotels, and transportation facilities.

Williamsburg is a delight as its costumed guides, tradesmen, and tavern workers lend drama and authenticity to one's colonial experience. Walking and carriage tours, courtroom presentations and political "discussions" by modern interpreters add to the ambience. Williamsburg is an education, each building and attraction with a story to tell. The visitor center (Site 1, Figure 32) houses an Educational Resource Center that

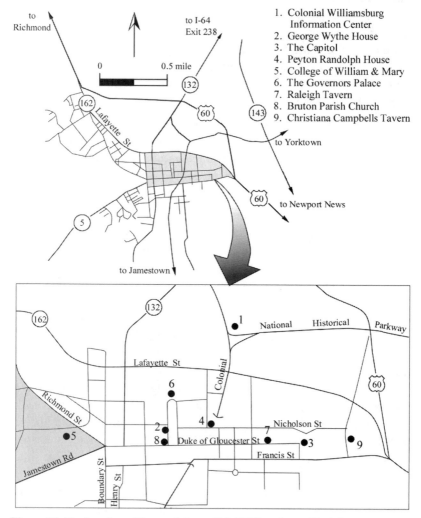

1. Colonial Williamsburg
   Information Center
2. George Wythe House
3. The Capitol
4. Peyton Randolph House
5. College of William & Mary
6. The Governors Palace
7. Raleigh Tavern
8. Bruton Parish Church
9. Christiana Campbells Tavern

Figure 32. The location of featured sites within Williamsburg, Virginia.

provides orientation programs and offers educators classroom materials and information on electronic field trips. *The Visitors Companion,* a free daily publication, contains site descriptions and schedules of special events. Three separate museums are in or near the historic district: The Abby Aldrich Rockefeller Folk Art Center features Mrs. Rockefeller's collection of American folk art; Bassett Hall provides audio tours of an eighteenth-century house the Rockefellers adapted as their Williamsburg home; and The Dewitt Wallace Decorative Arts Gallery features a permanent collection of English and American decorative art.

PUBLIC USE: *Colonial Williamsburg Information Center:* **Season and hours:** 9 AM–5 PM daily. **Admission fee:** Tickets are available at the Visitor Center on Colonial Parkway or at the Merchants Square Information Center. **Gift shops. Food service. For people with disabilities:** Most buildings are accessible.

FOR ADDITIONAL INFORMATION: Contact: Colonial Williamsburg Foundation, Box 1776, Williamsburg, Virginia 23187; 800-HISTORY. **Web site:** *www.colonialwilliamsburg.org.* **Read:** George Humphrey Yetter. 1988. *Williamsburg Before and After: The Rebirth of Virginia's Colonial Capital.*

23-2. GEORGE WYTHE HOUSE

PALACE GREEN, SOUTH OF PRINCE GEORGE STREET

George Wythe was a signer of the Declaration of Independence and a faculty member of the College of William and Mary. He was the first professor of law in an American college and his students included Thomas Jefferson, James Monroe, Henry Clay, and John Marshall. Wythe's home, built around 1750, is a simple house of the type popular in colonial Virginia, with a plain brick façade with no embellishments or adornments (Figure 33). The room in which he tutored students features a display of astronomical instruments imported from England, a collection that shows the depth of Wythe's interests. General George Washington stayed in the Wythe home preceding the Siege of Yorktown in September, 1781.

Figure 33. George Wythe House, Williamsburg, Virginia. (Photograph courtesy of Colonial Williamsburg Foundation)

23-3. THE CAPITOL

EASTERN END OF DUKE OF GLOUCESTER STREET

The reconstructed Capitol is a handsome three-story, H-shaped building that houses separate meeting chambers for the Governor's Council, the House of Burgesses, and the General Court. The Governor's Council, whose members were appointed from the colony's planter aristocracy, met in an elegant hall while the burgesses, elected by popular vote from white male property owners, were relegated to a more austere room lit by round windows. The burgesses, forerunners of today's elected representatives, were the most vocal critics of the colonial government through the 1760s and 1770s.

Visitors to the Capitol are intrigued by dramatizations of famous events that took place in that building — reenactments of debates between Thomas Jefferson and Patrick Henry over the Stamp Act and other British indignities, and the 1706 trial of Grace Sherwood for witchery. A shackled woman with stringy black hair, dressed in a shabby cotton shift, is led into the parliamentary chamber where the defense and prosecution present their cases and the modern audience votes on her guilt or innocence.

23-4. PEYTON RANDOLPH HOUSE
NICHOLSON STREET. CORNER OF NEW ENGLAND STREET

Peyton Randolph — lawyer, politician, and ardent patriot — was one of those influential Virginians prominent in America's early decision-making and nascent governance. The respect he engendered throughout the colonies culminated in his election as president of the first Continental Congress, a fact construed by some to mean he was in actuality the first President of the United States.

Randolph was a man of means as attested by his home, an imposing two-story frame mansion in which his friend George Washington was entertained on many occasions. Fine china, handsome silverware, exquisite woodwork, and paneled rooms reflect the high position in society enjoyed by the Randolph family.

23-5. COLLEGE OF WILLIAM AND MARY
WESTERN END OF DUKE OF GLOUCESTER STREET

The Wren Building of the College of William and Mary frames one end of Duke of Gloucester Street. It is the oldest American college building still in existence and has been restored to its appearance in 1716. It was named for famed architect Christopher Wren, but there is no evidence that he actually designed it even though it resembles his work — the English Renaissance style that would evolve into the Georgian architecture so popular in Virginia. The three-story, U-shaped edifice is still in use by the college.

Although he was not a college graduate, George Washington was deeply interested in education and fostered the idea of a national university. Washington received a number of honorary degrees (Harvard, Yale, Brown, Washington, and the University of

Pennsylvania) and served as Chancellor (an honorary position) of the College of William and Mary from 1788 until his death in 1799.

23-6. THE GOVERNORS PALACE
HEAD OF THE PALACE GREEN

The Governors Palace (Figure 34), home to seven royal governors, was designed by Royal Governor Nicholson in 1708. Completed in 1722, it was used by his colonial successors until 1771, and then by the first two governors of Virginia, Thomas Jefferson and Patrick Henry. The palace was abandoned when the capitol of Virginia was moved to Richmond but the building was restored in the 1930s to appear as it had during the tenure of Governor Botetourt (1768–1770). The entrance hall, designed to awe the colonials, contains a display of muskets, pistols, and swords that symbolized the might of the crown and in the center of the ceiling is a British military crest — a shield flanked by a crowned lion and a unicorn. Larger-than-life portraits of King George III and Queen Charlotte dominate the exquisite ballroom and the interior woodwork throughout is notable for its beauty and graceful lines. The exterior setting is impressive — a colorful green flanked by a wide driveway leads from Duke of Gloucester Street to the palace and its dependencies. The stately entrance leads to a landscaped forecourt topped by an elaborately scrolled heading flanked by the British lion and unicorn. The palace, three stories high in the Georgian style, has many-paned windows and a simple square-transomed doorway beneath a centered wrought-iron balcony.

23-7. RALEIGH TAVERN
DUKE OF GLOUCESTER STREET

Raleigh Tavern (Plate 6) was the unofficial capitol of Virginia — the place where the burgesses and gentry met to exchange informal views and engage in political gossip. The most famous infor-

Figure 34. The Governors Palace, Williamsburg, Virginia. (Photograph courtesy of Colonial Williamsburg Foundation)

mal meeting at the Raleigh Tavern was in 1769 when Royal Governor Botetourt dissolved the Assembly of Burgesses as it was about to vote on a measure to boycott British goods. Unperturbed, George Washington, in one of his first major political moves, led the burgesses down the street to the Raleigh Tavern where they formed the Virginia Non-Importation Association, designed to accomplish the same purpose, a boycott of selected British goods.

In 1774, then-Governor Dunmore dissolved the body and again the burgesses met at the Raleigh where they passed a resolution "to consider means of stopping exports and of securing the constitutional rights of America."[63] That resolution gave effective notice that Virginia had a common cause with the patriots in Boston who had conducted the Boston Tea Party.

23-8. BRUTON PARISH CHURCH

DUKE OF GLOUCESTER STREET AND PALACE GREEN

Bruton Church, designed by Royal Governor Alexander Spotswood, was consecrated in 1715. The church is a mellow red brick building, built in the shape of a cross, consistent with then-current architectural styling. Tall, white-shuttered windows run along the sides and the eastern end, and an octagonal steeple rises above the tower. The tower bell, installed in 1761, calls worshippers to services today as it did over two hundred years ago. George Washington, Thomas Jefferson, James Monroe, and other assembly members worshipped at Bruton when in Williamsburg. Interestingly, Martha Washington's great-great grandfather was the first rector of Bruton, the oldest active Anglican Church in America. **Read:** Reverend W. A. R. Goodwin. 1941. *The Record of Bruton Parish Church.*

23-9. CHRISTIANA CAMPBELLS TAVERN

WALLER STREET

George Washington was known to have dined and lodged at Christiana Campbells Tavern on many occasions and one of his receipts is reproduced on the menu. Today the tavern is a seafood restaurant, known for its sweet potato muffins and hot spoon bread. Christiana Campbells is one of four taverns within the Williamsburg Historic District; the others are Shields Tavern, Josiah Chowning Tavern, and Kings Arms Tavern. At all of them, costumed waitpersons serve colonial-style food — meat pastries, game pie, oysters, and ale — although they also offer more contemporary fare for the less adventurous. Reservations to any of the taverns may be made by calling 757-229-2141.

24. CARTERS GROVE PLANTATION

WILLIAMSBURG, VIRGINIA

The mansion at Carters Grove Plantation was completed shortly after 1750 by Carter Burwell, grandson of Robert "King" Carter, one of Virginia's most prosperous tobacco planters. In the colonial period the house was not only the centerpiece of an immense 300,000-acre plantation, but served as a social gathering place for students at William and Mary, many of them political activists. Legend tells us that George Washington proposed marriage to Betsy Cary, and Thomas Jefferson to Rebecca Burwell, in the drawing room of Carters Grove — and that both were rejected! That room is referred to fondly as "The Refusal Room."

The elegant brick mansion features attached flanking dependencies and a remarkable series of carved, paneled rooms. A master woodworker imported from England required four years to complete the hall, stairway, and nine rooms. One architectural historian called the magnificent carved stairway and entrance hall "a masterpiece — early Georgian brought to its finest maturity."[64] Carters Grove is a symbol of the owner's prominence in the Virginia Colony — the center of an agricultural enterprise that encompasses a huge expanse of land rolling to the banks of the James River.

Through the years a series of owners battled deterioration of the estate until a complete restoration was initiated in 1928 by owners Mr. and Mrs. Archibald McCrea, who transformed the house into a symbol of their personal wealth, social standing, and interest in historic preservation. Carters Grove was acquired from the McCrea estate by the Colonial Williamsburg Foundation in 1963. Carters Grove Plantation, located outside the main historic district of Williamsburg, operates a separate visitation schedule.

Archaeological studies are being conducted to the rear of the manor house, an area believed to be the site of Wolstenholme Towne, an English settlement destroyed by Indians in 1622. The Winthrop Rockefeller Archaeology Museum, located on the grounds, uses excavated artifacts to tell the story of Wolstenholme Towne. The Slave Quarter at Carters Grove allows visitors to experience buildings and outdoor spaces that reveal much about the lives of slaves whose forced labors enabled eighteenth-century plantations to be successful.

DIRECTIONS: Carters Grove is on US 60 about 2 miles south of the US 60/SR 199 intersection (Figure 35).

PUBLIC USE: Season and hours: Mid–March–October 31, Tuesday–Sunday, 9 AM–5 PM. November 1–December 3, Tuesday–Sunday, 9 AM–4 PM. Closed January 5 to mid-March. **Admission fee. Visitor center. Gift shop. Food service:** Snack bar. **For people with disabilities:** The second floor of the mansion is not accessible, but a video is available showing its features.

FOR ADDITIONAL INFORMATION: Contact: Colonial Williamsburg Foundation, Box 1776, Williamsburg, Virginia 23187; 800-HISTORY. **Web site:** *www.colonialwilliamsburg.org.* **Read:** Fiske Kimball. 1922. *Domestic Architecture of the American Colonies and of the Early Republic.*

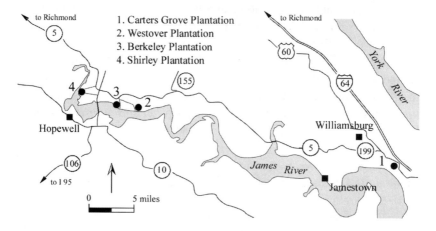

Figure 35. The location of Carters Grove, Westover, Berkeley, and Shirley plantations along the James River in southeastern Virginia.

25. GREAT DISMAL SWAMP NATIONAL WILDLIFE REFUGE

SUFFOLK, VIRGINIA

In the eighteenth century, the Great Dismal Swamp, a huge 200-square-mile wetland on the border of southeastern Virginia and northeastern North Carolina, was described as:

> *a very large swamp or bogg . . . . horrible desart . . . . the foul Damps ascend without ceasing, corrupt the Air, and render it unfit for Respiration . . . . never was Rum, that cordial of life, found more necessary than in this dirty place.*[65]

That description notwithstanding, in 1763 George Washington made the first of at least six trips to the Great Dismal, an area he described as a "glorious paradise."[66] He and a group of investors formed a company with the intention of draining the swamp and converting it to farmland. He also envisioned a canal to connect Chesapeake Bay with Albemarle Sound and initiated the project by supervising the digging of a five-mile-long canal that extended from the western edge of the swamp to Lake Drummond in the center.

According to author Douglas Southall Freeman, "In 1794 he considered it of all his speculations the most promising. The idea was indeed sound, if visionary at the time."[67] Washington and his partners eventually held title to 40,000 acres of the swamp, but the agricultural venture failed and the company turned its attention to lumbering and the manufacture of shingles. The Great Dismal canal and lumber venture staggered on through Washington's lifetime and at one point he became so disenchanted that he tried, unsuccessfully, to sell his shares which eventually passed to his heirs. The major canal he had foreseen was completed in 1828.

Vestiges of the original canal known as "Washington Ditch" may be seen as part of the remaining 109,000 acres of the Great Dismal — a remote morass of peat bogs and dense undergrowth of briars and vines threaded by innumerable canals and ditches. The swamp is a wildlife refuge administered by the US Fish and Wildlife Service. Trails are open for hiking and biking.

The State of North Carolina recently opened a visitor center at South Mills on the east side of the swamp, along the banks of the current Dismal Swamp Canal, part of the Atlantic Intracoastal Waterway.

DIRECTIONS: The Great Dismal is bounded generally by US 17 on the east, SR 32 on the west, US 13 on the north, and US 158 on the south. To reach the refuge headquarters from Suffolk, Virginia, take SR 604 southbound for 4.5 miles, then follow the signs (Figure 36).

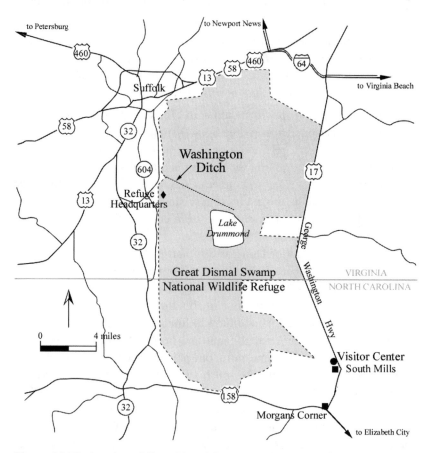

Figure 36. The location of Great Dismal Swamp National Wildlife Refuge in North Carolina and Virginia.

FOR ADDITIONAL INFORMATION: Contact: Great Dismal Swamp National Wildlife Refuge, PO Box 349, Suffolk, Virginia 23439-0349; 757-986-3705 *or* Dismal Swamp Canal Visitor Center, 2356 US Highway 17 North, South Mills, North Carolina 27976-9425; 252-771-8333. **Web sites:** *www.albemarle-nc.com/gates.gdsnwr; www.icw-net.com/ dscwelcome.* **Read:** Bland Simpson. 1990. *The Great Dismal.*

26. MICHAEL CRESAP HOME

OLDTOWN, MARYLAND

A stone house built around 1760 was the home of the eighteenth-century frontiersman and Revolutionary War hero, Michael Cresap. It is believed to be the oldest surviving pre-revolutionary building in Allegany County. The Cresap family was among the area's earliest settlers. Surveyor George Washington visited Colonel Thomas Cresap as early as 1748. Later, as a landowner, Washington's diary notes that he visited the Cresap home in Oldtown in October, 1770.

DIRECTIONS: The Cresap House is located in Oldtown1 block south of SR 51 (Figure 22).

PUBLIC USE: Season and hours: Open the first week in September, 12 N–5 PM daily. **For people with disabilities:** Partially accessible.

FOR ADDITIONAL INFORMATION: Contact: Michael Cresap Home, 19015 Opessa Street, SE, Oldtown, Maryland 21555-9702; 301-478-5154. **Read:** Bernarr Cresap and Joseph Ord. 1987. *The History of the Cresaps.*

27. GEORGE WASHINGTONS GRIST MILL PARK

PERRYOPOLIS, PENNSYLVANIA

When land in southwestern Pennsylvania became available in the mid-1700s, George Washington secured 1664 acres of prime agricultural land, much of the ground upon which modern-day Perryopolis sits. He first visited the property in 1770 and ordered the construction of a grist mill that was completed in 1776.

In 1992, the Perry Area Heritage Society initiated restoration of the original foundation of the mill, and rebuilt the framework in 1999. The Society sponsors several other nearby colonial attractions — Shreve's 1790s-era distillery; Fort Trial, a replica of a 1774 blockhouse; and a historic museum in downtown Perryopolis. A large brick house about one mile from the downtown area is known as Washingtons Farm, and may have been the primary residence of Gilbert Simpson, Washington's real estate partner. Washington's diary for September 13-17 and September 21, 1784, indicates that he stayed at Simpson's, but as Simpson owned several homes in the area, it is not clear in which house. Washingtons Farm is privately owned.

DIRECTIONS: From SR 51 at Perryopolis, go east on West Independence Street into town, then go south on Liberty Street to Columbia Street, then go east on Columbia to Layton Road then go east on Layton Road to George Washingtons Grist Mill Park (Figure 37).

PUBLIC USE: Season and hours: Late May-early September; Saturday only, 10 AM-12N, 1 PM-4 PM. **Admission fee. For people with disabilities:** Accessible.

FOR ADDITIONAL INFORMATION: Contact: Perry Area Heritage Society, PO Box 303, Perryopolis, Pennsylvania 15473-0303; 724-736-8080.

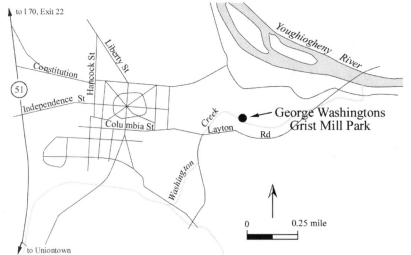

Figure 37. The location of George Washingtons Grist Mill Park near Perryopolis, Pennsylvania.

28. POINT PLEASANT BATTLE MONUMENT STATE PARK

POINT PLEASANT, WEST VIRGINIA

George Washington held a great interest in the west; he experienced exploration of the region at an early age, he surveyed land that was being taken up as the frontier of colonial settlement moved westward, and he recognized the economic potential of the Appalachian Mountains and the Ohio Valley beyond. Washington ventured into the western frontier on many occasions, but in 1770 he made what would become his most extensive foray into the Ohio Valley. Motivated by the promise of land due for military service rendered, and driven by personal ambition and the excitement of exploration, Washington traveled down the Ohio River from Fort Pitt to the point where the Kanawha River joins the Ohio at what is today Point Pleasant, West Virginia, and then journeyed a short distance up the Kanawha where he laid claim to several thousand acres of land to which he felt he was entitled as a result of his participation in the Virginia militia during the French and Indian War. Factually, Washington's journey to Point Pleasant represents the westernmost point he ever reached in his extensive travels. Symbolically, his journey to Point Pleasant demonstrates the geographic reach of his long-standing vision that the European colonists of the Atlantic Seaboard needed to look westward into the Ohio Valley for their long-term well being.

The land where the Kanawha and Ohio rivers merge was called Tu-Endie-wei by the Wyandotte Indians, a phrase meaning "the point between two waters." Washington's party had canoed past this point, and Washington himself had walked several miles overland upon and near the lowland at the confluence of the two streams. Four years later, on October 10, 1774, Virginia frontiersmen and Indians of the federated western tribes fought over control of this land in the Battle of Point Pleasant. The Indians had been goaded into hostilities by Royal Governor Dunmore, whose intention was to harass western colonists with Indian raids in an effort to keep their minds from grievances with onerous policies of the mother country. The day-long battle, won by the colonists under the leadership of Colonel Andrew Lewis, is recognized by some historians as the "First Battle of the Revolution," since it was fought six months before the more famous engagement at Lexington and Concord. An eighty-four-foot-high granite shaft with a statue of a Virginia woodsman at its base commemorates the battle in which 200 Indians and fifty settlers lost their lives.

The Mansion House Museum, the oldest hewn log house in the Kanawha Valley, was constructed as a tavern around 1796 and is preserved in the park as a museum featuring furniture and other artifacts of the post-revolution era including a large square piano believed to be one of the first transported over the Alleghenies. Two bedrooms are furnished with authentic four-poster beds over 150 years old. Point Pleasant Battle Monument State Park, also known as Tu-Endie-wei State Park, is operated by the state of West Virginia. The Mansion House Museum is maintained by the Colonel Charles Lewis Chapter, Daughters of the American Revolution.

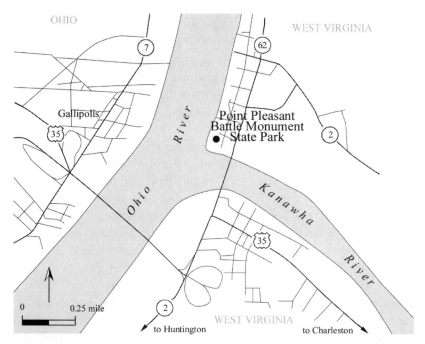

Figure 38. The location of Point Pleasant Battle Monument State Park in Point Pleasant, West Virginia.

DIRECTIONS: Point Pleasant Battle Monument State Park is located on the north side of the confluence of the Kanawha and Ohio rivers, immediately west of SR 2, in Point Pleasant, West Virginia (Figure 38).

PUBLIC USE: Season and hours: *Park:* Dawn–dusk daily. *Mansion House:* May–November, Monday–Saturday, 9 AM–4 PM; Sunday, 1 PM–4 PM. **For people with disabilities:** The grounds are accessible, the mansion is not.

FOR ADDITIONAL INFORMATION: Contact: Point Pleasant Battle Monument State Park (*aka* Tu-Endie-wei State Park), Point Pleasant, West Virginia 25550; 304-675-0869. **Web site:** *www.tu-endie-weistatepark.com.* **Read:** John G. Morgan. 1975. *A Point in History: The Battle of Point Pleasant.*

29. WESTOVER

CHARLES CITY, VIRGINIA

In the earliest days of Virginia, the James River was its most important commercial artery. After planter John Rolfe perfected profitable tobacco cultivation at the Jamestown Colony, farms and great plantations sprang up along the James where deep water enabled cargo ships to load and unload at private docks. Fortunately, some of the rich plantation homes along the James have survived — Berkeley, Westover, Evelynton, Shirley, Belle Air, and Sherwood Forest, the retirement home of President John Tyler — and all have been preserved and are open to visitation. George Washington served in the House of Burgesses with many of the owners and his diary indicates that he visited several of the homes in 1773 when he was the guest of William Byrd of Westover.

Westover, an elegant plantation home famous for its proportions and fine early eighteenth-century gates, was built around 1730 by William Byrd II, the founder of Richmond and Petersburg. Connoisseurs of historic homes consider Westover the finest example of Georgian domestic architecture in the United States. The lawn, with century-old tulip poplar trees, offers a commanding view of the majestic James River and the riverfront entry of the house is thought to be the most photographed doorway in the country. The house is complemented by exquisite gar-

dens and handsome outbuildings as well as by a unique clairvoyee embel-
lished with stone finials and wrought-iron gates.

The interior of Westover is a classic Georgian layout with a center
hall that doubled as a ballroom. The beautifully proportioned rooms have
ornately-carved ceilings and there is an unusual black mantelpiece in the
parlor. As Westover is privately owned, the interior is open only during
Virginia Garden Week or by special appointment. The grounds are open
year-round.

DIRECTIONS: Westover is south of SR 5; the entrance is about 2 miles
east of the intersection of SR 5 and SR 106 (Figure 35).

PUBLIC USE: Season and hours: *House:* Guided tours are conducted
daily during Virginia Garden Week, 10 AM–5 PM. Group tours are available the rest of the year by appointment only. *Grounds:* 9 AM–6 PM
daily. **Admission fee. For people with disabilities:** Call ahead for assistance.

FOR ADDITIONAL INFORMATION: Contact: Westover, 7000
Westover Road, Charles City, Virginia 23030; 804-829-2882. **Web site:**
www.jamesriverplantations.com.

30. BERKELEY PLANTATION
CHARLES CITY, VIRGINIA

On December 4, 1619, a small band of English adventurers calling
themselves the Berkeley Company landed in Virginia, their first act one of
thankful prayer for a safe end to an arduous journey, the first official
Thanksgiving in America. Unfortunately, their good luck did not last as
an Indian uprising wiped out the little colony in 1622.

The Harrisons, a family of great energy and ambition who had been
in Virginia for two generations, acquired the Berkeley property in 1691
and, under their dynamic leadership, Berkeley Plantation was expanded
to include a shipyard and tobacco export warehouse. In 1726, Benjamin
Harrison IV married Anne Carter, daughter of Robert "King" Carter, a
marriage that symbolized the colonial "web of kinship" that intimately
connected Virginia's powerful ruling class. In honor of the marriage,

Harrison began work on a Georgian home, now said to be the oldest three-story brick house in Virginia. The construction date is proved by a round date stone, carved above a side door, that contains the date, 1726, and the initials of Benjamin and Anne etched above a heart.

The Berkeley manor house is the centerpiece of a 1400-acre working plantation situated atop a landscaped and terraced hill overlooking the James River, with a formal boxwood garden and textured lawns sloping from the front door to the bank of the river. Handsome Adam woodwork and double arches in the "Great Rooms" were installed at the direction of Thomas Jefferson and all of the interior rooms are furnished with authentic furniture and fine antiques.

Benjamin and Anne's son, Benjamin Harrison V, was a three-time governor of Virginia, a signer of the Declaration of Independence, a moving force in the Continental Congress, and a close friend of George Washington who dined with the Harrisons at Berkeley on November 2, 1773. Harrison's youngest son, William Henry, ninth President of the United States, was born at Berkeley in 1773 and his grandson, Benjamin, was elected twenty-third president. Visitors to Berkeley are always interested in the bedroom in which William Henry was born, the same room in which he wrote his inaugural address at a simple desk that remains in place.

Berkeley is also noted for its Civil War history as it was once appropriated as headquarters for General George McClellan when he led the Army of the Potomac. During the bivouac, General Daniel Butterfield composed the plaintive *Taps,* played for the first time at Berkeley by bugler O.W. Norton. President Abraham Lincoln visited Berkeley in 1862 to review the 140,000 troops stationed on the grounds and in the surrounding area.

After the Civil War Berkeley began to decline until 1907 when it was purchased by Scottish-born John Jamison who, as an immigrant, had served in the Army of the Potomac as a drummer boy. John's son Malcolm and daughter-in-law Grace were responsible for the detailed, magnificent restoration of Berkeley that appears today as in its glory days under the Harrisons.

DIRECTIONS: Berkeley is south of SR 5; the entrance is about 2 miles east of the intersection of SR 5 and SR 106 (Figure 35).

PUBLIC USE: Season and hours: 8 AM–5 PM daily. Closed Christmas Day. **Admission fee. Visitor center. Gift shop. Food service:** The

Coach House Restaurant is in a restored outbuilding 100 yards from the manor house. Telephone 804-829-6603. **For people with disabilities:** Accessibility is limited. Some assistance is available with advance notice.

FOR ADDITIONAL INFORMATION: Contact: Berkeley Plantation, 12602 Harrison Landing Road, Charles City, Virginia 23030; 804-829-6018. **Web site:** *www.berkeleyplantation.com.* **Read:** (1) Parke Rouse, Jr. and Susan T. Burtch. 1980. *Berkeley Plantation and Hundred.* (2) Bruce Roberts. 1990. *Plantation Homes of the James River.*

31. SHIRLEY PLANTATION

CHARLES CITY, VIRGINIA

Founded in 1613 by Sir Thomas West, Shirley is the oldest plantation in Virginia. The property was originally granted to Edward Hill whose grandson, Edward Hill III, began construction of the present mansion house in 1723 for his daughter Elizabeth and her husband, John Carter, thus initiating the unbroken continuity of occupancy by one family. Today, Shirley is occupied by the tenth and eleventh generations descended from its founders.

Shirley was completed in 1738, an architectural treasure largely in its original state. A flying staircase, the only one in the nation, rises three stories with no visible means of support. The interior is graced with hand-carved woodwork, family portraits, silver, furniture, and other exquisite decorations. The exterior contains four brick outbuildings — a kitchen house, laundry house, and two L-shaped barns — that form a Queen Anne forecourt, a rare remembrance of that architectural style. The grounds comprise 800 acres that contain a stable, smokehouse, root cellar, and dovecote.

Since colonial times, Shirley has been a center of gracious living. The mansard roof is appropriately graced by a 3½-foot wooden pineapple, the symbol of hospitality for over 250 years. In 1773, during his time in the James River area, George Washington rode from Westover to Shirley Plantation to visit owner Charles Carter with whom he shared a keen interest in experimental farming.

DIRECTIONS: Shirley is located south of SR 5, immediately west of the intersection of SR 5 and SR 106 (Figure 35).

PUBLIC USE: Season and hours: 9 AM–5 PM daily, with the last ticket sold at 4:45 PM. Grounds close at 6 PM. Closed Thanksgiving Day and Christmas Day. Call for January–February tour hours. **Admission fee. Gift shop. For people with disabilities:** Call ahead for information regarding assistance.

FOR ADDITIONAL INFORMATION: Contact: Shirley Plantation, 501 Shirley Plantation Road, Charles City, Virginia 23030-2907; 800-232-1613. **Web site:** *www.shirleyplantation.com.* **Read:** Joanne B. Young. 1981. *Shirley Plantation: A Personal Adventure for Ten Generations.*

∾

THE ROAD TO PHILADELPHIA

In the mid-eighteenth century, growing unrest with British colonial policies began to produce increased cooperation between the colonies. Although George Washington had served in the Virginia Assembly as a burgess for over fifteen years, his participation in the affairs of the colony had been minimal as he had apparently been concerned with local, regional, and personal issues — his chief interest to amass and protect his personal fortune. In 1769, however, he finally spoke out with criticism of British policies as ill-advised, a deliberate attack on colonial liberty. His motives were uncertain, but from that point on he became increasingly vocal and took a more active role in the colonies' faltering steps toward total freedom. Along with Patrick Henry, Thomas Jefferson, George Mason, and others, George Washington assumed a leadership role in Virginia's evolving position on freedom from Great Britain.

Both the First and Second Continental Congresses were held in Philadelphia, the focal point of colonial cooperation and activity, due in large part to its central location. During the first, in 1774, representatives of the colonies met to discuss issues of unity and mutual concern. During the second, a year later, the representatives took the bold and dramatic action of authorizing a Continental Army and named George Washington as its commander-in-chief. Throughout the war years that followed, Philadelphia remained the center of government for the loosely consolidated, tenuously independent thirteen colonies.

Except for his years at Mount Vernon, George Washington spent more time in Philadelphia than anywhere else — attending the two continental congresses, spending months in and near the city during the war (Washington Crossing, Brandywine, Germantown, Valley Forge), participating in the post-war Constitutional Congress, and then in residence as president when Philadelphia was the national capital.

Travel to Philadelphia (or anywhere else) was adventurous. The busy road from Philadelphia to New York was passable, but the roads from the south were mostly ruts, muddy in the summer and frozen rock hard in winter. The main route from Mount Vernon to Philadelphia involved crossing the Potomac, then riding to Annapolis, turning north across the Patapsco River via the Gunpowder and Susquehanna ferries to pick up an easily traveled road from Elk River to Brandywine Ferry to Chester and across the Schuylkill River to Philadelphia. Lodgings for a journey that lasted three or four days were at scattered "ordinaries" or, with luck, in homes of friends. George Washington traveled these roads often and, over time, he came to know them well (Figure 39, Table 4).

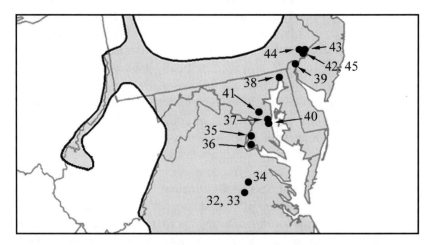

Figure 39. George Washington became increasingly involved with the growing discontent toward British colonial rule in the years leading up to the outbreak of the Revolutionary War. His political activism took him from the centers of political ideology in Virginia to Philadelphia which had become the seat of revolutionary political thought for the British American colonies collectively. The names and page numbers for descriptions of the numbered sites shown here are given in Table 4.

Table 4. Publicly accessible sites identified with George Washington's activities during the years immediately preceding the Revolutionary War.

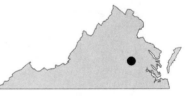

32. Saint Johns Church

RICHMOND, VIRGINIA

Saint Johns is the oldest church in Richmond and, since Henrico Parish began in 1611, is the mother of all Episcopal churches in the area. The present building is either the fourth or fifth Henrico parish church and its oldest portion, the existing east-west transepts, was erected in 1741 on land donated by William Byrd II, the founder of Richmond. There have been changes through the years, but the interior still retains thirty colonial pews and a colonial-era pulpit with a remarkable sounding board. The parish also owns and displays a chalice from 1718, a baptismal bowl from 1694, and various other treasures from the eighteenth century. In 1941, Great Britain's King George VI presented the parish with a copy of the 1662 Book of Common Prayer that had been bound for Queen Anne.

It is uncertain how many times George Washington visited Richmond, but we do know that the Second Virginia Convention was held at Saint Johns during the week of March 20, 1775, and that burgesses George Washington and Thomas Jefferson were in attendance. During a debate on raising a Virginia militia, delegate Patrick Henry delivered his fiery "Give me Liberty or Give me Death" speech which narrowly swayed

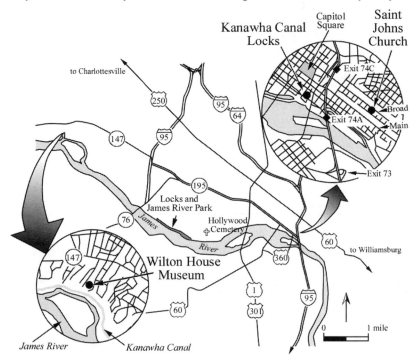

Figure 40. The location of Saint Johns Church, Wilton House Museum, and the Kanawha Canal Locks in Richmond, Virginia.

184

the vote in support of the resolution. Reenactments of the convention and Henry's speech are held on Sunday afternoons at 2 PM, from the last Sunday in May through the first Sunday in September.

Saint Johns conducts regular Sunday services at 11 AM.

DIRECTIONS: From I 95, take Exit 74C and go eastbound on US 60 (East Broad Street) 1 mile to the church on the south side of the street between 24th Street and 26th Street (Figure 40).

PUBLIC USE: Season and hours: Guided tours are conducted Monday–Saturday, 10 AM–3:30 PM; Sunday, 1 PM–3:30 PM. Closed Easter Sunday, Thanksgiving Day, Christmas Eve Day, Christmas Day, New Year's Eve Day, and New Year's Day. **Admission fee. Gift shop. For people with disabilities:** Partially accessible. Call ahead for assistance.

FOR ADDITIONAL INFORMATION: Contact: Saint Johns Church, 2401 East Broad Street, Richmond, Virginia 23223; 804-648-5015. **Read:** (1) Henry Mayer. 1986. *A Son of Thunder: Patrick Henry.* (2) Sue St. Amand. 1996. *St. John's: A Pictorial History.*

33. WILTON HOUSE MUSEUM

RICHMOND, VIRGINIA

Wilton, an impressive example of an elegant eighteenth-century Georgian home, was built in 1750 by William Randolph III on a 2000-acre James River plantation called "World's End." Built of warm and mellow rosy brick and decorated in contemporary style with Chippendale and Queen Anne furniture, Wilton is an outstanding representation of opulent Virginia plantation life. For example, all the walls — in every room, hall and even closets — are paneled from floor to ceiling. George Washington stayed at Wilton for two days, March 25 and 26, 1775, when attending the Second Virginia Convention held at nearby Saint Johns Church. The upstairs guest bedroom is called the "Washington Room" in honor of his visit.

Threatened by industrial encroachment in 1933, Wilton was purchased by the National Society of the Colonial Dames who had it moved brick by brick and reconstructed on the banks of the James River fifteen miles from its original location. In their written history of Wilton, the dames say that:

> *Wilton stands as a testimonial to colonists such as Randolph
> and his wife Anne Carter Harrison of Berkeley Plantation and
> bears witness to the colonists' determination to create a cultured
> life style in the new world.*[68]

DIRECTIONS: From downtown Richmond, take Main Street westbound
to a dead end at Thompson Street, turn south on Thompson for 1 block
to SR 147 (Cary Street), then go west on SR 147 to South Wilton Road
(5400 block of Cary), then go south on South Wilton Road to Wilton
House at the end of the street (Figure 40).

PUBLIC USE: Season and hours: March–January, guided tours are
conducted Tuesday–Saturday, 10 AM–4:30 PM; Sunday, 1:30 PM–4:30
PM; Monday, by appointment. Closed national holidays. February, open
by appointment. **Gift shop. Admission fee. For people with disabilities:** First floor accessible with assistance needed to traverse several
front steps.

FOR ADDITIONAL INFORMATION: Contact: Wilton House Museum, South Wilton Road, PO Box 8225, Richmond, Virginia 23226;
804-282-5936. **Web site:** *www.wiltonhousemuseum.org.* **Read:** Wade
Tyree Kinnard. 1994. *Wilton.*

34. HANOVER TAVERN

HANOVER, VIRGINIA

Hanover Tavern, built around 1732, is part of the Hanover Courthouse Historic District that lies on the colonial route of the Great Northern Post Road between Fredericksburg and Richmond. The historic district includes the tavern, the 1735 courthouse, a jail, and the county
clerk's office. It is documented that many historic figures tarried at
Hanover Tavern, a two-story clapboard house with two chimneys. George
Washington stopped at Hanover on his many journeys south, but perhaps
his most notable stop was when he traveled with General Rochambeau
as their armies moved toward their destiny at Yorktown.

Hanover Tavern, which has evolved through five phases of construction, is owned by the Hanover Tavern Foundation. The foundation

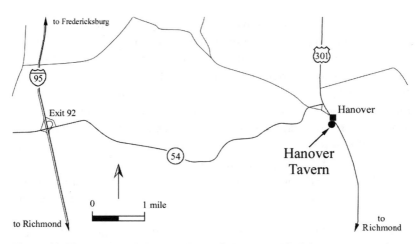

Figure 41. The location of Hanover Tavern in Hanover, Virginia.

is currently (2002) conducting a capital fundraising and restoration effort on behalf of this important national treasure.

DIRECTIONS: Exit I 95 at Exit 92 onto SR 54 eastbound, go about 5 miles to US 301, then go south on US 301 0.1 mile to the historic district. Hanover Tavern is on the west side of US 301 (Figure 41).

PUBLIC USE: Season and hours: Hanover Tavern is open by appointment only. **Admission fee.**

FOR ADDITIONAL INFORMATION: Contact: Hanover Tavern Foundation, PO Box 487, Hanover, Virginia 23069; 804-537-5050. **Web site:** *www.hanovertavern.org.*

35. SMALLWOODS RETREAT

MARBURY, MARYLAND

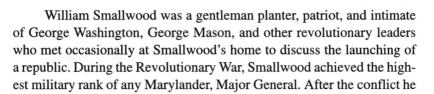

William Smallwood was a gentleman planter, patriot, and intimate of George Washington, George Mason, and other revolutionary leaders who met occasionally at Smallwood's home to discuss the launching of a republic. During the Revolutionary War, Smallwood achieved the highest military rank of any Marylander, Major General. After the conflict he served as the state's fourth governor and occupied that office at the time Maryland ratified the Constitution of the United States.

In honor of General Smallwood's service to Maryland and the nation, the Smallwood Foundation, Inc. rebuilt his modest stone home in the mid-1950s as the centerpiece of a 528-acre state park named for him. The house is furnished with eighteenth-century furniture and other artifacts. General Smallwood's grave is in a copse near the house.

DIRECTIONS: Smallwood State Park is located west of SR 224 about 2 miles south of Marbury (Figure 42).

PUBLIC USE: Season and hours: Daily, 7 AM–dusk. **Admission fee:** May 1–September 30; Saturday, Sunday, and holidays. **For people with disabilities:** The house is not accessible.

FOR ADDITIONAL INFORMATION: Contact: Smallwoods Retreat, Smallwood State Park, Route 1, Box 54, Marbury, Maryland 20653; 301-743-7613.

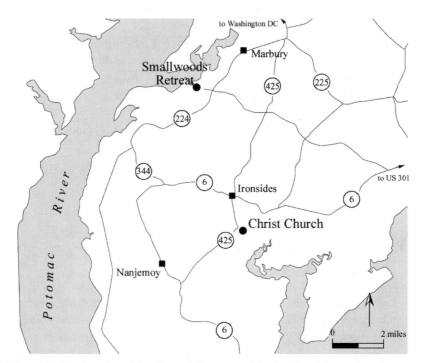

Figure 42. The location of Smallwoods Retreat and Christ Church in southern Maryland.

36. CHRIST CHURCH, DURHAM PARISH

NANJEMOY, MARYLAND

Durham was the parish of General Smallwood who attended services with his friend George Washington in the tiny, square-shaped, steepleless, brick building. Christ Church is an active church that conducts Sunday services at 11 AM.

DIRECTIONS: From US 301 at La Plata, Maryland, take SR 6 westbound to Ironsides, then SR 425 southbound to the church (Figure 42).

FOR ADDITIONAL INFORMATION: Contact: Christ Church, Durham Parish, 8685 Ironside Road, Nanjemoy, Maryland 20662; 301-743-7099.

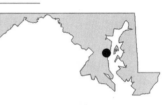

37. RISING SUN INN

CROWNSVILLE, MARYLAND

The Rising Sun Inn, built around 1753, was a popular stopping place for George Washington and other travelers on the historic post road between Annapolis and Baltimore, the busiest highway in colonial Maryland. Time and the construction of modern roads took their toll and the Rising Sun fell into decline. In almost total decay, the building was rescued in 1916 by the Ann Arundel Chapter, Daughters of the American Revolution, who restored, refurbished, and filled it with a collection of colonial period furniture and china. The two-story frame and brick tavern is maintained by the chapter as its headquarters.

DIRECTIONS: The Rising Sun Inn is located on SR 178 north of Crownsville. Exit I 97 at Exit 5, go east on SR 32 to SR 178, then go north on SR 178 for 0.7 mile to the inn, located on the west side of the highway. Use the driveway and parking area on the north side of the structure (Figure 43).

PUBLIC USE: Season and hours: The Rising Sun Inn is open to the public the second Sunday of each month except December–February, and by appointment. **For people with disabilities:** Not accessible.

FOR ADDITIONAL INFORMATION: Contact: Rising Sun Inn, 1090 Generals Highway, Crownsville, Maryland 21032; 410-923-0316. **Web site:** *www.rootsweb.com/~mdaadar/history-right.html.*

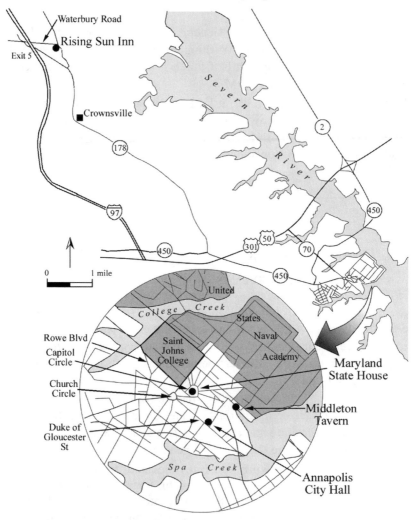

Figure 43. The location of Rising Sun Inn in Crownsville, and featured sites in Annapolis, Maryland.

38. RODGERS TAVERN

PERRYVILLE, MARYLAND

Rodgers Tavern (Plate 7), a two-story brick building with a wide front veranda, was built sometime before 1750 and survived as a working tavern/restaurant for over two hundred years. George Washington's correspondence tells of more than thirty trips on the Lower Susquehanna Ferry to Perryville where he usually stayed with ferry operator and tavern owner John Rodgers. Rodgers became a Revolutionary War hero and his son, Commodore John Rodgers, is recognized as a founder of the United States Navy. Other travelers who rested at Rodgers Tavern included Thomas Jefferson and James Madison. Rodgers Tavern was purchased in 1996 by the town of Perryville which opens the building for special civic events and for visitation by the public by advance reservation.

DIRECTIONS: From I 95, take Exit 93 and proceed southbound on SR 275 to Perryville. Turn west on SR 7 and follow the street to its end at

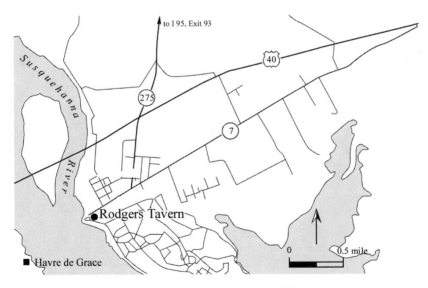

Figure 44. The location of Rodgers Tavern in northern Maryland.

191

the Susquehanna River. Rodgers Tavern is on the south side of the street (Figure 44).

FOR ADDITIONAL INFORMATION: Contact: Rodgers Tavern, Old Post Road, Perryville, Maryland 21903; 410-642-6066. **Read:** Mim Crowl. 1970. "Guess Who Slept Here."

39. ROBINSON HOUSE

CLAYMONT, DELAWARE

From time to time George Washington lodged at the Robinson "ordinary" during journeys between Baltimore and Philadelphia and it is believed he stayed there while on the military march from Philadelphia to the Brandywine battlefield. The Robinson house, built around 1723, is a typical 1½-story farmhouse/tavern of the period — plaster over lath with

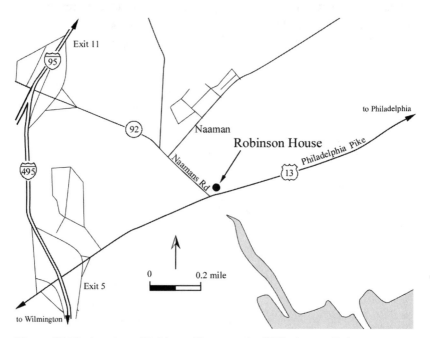

Figure 45. The location of Robinson House north of Wilmington, Delaware.

192

a large open fireplace dominating the public room. The Robinson House is owned by the State of Delaware but leased to the Naamans Kill Chapter of the Questers who open Robinson House as a house museum furnished as it was in the colonial period.

DIRECTIONS: From I 95, take Exit 11 and go eastbound on SR 92 (Naamans Road) to US 13 (Philadelphia Pike). The Robinson House is on the north side of the US 13/SR 92 intersection (Figure 45).

PUBLIC USE: Season and hours: Sundays, 1 PM–4 PM, or by appointment. **Admission fee. For people with disabilities:** Accessible.

FOR ADDITIONAL INFORMATION: Contact: The Questers, The Robinson House, 1 Naamans Road, Claymont, Delaware 19703; 302-792-0285.

40. MIDDLETON TAVERN

ANNAPOLIS, MARYLAND

George Washington spent a great deal of social time in Annapolis and as a rest stop on trips between Mount Vernon and Philadelphia. Few buildings from Washington's time remain, but we know from his journals that he often stayed at Middleton Tavern, the center of Annapolis social life. Middleton Tavern was built around 1750 by Samuel Middleton, who ran a ferry service between Rock Hall on the Eastern Shore and a dock conveniently located in front of the tavern. One famous story told by Washington himself was that Middleton's ferry once ran aground offshore, unable to move until the next favorable tide. President Washington, on board, spent an uncomfortable night crammed into a bunk "too short by a head, covered only by greatcoat and boots."[69] It is not reported whether Samuel Middleton ever bragged that "Washington slept here."

Middleton Tavern has had many owners and purposes since colonial days, serving at times as a meat market and then as a general store. In 1968, it was purchased by restaurateur Jerry Hardesty who restored the original name. Refurbished and renovated, today's Middleton Tavern reflects colonial-style décor yet provides the same brand of hospitality, service, and refreshment enjoyed by our founding fathers when Annapolis was called the "Athens of America."

DIRECTIONS: Middleton Tavern is at the head of City Dock, directly across from the Market House in the heart of the Annapolis Historic District (Figure 43).

FOR ADDITIONAL INFORMATION: Contact: Middleton Tavern, 2 Market Space, Annapolis, Maryland 21401; 410-263-3323. **Web site:** *www.middletontavern.com.*

41. MONTPELIER MANSION

LAUREL, MARYLAND

Planter Thomas Snowden built Montpelier, one of the finest examples of eighteenth-century Georgian architecture, on a knoll overlooking the Patuxent River. Its proximity to a main road from the south to Philadelphia made it a convenient stopping place for travelers such as Snowden's close friend George Washington who visited the plantation when traveling between Mount Vernon and Philadelphia. Abigail Adams once stayed at Montpelier, describing it as a "Large, Handsome, Elegant house, where I was received with what we might term true English Hospitality."[70]

Montpelier exhibits the formal symmetry and balance of Georgian architecture so popular in Maryland and Virginia in the 1760s and 1770s. The mansion's furnishing plan is based on a room by room inventory of the possessions of Snowden's son, Nicholas. Select rooms have been researched and furnished as they would have appeared from the 1790s to 1830s. Large trees and boxwood grace the landscape that boasts of an original eighteenth-century summerhouse, one of only two in the United States known to have survived. The Friends of Montpelier, a volunteer organization, conducts a year-round program of history lectures, tours, and other special events. Formal afternoon tea served on the second and fourth Friday of each month has become Montpelier's most popular tourist attraction.

Montpelier is owned and operated by the Maryland-National Capital Park and Planning Commission.

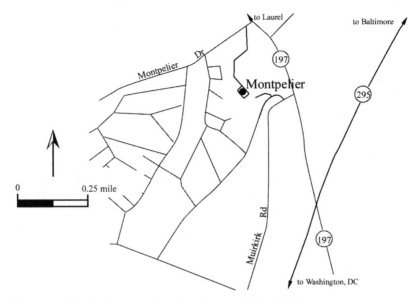

Figure 46. The location of Montpelier in central Maryland.

DIRECTIONS: From SR 295 (Baltimore-Washington Parkway), exit at SR 197 and drive north for 0.25 mile to Muirkirk Road. Turn west on Muirkirk Road and take the first right onto the estate grounds (Figure 46).

PUBLIC USE: Season and hours: Guided tours are conducted from March–November, Sunday 12 N–4 PM. Group tours by appointment. **Admission fee. Gift shop. For people with disabilities:** The first floor is accessible with a videotape available showing the second floor.

FOR ADDITIONAL INFORMATION: Contact: Montpelier Mansion, 9401 Montpelier Drive, Laurel, Maryland 20707; 301-953-1376. **Web** *site:www.pgparks.com.* **Read:** G. E. Smith Kidder. 1981. *The Architecture of the United States.*

42. BLUE BELL INN

PHILADELPHIA, PENNSYLVANIA

The Blue Bell Inn, built in 1766, was ten miles south of central Philadelphia on the King's Highway, the stagecoach road that connected the southern colonies with Philadelphia. The "highway" was actually a dirt road filled with deep ruts and washed-out gullies and a journey of five days between Baltimore and Philadelphia was not uncommon. The Blue Bell Inn became a welcome stopping place for weary travelers and it is known that George Washington was a guest, including a visit during his presidency. A charming story about that visit, as recounted by M. Lafitte Viera in *West Philadelphia,* said:

> *Washington remained musing in front of the fireplace long after the house was quiet. The Misses Lloyds, daughters of the owner, who had been at a dance, returned about midnight and repaired to the kitchen for refreshments and to talk over the conquests of the evening. The door was slightly ajar, Washington unconsciously listening to their gay prattle. Suddenly the sound of his own name attracted his attention and he heard one of the girls laughingly remark that she would like to see if a kiss would dispel the sober look on the General's face.*
>
> *Washington sprang to his feet, and much to the embarrassment of the party, opened the door and confronted the trio. Despite merry teasing, Washington could not succeed in persuading the culprit to acknowledge the speech, so amid much laughter and many protests he declared that he should have to kiss all and in the proper manner customary in the old colonial days.[71]*

The Blue Bell fell into disrepair until rescued from demolition in the 1980s by the Friends of the Blue Bell, a non-profit organization with a mandate to restore the inn to its original condition. The two-story stone building was structurally sound, although burned-out floors had to be repaired, fireplaces refinished, and windows and shutters replaced.

The Road to Philadelphia

With financial help from the City of Philadelphia, plus private and public donations, they are well on their way to saving another important landmark in America's early history.

DIRECTIONS: From I 95, exit onto Island Avenue northbound. The inn is on the northwest corner of the intersection of Island and Woodland avenues (Figure 47).

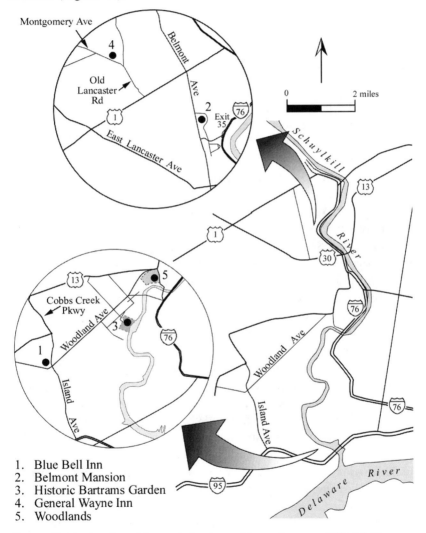

1. Blue Bell Inn
2. Belmont Mansion
3. Historic Bartrams Garden
4. General Wayne Inn
5. Woodlands

Figure 47. The location of featured sites located in southwestern Philadelphia.

PUBLIC USE: Season and hours: May–October, Saturday, 1 PM–4 PM. **For people with disabilities:** Not accessible.

FOR ADDITIONAL INFORMATION: Contact: Blue Bell Inn, 7303 Woodland Avenue, Philadelphia, Pennsylvania 19153; 215-365-5927. **Read:** John T. Faris. 1917. *Old Roads Out of Philadelphia.*

43. PHILADELPHIA, PENNSYLVANIA

No city has been part of more critical events in early American history than Philadelphia. The United States of America was born there on July 4, 1776, when the Declaration of Independence was adopted, and later when the Constitution, also drafted in Philadelphia, laid the foundation for the nation's future. And the city served as the new nation's capital from 1790 to 1800.

In 1682, William Penn founded Philadelphia, Greek for "City of Brotherly Love," under charter from King Charles II. Penn, a convert to the persecuted Society of Friends (Quakers), envisioned a society in which people of all faiths would live together in harmony and freedom. Under his leadership, every taxpayer had a vote, prisoners had a right to a hearing, accused persons were provided a trial by jury, and taxation was by law. As an example of inspired urban planning, the city of Philadelphia was explored, surveyed, and laid out street by street, open space by open space, before settlers were allowed to build homes or shops.

By the 1760s, Philadelphia had grown to a population of 25,000 — the largest, most sophisticated, and progressive city in America, due in great measure to the efforts and persuasive powers of its premier citizen, Benjamin Franklin, whose energy and vision manifested in Philadelphia's development from Penn's simple Quaker town to a major metropolis, seaport, and gateway to the west by the late eighteenth century. Among Franklin's innovations were the first fire-fighting company in America, street lighting and paving, recruitment of local militia, and construction of the city's first hospital. He was involved with dissemination of knowledge, the founding of the University of Pennsylvania (where Commander-in-Chief Washington attended commencement on March 21, 1781), and the establishment of the first subscription library in the country. Politically, Franklin was an early advocate of confederation, a prime mover at both Continental Congresses and the Constitutional Convention, and an effective ambassador to European countries. His success in persuading the French to join the war against England was unquestionably the single most important American foreign diplomacy triumph of the Revolutionary War period.

Today, Philadelphia is a melange of modern city life and colonial charm. Historic landmarks are mixed with glass office towers; narrow cobblestone streets intersect broad boulevards clogged with traffic, and eighteenth-century homes are tucked away just blocks from the busy business district. Due to the foresight of national and city leaders, many historic buildings have been preserved, a number of them concentrated in Independence National Historical Park (Figure 48).

FOR ADDITIONAL INFORMATION: Contact: Philadelphia Convention and Visitors Bureau, 1515 Market Street, Philadelphia, Pennsylvania 19102; 800-537-7676. **Read:** Russell F. Weigley, ed. 1982. *Philadelphia, a 300-Year History.*

43-1. INDEPENDENCE NATIONAL HISTORICAL PARK

Independence National Historical Park (Figure 49) is a National Park Service facility covering forty-five acres of the "Old City" that includes refurbished and replicated places associated with the nation's early political history and the men who lived it — George Washington, John Adams, Samuel Adams, Thomas Jefferson, James Madison, Benjamin Franklin, and others. One can almost feel their presence when visiting the government buildings where they conferred and acted, worshipping at the churches they attended, strolling the streets they walked, or dining at the taverns where they dined, drank, gambled — and politicked.

The National Park Service suggests that tours of Independence Park begin at the visitor center with a screening of the film *Independence* and where rangers are stationed to answer questions and provide the latest information regarding hours of operations, admission fees (there

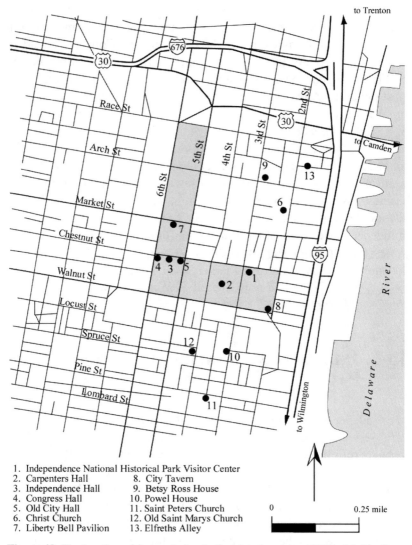

1. Independence National Historical Park Visitor Center
2. Carpenters Hall
3. Independence Hall
4. Congress Hall
5. Old City Hall
6. Christ Church
7. Liberty Bell Pavilion
8. City Tavern
9. Betsy Ross House
10. Powel House
11. Saint Peters Church
12. Old Saint Marys Church
13. Elfreths Alley

Figure 48. The location of featured sites in the historic center of Philadelphia, Pennsylvania.

are selective fees for some attractions), and other matters. Most historic buildings are open from 9 AM to 5 PM, but the hours are subject to change and some sites are open only for guided tours that require tickets, available at the visitor center on a first come, first served basis.

Figure 49. Independence National Historical Park in Philadelphia, Pennsylvania, featuring Independence Hall in the center. (Photograph courtesy of National Park Service)

DIRECTIONS: From I 76, I 95, I 676, and US 30, exit and go to Chestnut and 2nd streets for the parking garage (Figure 48).

PUBLIC USE: Season and hours: Most park buildings are open from 9 AM to 5 PM daily, with extended hours for some buildings during weekends in the spring and weekdays in July and August. **Admission fee.** Admission is free to most buildings but some attractions require tour tickets, available at the Visitor Center. **Visitor center. Gift shop. For people with disabilities:** Most sites are first-floor accessible.

FOR ADDITIONAL INFORMATION: Contact: Independence National Historical Park, 311–313 Walnut Street, Philadelphia, Pennsylvania 19106; 215-597-8974. **Web site:** *www.nps.gov/inde.* **Read:** (1) National Park Service. 1962. *A Guide to Independence National Historical Park.* (2) Paul Hogarth. 1976. *Walking Tours of Old Philadelphia.*

43-2. CARPENTERS HALL

320 CHESTNUT STREET

When the First Continental Congress met in 1774, it was logical that Philadelphia be the site for the deliberations. As the principal city of the colonies it offered the necessary amenities and was centrally located between the northern and southern colonies, an important consideration in an era of tedious and often uncomfortable travel. The Pennsylvania State House was originally intended to be the meeting site but the delegates voted for neutrality and chose a building lent by the Carpenters Company of Philadelphia, an association of master builders. Almost three centuries later, the Carpenters Company's primary mission is the preservation of Carpenters Hall, maintaining its historical significance, and the company's own history. The distinguished brick structure with a weather vane contains a museum of carpentry featuring some of the original chairs used by the Continental Congress as the delegates deliberated the most momentous matters in the history of this nation.

FOR ADDITIONAL INFORMATION: Read: Carpenters' Company. 1876. *Carpenters' Hall and its Historic Memories.*

43-3. INDEPENDENCE HALL

CHESTNUT STREET BETWEEN 5TH AND 6TH

Independence Hall (Figure 49), built as the Pennsylvania State House between 1752 and 1756, is the single most important building in the early political history of the United States — the place where the Declaration of Independence was adopted, where George Washington was named Commander-in-Chief of the Continental Army at the Second Continental Congress, and where the Constitution of the United States was drafted in 1787.

The two-story brick building with a massive clock and bell tower is a masterpiece of symmetry and grace and the interior has been magnificently restored. The Assembly Room contains two original artifacts — the inkstand used by signers of both the Declaration of Independence and the Constitution — and the chair occupied by George Washington, presiding officer of the Constitutional Convention. The sun carving on the back of the chair fascinated delegate Benjamin Franklin who, after the Constitution had been signed, declared the design to be a rising, and not a setting, sun.

The Pennsylvania Supreme Court Chamber lies across the hall from the Assembly Room; the Governor's Council Chamber and The Long Gallery are on the second floor. The Council Chamber is where the descendants of William Penn presided over the Provincial Council while The Long Gallery was the site of banquets and balls honoring events of importance for both American and British occupiers.

PUBLIC USE: Guided tours of Independence Hall are conducted 10 AM–3:45 PM daily. Open house is 9 AM–10 AM and 4 PM–5 PM daily. **Read:** Edward M. Riley. 1990. *Starting America: The Story of Independence Hall.*

43-4. CONGRESS HALL

6TH AND CHESTNUT

Congress Hall, one of the buildings flanking Independence Hall, was the home of the United States Congress from 1790 until 1800 when the capital was moved to Washington, DC. The compact brick building with simple lines was meant to be functional rather than dramatic although the chamber of the House of Representatives on the first floor is handsomely furnished with mahogany tables and studded elbow chairs. The Senate Chamber on the second floor is even more elegant, with red leather chairs and mahogany desks.

Congress Hall was the site of George Washington's second inauguration and that of John Adams as second president of the United States. The First Bank of the United States and the Federal Mint were chartered here, and the controversial Jay Treaty with Great Britain was debated and ratified in Congress Hall. Here the United

States Congress established its prominence as being truly representative of the people.

FOR ADDITIONAL INFORMATION: Read: National Park Service. 1990. *Congress Hall, Capitol of the United States, 1790–1800.*

43-5. OLD CITY HALL

5TH AND CHESTNUT

Old City Hall, a plain boxlike structure with a peaked roof and a cupola, flanks Independence Hall opposite Congress Hall. Shortly after its construction, the City of Philadelphia offered the building to the federal government which utilized it to house the Supreme Court from 1791 to 1800. When the government moved to Washington, DC, the building reverted to its original role as Philadelphia's City Hall. The city government moved to new headquarters in 1874 and Old City Hall fell into neglect until its restoration by the National Park Service in 1973.

The Supreme Court Chamber has been restored to its original condition and the first floor contains exhibits on the Supreme Court's use of the building. Another interesting exhibit tells the story of Philadelphia's devastating yellow fever epidemic of 1793.

43-6. CHRIST CHURCH

22–26 NORTH 2ND STREET

Christ Church, established in 1695, was the Episcopal pastoral home for many patriots including fifteen signers of the Declaration of Independence. The present church building, completed in 1744, is an outstanding example of colonial Georgian architecture and features one of the oldest Palladian windows in America, the original chandelier, and an unusual "wine-glass" pulpit. Many of the church's priceless treasures are part of its daily life; the communion vessels used on Christmas Day and Easter Sunday were gifts from Queen Anne. The baptismal font, a gift from All Hallows Church Barking-by-the-Tower in London, is the one in which William Penn was baptized in 1644. The tower and steeple were financed in part by lotteries managed by parishioner Benjamin Franklin whose pew is marked by a brass plaque, as are those of Betsy Ross and George and Martha Washington.

FOR ADDITIONAL INFORMATION: Contact: Christ Church, 22–26 N. 2nd Street, Philadelphia, Pennsylvania 19106; 215-922-1695. **Read:** Benjamin Dorr. 1841. *A Historical Account of Christ Church, Philadelphia.*

43-7. LIBERTY BELL PAVILION
MARKET STREET BETWEEN 5TH AND 6TH

The Liberty Bell, hung in the brand-new Pennsylvania State House in 1752, is inscribed with the words, "Proclaim Liberty throughout all the Land." Known as the State House Bell, it was used to inform city residents of special events, announcements, and celebrations. By 1846, however, a small crack had enlarged to the point where the bell could no longer be sounded; it was last rung in celebration of George Washington's birthday in 1846.

The most enduring symbol of America's struggle for freedom, the Liberty Bell is housed in a clear glass building where every American can view and draw inspiration from it. In the spring of 2003, the bell will be moved to the southwest corner of 6th and Chestnut streets, directly across the street from Congress Hall.

FOR ADDITIONAL INFORMATION: Read: David Kimball. 1989. *Venerable Relic: The Story of the Liberty Bell.*

43-8. CITY TAVERN
2ND AT WALNUT

The City Tavern in Philadelphia was erected at a great expense by a voluntary subscription of the principal gentlemen of the city for the convenience of the public, and is much the largest and most elegant house occupied in that way in America.

— Pennsylvania Packet, 1774 [72]

An eighteenth-century tavern was much more than a place to quench one's thirst. In towns and cities where most men worked at home or in small offices and where there were no office buildings, banks, stock exchanges, or convention centers, taverns served many of those functions. Social affairs were equally important so taverns were the sites for dinners of fraternal societies, meetings of political friends and foes, dances, concerts, and other gatherings. News brought in by riders reached taverns more quickly than did newspapers, and thus added to the tavern's popularity as a meeting place.

City Tavern, one of the most elegant buildings in Philadelphia, was an immediate success due to its convenient location on a main thoroughfare. According to the National Park Service, the three-story-high building boasted of:

> . . . *several large club rooms, two of which being thrown into one make a spacious room of near fifty feet in length for public entertainment. [There were] several commodious lodging rooms, for the accommodation of strangers, two large kitchens, and every other conveniency for the purpose.*[73]

City Tavern was the most popular watering hole in Philadelphia for early patriots and politicians. Following exhaustive research, the tavern was authentically reconstructed in 1975 to reflect its glory as America's finest colonial dining place. Under private concession, City Tavern remains a working restaurant enabling today's visitors to experience the ambience of the past and to share in the atmosphere of gentility, hospitality, and good cheer enjoyed by our nation's founders.

FOR ADDITIONAL INFORMATION: Contact: City Tavern, 138 S. 2nd Street at Walnut, Philadelphia, Pennsylvania 19106; 215-413-1443. **Read:** John David Ronalds Platt. 1973. *The City Tavern: Independence National Historical Park.*

Independence Park includes other sites of historical significance, but a direct association with George Washington has not been proven for these structures. It stands to reason, however, that since he spent so many years in Philadelphia, he visited the

Bishop White House and Todd House on Walnut Street. William White, Pennsylvania's first Protestant Episcopal Bishop, served as Chaplain to the Continental Congresses and the Todd House was the home of Dolley Payne Todd before her marriage to James Madison. The Todds and Whites were families from different economic levels who shared the same neighborhood and experienced the joys and sorrows of life in the capital of the young nation. A special tour of the two houses is available.

The Free Quaker Meeting House at 5th and Arch, The First Bank of the United States, and Philosophical Hall on South 5th Street are undoubtedly places visited by Washington as is Declaration House at 7th and Market, the home in which Thomas Jefferson wrote the Declaration of Independence. The New Hall Museum on Chestnut Street is in the former home of Joseph Pemberton, Quaker merchant, civic leader, and friend of George Washington.

In addition to the places just mentioned, there are several important sites associated with George Washington that are not part of Independence Park, but are within three blocks of the park and are open for visitation.

43-9. BETSY ROSS HOUSE

239 ARCH STREET

A narrow, two-story colonial structure (Figure 50) houses the home and shop where, according to legend, twenty-five-year-old widow Betsy Ross stitched the first flag of the United States at the request of George Washington. Since Betsy was a manufacturer of naval flags, it is more likely that the flag was sewn at the request of the naval fleet defending Philadelphia but, legend or not, the flag remains America's most prominent symbol of national unity and common purpose. Hardworking, industrious Betsy Ross will stand forever as an American heroine who made an enduring contribution to American history.

Her house, restored and furnished in the middle-class manner of the period, is owned and managed by Historic Philadelphia, Inc.

Figure 50. The Betsy Ross House in Philadelphia, Pennsylvania. (Photograph by William G. Clotworthy)

Her workroom features lifesized wax figures of Betsy at work on the first flag, with General Washington in attendance.

PUBLIC USE: Season and hours: Memorial Day through Labor Day, 10AM–5 PM; other times, Tuesday–Sunday, 10 AM–5 PM. Open Monday holidays; closed Thanksgiving Day, Christmas Day, and New Year's Day. **Gift shop.**

FOR ADDITIONAL INFORMATION: Contact: Betsy Ross House, 239 Arch Street, Philadelphia, Pennsylvania 19106; 215-627-5343. **Read:** Eve Spencer. 1993. *A Flag for Our Country.*

43-10. POWEL HOUSE

244 S. 3RD STREET

The residence of Samuel Powel, Philadelphia's last mayor under the crown and first mayor in the new republic, is an elegant Georgian brick townhouse dating to 1765. The house presents a three-bay, side-passage plan typical of the period with interior appointments of exquisite beauty. As described in their literature, the Powel House contains "The original staircase of Santo Domingo mahogany rises gracefully from a paneled and columned entrance hall leading to the second floor and Mrs. Powel's 'parlor upstairs,' a spacious, elegant and finely ornamented room."[74] Another outstanding feature of the property is a formal garden to the rear of the house.

Mrs. Elizabeth Powel was Philadelphia's most brilliant and gracious hostess whose hospitality extended to George Washington, other politicians, and foreign dignitaries. Washington and Mrs. Powel became close friends and continued a friendly correspondence for many years. The Powel House is owned and maintained by the Philadelphia Society for the Preservation of Landmarks.

PUBLIC USE: Season and hours: Thursday–Saturday, 12 N–5 PM; Sunday, 1 PM–5 PM. Closed holidays. **Admission fee. Gift shop. For people with disabilities:** Limited access.

FOR ADDITIONAL INFORMATION: Contact: Powel House, 244 S. 3rd Street, Philadelphia, Pennsylvania 19106; 215-627-0364. **Read:** Arnold Nicholson. 1965. *American Houses in History.*

43-11. SAINT PETERS CHURCH
313 PINE STREET

Reverend William White, the provost of the University of Pennsylvania, delivered the dedication sermon at Saint Peters in 1761. He described the church as "decently neat and plain,"[75] an appropriate description of the building, a pure example of Georgian symmetry and craftsmanship. An unusual feature of the interior is its double-ended seating plan; an altar at one end for one part of the service and a wineglass pulpit for the sermon at the other end. Four signers of the Declaration of Independence attended Saint Peters as their Philadelphia home church, and George Washington, although a member of Christ Church, worshipped at Saint Peters several times, accompanied by his compatriot Samuel Chew, Chief Justice of Pennsylvania.

FOR ADDITIONAL INFORMATION: Contact: Saint Peters Church, 313 Pine Street, Philadelphia, Pennsylvania 19106; 215-925-5968.

43-12. OLD SAINT MARYS CATHOLIC CHURCH
252 SOUTH 4TH STREET

Washington's diary for October 9, 1774, notes, "Went to popish church in afternoon."[76] It is thought that he meant Saint Marys, founded in 1763, which was the principal Catholic church in Philadelphia during the revolutionary period. The church has been greatly expanded and refurbished over the past two centuries but the sanctuary is the same as when General Washington visited. The plain exterior of the church conceals a rich ornamental interior that has an elaborate high altar and Victorian Crucifixion window.

FOR ADDITIONAL INFORMATION: Contact: Old Saint Mary's Catholic Church, 252 South 4th Street, Philadelphia, Pennsylvania 19106; 215-923-7930.

44. BELMONT MANSION
PHILADELPHIA, PENNSYLVANIA

Belmont Mansion, a three-story brick masterpiece, lies in Fairmount Park, one of America's great urban open spaces. The mansion is a poignant reminder of difficult personal divisions caused by the American Revolution. Belmont was built by William Peters, a corrupt Tory land speculator who fled to England, after which the estate became the property of his son Richard, a staunch patriot prominent in civic and national affairs. Richard Peters served as a judge of the United States District Court for almost forty years. George Washington often visited his friend Peters and, on one occasion, dug a hole in the ground with his walking stick and planted a Spanish Chestnut tree, a descendant of which still lives by the side of the mansion.

Noting the deterioration of Belmont in 1986, a group of women formed The American Women's Heritage Society to "work to provide a showcase for contributions to the growth and development of Philadelphia and the country, and to continue the restoration of this historic house."[77] The society is the only African-American Women's organization to administer a historic mansion. Renovations of Belmont are continuous, with plans underway (2002) to open the house for public visitation within a year. Belmont is currently open only for special events contracted for in advance.

DIRECTIONS: Exit I 76 at Exit 35, go west on Montgomery Drive 0.5 mile, then north on Belmont Drive 0.5 mile to Belmont Mansion on the west side of the street (Figure 47).

FOR ADDITIONAL INFORMATION: Contact: Belmont Mansion, 2000 Belmont Mansion Drive, Fairmount Park, Philadelphia, Pennsylvania 19131; 215-878-8844. **Web site:** *www.awhsinc.org.*

45. Historic Bartrams Garden

Philadelphia, Pennsylvania

In 1748, John Bartram, sometimes described as America's first native botanist, planted a flower and herb garden on a prosperous farm overlooking the Schuylkill River. Self-taught, Bartram published the first comprehensive catalogue of American plants, a broadside listing 220 species of trees, shrubs, and vines, many of which are still grown at Bartrams Garden. Bartram's professional reputation spread to Europe where scientists, philosophers, and politicians respected his research. Benjamin Franklin and George Washington visited and admired Bartram's home and gardens and it is believed that Washington purchased seedlings from Bartram to be planted at Mount Vernon.

In 1893, several descendants of Bartram formed the John Bartram Association to assist in the preservation of the gardens that are now operated as a museum and public garden which encompasses twenty-seven acres of color — the blossoms and herbs descended from Bartram's

Figure 51. John Bartrams Home, Bartrams Garden, Philadelphia, Pennsylvania. (Photograph by William G. Clotworthy)

original cuttings. His comfortable stone house (Figure 51) has been renovated to appear as it did in the 1700s. Historic Bartrams Garden is situated in a public park managed by the City of Philadelphia. According to their mission statement, "...the John Bartram Association is to preserve and develop Historic Bartrams Garden as a museum and public garden, fostering environmental awareness through education and outreach."[78]

DIRECTIONS: From Gray's Ferry Avenue, immediately west of the Schuylkill River, go south on Paschall Avenue, then go southeast onto 49th Street and follow the trolley tracks (as the street changes to Gray's Avenue and Lindbergh Boulevard) past the sign for 54th Street, then make a sharp left (heading southeast) just beyond the Amoco Station and railroad bridge (the entrance is not visible until after crossing the bridge) into Bartrams Garden (Figure 47).

PUBLIC USE: Season and hours: *Historic Garden:* 10 AM–5 PM daily. Closed major holidays. *Bartram House:* Tours are conducted March through December, Tuesday–Sunday, 12:10 PM, 1:10 PM, 2:10 PM, 3:10 PM. Group tours are available throughout the year by advance reservation. **Admission fee:** For house tour only. **Gift shop. For people with disabilities:** First floor partially accessible.

FOR ADDITIONAL INFORMATION: Contact: Historic Bartrams Garden, 54th Street and Lindbergh Boulevard, Philadelphia, Pennsylvania 19143; 215-729-5281. **Web site:** *www.bartramsgarden.org.* **Read:** William Bartram. 1996. *Bartram: Travels and Other Writings.*

∼

THE REVOLUTIONARY WAR

Portentous events were taking place in the colonies when the Second Continental Congress met in Philadelphia in May, 1775. The battle at Lexington and Concord in Massachusetts a few weeks earlier had provoked "the shot heard round the world" that led a ragtag army of New England militia and volunteers to infest the hills and surround the British Army that occupied Boston.

Delegate George Washington, for whatever reason, wore his military uniform to the Congress, perhaps expecting to be named commander of Virginia forces if that colony were to join the incipient rebellion. Rumors circulated in Congress, however, that he might be named commander of a continental army, one rumor he was quick to dispel. It became fact, of course, when the forty-two-year-old Virginian was elected commander-in-chief of an army that barely existed. He immediately left for Massachusetts to take command of his new charge. Just before his departure, he was informed of the Battle of Bunker Hill in which the British had defeated the Americans but had sustained such heavy losses that they were forced back into Boston.

George Washington had traveled to New England only once before, to meet Royal Governor Shirley in Boston in 1756. During the Revolutionary War he journeyed to Boston, Newport, Rhode Island, and Wethersfield, Connecticut, and made two visits to New England as president. Thus New England is rich with sites where Washington commanded or visited or worshipped, none more interesting historically than those that date to 1775 when he assumed command of the Continental Army. The entire Boston area that includes Cambridge, Concord, and Lexington is justly proud of its role in the Revolution, and has been careful to preserve many of the places associated with that phase of our national heritage.

General George Washington arrived in Cambridge in June, in the middle of a rainstorm. His new command, dispersed by the weather, was unprepared to greet him with proper respect and honors although lodgings/headquarters had been readied at Wadsworth House, the home of the president of Harvard University, Samuel Langdon. The brick Wadsworth House, built in 1726, was named for Benjamin Wadsworth, a former president of Harvard University. Washington used the house only briefly before moving to a larger and more suitable house. The Wadsworth House on Harvard Square is currently used for university offices and is closed to the public.

George Washington has been criticized as a second-rate general, a charge that overlooks the fact that he won. His brilliance is that he won with what he had, which at the beginning was an informal, undisciplined, and sometimes disorganized mob of militia and other volunteers. Washington took immediate steps to rectify myriad problems — political, military, disiplinary, material, and others — while his troops continued to fortify the hills and pressed the American siege of Boston. The siege was successful, and when British General Lord Howe's army evacuated Boston by sea in March, 1776, it marked George Washington's first great military victory.

Washington assumed that Britain's next objective would be New York, so he led his revitalized army south to prepare that city's defenses from attack by the British armada and trained professional army led by a frustrated and determined Lord Howe whose orders were to restore the King's peace — at any cost. The War for American Independence was soon to begin in earnest.

General George Washington spent over half of the war in New Jersey and Pennsylvania, thus several pivotal American victories — Saratoga, Kings Mountain, Cowpens — were accomplished without his direct presence. He was, however, at Valley Forge, Morristown, Trenton, Princeton, Monmouth, and Yorktown. Those encampments, battlefields, headquarters buildings and many other places have been preserved by the federal or state governments or by national, state, and local historical societies whose efforts enable us to recreate Washington's itinerary and to visit the sites of defeat, hardship, victory, and joy experienced by him and his armies between 1775 and 1783 (Figure 52, Table 5).

From Cambridge and Dorchester Heights to New York, across New

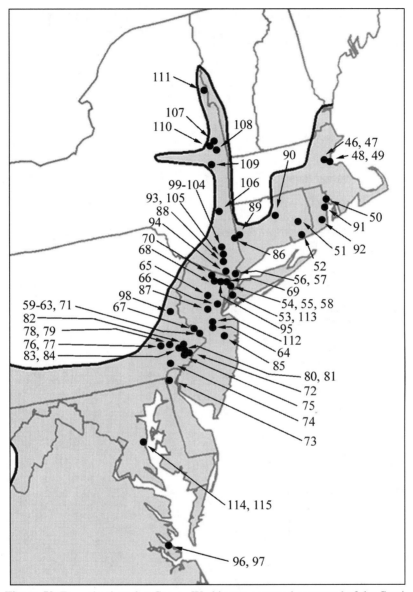

Figure 52. From the time that George Washington assumed command of the Continental Army in the summer of 1775 until he resigned his command late in 1783, most of his time was spent in what are now the states of Pennsylvania, New Jersey, and New York. The names and page numbers for descriptions of the numbered sites shown here are given in Table 5.

Table 5. Publicly accessible sites identified with George Washington's activities during the Revolutionary War.

Map Number	Site Name	Page Number for Site Account
46.	Longfellow National Historic Site	218
47.	Christ Church	220
48.	Dorchester Heights Soldiers Monument	221
49.	Boston National Historical Park	222
	The Freedom Trail	223
	Kings Chapel	224
	Old State House	225
	Faneuil Hall	226
	Old North Church	227
50.	Governor Stephen Hopkins House	228
51.	Governor Jonathan Trumbull House	229
52.	Shaw Mansion	230
53.	Empire-Fulton Ferry State Park	232
54.	Morris-Jumel Mansion	233
55.	Van Cortlandt House Museum	234
56.	Washingtons Headquarters Museum	237
57.	The Purdy House	237
58.	Fort Lee Historic Park	239
59.	Historic Summerseat	240
60.	Washington Crossing Historic Park	242
61.	Washington Crossing State Park	244
62.	Johnson Ferry House State Historic Site	245
63.	Old Barracks Museum	245
64.	Princeton Battlefield State Park	247
65.	Morristown National Historical Park	248
66.	Drake House Museum	251
67.	Holcombe-Jimison Farmstead Museum	252
68.	Van Allen House	253
69.	Steuben House	254
70.	Ringwood State Park	255
71.	Moland House Historical Park	256
72.	Elfreths Alley	257
73.	Hale-Byrnes House	258
74.	Brandywine Battlefield State Park	259
75.	General Wayne Inn	261
76.	Pottsgrove Manor	262
77.	Historic Antes House	263
78.	Pennypacker Mills and Mansion	265
79.	Peter Wentz Farmhouse	266
80.	Cliveden	267
81.	Stenton	269
82.	Hope Lodge	270

(table continued on page 217)

Table 5 *(continued)*

Jersey into Pennsylvania and back, from defeats at Brandywine and Germantown to the horrors of Morristown and Valley Forge — from the brilliant achievement of the Delaware River crossing and victories at Trenton and Princeton, to Monmouth, West Point, and Yorktown — these and other places will live forever in the hearts, minds, and souls of every American who reveres the name and accomplishments of George Washington.

The sites in this section begin with those related to General Washington's arrival in Cambridge in June, 1775, and end with the place at which he resigned his command of the military on December 23, 1783, in Annapolis, Maryland. The battles, the bleak encampments, the struggles with Congress, and the difficulties inherent in supplying and maintaining the Continental Army are described within the context of the places where he lived and fought.

46. LONGFELLOW NATIONAL HISTORIC SITE
CAMBRIDGE, MASSACHUSETTS

The Wadsworth House proved inadequate as headquarters for Washington and his staff, so they moved into a large Georgian-style dwelling that had been the home of Major John Vassall, a wealthy Tory forced to flee on the eve of the revolution. The house (Plate 8) served as Washington's headquarters for nine months and it is where he planned the siege of Boston and, more happily, where he and Martha celebrated their seventeenth wedding anniversary in January, 1776.

In 1837, the house became the home of poet Henry Wadsworth Longfellow when he taught at Harvard and is where he wrote his most famous works, *The Song of Hiawatha* and *The Children's Hour.* Professor and Mrs. Longfellow had a deep appreciation of the history of the house and passed that respect to their children who bequeathed it to the federal government — to preserve, protect, and interpret the home of one of America's best-loved literary figures, and its most famous military and political figure. Longfellow's books, furniture, and artwork collections are displayed in the house that is maintained by the National Park Service.

The Longfellow House recently (2002) completed extensive reno-vations that included environmental controls designed to preserve more than 600,000 historic documents and artifacts, and alterations to the car-riage house provided new facilities for education programs, exhibits and workshops.

DIRECTIONS: From SR 2A (Massachusetts Avenue) at Harvard Square, Cambridge, go north 2 blocks to Garden Street, go west on Garden 2 blocks to Mason Street, go west on Mason 1 block to Brattle Street, then go west on Brattle 0.1 mile to the Longfellow House at #105 (Figure 53).

PUBLIC USE: Season and hours: Guided tours are conducted mid-March–May, November, and December, Wednesday–Friday, 12 N–4:30 PM; Saturday and Sunday, 10 AM–4:30 PM. June–October, Wednes-day–Sunday, 10 AM–4:30 PM. **Admission fee. Visitor center. Gift shop. For people with disabilities:** Call ahead for assistance. The sec-ond floor is not accessible.

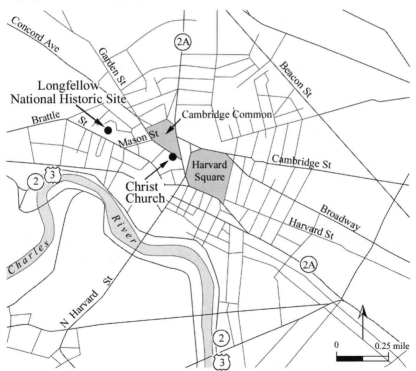

Figure 53. The location of Longfellow National Historic Site and Christ Church in Cambridge, Massachusetts.

FOR ADDITIONAL INFORMATION: Contact: Longfellow National Historic Site, 105 Brattle Street, Cambridge, Massachusetts 02138; 617-876-4491. **Web site:** *www.nps.gov/long/.* **Read:** (1) Samel Adams Drake. 1900. *The Historic Mansions and the Highways Around Boston.* (2) Arvin Newton. 1963. *Longfellow: His Life and Work.*

47. CHRIST CHURCH

CAMBRIDGE, MASSACHUSETTS

Peter Harrison, architect of Kings Chapel in Boston, designed Christ Church, the oldest church building in Cambridge. At the outset of the revolution, the rector and Tory members of the congregation were forced to flee Cambridge and the Episcopal church building was converted to a military barracks where it is told that Connecticut troops melted the organ pipes to make bullets. On New Year's Eve, 1775, the church reopened for a special service attended by George and Martha Washington (Pew # 93 is marked). Except for a single funeral (of a British officer!), the church was not reopened for regular religious services until 1790.

The park across the street was the location of the Washington Elm under the branches of which Washington took command of the Continental Army. The tree died in 1923.

DIRECTIONS: From Harvard Square in Cambridge, proceed north on SR 2A 2 blocks to Garden Street and Christ Church on the left (Figure 53).

PUBLIC USE: Season and hours: Open early morning until evening. **Admission fee. For people with disabilities:** Accessible.

FOR ADDITIONAL INFORMATION: Contact: Christ Church, 0 Garden Street, Cambridge, Massachusetts 02138; 617-876-0200. **Web site:** *www.cccambridge.org.*

48. DORCHESTER HEIGHTS SOLDIERS MONUMENT

BOSTON, MASSACHUSETTS

On the night of March 4, 1776, colonial militia and local volunteers fortified the summit of Dorchester Heights south of Boston, heights that overlooked the city of Boston, and trained their cannons on the British garrison below. The British cannons could not reach the Americans holding the heights, so rather than attempt a frontal assault (General Howe remembered the devastating losses suffered by the British soldiers at Bunker Hill) the British decided to evacuate the city. The British retreat was the first major military victory, and a bloodless one, for Commander-in-Chief George Washington and it served to raise the morale of the embattled colonists.

In 1898, the General Court of Massachusetts commissioned a white

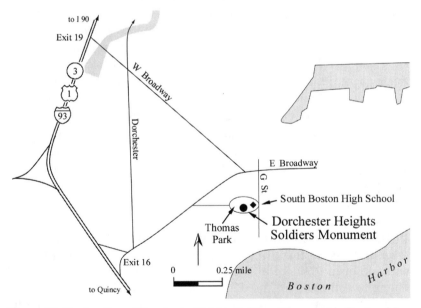

Figure 54. The location of Dorchester Heights Soldiers Monument in Boston, Massachusetts.

marble Georgian Revival tower monument to commemorate the victory. It was placed on the remaining hill of Dorchester Heights. In 1976 the city of Boston transferred the monument to the National Park Service as part of Boston National Historical Park. The Dorchester Heights Soldiers Monument stands in city-owned Thomas Park.

DIRECTIONS: From I 93, take Exit 19 onto Broadway eastbound to G Street, then go south on G Street about 0.25 mile to South Boston High School. Thomas Park and Dorchester Heights Soldiers Monument is to the west of the high school (Figure 54).

PUBLIC USE: Season and hours: *Grounds:* Dawn–dusk daily. *Monument:* Mid-June–August, open on a limited schedule.

49. BOSTON NATIONAL HISTORICAL PARK

BOSTON, MASSACHUSETTS

Following the British retreat from Boston, General Washington inspected the city briefly. It was not until his presidential tour in 1789 that he spent much time there. Boston's rich revolutionary history, however, is delineated at Boston National Historical Park, a combination of many sites that provide a comprehensive view of Boston's role in our revolutionary heritage. Three — Bunker Hill Monument, the Charlestown Navy Yard, and Dorchester Heights — are owned by the federal government, while Faneuil Hall, Old North Church, Old South Meeting House, Old State House, the Paul Revere House, and others are either privately owned or managed by the City of Boston. Boston National Historical Park represents a significant cooperative effort between federal, state, municipal, and private enterprises to provide the public with an overview of one city's important contribution to American history. The National Park Service administers the complex.

PUBLIC USE: Season and hours: *National Park visitor centers (downtown and Charlestown Navy Yard):* 9 AM–5 PM daily. Most historic sites are open 9:30–5 PM during the peak season and 10 AM–4 PM during the off season. Closed Thanksgiving Day, Christmas Day, New Year's Day. **Admission fee:** There is no fee at the federally owned sites but fees may be collected at privately owned and operated sites.

FOR ADDITIONAL INFORMATION: Contact: Boston National Historical Park Visitor Center, 15 State Street, Boston, Massachusetts 02113; 617-242-5642 *or* Superintendent, Boston National Historical Park, Charlestown Navy Yard, Boston, Massachusetts 02129-4543; 617-242-5644. **Web site:** *www.nps.gov/bost/.* **Read:** (1) Donald Barr Chidsey. 1966. *The Siege of Boston.* (2) Brendan Morrissey. 1994. *Boston 1775.* (3) Barbara Clark Smith. 1998. *Boston and the American Revolution.*

49-1. THE FREEDOM TRAIL

The Freedom Trail is a 2½-mile walking tour of sixteen important sites and structures that represent the historical and cultural heritage of Boston (Figure 55). The trail winds through the Italian neighborhood of the North End, the "Old Boston" of Beacon Hill, and the Irish community of Charlestown, touching places familiar to every American — the Old North Church where two lanterns in the steeple sent Paul Revere on a ride to warn patriots that the British were coming by sea; Paul Reveres House, the oldest wooden structure in Boston; Old Ironsides, the oldest commissioned warship afloat in the world; the Bunker Hill Monument that commemorates the first major battle of the Revolution; and the Old South Meeting House where the Boston Tea Party was planned. The Freedom Trail, administered by the National Park Service, is a walk not only through history but through the ethnic melting pot that is Boston.

The trail begins at Boston Common, the oldest public park in the United States, used by the English colonists from 1634 as a "cow pasture and training field" for the militia, and where British soldiers mustered before the Battle of Bunker Hill in 1775. The Arlington Avenue entrance to the park is enhanced by Thomas Ball's larger-than-life bronze equestrian statue of George Washington. A number of sites on the Freedom Trail were visited by George Washington when he was in Boston during his presidential tour in 1789. National Park Service rangers conduct guided tours of the downtown portion of the Freedom Trail daily, from mid-April through November. **Read:** Charles Bahne. 1993. *Complete Guide to Boston's Freedom Trail.*

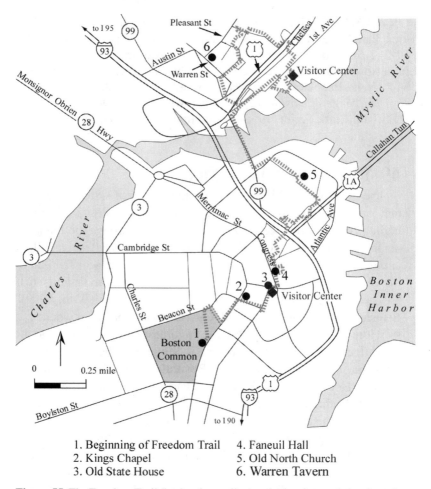

1. Beginning of Freedom Trail   4. Faneuil Hall
2. Kings Chapel   5. Old North Church
3. Old State House   6. Warren Tavern

Figure 55. The Freedom Trail (broken heavy line) and other featured sites in and near the center of Boston, Massachusetts.

49-2. KINGS CHAPEL

The first Anglican Church in Boston, dating to 1754, became America's first Unitarian church after the Revolution. The light and airy interior designed by Peter Harrison is considered one of the most beautiful in the United States. Governors, prominent citizens, and many of the founders of Massachusetts are interred in Kings Chapel Burying Ground adjoining the church. President Washington attended an oratorio at Kings Chapel on October 27, 1789.

Plate 1. *George Washington Birthplace National Monument, Washingtons Birthplace, Virginia.*

Plate 2. *Saint Pauls Episcopal Church, King George, Virginia.*

Plate 3. *Historic Kenmore, Fredericksburg, Virginia.*

Plate 4. *River Farm, Alexandria, Virginia.*

Plate 5. *Natural Bridge, Natural Bridge, Virginia.*

Plate 6. *Raleigh Tavern, Williamsburg, Virginia.*

Plate 7. *Rodgers Tavern, Perryville, Maryland.*

Plate 8. *Longfellow National Historic Site, Cambridge, Massachusetts.*

Plate 9. *Ford Mansion, Morristown National Historical Park, Morristown, New Jersey.*

Plate 10. *Valley Forge National Historical Park, Valley Forge, Pennsylvania.*

Plate 11. *Great Falls Park, Great Falls, Virginia.*

Plate 12. *Harpers Ferry National Historical Park, Harpers Ferry, West Virginia.*

Plate 13. *Lee House National Historic Landmark, Marblehead, Massachusetts.*

Plate 14. *The Old Exchange Building and Provost Dungeon, Charleston, South Carolina.*

Plate 15. *John Rutledge House Inn, Charleston, South Carolina.*

Plate 16. *Mount Rushmore National Memorial, Keystone, South Dakota.*

PUBLIC USE: Season and hours: May–October, Tuesday–Saturday, 10 AM–4 PM. November–April, Tuesday–Friday, 10 AM–2 PM; Saturday, 10 AM–4 PM. **For people with disabilities:** Accessible.

FOR ADDITIONAL INFORMATION: Contact: Kings Chapel, 58 Tremont Street, Boston, Massachusetts, 02113; 617-227-2155.

49-3. OLD STATE HOUSE

The Old State House (Figure 56), the oldest public building in Boston, stands on the site of the first Boston Town House that burned in 1711. Rebuilt in 1713, the new building featured a merchants' exchange on the ground floor with government offices on the second. On March 4, 1770, five American colonists were killed across the street when a squad of British regulars clashed with an unruly mob of citizens, an action that became known as the Boston Massacre.

Figure 56. The Old State House, Boston, Massachusetts. (Photograph courtesy of National Park Service)

The State House's proudest moment occurred when President George Washington reviewed a parade of citizens from its steps. A commemorative plaque states:

> *In celebration of America's independence, President George Washington's triumphal visit to the Old State House marked the transition of Massachusetts from Colony to Commonwealth and the emergence of a new nation. Despite the many changes it has since witnessed, the Old State House survives today as a revered symbol of American independence and freedom.*[79]

The state government moved to Beacon Hill in 1798 and the Old State House underwent several lives as retail stores, Boston's City Hall, and commercial office space. It was saved from destruction in 1881 by The Bostonian Society, a group of determined citizens who restored the building and manage it today as Boston's History Museum. A reference library on the third floor contains over 6000 volumes and 20,000 photographic views of Boston.

PUBLIC USE: Season and hours: 9:30 AM–5 PM daily. Closed Easter Sunday, Thanksgiving Day, Christmas Day, and New Year's Day. **Admission fee. Gift shop. For people with disabilities:** First floor accessible.

FOR ADDITIONAL INFORMATION: Contact: Old State House, 206 Washington Street, Boston, Massachusetts 02113; 617-720-3290.

49-4. FANEUIL HALL

Huguenot merchant Peter Faneuil marked his financial success by building a central food market as the hub of his commercial empire in 1742. Faneuil Hall included an open-air market on the ground level and a large room for town meetings on the second floor — a marketplace for food on one level and a marketplace for ideas on another. As Francis Hatch wrote:

> *Here orators in ages past*
> *Have mounted their attacks*
> *Undaunted by proximity*
> *Of sausage on the racks.* [80]

The Marquis de Lafayette called Faneuil Hall "The Cradle of Liberty," as it was the scene of many dramatic meetings during the revolutionary movement. The present hall, doubled in size since colonial days, remains an active gathering place for Bostonians where restaurants and food stalls serve thousands each day. An upstairs meeting room contains paintings of revolutionary battles and the third floor houses the museum and armory of the Ancient and Honorable Artillery Company of Massachusetts, a military company founded in 1638 for the defense of the Colony. President Washington dined at Faneuil Hall during his New England tour.

PUBLIC USE: Season and hours: *Museum:* 10 AM–4 PM daily. Closed Thanksgiving Day, Christmas Day, and New Year's Day. *Second floor meeting room:* 9 AM–5 PM daily. **For people with disabilities:** Accessible.

FOR ADDITIONAL INFORMATION: Contact: Faneuil Hall, Merchants Row, Boston, Massachusetts 02113; 617-242-5642.

49-5. OLD NORTH CHURCH

Old North dates to 1723, the oldest church in Boston — one of the few remaining examples of the Georgian style made famous by Christopher Wren. Old North is a rare and beautiful building where art, history, and faith converge, its interior flooded with light from magnificent arched windows. The steeple of Old North Church is where sexton Robert Newman hung the lanterns that signaled Paul Revere to begin the ride that ignited the Revolutionary War. A new steeple was erected in 1955, but the window from which the signal lanterns flashed was retrieved and incorporated into the new tower.

PUBLIC USE: Season and hours: 9 AM–5 PM daily. **Gift shop. For people with disabilities:** Accessible.

FOR ADDITIONAL INFORMATION: Contact: Old North Church, 193 Salem Street, Boston, Massachusetts 02113; 617-523-6676.

50. GOVERNOR STEPHEN HOPKINS HOUSE

PROVIDENCE, RHODE ISLAND

A red clapboard house with an eighteenth-century parterre garden was the home of Stephen Hopkins, ten-time governor of Rhode Island, and a signer of the Declaration of Independence. As he inscribed his name to the Declaration, he said, "My hand trembles, but my heart does not."[81]

Hopkins entertained George Washington in his home twice, once following the British evacuation of Boston in 1776 and later when Washington was in the Rhode Island Colony to confer with French general Rochambeau. The house is owned by the state of Rhode Island and administered by the Colonial Dames of America.

DIRECTIONS: From I 195, take Exit 2 to Benefit Street northbound

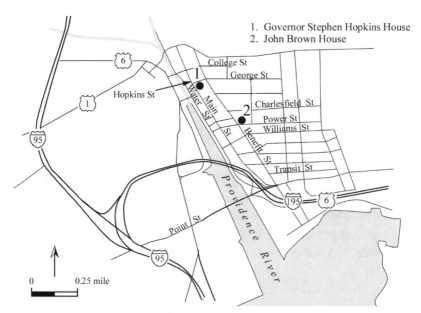

Figure 57. The location of the Governor Stephen Hopkins House and John Brown House in Providence, Rhode Island.

and go about 0.75 mile to the house at the corner of Benefit and Hopkins streets (Figure 57).

PUBLIC USE: Season and hours: April–December 1, Wednesday–Saturday, 1 PM–4 PM. **Admission fee. For people with disabilities:** Not accessible.

FOR ADDITIONAL INFORMATION: Contact: Governor Stephen Hopkins House, 15 Hopkins Street, Providence, Rhode Island 02903; 401-751-7067. **Web site:** *www.ritourism.com.*

51. Governor Jonathan Trumbull House, Wadsworth Stable, and The War Office
Lebanon, Connecticut

Jonathan Trumbull, Governor of Connecticut during the Revolutionary War, was purported to be the only colonial governor who supported the rebellion. Trumbull served as a counselor to George Washington, and Washington used the governor's residence to hold strategy sessions. A small dependency was called The War Office. Wadsworth Stable was the home for Washington's horse, Nelson.

The Trumbull House, built in 1735, is a red clapboard house with a number of unusual design features and is furnished in period. The Trumbull House and Wadsworth Stable are owned and maintained by the Daughters of the American Revolution while the War Office is a property of the Sons of the American Revolution.

DIRECTIONS: From the intersection of SR 207 and SR 87 in Lebanon, go west on SR 207 1 block, then north on West Town Street about 0.05 mile to the Trumbull house, stable, and war office (Figure 58).

PUBLIC USE: Season and hours: *The War Office:* June–August, Saturday–Sunday, 1–4 PM. *Trumbull House:* Mid-May–mid-October, Tuesday–Saturday, 1 PM–5 PM. **Admission fee. For people with disabilities:** Accessible.

FOR ADDITIONAL INFORMATION: Contact: Governor Jonathan Trumbull House, 169 West Town Street, Lebanon, Connecticut 06249; 860-642-7558. **Web site:** *www.erols.com/shawnmcf/ctdar/dar.htm.*

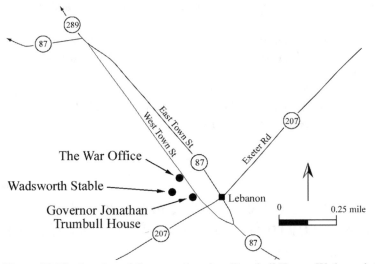

Figure 58. The location of Governor Jonathan Trumbull House, Wadsworth Stable, and The War Office in Lebanon, Connecticut.

52. SHAW MANSION

NEW LONDON, CONNECTICUT

The impressive Shaw Mansion, a three-story granite building of Georgian design, was constructed by sea captain Nathaniel Shaw in 1756. His son was New London's marine agent during the revolution and the house served as Connecticut's Naval Office. George Washington visited the Shaw home for conferences and remained overnight on April 9, 1776, during his journey from Boston to New York. The Shaw Mansion is currently the home of the New London Historical Society that conducts guided tours with an emphasis on the West Indian trade and the history of early New London.

DIRECTIONS: From I 95, take Exit 84 and go south on Huntington Street, which becomes Tilley Street, to a dead end at Bank Street, then

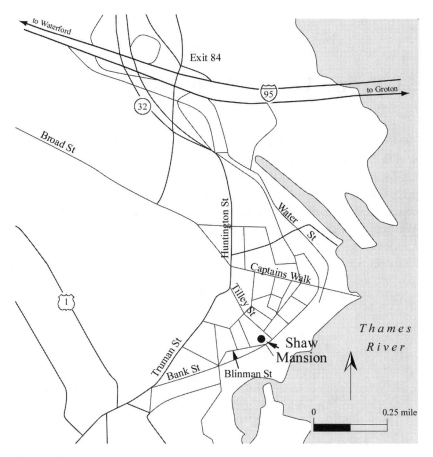

Figure 59. The location of Shaw Mansion, New London, Connecticut.

go west on Bank Street to Blinman Street, then go west on Blinman and Shaw Mansion at #11, immediately on the right (Figure 59).

PUBLIC USE: Season and hours: Guided tours are conducted Wednesday–Friday, 1–4 PM; Saturday, 10 AM–4 PM. Closed major holidays. **Admission fee. Gift shop. For people with disabilities:** Only the first floor is accessible.

FOR ADDITIONAL INFORMATION: Contact: Shaw Mansion, 11 Blinman Street, New London, Connecticut 06320; 860-443-1209. **Web site:** *www.newlondongazette.com/newlondongazette.html.*

53. EMPIRE-FULTON FERRY STATE PARK

BROOKLYN, NEW YORK

George Washington's first major defeat in the Revolutionary War was at the Battle of Long Island on August 27, 1776, wherein the Americans were outflanked by British General Howe. Howe failed to immediately follow up the victory, however, an error that allowed the Americans to escape to Manhattan Island. The retreat, in retrospect, was one of Washington's great military coups as, under cover of darkness and fog, he moved his army across the East River to safety, ready to fight again. The debarkation spot (and legend has it that the General was the last man

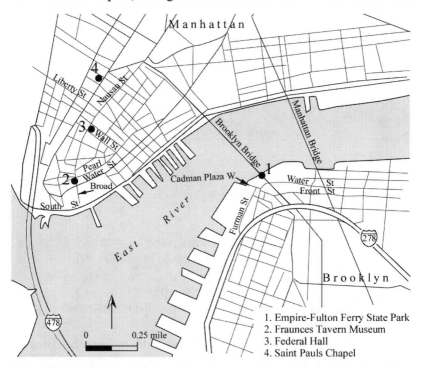

1. Empire-Fulton Ferry State Park
2. Fraunces Tavern Museum
3. Federal Hall
4. Saint Pauls Chapel

Figure 60. The location of featured sites in western Long Island and southern Manhattan, New York City, New York.

to leave Brooklyn) is in a nine-acre riverside park located under the supports of the Brooklyn Bridge. The park features a boardwalk that enables strollers to enjoy a magnificent view of downtown Manhattan or to watch ships traverse the East River. A plaque marks the area where General Washington and his army embarked for the safety of Manhattan Island.

DIRECTIONS: From Cadman Plaza, walk westbound on Cadman Plaza West to Water Street, then go right on Water to New Dock, then go left to the East River (Figure 60).

FOR ADDITIONAL INFORMATION: Empire-Fulton Ferry State Park, 26 New Dock Avenue, Brooklyn, New York 11215; 718-858-4708. **Read:** (1) Eric I. Manders. 1978. *The Battle of Long Island.* (2) John J. Gallagher. 1995. *The Battle of Brooklyn, 1776.*

54. MORRIS-JUMEL MANSION
NEW YORK, NEW YORK

The Morris-Jumel Mansion, built around 1765, is one of New York's oldest houses, the most important surviving landmark of the Battle of Harlem Heights (Figure 61). Roger Morris's Georgian masterpiece, appropriated as headquarters by General Washington following the retreat from Long Island, is preserved as a house museum filled with Colonial, Federal, and American Empire furniture. It is maintained by the Historic House Trust of New York City, a not-for-profit organization created to preserve and promote sixteen historic house museums located in New York City parks.

DIRECTIONS: The Morris-Jumel Mansion is within Roger Morris Park, bounded by 160th and 162nd streets, Edgecomb Avenue and Jumel Terrace in northern Manhattan (Figure 62).

PUBLIC USE: Season and hours: Tuesday–Sunday, 10 AM–4 PM. Closed major holidays. **Admission fee. Gift shop. For people with disabilities:** There are five steps into the mansion. The second floor of the house is not accessible, although an orientation film showing the second floor is available.

FOR ADDITIONAL INFORMATION: Contact: Morris-Jumel Mansion, 65 Jumel Terrace, New York, New York 10032; 212-923-8008.

Figure 61. Morris-Jumel Mansion, New York, New York.

Web site: *www.nychistory.org.* **Read:** (1) Bruce Bliven, Jr. 1956. *Battle for Manhattan.* (2) Constance Greiss. 1995. *Morris-Jumel Mansion: A Documentary History.*

55. VAN CORTLANDT HOUSE MUSEUM
BRONX, NEW YORK

Van Cortlandt House (Figure 63) has stood since 1748 as a symbol of New York City's colonial past — at that time a prosperous estate with lush fields, livestock, grist mill, and a resident community of craftsmen and farm workers who exemplified plantation life in the Lower Hudson Valley. During the Revolutionary War, the house sat near or behind enemy lines and George Washington used it as headquarters twice. The Van Cortlandt House is operated by the National Society of Colonial Dames as a house museum furnished with decorative arts and family collections from the Colonial and Federal periods. Today's visitors tour the family's

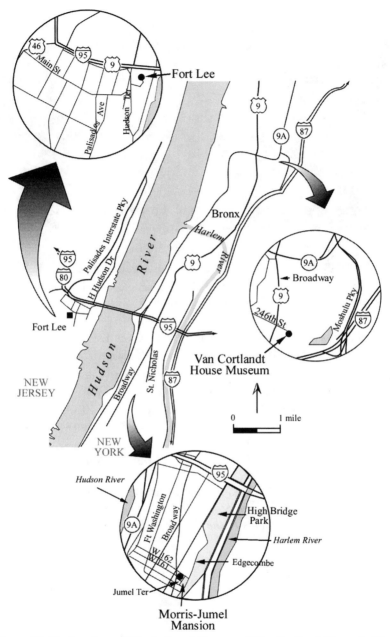

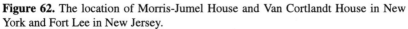

Figure 62. The location of Morris-Jumel House and Van Cortlandt House in New York and Fort Lee in New Jersey.

235

Figure 63. Washingtons Headquarters, Van Cortlandt House Museum, New York, New York. (Photograph by William G. Clotworthy)

formal and private rooms as well as the kitchen and slave bedchamber, a tour that shows the diverse family life of those who lived there.

DIRECTIONS: Van Cortlandt House Museum lies within Van Cortlandt Park at US 9 (Broadway) and 246th Street (Figure 62).

PUBLIC USE: Season and hours: Tuesday–Friday, 10 AM–3 PM; Saturday–Sunday, 11 AM–4 PM. Closed holidays. **Admission fee. Gift shop. For people with disabilities:** Restricted.

FOR ADDITIONAL INFORMATION: Contact: Van Cortlandt House Museum, Broadway at 246th Street, Bronx, New York 10471; 718-543-3344. **Web site:** *www.nychistory.org.* **Read:** Gordon P. Stillman. 1996. *100 Years in New York, the Story of the First Century of the National Society of Colonial Dames in the State of New York.*

56. WASHINGTONS HEADQUARTERS MUSEUM
NORTH WHITE PLAINS, NEW YORK

George Washington used the farmhouse of Elijah Miller as headquarters when directing the final engagements of the Battle of White Plains in October, 1776. The table and chairs used by Washington have been preserved, and remains of defensive earthworks are visible on the hill behind the house, supposedly where the last artillery shots of the battle were fired. The house, built in 1738, is of a style common to the area in the eighteenth century — a simple, one-story frame building bespeaking the sparseness of the times, with several small rooms, a buttery, sloping roof, and front porch. A sycamore tree in the front has been a witness to history for over 300 years. The Miller House is owned by Westchester County which uses it as a center for educational programs designed to bring the lifestyle of the eighteenth century alive through hands-on interpretive programs.

DIRECTIONS: From the Bronx River Parkway in North White Plains, exit onto Virginia Road northbound for about 1 mile to the Miller House (Figure 64).

PUBLIC USE: Season and hours: Open by appointment only, except for monthly living history programs. Call for schedule. **For people with disabilities:** Accessible.

FOR ADDITIONAL INFORMATION: Contact: Washingtons Headquarters Museum, 140 Virginia Road, North White Plains, New York 10603; 845-949-1236. **Web site:** *www.westchesterny.com.*

57. THE PURDY HOUSE
WHITE PLAINS, NEW YORK

There is controversy within White Plains historical circles regarding the location of Washington's Headquarters during the Battle of White

Plains. Some say it was the Miller farmhouse while the White Plains Historical Society insists it was the 1721 Purdy House on the crest of Purdy Hill facing Chatterton Hill, across the Bronx River from the battle site. According to the historical society, Washington used Purdy's house from October 23rd to October 31st, prior to and during the battle. The following year, 1778, he used it from July 27th to September 16th, when he anticipateed a British assault on New York City. The Purdy House is a simple 1½-story, shingled building furnished in period.

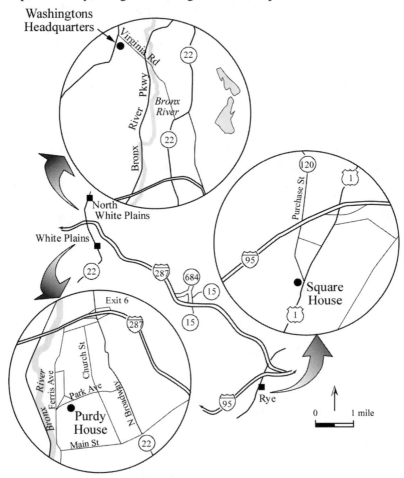

Figure 64. The location of Washingtons Headquarters Museum in North White Plains, Purdy House in White Plains, and Square House in Rye, New York.

DIRECTIONS: From I 287 (Cross-Westchester Parkway), take Exit 6 onto North Broadway southbound to Park Avenue, then go west on Park about 1 mile to the Purdy House (Figure 64).

PUBLIC USE: Season and hours: The Purdy House is open by appointment only. **For people with disabilities:** Accessible.

FOR ADDITIONAL INFORMATION: Contact: The Purdy House, 60 Park Avenue, White Plains, New York 10603; 914-328-1776. **Web site:** *www.westchesterny.com.*

58. FORT LEE HISTORIC PARK

FORT LEE, NEW JERSEY

Fort Lee, named for General Charles Lee, was a major link in the American fortifications that defended New York City and the Hudson River. Late in 1776, after the Continental Army had been defeated at Long Island, New York City, and White Plains, Americans remained in control of only two forts in the area — Fort Lee, west of the Hudson River in New Jersey, and Fort Washington, directly across the Hudson, in Manhattan. On November 16th, Fort Washington fell to an overwhelming British assault which left Fort Lee isolated and vulnerable.

A few days after Fort Washington was captured, British General Cornwallis led an expeditionary force across the Hudson River five miles north of Fort Lee, a move that forced Washington's army to abandon the fort and retreat across New Jersey into Pennsylvania. The loss of the two forts was a major blow to the revolutionary cause, a defeat that inspired Thomas Paine's famous words, "These are the times that try men's souls."[82]

A replica of Fort Lee has been constructed fourteen miles east of its original location, with earthworks and redans built on the dramatic palisades close to the New Jersey side of the George Washington Bridge. Fort Lee Historic Park, in which the reconstruction is located, blends history and scenic beauty, and a visitor center with two floors of audio-visual displays, detailed exhibits, and a short film, provides dramatic background to the role of Fort Lee in the revolution. The Palisades Interstate

Park Commission operates Fort Lee Historic Park.

Fort Washington is now Fort Washington Park, a New York City recreation facility at 170th Street and the Hudson River.

DIRECTIONS: From I 95 at the west end of the George Washington Bridge, take the Fort Lee Exit . Bear right down the ramp and turn right at the light. The entrance is 50 feet beyond the next light. From US 4/46 and I 80/95, take the exit for Fort Lee/Palisades Interstate Parkway and proceed on Bridge Plaza southbound past five traffic lights. At the next light, turn right onto Hudson Terrace. The park entrance is 50 feet south on the left side (Figure 62).

PUBLIC USE: Season and hours: March–December, 9 AM–5 PM. Closed Monday and Tuesday. **Admission fee:** There is a parking fee in the summer. **Museum. Visitor center. For people with disabilities:** Accessible.

FOR ADDITIONAL INFORMATION: Contact: Fort Lee Historic Park, Hudson Terrace, Fort Lee, New Jersey 07024; 201-461-1776. **Web site:** *www.fieldtrip.com/nj.* **Read:** Earl Schenck Miers. 1971. *Crossroads of Freedom.*

59. HISTORIC SUMMERSEAT

MORRISVILLE, PENNSYLVANIA

Summerseat, built in 1760, is a sturdy eight-room colonial house used as a summer home for wealthy Philadelphians. General Washington lived at Summerseat from December 8 to 14, 1776, just prior to the dramatic crossing of the Delaware River on Christmas Day. Summerseat was owned at different times by Robert Morris and George Clymer, men who signed both the Declaration of Independence and the Constitution. Furnished in period, Historic Summerseat is owned and operated as a colonial house museum by the Historic Morrisville Society.

DIRECTIONS: From US 1 in Morrisville, go north on Pennsylvania Avenue to Hillcrest Avenue, go west on Hillcrest to Legion Avenue, then go south on Legion to Historic Summerseat (Figure 65).

PUBLIC USE: Season and hours: Open the first Saturday of each month, 9 AM–2 PM. **For people with disabilities:** The first floor is accessible after three steps into home.

FOR ADDITIONAL INFORMATION: Contact: Historic Summerseat, Hillcrest and Legion Avenues, Morrisville, Pennsylvania 19067; 215-295-7339.

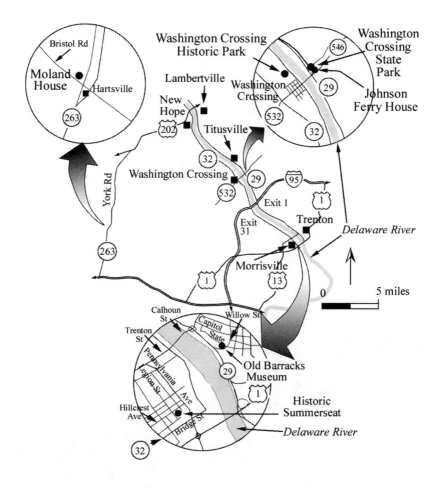

Figure 65. The location of featured sites along the Delaware River in New Jersey and Pennsylvania.

241

60. WASHINGTON CROSSING HISTORIC PARK

WASHINGTON CROSSING, PENNSYLVANIA

In the winter of 1776, the Continental Army was in disarray. A sense of foreboding settled on George Washington as he led a retreat from New Jersey into Pennsylvania. Harsh weather conditions and the lack of supplies and civilian support were eroding army morale. A victory was needed desperately, so Washington and his staff devised a bold plan to cross the Delaware River and attack the Hessian barracks at Trenton, a small but strategically situated city in New Jersey. On Christmas Night, 1776, 2400 men crossed the river near McConkey's Ferry (Figure 66) to begin a march that culminated in a successful assault on Trenton, a victory that re-ignited the flame of freedom and gave new life to the American Revolution.

Figure 66. New Jersey as seen across the Delaware River from Washington Crossing Historic Park, Washington Crossing, Pennsylvania. (Photograph by William G. Clotworthy)

Washington Crossing is where the Continental Army embarked for New Jersey that fateful Christmas night and where a 500-acre Pennsylvania State Park is now dedicated to the memory of George Washington and the tiny army that accomplished so much. The park, connected to New Jersey's Washington Crossing State Park by the Titusville Bridge, consists of two sections, Thompsons Mill and McConkeys Ferry. The Thompsons Mill section to the north features a wildflower preserve with natural history exhibits, Bowmans Hill Tower with a commanding view of the Delaware Valley, and the Thompson-Neely House, built in 1702. Recognized as a fine example of early eighteenth-century colonial architecture, the home of Robert and Hannah Thompson served as headquarters for American general Lord Stirling who was in charge of troops stationed along the Delaware to prevent the British from crossing that river.

The McConkey Ferry Inn, a restored stone house in which Washington and his officers ate Christmas dinner prior to the crossing, centers the McConkeys Ferry section on the south. A memorial building serving as a visitor center features exhibits and a film that depicts the crossing. The McConkeys Ferry section also contains restored homes and a grist mill, a general store, and blacksmith shop. The Washington Crossing Park Commission, in conjunction with the Pennsylvania Historical and Museum Commission and the Washington Crossing Foundation, administers Washington Crossing Historic Park. Several of the historic buildings provide demonstrations of colonial crafts such as spinning, weaving, and blacksmithing. The Bowman Hill Wildflower Preserve features miles of trails and a variety of programs, special events, and exhibits.

DIRECTIONS: Washington Crossing Historic Park is located on SR 32 immediately north of Washington Crossing, Pennsylvania (Figure 65).

PUBLIC USE: Season and hours: Monday–Saturday, 9 AM–5 PM; Sunday, 12 N–5 PM. Closed certain holidays, except Memorial Day, July 4, and Labor Day. **Admission fee. Visitor center. Gift shop. For people with disabilities:** The first floors of the historic houses are accessible. Books describing the second floors are available.

FOR ADDITIONAL INFORMATION: Contact: Washington Crossing Historic Park, 1112 River Road, Box 103, Washington Crossing, Pennsylvania 18977; 215-493-4076. **Read:** Robert Leckie. 1992. *George Washington's War.*

61. WASHINGTON CROSSING STATE PARK

TITUSVILLE, NEW JERSEY

General Washington picked the Christmas Day embarkation and landing places carefully. The area was remote and would hopefully allow the army to cross the Delaware River without detection. After crossing the ice-choked river, the Americans landed in New Jersey eight miles above Trenton. After a short rest, the army marched to Trenton over Continental Lane, now part of Washington Crossing State Park, an 850-acre state park established by New Jersey in 1912 and dedicated to the memory of Washington's army and their heroics.

A modern visitor center, dedicated in 1976 as part of our country's bicentennial celebration, contains collections and displays that interpret the "Ten Critical Days" — December 24, 1776, through January 3, 1777 — the successful assault on Trenton through the subsequent victory at Princeton. The visitor center also houses the Swan Collection of the American Revolution, an impressive collection of authentic Revolutionary War artifacts interpreting the critical events leading up to and during the Battle of Trenton. Each Christmas Day, a group of dedicated history buffs in period uniforms reenacts the historic event of 1776 by crossing the Delaware in replicas of the famous flat-bottomed Durham Boats used by the Continental Army.

DIRECTIONS: Washington Crossing State Park is located on SR 29 immediately north of SR 546 and Washington Crossing, New Jersey (Figure 65).

PUBLIC USE: Season and hours: *Grounds:* Memorial Day–Labor Day, 8 AM–8 PM; Labor Day-Memorial Day, 8 AM–4:30 PM. *Visitor center:* Wednesday–Sunday, 9 AM–4 PM. **Admission fee:** Parking. **For people with disabilities:** Visitor center accessible.

FOR ADDITIONAL INFORMATION: Contact: Washington Crossing State Park, Route 546, 355 Washington Crossing Penn Road, Titusville, New Jersey 08560; 609-737-0623. **Web site:** *www.fieldtrip.com/nj.* **Read:** Ann Hawkes Hutton. 1983. *Portrait of Patriotism: Washington Crossing the Delaware.*

62. JOHNSON FERRY HOUSE STATE HISTORIC SITE

TITUSVILLE, NEW JERSEY

A small stone tavern at the north end of Continental Lane sheltered General Washington after the crossing of the Delaware River. Built around 1740, it has been restored and furnished with local period pieces as in the "keeping" room and bedroom. The site includes a kitchen garden and an orchard with fruit trees representative of the eighteenth century. Living history demonstrations of foodways, textiles, woodworking, and early American music are frequently held on summer weekends.

DIRECTIONS: Johnson Ferry House is located on SR 29 immediately north of SR 546 and Washington Crossing, New Jersey (Figure 65).

PUBLIC USE: Season and hours: Wednesday–Saturday, 10 AM–4 PM; Sunday, 1 PM–4 PM. Closed holidays. **For people with disabilities:** Accessible.

FOR ADDITIONAL INFORMATION: Contact: Johnson Ferry House State Historic Site, Washington Crossing State Park, Titusville, New Jersey 08560; 609-737-2515.

63. OLD BARRACKS MUSEUM

TRENTON, NEW JERSEY

The British colonial barracks at Trenton (Figure 67) was manned by a contingent of Hessian mercenaries when George Washington led his troops in a surprise attack the day after Christmas, 1776 — a daring raid that was an important military and psychological victory for the patriots. Twenty-one Hessians were killed and over nine hundred taken prisoner while American losses were slight — only four or five men were wounded, one of whom was Lieutenant James Monroe, the future fifth president of the United States.

Figure 67. Old Barracks Museum, Trenton, New Jersey. (Photograph by William G. Clotworthy)

One hundred years after the battle, the unused barracks was in a state of deterioration. A determined group of ladies who called themselves The Purchase Fund, later incorporated as the Old Barracks Association, persuaded the State of New Jersey to acquire the barracks building and repair it. The reconstructed building, owned by the state, is managed by the Old Barracks Association. A cultural history museum contains rooms with eighteenth-century furnishings and there is a restored squad room where costumed interpreters portray New Jersey residents of the revolutionary period.

DIRECTIONS: Old Barracks Museum is located on Barrack Street adjacent to the New Jersey State House. From I 95, take Exit 1 onto SR 29 southbound to the Willow/Barrack Exit, exit onto Willow and go about 0.25 mile to the New Jersey State House and Old Barracks Museum on the west side of the street (Figure 65).

PUBLIC USE: Season and hours: 10 AM–5 PM daily. Closed Thanksgiving Day, Christmas Eve Day, Christmas Day, New Year's Day, and Easter Sunday. **Admission fee. Gift shop. For people with disabilities:** Fully accessible.

FOR ADDITIONAL INFORMATION: Contact: Old Barracks Museum, Barrack Street, Trenton, New Jersey 08608; 609-396-1776. **Web site:** *www.barracks.org.* **Read:** (1) William M. Dwyer. 1983. *The Day is Ours! An Inside View at the Battles of Trenton and Princeton, November 1776–January 1777.* (2) Martin McPhillips. 1985. *The Battle of Trenton.*

64. PRINCETON BATTLEFIELD STATE PARK

PRINCETON, NEW JERSEY

A week after victory at Trenton, General Washington pressed his military and psychological advantage with yet another surprise attack, this on a British outpost at Princeton, New Jersey. The initial thrust was driven back, but Washington rallied his troops and drove off the enemy. With superior British reinforcements rushing to the battlefield, however, Washington wisely decided to withdraw. Significant American losses were incurred at Princeton, but the twin victories at Trenton and Princeton helped restore army and civilian morale so essential to the flagging cause of independence.

Princeton Battlefield State Park commemorates the historic battle, part of the "Ten Critical Days," from Trenton to Princeton — a major turning point in the Revolution. During the battle, George Washington's close friend General Hugh Mercer, the physician from Fredericksburg, received seven bayonet wounds and was carried to the Thomas Clarke House where he expired, his death a crushing personal blow to General Washington. The Clarke House, built around 1770, is a 2½-story Georgian converted to a modern museum with three rooms on the first floor and four on the second, which are furnished with period pieces donated by local historical societies and private families. Several rooms contain military artifacts, exhibits, and a research library of eighteenth-century military, political, and domestic subjects. The State of New Jersey, Division of Environmental Protection, maintains Princeton Battlefield and the Clarke House.

In addition to the Princeton Battlefield State Park, the Village of Princeton honored the victory by commissioning a striking Battlefield Monument at the junction of Mercer, Stockton, and Nassau streets in the downtown area.

DIRECTIONS: Princeton Battlefield State Park is 3 miles south of Princeton on SR 583 (Princeton Pike; Mercer Street in Princeton) (Figure 68).

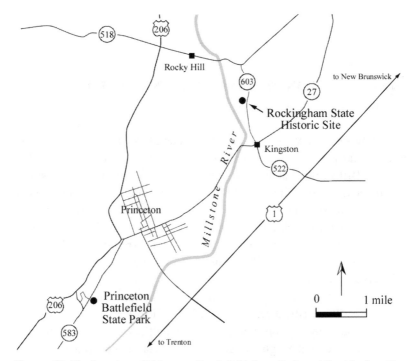

Figure 68. The location of Princeton Battlefield State Park and Rockingham State Historic Site in central New Jersey.

PUBLIC USE: Season and hours: *Grounds:* Dawn to dusk. *Clarke House:* Wednesday–Saturday, 10 AM–12 N and 1–4 PM; Sunday, 1–4 PM. **For people with disabilities:** The first floor of the Clarke House is accessible.

FOR ADDITIONAL INFORMATION: Contact: Princeton Battlefield State Park, 500 Mercer Road, Princeton, New Jersey 08542; 609-921-0074. **Read:** Richard Ketchum. 1973. *The Winter Soldiers.*

65. Morristown National Historical Park

Morristown, New Jersey

Morristown was the main encampment for the Continental Army from January through May, 1777, and again during the bitter winter of

1779–1780. The surrounding mountains afforded natural protection from the British but not from the elements — the army suffered terribly from cold, starvation, disease, and even mutiny.

Morristown National Historical Park was created in 1933, the first historic park authorized by Congress. It consists of three sections: Washington's Headquarters and Historical Museum and Library, Fort Nonsense, and the Jockey Hollow encampment area. During the first encampment, Washington resided at a tavern that no longer exists. His headquarters during the second encampment was the Ford Mansion (Plate 9), considered Morristown's finest home and generously offered to General and Mrs. Washington by Mrs. Jacob Ford, Jr., a widow with four small children. Innumerable meetings and discussions conducted by staff officers filled every day and every room, and forced the Ford family into two rooms of the house. It must have been a long winter for Mrs. Ford. The home, which dates to 1772, has been furnished to represent the time of Washington's residency. The adjoining museum and library houses 40,000 manuscripts and 20,000 printed works dealing with the revolutionary era and material relating to the Morristown encampments.

Fort Nonsense is the site of an earthern fort overlooking Morristown. The earthworks became known as Fort Nonsense due to a soldier's story that its only purpose was to keep the troops busy. Jockey Hollow, five miles west of the Ford House, was home to 10,000 soldiers of the Continental Army. Dogged by hunger and cold, the soldiers kept busy with drills, training and work details and spent their free time huddled around the fireplaces. Up to twelve men shared each of over 1,000 rude huts in Jockey Hollow. Today, Jockey Hollow contains trenches, redans, and five reconstructed huts. The park's museum is an important orientation point for the events that happened at Morristown. Exhibits of numerous military and other artifacts afford a glimpse of the Continental Army in winter quarters.

Washington Rock State Park in nearby Plainfield is a picturesque forty-five-acre park, just off SR 22. It is the site of a vantage point in the Watchung Mountains from which Washington's army at Morristown could observe British troop movements in the valley below. The lookout post is marked with a commemorative plaque.

DIRECTIONS: *Ford Mansion:* From I 287, take Exit 36 eastbound; the mansion is to the immediate north. *Fort Nonsense:* From I 287, take Exit

35 westbound on South Street 1 mile to Western Avenue, then go south on Western 0.1 mile to Ann Street and the entrance to Fort Nonsense. *Jockey Hollow:* From I 287, take Exit 33 westbound on Harter Road 1 mile, then go south on Mount Kemble Avenue about 2.5 miles to Glen Alpin Road, then go west on Glen Alpin about 1 mile to the Jockey Hollow Visitor Center (Figure 69).

PUBLIC USE: Season and hours: 9 AM–5 PM daily. Closed Thanksgiving Day, Christmas Day, and New Year's Day. **Admission fee. For people with disabilities:** Most exhibits, Jockey Hollow Visitor Center, and the Washington Headquarters Museum are accessible.

FOR ADDITIONAL INFORMATION: Contact: Morristown National Historical Park, Washington Place, Morristown, New Jersey 07960; 973-539-2085. **Web site:** *www.nps.gov/morr.* **Read:** (1) James Elliott Lindsley. 1874. *A Certain Splendid House.* (2) Joseph Plumb Martin. 1962. *Private Yankee Doodle, A Narration of Some of the Adventures, Dangers and Sufferings of a Revolutionary Soldier.* (3) Linda Grant DePauw. 1975. *Founding Mothers: Women in America in the Revolutionary Era.*

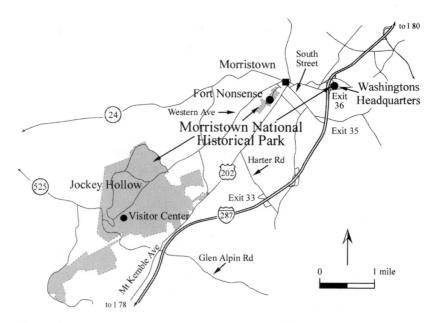

Figure 69. The location of Morristown National Historical Park, Morristown, New Jersey.

66. DRAKE HOUSE MUSEUM

PLAINFIELD, NEW JERSEY

George Washington stayed at the home of his friend, Reverend Nathaniel Drake, when planning and then fighting the Battle of Short Hills, June 25–27, 1777. The clapboard farmhouse, built in 1746, was a typical 1½-story building with four rooms and a loft. Considerable architectural changes including extensive additions have been effected over the last two centuries. The Drake House is headquarters for the Plainfield Historical Society that maintains the home's early ambience with colonial period furnishings and artifacts.

DIRECTIONS: From I 78, take Exit 40 eastbound on SR 531 to West Front Street, then go south on West Front Street 0.5 mile to the Drake House Museum on the west side of the street (Figure 70).

PUBLIC USE: Season and hours: Sunday, 2–4 PM except holidays. **For people with disabilities:** The first floor is accessible.

FOR ADDITIONAL INFORMATION: Contact: Drake House Museum, 602 West Front Street, Plainfield, New Jersey 07060; 908-755-5831.

Figure 70. The location of Drake House Museum, Plainfield, New Jersey.

67. HOLCOMBE-JIMISON FARMSTEAD MUSEUM

LAMBERTVILLE, NEW JERSEY

General Washington used this 1733 colonial farmhouse as headquarters from July 18 to July 31, 1777, and again on June 21 and 22, 1778. The house, barn, and other outbuildings have been transformed into a museum of colonial farming that features the extensive tools and equipment collection of the Hunterton County Historical Society. Holcombe-Jimison is owned and operated by the Holcombe-Jimison Farmstead Museum, Inc.

DIRECTIONS: The museum is on the east side of SR 29 about 0.2 mile north of US 202 (Figure 71).

PUBLIC USE: Season and hours: First Sunday in May to last Sunday in October, Sunday, 1–4 PM, Wednesday, 9 AM–12 N. **Admission fee. For people with disabilities:** All buildings are accessible with the exception of the third floor of the barn.

FOR ADDITIONAL INFORMATION: Contact: Holcombe-Jimison Farmstead Museum, 1605 Daniel Bray Highway, Box 588, Lambertville, New Jersey 08530; 609-397-2752.

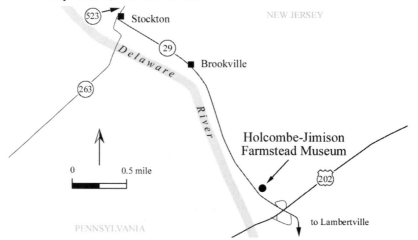
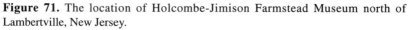

Figure 71. The location of Holcombe-Jimison Farmstead Museum north of Lambertville, New Jersey.

68. VAN ALLEN HOUSE

OAKLAND, NEW JERSEY

The Van Allen House, a small stone and clapboard farmhouse, was Washington's headquarters in August, 1777, when he received the distressing news that British General Burgoyne had captured Fort Ticonderoga. The house is owned by the city and operated as a colonial house museum by the Oakland Historic Society.

DIRECTIONS: From I 287, take Exit 58 northbound on Ramapo Valley Road 0.1 mile to Franklin Street, then go eastbound on Franklin 0.1 mile to the Van Allen House (Figure 72).

PUBLIC USE: Season and hours: Open the fourth Sunday of each month, 1–4 PM. **For people with disabilities:** Accessible.

FOR ADDITIONAL INFORMATION: Contact: Van Allen House, Oakland Historic Society, Franklin Avenue, Box 296, Oakland, New Jersey 07436; 201-337-3472.

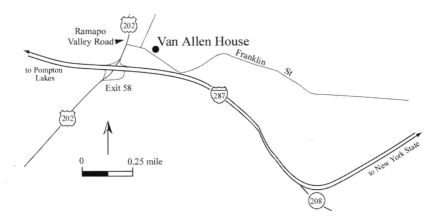

Figure 72. The location of Van Allen House, Oakland, New Jersey.

69. STEUBEN HOUSE

RIVER EDGE, NEW JERSEY

Baron von Steuben, purportedly a former Prussian army officer, joined George Washington at Valley Forge and is credited with bringing military discipline and European training methods to the Continental Army. After the war, a grateful nation presented von Steuben with a 1713 Bergen Dutch mansion as partial payment for his distinguished service. During the conflict itself, both Washington and Lord Cornwallis used the house as headquarters. Today the house displays the museum collection of the Bergen County Historical Society as well as artifacts from the area's 1650 New Jersey Dutch population.

DIRECTIONS: From SR 4, exit onto Hackensack Avenue northbound, go about 0.4 mile to Main Street, then go east on Main 0.25 mile to the Steuben House (Figure 73).

PUBLIC USE: Season and hours: Wednesday–Saturday, 10 AM–12 N and 1–5 PM; Sunday, 2–5 PM. Closed Thanksgiving Day, Christmas Day, and New Year's Day. **Gift shop. For people with disabilities:** The first floor is accessible.

FOR ADDITIONAL INFORMATION: Contact: Steuben House, 1209 Main Street, River Edge, New Jersey 07661; 201-487-1739.

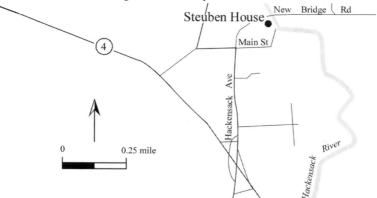

Figure 73. The location of Steuben House, River Edge, New Jersey.

70. RINGWOOD STATE PARK

RINGWOOD, NEW JERSEY

Mines in the Ramapo Mountains of New Jersey produced iron ore as early as 1740 and by the 1760s mines and forges were in full operation. Ironmaster Robert Erskine, Surveyor General for the Continental Army, owned some of the forges that produced munitions essential to the military effort. General George Washington stayed at Erskine's mansion, Ringwood Manor, during several inspection trips to the area.

The present Ringwood Manor dates to the middle of the nineteenth century. The structure is a grand masterpiece of seventy-eight rooms surrounded by lush, decorative gardens filled with impressive statuary. Twenty-one of the mansion's rooms have been restored and converted to a museum devoted to the life and career of Robert Erskine and to the history of the iron industry.

DIRECTIONS: From I 87 (New York State Thruway), take Exit 15 onto SR 17 northbound, go about 3 miles to Sterling Mine Road, then go

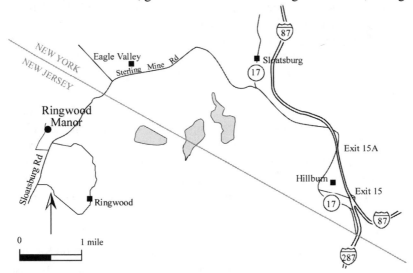

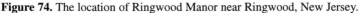

Figure 74. The location of Ringwood Manor near Ringwood, New Jersey.

west on Sterling Mine Road (which becomes Sloatsburg Road) for about 4 miles to Ringwood State Park (Figure 74).

PUBLIC USE: Season and hours: *Mansion:* Wednesday–Sunday, 10 AM–4 PM. *Grounds:* Dawn–dusk daily. **Visitor center. Gift shop. For people with disabilities:** The first floor of the mansion is accessible. A slide show shows the other floors.

FOR ADDITIONAL INFORMATION: Contact: Ringwood State Park, 1304 Sloatsburg Road, Ringwood, New Jersey 07456; 201-962-7031. **Web site:** *www.state.nj.us/dep/forestry.*

71. MOLAND HOUSE HISTORICAL PARK

HARTSVILLE, PENNSYLVANIA

In the summer of 1777, George Washington led his troops southward from the Morristown encampment, unsure of the intentions of British Commanding General Howe whose army had left New York City by sea, its destination unknown. On August 10th, Washington set up headquarters at the farmhouse of the widow Moland north of Philadelphia. On the 22nd, news arrived that Howe's fleet had been sighted on Chesapeake Bay. Washington, convinced that Philadelphia was Howe's intended target, left immediately to face that danger.

Legend has it that the American flag sewn by Betsy Ross was first flown at the Moland House, although it is but one of several locations that claim that honor. We do know that it was here that Washington was introduced to the Marquis de Lafayette, a newly arrived volunteer from France.

The Moland House, situated on a twelve-acre site, had been neglected through the years, but was acquired in 1996 by Warwick Township which initiated an ambitious refurbishing project conducted under the supervision of the Warwick Township Historical Society. As of 2002, the exterior of the house has been restored, although work on the interior plus reconstruction and repair of several outbuildings is estimated to take several more years.

DIRECTIONS: Hartsville is 20 miles north of Philadelphia on SR 263. The Moland House Historical Park is 1 block west of SR 263, north of Bristol Road (Figure 65).

PUBLIC USE: Season and hours: Open by appointment.

FOR ADDITIONAL INFORMATION: Contact: Warwick Township Historical Society, Moland House Historical Park, 1641 Old York Road, Hartsville, Pennsylvania 18974; 215-343-6439. **Web site:** *www.voicenet.com/~pstav.*

72. ELFRETHS ALLEY

PHILADELPHIA, PENNSYLVANIA

Elfreths Alley, which dates to 1702, is considered the oldest residential street in Philadelphia — a narrow, one-block-long, cobblestoned street containing thirty houses, none more than sixteen feet wide (Figure 75). Preserved by the Elfreths Alley Association and the residents, the

Figure 75. The western end of Elfreths Alley, Philadelphia, Pennsylvania. (Photograph by William G. Clotworthy)

homes reflect a mixture of urban, middle class architecture of the eighteenth and early nineteenth centuries. Number 126 Elfreths Alley is a "trinity" house with its single rooms, three-stories high. It has been combined with next door neighbor, number 124, to form a charming museum of colonial life with period furniture and changing exhibits.

As the British army moved toward Philadelphia from the Chesapeake in August, 1777, General George Washington, in an attempt to boost the morale of the city's populace, marched the Continental Army through Elfreths Alley on the way to engage the British south of the city.

DIRECTIONS: Elfreths Alley extends between 2nd Street and Front Street in central Philadelphia (Figure 48).

PUBLIC USE: Season and hours: *Museum:* March to December, Monday–Saturday, 10 AM–4 PM; Sunday, 12 N–4 PM. January and February, open weekends only. **Admission fee. Gift shop. For people with disabilities:** Accessible.

FOR ADDITIONAL INFORMATION: Contact: Elfreths Alley Association, 124–126 Elfreths Alley, Philadelphia, Pennsylvania 19106; 215-574-0560. **Web site:** *www.elfrethsalley.org.*

73. HALE-BYRNES HOUSE
NEWARK, DELAWARE

Potter Samuel Hale built a home workshop on the bank of Christina Creek around 1750, and later sold the house to Daniel Byrnes. The house is a fine example of eighteenth-century brick architecture, with back-to-back corner fireplaces and a large well-appointed kitchen fireplace. On September 3, 1777, George Washington held a council of war in the house with generals Lafayette and Wayne preceding the Battle of Brandywine. The Delaware Society for the Preservation of Antiquities operates the Hale-Byrnes House as a house-museum.

DIRECTIONS: From I 95, take Exit 4 onto SR 7 northbound to Stanton-Christiana Road, then go north on Stanton-Christiana Road to the Hale-Byrnes House on the east side of the road (Figure 76).

PUBLIC USE: Season and hours: Open by appointment only. **For people with disabilities:** Accessible.

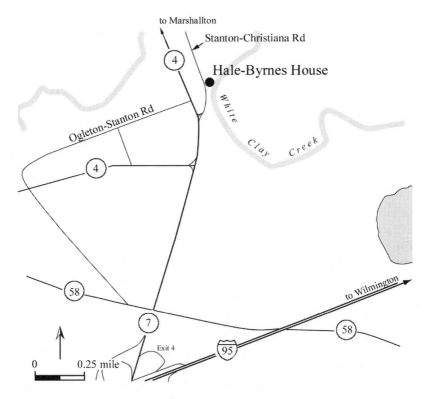

Figure 76. The location of Hale-Byrnes House, Newark, Delaware.

FOR ADDITIONAL INFORMATION: Contact: Hale-Byrnes House, 606 Stanton-Christiana Road, Newark, Delaware 19713; 302-998-3792. **Read:** John F. Reed. 1965. *Campaign to Valley Forge.*

74. BRANDYWINE BATTLEFIELD STATE PARK

CHADDS FORD, PENNSYLVANIA

In the Battle of Brandywine, fought on September 11, 1777, British General Howe outmaneuvered General Washington and only a last-minute defensive action by the forces of General Nathaneal Greene enabled the

Americans to retreat to safety in an orderly manner, preserving the army to fight another day. As a result of the defeat, however, Philadelphia was vulnerable to British occupation. On the other hand, the courageous stand of the Continental Army helped convince France to form an alliance with the colonials — a union that was instrumental in turning the tide of the conflict.

A fifty-acre state park contains the houses used as headquarters by George Washington and General Lafayette before and during the battle. Washington was quartered in an early eighteenth-century stone house that was later lost to fire, then rebuilt on the same site. Lafayette's head-quarters was a farmhouse that belonged to Quakers Gideon and Sarah Gilpin.

Brandywine Battlefield State Park is owned and operated by the Pennsylvania Historical and Museum Commission that sponsors a comprehensive twenty-three-mile driving tour of the battlefield. The trip encompasses the headquarters buildings and some important sites outside the park such as British General Howe's headquarters, now a private residence, and Jeffries Ford on Brandywine Creek, where a British flanking movement turned a probable American victory into defeat.

Brandywine Springs Park, 20 miles south of Brandywine Battefield on Faulkland Road in Wilmington, Delaware, is on the site of a once-famous hostelry where Washington and Lafayette were said to have met to prepare strategy for the impending battle.

DIRECTIONS: Brandywine Battlefield State Park is on the north side of US 1, 1 mile east of Chadds Ford (Figure 77).

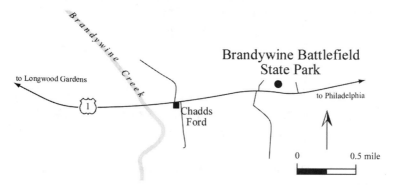

Figure 77. The location of Brandywine Battlefield State Park, Chadds Ford, Pennsylvania.

PUBLIC USE: Season and hours: *Grounds:* 9 AM–8 PM daily. Closed major holidays. *Visitor center and buildings:* Tuesday–Saturday, 9 AM–5 PM; Sunday, 12 N–5 PM. Extended hours in the summer. Closed Mondays and holidays except Memorial Day, July 4, and Labor Day. **Admission fee:** Tours of the historic buildings only. **Gift shop. For people with disabilities:** The visitor center is accessible.

FOR ADDITIONAL INFORMATION: Contact: Brandywine Battlefield State Park, US 1, Box 202, Chadds Ford, Pennsylvania 19317; 610-459-3342. **Read:** Henry Seidel Canby. 1946. *The Brandywine.*

75. GENERAL WAYNE INN

MERION, PENNSYLVANIA

In 1704, Robert Jones built a tavern that adjoined the Merion Friends Meeting House, the oldest existing house of worship in Pennsylvania. The tavern was host to Washington in September, 1777, following the Battle of Brandywine. A history of the tavern notes that his party ate "a hearty breakfast of boiled river fish and mountains of meat chops swimming in thick brown gravy with corn and greens" before they retreated to the west.[83]

The tavern, originally called Wayside Inn, has known many owners. The name was changed to General Wayne Inn following a reception held in honor of General "Mad Anthony" Wayne upon his return home from a victory over hostile Indians at the Battle of Fallen Timbers in 1795. The General Wayne Inn remains a popular dining spot.

DIRECTIONS: From US 1, turn north onto Old Lancaster Road and at the second light turn west on Montgomery Avenue. The General Wayne Inn is located on the north side of Montgomery Avenue (Figure 47).

FOR ADDITIONAL INFORMATION: Contact: General Wayne Inn, 625 Montgomery Avenue, Merion, Pennsylvania 19066; 610-667-3330.

76. POTTSGROVE MANOR

POTTSTOWN, PENNSYLVANIA

Following the Battle of Brandywine, General Washington led his troops west to Evansburg, Pennsylvania, then to Camp Pottsgrove in the Crooked Hills, from where the Americans could control roads leading to supply depots in nearby Reading. During the encampment, Washington utilized the home of Colonel Frederick Antes as headquarters but the Potts family records indicate that he visited Pottsgrove Manor (Figure 78) on occasion.

The town of Pottstown was founded by ironmaster John Potts who constructed a sturdy Georgian home in 1752, a mansion that rivaled any house in Philadelphia for refinement and the value of its furnishings. The sandstone exterior and handsome interior woodwork have withstood the passage of over two centuries, enabling visitors today to experience an authentic picture of fine living in the eighteenth century.

Figure 78. Pottsgrove Manor, Pottstown, Pennsylvania. (Photograph courtesy of Pottsgrove Manor)

Pottsgrove Mansion is owned by the Commonwealth of Pennsylvania that has restored the house and its eighteenth-century herb and flower garden. The Montgomery County Department of History and Cultural Arts maintains Pottsgrove and sponsors a twenty-five-mile self-guided auto tour of the historic Camp Pottsgrove encampment area that includes visits to the manor house, Washington's headquarters in the Antes House, two churches that served as hospitals, monuments, and commemorative plaques.

DIRECTIONS: From US 422 at Pottstown, exit onto SR 100 northbound to King Street, then go east on King to Pottsgrove Manor on the south side of the street (Figure 79).

PUBLIC USE: Season and hours: Tuesday–Saturday, 10 AM–4 PM; Sunday, 1–4 PM. Closed major holidays. **Gift shop. For people with disabilities:** The first floor of the mansion is accessible.

FOR ADDITIONAL INFORMATION: Contact: Pottsgrove Manor, 100 West King Street, Pottstown, Pennsylvania 19464; 610-326-4014. **Web site:** *www.montcopa.org.* **Read:** Mrs. Thomas Potts James. 1874. *The Memorial of Thomas Potts, Jr.*

77. HISTORIC ANTES HOUSE
PERKIOMENVILLE, PENNSYLVANIA

During the Pottsgrove encampment, General Washington headquartered at the farmhouse of Frederick Antes from September 22 to 26, 1777. Antes, a colonel of the Pennsylvania Militia, was the son of Henry Antes, who was one of the great master builders of the early colonial period, responsible for many early Moravian structures. Henry Antes's own house, a 2½-story stone building built in 1736, was considered a mansion with medieval quality — a steeply sloping roof, central chimney, and a traditional three-room floor plan. Through the years, significant and not always attractive changes were made that tended to destroy the character of the original architecture. In 1988, the Goschenhopper Historians, a group of dedicated private volunteers, purchased the house and initiated an extensive restoration project that will eventually return the home to its appearance at the time of George Washington's occu-

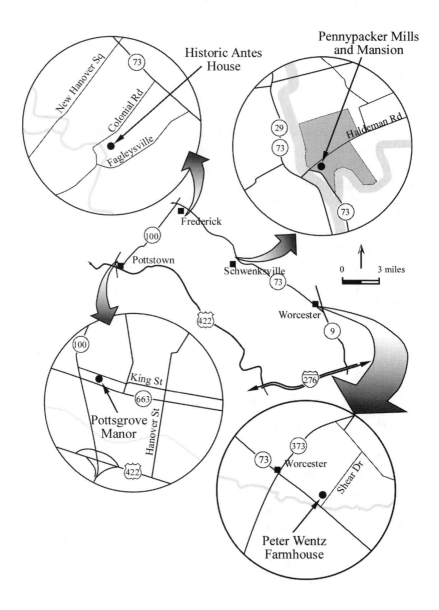

Figure 79. The location of Pottsgrove Manor, Historic Antes House, Pennypacker Mills and Mansion, and Peter Wentz Farmhouse in southeastern Pennsylvania.

pancy. When completed, the historians plan to open the house as an educational center and museum for regular visitation. The house is currently open only for group tours by appointment.

DIRECTIONS: From SR 73 at Frederick, go south on Colonial Road 1.5 miles to the Antes House on the east side of the road (Figure 79).

PUBLIC USE: Season and hours: Open by appointment only.

FOR ADDITIONAL INFORMATION: Contact: Historic Antes House, 318 Colonial Road, Perkiomenville, Pennsylvania 18074; 215-234-8953. **Web site:** *www.goschenhoppen.org.* **Read:** Ruth Hoover Seitz and Blair Seitz. 1989. *Pennsylvania's Historic Places.*

78. PENNYPACKER MILLS AND MANSION

SCHWENKSVILLE, PENNSYLVANIA

Pennypacker Mansion was Washington's headquarters from September 26 to 30, 1777, when he prepared for the Battle of Germantown. He returned to the house for a few days following that bitter defeat.

In 1900, Pennsylvania Governor Samuel W. Pennypacker purchased the property as it embodied important personal and patriotic symbols for him — early settlement, Revolutionary War history, and a genealogical link through ancestors who had owned the house prior to 1750. Extensive reconstruction and refurbishing transformed the typical stucco-over-stone German farmhouse into a Georgian-style colonial mansion with an interior that reflects preferences of the nineteenth-century middle class. Only the shell remains from colonial times, yet Pennypacker Mills is an important example of America's architectural taste in the Victorian era. Pennypacker Mills is operated as a house museum of the Montgomery County Department of History and Cultural Arts.

DIRECTIONS: Pennypacker Mills is on the corner of SR 73 and Haldeman Road in Schwenksville (Figure 79).

PUBLIC USE: Season and hours: Tuesday–Saturday, 10 AM–4 PM; Sunday, 1–4 PM. Closed major holidays. **Gift shop. For people with disabilities:** The first floor of the mansion is accessible.

FOR ADDITIONAL INFORMATION: Contact: Pennypacker Mills and Mansion, 5 Haldeman Road, Schwenksville, Pennsylvania 19473; 610-287-9349. **Web site:** *www.montcopa.org.*

79. PETER WENTZ FARMHOUSE

WORCESTER, PENNSYLVANIA

General Washington utilized farmer Peter Wentz' colonial house (Figure 80) as temporary headquarters before and after the Battle of Germantown. The main house, built around 1758, reflects Georgian architecture that was popular with the colonial gentry, with added fillips such as a tile roof over a beehive bake oven and bright colors reflecting the owner's German heritage. The Peter Wentz Farmhouse is a historic replication of an eighteenth-century working farm with colonial craft and farming demonstrations conducted by costumed guides on Saturdays in season. The Peter Wentz Farm is owned and operated by Montgomery County.

Figure 80. Peter Wentz Farmhouse, Worcester, Pennsylvania. (Photograph by William G. Clotworthy)

DIRECTIONS: The Wentz farmhouse is at the corner of SR 73 and Shear Road, 0.75 mile east of the intersection of SR 73 and SR 373 (Figure 79).

PUBLIC USE: Season and hours: Tuesday–Saturday, 10 AM–4 PM; Sunday, 1–4 PM. Closed Thanksgiving Day, Christmas Day, New Year's Day, July 4th, and Easter Sunday. **Visitor center. Gift shop. For people with disabilities:** Partially accessible.

FOR ADDITIONAL INFORMATION: Contact: Peter Wentz Farmhouse, Box 240, Worcester, Pennsylvania 19490; 610-584-5104. **Web site:** *www.montcopa.org.*

80. CLIVEDEN

GERMANTOWN, PENNSYLVANIA

The Cliveden mansion was the scene of pivotal action between the forces of George Washington and British troops during the Battle of Germantown on October 4, 1777. Poor timing, decreased visibility due to fog, and a determined British defense of the house contributed to an American defeat. Monumentalized by the battle, it is easy to overlook the fact that Cliveden is important architecturally and historically, speaking as it does of seven generations of a notable Philadelphia family and how they determined their places in the world.

Pennsylvania's colonial Chief Justice Benjamin Chew built Cliveden in the 1760s to escape the summer heat and congestion of Philadelphia. He situated the imposing three-story house on a slope above the more modest homes of Germantown. Its height was exaggerated by laying courses of progressively thinner dressed stones from the foundation to the roof. The interior reflects family living wherein original eighteenth and nineteenth century pieces of furniture, glassware, silver, and paintings trace two centuries of Chew family history and art collecting. Cliveden's curator of education says, "We're not talking about the rich Chews who lived here, we flesh out the story from the perspective of the women, children, servants, and slaves who lived here. We talk about people we have come to know through our research."[84] Thus Cliveden becomes a symbol of family life through the history of America. Cliveden is a museum property of the National Trust for Historic Preservation.

DIRECTIONS: From US 1 (Roosevelt Boulevard), go westbound onto Wissahickon Avenue, take Wissahickon to Johnson Street, then take Johnson northbound to Germantown Avenue, then take Germantown westbound 1 block to Cliveden Street, and then take Cliveden northbound 1 block to the entrance gate (Figure 81).

PUBLIC USE: Season and hours: April–December, Thursday–Sunday, 12 N–4 PM. Closed Thanksgiving Day and Christmas Day. **Admission fee. Visitor center. Gift shop. For people with disabilities:** Call ahead for assistance.

FOR ADDITIONAL INFORMATION: Contact: Cliveden, 6401 Germantown Avenue, Philadelphia, Pennsylvania 19144; 215-848-1777. **Web site:** *www.cliveden.org.* **Read:** Thomas J. McGuire. 1994. *The Surprise of Germantown.*

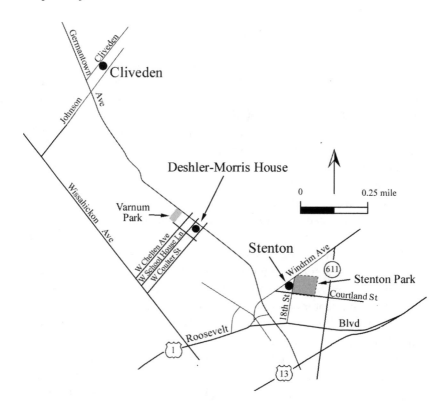

Figure 81. The location of Cliveden, Stenton, and Deshler-Morris House in western Philadelphia, Pennsylvania.

81. STENTON

GERMANTOWN, PENNSYLVANIA

In 1728, James Logan, secretary to William Penn, built Stenton (Figure 82) as a summer home and named it for his father's birthplace in Scotland. It has a simple elegance in the Quaker tradition with a wide central hallway and two paneled parlors on the ground floor. Logan was a leading political figure, particularly known for his skill in handling Indian affairs and it is told that Indian delegates often visited and set up camp on the grounds.

The three-story Georgian masterpiece served as military headquarters at times for both George Washington and British General Richard Howe.

Figure 82. Washingtons Headquarters, Stenton, Philadelphia, Pennsylvania. (Photograph by William G. Clotworthy)

Stenton, essentially unaltered, is a museum property of the National Society of the Colonial Dames of America who have furnished the house with William and Mary and Queen Anne pieces similar to those Logan is known to have owned. A rubblestone barn is a fine example of a Pennsylvania bank barn.

DIRECTIONS: From US 1 (Roosevelt Boulevard), exit onto SR 611 northbound 0.25 mile to Courtland Street, go west on Courtland to 18th Street. Then go north on 18th Street to Stenton located on the west side of the street opposite Stenton Park (Figure 81).

PUBLIC USE: Season and hours: Thursday–Saturday, 1–4 PM. Open by appointment Tuesdays and Wednesdays. Closed national holidays. **Admission fee. Gift shop. For people with disabilities:** The first floor is accessible.

FOR ADDITIONAL INFORMATION: Contact: Stenton, 4601 N. 18th Street, Philadelphia, Pennsylvania 19144; 215-319-7312. **Web site:** *www.stenton.org.*

82. HOPE LODGE

FORT WASHINGTON, PENNSYLVANIA

Hope Lodge (Figure 83) was built in 1750 by Samuel Morris, a prosperous Quaker farmer and entrepreneur. During the Whitemarsh encampment, George Washington's Surgeon General, John Cochran, requisitioned Hope Lodge as his headquarters, and it is more than likely that General Washington was a visitor.

Hope Lodge is an excellent example of early Georgian architecture — balanced and symmetrical. Owners over the last two centuries have been scrupulous in retaining the flavor, ambience, and structural integrity of the historic home. Its most recent owners, William and Alice Degn, preserved the house and added to its valuable furnishings before they bequeathed it to the public "in perpetuity for the enjoyment and education of the people of the Commonwealth of Pennsylvania and others, as a museum and permanent exhibit typical of the architecture and furnishings of the colonial period of America."[85] Thanks to their generosity, visitors are privileged to experience one of America's great homes in its near-pristine glory.

Figure 83. Hope Lodge, Fort Washington, Pennsylvania. (Photograph by William G. Clotworthy)

Hope Lodge is close to Fort Washington State Park, which includes an area where Washington's disconsolate soldiers built a fort to defend the Whitemarsh encampment.

DIRECTIONS: From I 276 (Pennsylvania Turnpike), take Exit 26 (Fort Washington), go south on SR 309 1.25 miles, then go north on SR 73 (Church Road) 0.75 mile to Bethlehem Pike, then go north on Bethlehem Pike 0.5 mile to Hope Lodge on the east near Fort Washington State Park (Figure 84).

PUBLIC USE: Season and hours: Tuesday–Saturday, 9 AM–5 PM; Sunday, 12 N–5 PM. Closed Thanksgiving Day, Christmas Day, and New Year's Day. **Admission fee. Gift shop. For people with disabilities:** Call ahead for assistance.

FOR ADDITIONAL INFORMATION: Contact: Hope Lodge, 553 Bethlehem Pike, Fort Washington, Pennsylvania 19034; 215-646-1595. **Web site:** *www.ushistory.org/hope.* **Read:** Paul A. W. Wallace. 1962. "Historic Hope Lodge."

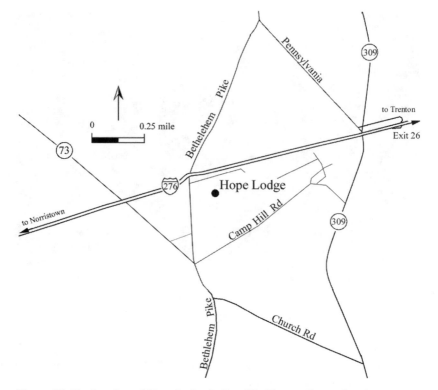

Figure 84. The location of Hope Lodge in Fort Washington, Pennsylvania.

83. Valley Forge National Historical Park

Valley Forge, Pennsylvania

Valley Forge, west of Philadelphia, was the location of the Continental Army's winter encampment from December 19, 1777, to June 19, 1778 — a time and place of terrible suffering and deprivation where over 2000 men died from disease brought on by harsh winter weather, lack of food, and poor sanitation. The site had been picked because the terrain was defensible, it protected important munitions factories to the west, and it enabled the army to counter possible British movements from the east. The army not only survived its trying ordeal, but under Washington's leadership became better organized and a more efficient military force, due in no small measure to the training regimen installed by Baron von Steuben.

Self-guided driving tours of the 3500-acre park start at a modern visitor center, then wind past extensive remains and reconstructions of the earthworks, Artillery Park, Washington's Headquarters, his officer's quarters, and the Grand Parade where von Steuben drilled the army. An impressive National Memorial Arch contains an inscription of Washington's heartfelt words of respect for the army, "Naked and starving as they are, we cannot enough admire the incomparable patience and fidelity of the soldiery."

Washington's headquarters (Figure 85) was the rented home of Isaac Potts, a member of the famous Pennsylvania iron works family. Comfortable as a private, single-family house, it was barely adequate since the five-room fieldstone building housed at least twenty people — General and Mrs. Washington plus Washington's military staff. Devoted

Figure 85. Washingtons Headquarters, Valley Forge National Historical Park, Valley Forge, Pennsylvania. (Photograph courtesy of National Park Service)

maintenance over the years has kept the two-story house looking much as it did over two hundred years ago.

The Muhlenburg Brigade area of Valley Forge contains five reproduced log cabins (Plate 10), constructed to the exact specifications prescribed by General Washington for structures to accommodate twelve men — fourteen feet wide by sixteen feet long with 6½-foot side walls and a fireplace opposite the front door. These reproductions are representative of the hundreds of huts built to accommodate the thousands of people who lived and worked at Valley Forge during the winter of 1777-1778.

Varnum's Quarters, occupied by General James Varnum of Rhode Island, is an example of early eighteenth-century architecture — a tall, narrow stone building with a steep roof and randomly placed windows. The house is heavily restored but most of the stonework and some of the woodwork are thought to be original. Varnum's Quarters is typical of the small farmhouses in which many of Washington's generals, and Washington himself, were quartered during the encampment.

The Museum of the Valley Forge Historical Society is located on private property within the park, between the Memorial Chapel and the Bell Tower. The museum contains an unsurpassed collection of more than 3000 artifacts, many once possessed by George Washington. The spirit (and difficulty) of life at Valley Forge is documented with galleries, displays, and exhibits offering visitors an opportunity to visualize and better understand the attitude, sacrifice, and dedication of the 12,000 brave men and women who lived at Valley Forge during the harsh winter. The National Park Service Visitor Center has information regarding the encampment. The George C. Neumann Collection of firearms, swords, and accessories is the focal point of an exhibit area in the visitor center.

DIRECTIONS: From I 76, take Exit 24 onto US 422 northbound 1 mile to SR 23, then go west on SR 23 and immediately enter Valley Forge National Historical Park (Figure 86).

PUBLIC USE: Season and hours: *Park:* 6 AM–10 PM daily. *Visitor center and Washingtons headquarters:* 9 AM–5 PM daily. Closed Christmas Day. *Museum:* Monday–Saturday, 9:30 AM–4 PM; Sunday, 1–4 PM. **Admission fee:** Museum only. **Gift shop. For people with disabilities:** The historic buildings are partially accessible. The visitor center and museum are accessible.

FOR ADDITIONAL INFORMATION: Contact: Valley Forge National Historical Park, Box 953, Valley Forge, Pennsylvania 19482; 610-783-

1077. **Web site:** *Park:* *www.nps.gov/vafo.* **Museum:** *www.valleyforgemuseum.com.* **Read:** (1) Donald Barr Chidsey. 1959. *Valley Forge.* (2) Noel F. Busch. 1974. *Winter Quarters.* (3) John W. Jackson. 1992. *Valley Forge: Pinnacle of Courage.* (4) Barbara Pollamine. 1993. *Great and Capitol Changes: An Account of the Valley Forge Encampment.*

84. HISTORIC YELLOW SPRINGS
CHESTER SPRINGS, PENNSYLVANIA

Yellow Springs is a 145-acre complex of eighteenth- and nineteenth-century hotels, residences, and a bathhouse that opened in 1722 as a health spa which was fed by mystical yellow water thought to have curative powers. During the Revolutionary War, the site was commissioned by the Continental Congress to serve as a hospital providing medical aid to the army camped at nearby Valley Forge. General and Mrs. Washington visited troops hospitalized at Yellow Springs on many occasions.

Restored stone ruins mark the site of a Revolutionary War Memorial and an authentic colonial-era medicinal herb garden. Several buildings have been restored by Historic Yellow Springs, Inc., a non-profit organization with the mandate to act as:

> *. . . a curator of a historic site and conservator of open space; to develop and offer programs which interpret its unique history; provide a quality historical and educational resource center that serves local, regional and national common-interest groups; and serve as a center for community activities.*[86]

DIRECTIONS: From I 76, take Exit 23 onto SR 100 southbound to Lionville, then go north on SR 113 about 4 miles to Chester Springs, then go north on Yellow Springs Road 0.5 mile to Art School Road, then go east on Art School to Historic Yellow Springs immediately ahead on the north side of the road (Figure 86).

PUBLIC USE: Season and hours: Pre-arranged guided tours are conducted Monday–Friday, 9 AM–4 PM. Closed major holidays. **Food service:** The Inn at Historic Yellow Springs, open for dinner and Sunday brunch, is on the grounds. Call 610-827-7477 for reservations. **For people with disabilities:** Partially accessible.

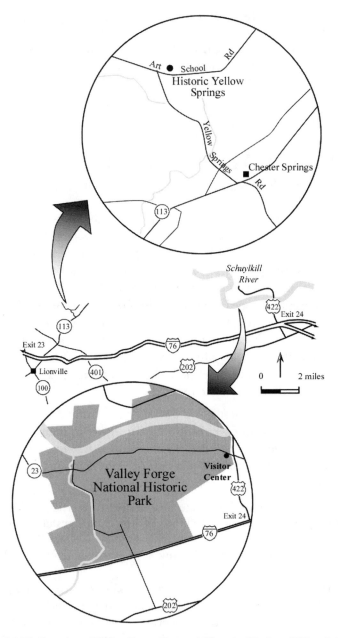

Figure 86. The location of Valley Forge National Historical Park and Historic Yellow Springs in eastern Pennsylvania.

FOR ADDITIONAL INFORMATION: Contact: Historic Yellow Springs, 1685 Art School Road, Box 62, Chester Springs, Pennsylvania 19425; 610-827-7414. **Read:** Ricardo Torres-Reyes. 1971. *1779–80 Encampment: A Study of Medical Services.*

85. MONMOUTH BATTLEFIELD STATE PARK

MANALAPAN, NEW JERSEY

One of the longest battles of the Revolutionary War was fought on June 28, 1778, between the forces of George Washington and British General Sir Henry Clinton at Monmouth Courthouse, New Jersey. Clinton was headed for New York City from Philadelphia when his army was beset by Washington's troops from Valley Forge. An inexplicable retreat ordered by American General Charles Lee prevented a total American victory, but the vicious fighting proved the value of the military discipline and training that had been instilled in the Americans by Baron von Steuben at Valley Forge. The battle was thus a moral and political triumph for the Americans as they met the British on the open field and forced them to retreat — the British suffered several times more casualties than the Americans. The Battle of Monmouth was fought in oppressive summer heat that took a worse toll than bullets. Local ladies took fresh water to the Continentals during the battle, and one of them, Mrs. Mary Hays, became famous as "Molly Pitcher," who not only carried water, but is reputed to have loaded and fired a cannon after her artilleryman husband was overcome by heat exhaustion.

Monmouth Battlefield State Park commemorates the battle and the men who fought there. The park preserves a splendid rural landscape with miles of hiking and equestrian trails, picnic areas, a restored revolutionary-era farmhouse, and a visitor center that stands on Combs Hill, the command post of the American artillery. Inside is an interpretive display area where two slide booths and a fiber-optic map interpret the battle and recovered artifacts are displayed. The New Jersey Park Service maintains Monmouth Battlefield.

DIRECTIONS: From the New Jersey Turnpike, take Exit 8A onto SR

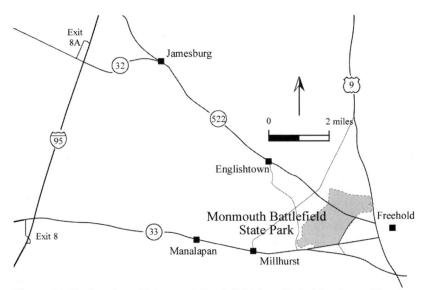

Figure 87. The location of Monmouth Battlefield State Park, Manalapan, New Jersey.

32 eastbound to Jamesburg, then take CR 522 southeast about 8 miles to Monmouth Battlefield State Park (Figure 87).

PUBLIC USE: Season and hours: 9 AM–4 PM daily. **Visitor center. Gift shop:** Seasonal. **Food service:** Seasonal. **For people with disabilities:** The visitor center and recreational facilities are partially accessible. Please call ahead for arrangements.

FOR ADDITIONAL INFORMATION: Contact: Monmouth Battlefield State Park, 347 Freehold-Englishtown Road, Manalapan, New Jersey 07726; 732-462-9616. **Web site:** *www.state.nj.us.* **Read:** (1) Mary Beth Norton. 1980. *Liberty's Daughters: The Revolutionary Experience of American Women, 1750–1780.* (2) Irvin Haas. 1987. *America's Historic Battlefields.*

86. JOHN KANE HOUSE

PAWLING, NEW YORK

Following the British evacuation of Philadelphia and the Battle of Monmouth in the autumn of 1778, a large part of the Continental Army moved to the Pawling area to fill in a defensive line that extended from Danbury, Connecticut, to Newburgh, New York. From September 12th to November 23rd, George Washington's headquarters was the home of John Kane, a Tory stripped of his property and forced to leave home to seek British protection.

The kitchen wing is believed to be the portion used by Washington. It dates to 1760 and is the sole remaining part of the original house that was replaced by a Federal-style structure. Following a succession of owners, the house was acquired by the Historical Society of Quaker Hill and Pawling which displays an eclectic collection of artifacts and memorabilia of the colonial period and local Pawling history. Exhibits in one room are devoted to one of Pawling's favorite sons, broadcaster and world traveler Lowell Thomas.

The goal of the Historical Society is to "bring the past rich heritage of the Pawling area to life. To that end, we maintain our historic buildings, sponsor programs, and collect, preserve and present for public viewing books, papers and memorabilia."[87]

The Historical Society also maintains the Oblong Meeting House in the Quaker Hill section of Pawling. It dates to 1764, a rare example of strong Quaker influence in the community during the eighteenth and nineteenth centuries. It was utilized as a hospital in 1778 by Washington's troops, some of whom are buried in a graveyard across the road.

DIRECTIONS: From SR 22 northbound, exit onto Main Street and go 1 mile to the Kane House on the east side of the road. From SR 22 southbound, exit on Coulter Avenue and go south about 0.4 to Main Street, then go south on Main Street. The Kane House is immediately to the east (Figure 88).

PUBLIC USE: Season and hours: Saturday and Sunday, 2–4 PM.

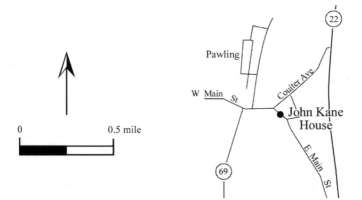

Figure 88. The location of John Kane House, Pawling, New York.

Groups by appointment. **Gift shop. For people with disabilities:** Accessible.

FOR ADDITIONAL INFORMATION: Contact: John Kane House, East Main Street, Box 9, Pawling, New York 12564; 845-855-9316.

87. WALLACE HOUSE STATE HISTORIC SITE AND OLD DUTCH PARSONAGE STATE HISTORIC SITE

SOMERVILLE, NEW JERSEY

John Wallace was a fabric importer from Philadelphia who leased half of his eight-room colonial home to George and Martha Washington from December, 1778 to June, 1779, when the Continental Army was camped at nearby Middlebrook (now Somerville). At that time the house directly to the east was the manse for three Dutch Reformed Churches in the Raritan Valley served by Jacob Hardenbergh, also a member of the Provincial Congress. Hardenbergh was a leader in the founding of Queen's College (Rutgers University) and later functioned as its first president. He and neighbor Washington became friends and visited one another frequently.

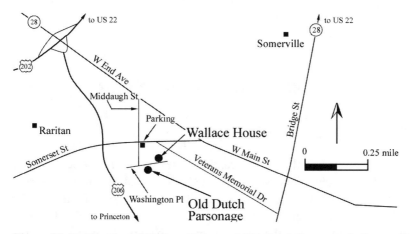

Figure 89. The location of Wallace House and Old Dutch Parsonage in Somerville, New Jersey.

The Old Dutch Parsonage was built in 1751 and the Wallace House was built in 1771. In 1947, the State of New Jersey opened the two historic structures to the public as museums; each was furnished with authentic eighteenth-century pieces. Both houses are now administered by the New Jersey Department of Environmental Protection, Division of Parks and Forestry.

DIRECTIONS: From US 287, take Exit 13 (US 202/206) onto US 206 southbound to Somerville. Go east on Somerset Street for 1 block to the visitors' parking area at 71 Somerset Street. The structures face onto Washington Place, one block south of Somerset Street (Figure 89).

PUBLIC USE: Season and hours: Wednesday–Saturday, 10 AM–12 N, 1–4 PM; Sunday, 1–4 PM. Closed state and federal holidays. **For people with disabilities:** The first floor of each home is accessible.

FOR ADDITIONAL INFORMATION: Contact: Wallace House State Historic Site, 71 Somerset Street, Somerville, New Jersey 08876; 908-725-1015. **Web site:** *www.vpa.org/museumsnj.html.*

88. STONY POINT BATTLEFIELD STATE HISTORIC SITE

STONY POINT, NEW YORK

In May, 1779, the British captured the Hudson River peninsula at Stony Point, New York, south of West Point, and began to construct fortifications that threatened American defenses at West Point and the Hudson Valley. General Washington marched north from Middlebrook, New Jersey, to combat the provocation. He observed the enemy works from nearby Buckberg Mountain and devised a bold plan to recapture Stony Point.

At midnight on July 15th, Brigadier General "Mad Anthony" Wayne led his regiment across marshes that separated Stony Point from the mainland and effected a daring bayonet attack that resulted in the surrender of the British garrison. One of the last major battles of the Revolutionary War fought in the north, the victory helped boost American morale although the combined might of the British army and navy forced the Americans to abandon Stony Point a few days later. The British, however, never threatened the Hudson Highlands again.

Stony Point Battlefield State Historic Site offers a wide variety of special events including guided and self-guided tours, as well as demonstrations of artillery, musketry, cooking, and camp life conducted by staff members in period dress.

DIRECTIONS: From US 9W north of Stony Point, go east on Park Road to Stony Point Battlefield State Historic Site (Figure 90).

PUBLIC USE: Season and hours: April 15–October 31, Wednesday–Saturday, 10 AM–5 PM; Sunday, 1–5 PM. Closed Mondays and Tuesdays except Memorial Day, Independence Day, and Labor Day. **For people with disabilities:** Partially accessible.

FOR ADDITIONAL INFORMATION: Contact: Stony Point Battlefield State Historic Site, Box 182, Stony Point, New York 10980; 845-786-2521. **Web site:** *www.nysparks.state.ny.us.*

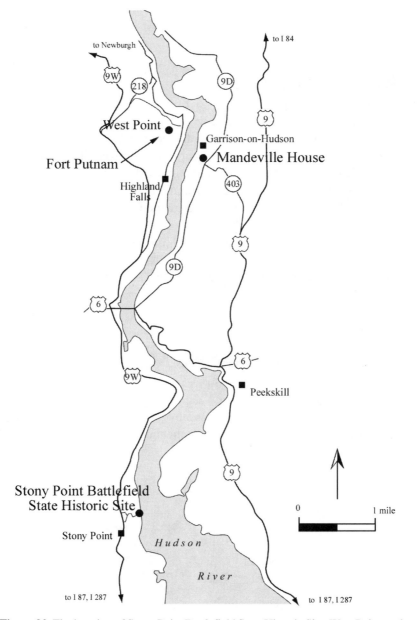

Figure 90. The location of Stony Point Battlefield State Historic Site, West Point, and the Mandeville House along the lower Hudson River in New York.

89. THE GREAT OAK

GAYLORDSVILLE, CONNECTICUT

On September 20, 1780, General George Washington, on his way to his first meeting with French General Rochambeau in Wethersfield, Connecticut, paused for rest and lunch under the spreading branches of a huge oak tree in Gaylordsville. A commemorative plaque has been installed at the Great Oak that is owned by the Connecticut Daughters of the American Revolution.

DIRECTIONS: From US 7 about 0.3 mile south of Gaylordsville, go southwest on Gaylord Road to the Great Oak on the south side of the road near the intersection with Newton Road (Figure 91).

90. WEBB-DEANE-STEVENS MUSEUM

WETHERSFIELD, CONNECTICUT

The Webb-Deane-Stevens Museum, part of the largest historic district in Connecticut, comprises three authentically restored and furnished

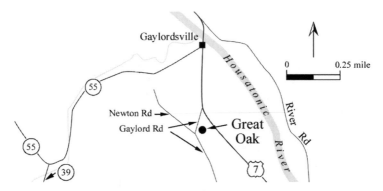

Figure 91. The location of the Great Oak, Gaylordsville, Connecticut.

eighteenth-century houses in the center of Wetherfield where 150 houses date from before 1850.

Joseph Webb was a prosperous merchant whose brick and clapboard house has a wide center hall, fine interior paneling, and a massive gambrel roof. General George Washington met French General Rochambeau at Webb's house on May 22 and 23, 1781, to formulate plans for an assault on Yorktown, Virginia. Washington's bedroom has been preserved, still decorated with the red-wool flocked wallpaper hung for his visit. An old map of the colonies is displayed in a conference room that contains a gateleg table ringed by antique chairs.

Silas Deane, a member of the Continental Congress who undertook many important diplomatic assignments, built a house next door in 1766. Many distinguished guests called on Deane, including his friend John Adams who wrote in 1774 of being entertained at Deane's ". . . most genteely with punch, wine and coffee."[88]

Leather tanner Isaac Stevens built his home in 1788. His account books and leather fire buckets remain on display in the house that contrasts with the Webb and Deane homes as it represents a later period when Stevens was part of an upwardly mobile middle class.

The Webb-Deane-Stevens Museum complex is owned and maintained by the National Society of Colonial Dames.

DIRECTIONS: From I 91, take Exit 26 and go west on Marsh Street to Main Street, then go south on Main to the homes on the west side of the street (Figure 92).

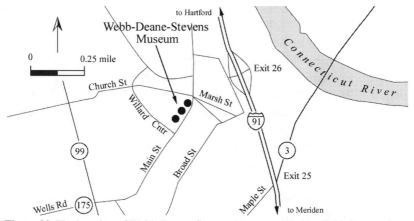

Figure 92. The location of Webb-Deane-Stevens Museum, Wethersfield, Connecticut.

PUBLIC USE: Season and hours: Guided tours on the hour, May 1–October 31, 10 AM–4 PM. Last tour at 3 PM. Closed Tuesdays. **Admission fee. Gift shop. For people with disabilities:** Only the Webb House is accessible.

FOR ADDITIONAL INFORMATION: Contact: Webb-Deane-Stevens Museum, 211 Main Street, Wethersfield, Connecticut 16109; 860-529-0612. **Web site:** *www.ohwy.com/ct/w/wedestmu.htm.*

91. GENERAL JAMES MITCHELL VARNUM MUSEUM

EAST GREENWICH, RHODE ISLAND

James Mitchell Varnum was a distinguished attorney whose fine two-story frame home, built in 1773, commands an excellent view of picturesque Greenwich Bay. The house reflects the finest architectural features of eighteenth century New England — hipped roof, modillioned cornices, and a central pedimented doorway with a columned porch.

Varnum was interested in military affairs and obtained a commission as colonel of the Rhode Island Militia at the beginning of the Revolution. By 1777, he was a brigadier general in the Continental Army in which he served with great distinction at Boston, Long Island, and Valley Forge. The Varnum house was used for strategy conferences between Washington, Lafayette, Rochambeau, and Greene, and it is believed that General Washington slept in the northeast bedroom.

The house and its gardens have been restored to reflect the home's glory as an example of gracious Rhode Island culture in the colonial period, its rooms filled with notable period pieces. The Varnum Continentals, a non-profit historical association, maintains the Varnum Museum.

DIRECTIONS: From I 95, take Exit 8 onto Division Street eastbound about 2 miles to Pierce Street, go south on Pierce 4 blocks to the Varnum House on the west side of the street. Parking is on Church Street (Figure 93).

PUBLIC USE: Season and hours: June 1–September 1, Tuesday, Friday, and Saturday, 1–4 PM. Month of September, Saturday, 1–4 PM.

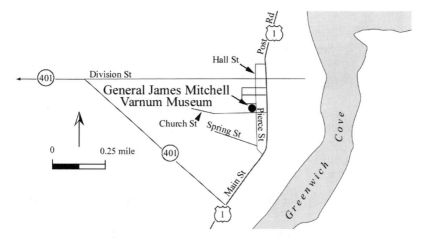

Figure 93. The location of General James Mitchell Varnum Museum, East Greenwich, Rhode Island.

Admission fee. Gift shop. For people with disabilities: The first floor is accessible.

FOR ADDITIONAL INFORMATION: Contact: General Varnum Museum, 57 Pierce Street, East Greenwich, Rhode Island 02818; 401-884-1776. **Web site:** *www.varnumcontinentals.org.*

92. KINGSTON FREE PUBLIC LIBRARY

KINGSTON, RHODE ISLAND

When Newport, the capital of Rhode Island, was occupied by the British during the Revolutionary War, the Rhode Island Assembly met in Kingstown (now Kingston) in a building that presently serves as the Kingston Free Public Library. The original exterior of the building has been covered by a Victorian façade but the interior has been refurbished to represent the colonial period. George Washington visited the temporary capitol building when traveling through Rhode Island colony in 1781.

DIRECTIONS: Kingston Free Public Library is located in central Kingston at the intersection of SR 138 and Upper College Road (Figure 94).

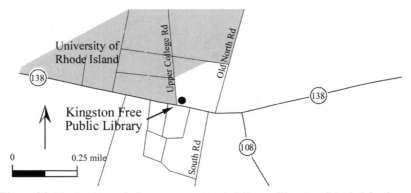

Figure 94. The location of Kingston Free Public Library, Kingston, Rhode Island.

PUBLIC USE: Season and hours: Monday–Tuesday, 10 AM–6 PM; Wednesday, 10 AM–8 PM; Thursday–Friday, 10 AM–5 PM; Saturday, 9:30 AM–5 PM (winter), 9:30 AM–1 PM (summer). **For people with disabilities:** Accessible.

FOR ADDITIONAL INFORMATION: Contact: Kingston Free Library, 2605 Kingstown Road, Kingston, Rhode Island 02881; 401-783-8254.

93. WEST POINT

WEST POINT, NEW YORK

West Point is the location of the United States Military Academy, founded in the early 1800s. During the Revolutionary War, West Point, the site of a fort built by General Thaddeus Kosciusko, was arguably the most strategically important defense facility in the colonies. Washington and the Congress considered it to be a key site as it protected the Hudson River, which bisected the colonies (Figure 95). The highlands at West Point were a natural place for fortifications as they overlooked a ninety-degree angle in the river where sailing ships were forced to slow down, thus becoming easy targets. As an additional deterrent, the Americans stretched a massive chain across the Hudson River from West Point to a small fort on Constitution Island that lay near the east bank of the river. The combined effect of the forts, the chain, and the bend in the river blocked British travel on the river during the war.

Figure 95. View of the Hudson River from the Hudson Highlands at the United States Military Academy, West Point, New York. (Photograph by William G. Clotworthy)

General Washington visited West Point on numerous occasions, but no visit was more dramatic than in 1780 when he was horrified to learn that General Benedict Arnold had offered the plans of West Point to the British. Arnold managed to escape to the safety of British lines, but his accomplice, British Major John Andre, was captured, given a military trial, and hanged.

The first monument built at West Point when it became the United States Military Academy was in honor of General Kosciusko. Elsewhere on the grounds of the academy is a piece of the Great Chain and a restoration of Fort Putnam.

West Point is open 24 hours a day, 365 days a year. Visitors are welcome during regular daylight hours when modern facilities such as the Cadet Chapel, Parade Ground, and Academy Museum are shown as part of regular guided tours. Constitution Island is open from mid-June to October and Fort Putnam from mid-May to mid-October. Visitors should contact the visitor center for current information.

DIRECTIONS: The United States Military Academy lies astride US 9W between Newburgh and Highland Falls. From 9W, go eastbound on SR 218 to reach the campus and historic areas (Figure 90).

PUBLIC USE: Season and hours: *Visitor center:* 9 AM–4:45 PM daily. Closed Thanksgiving Day, Christmas Day, and New Year's Day. **Admission fee. Guided tours only. Gift shop. For people with disabilities:** Accessible.

FOR ADDITIONAL INFORMATION: Contact: United States Military Academy, West Point, New York 10966; 845-938-2638. **Web site:** *www.usma.edu.* **Read:** Lincoln Diamant. 1989. *Chaining the Hudson.*

94. GEORGE WASHINGTON MASONIC SHRINE

TAPPAN, NEW YORK

General George Washington stayed at the home of Johannes DeWint four times during the Revolutionary War. It was during his second visit, from September 28 to October 7, 1780, that British Major John Andre, found guilty of spying, was executed within sight of the DeWint House. Washington had approved the execution but was not a witness, although it was reported that he requested the shutters of his room be closed at the time of the hanging. Those shutters are still in place.

The DeWint House, built around 1700, is an interesting example of Dutch-style architecture, with its steeply pitched roof, bricks from Holland, and purple tiles around the fireplace. Several small rooms are furnished in period and there is a separate museum featuring documents and artifacts pertaining to the Revolutionary War and Washington's visits to Tappan.

The DeWint House is owned and maintained by the Grand Lodge of Free and Accepted Masons of the State of New York.

DIRECTIONS: From the Palisades Interstate Parkway, take Exit 5 onto SR 303 southbound about 1.5 miles to Oak Tree Road, then go west on Oak Tree 0.2 mile to Livingston Avenue, then go south on Livingston to the shrine on the west side of the street (Figure 96).

PUBLIC USE: Season and hours: 10 AM–4 PM daily. Closed Thanksgiving Day, Christmas Day, and Easter Sunday. **For people with disabilities:** Accessible.

FOR ADDITIONAL INFORMATION: Contact: George Washington

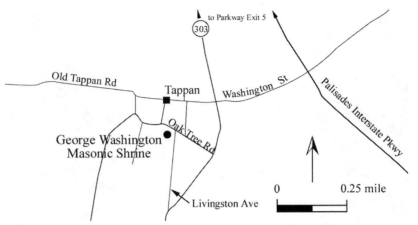

Figure 96. The location of George Washington Masonic Shrine, Tappan, New York.

Masonic Shrine, DeWint House, 20 Livingston Avenue, Tappan, New York 10983; 845-359-1359. **Read:** James Thomas Flexner. 1975. *The Traitor and the Spy.*

95. DEY MANSION/WASHINGTONS HEADQUARTERS MUSEUM

WAYNE, NEW JERSEY

A brick and brownstone Georgian house of eleven rooms was the home of Theunis Dey, a county and colony official and colonel of the Bergen County Militia during the Revolutionary War. General George Washington took possession of Dey's home in July, 1780, when the American army was encamped nearby. He returned in October, following an active summer of meetings with French allies, campaigns in the Hudson Highlands, and the development of an uncertain military situation after Benedict Arnold's defection.

The Dey Mansion (Figure 97) has been open as a house museum since 1934, its rooms filled with antiques and colonial artifacts from the time of Washington's residency. A blacksmith shop and plantation house are among several reconstructed outbuildings. Dey Mansion is owned and operated by the Passaic County Department of Parks and Recreation.

Figure 97. Dey Mansion/Washingtons Headquarters Museum, Wayne, New Jersey. (Photograph by William G. Clotworthy)

DIRECTIONS: From I 80, take Exit 54 northbound onto Minnisink Road about 0.75 mile to Totowa Road, then take Totowa westbound about 1 mile to Passaic County Golf Course, then go north into the golf course to the Dey Mansion immediately on the west side of the road (Figure 98).

PUBLIC USE: Season and hours: Wednesday–Friday, 1 PM–4 PM; Saturday–Sunday, 10 AM–12 N, 1–4 PM. Closed Thanksgiving Day, Christmas Day, New Year's Day, and Easter Sunday. **Admission fee. Gift shop. For people with disabilities:** The first floor is partially accessible.

FOR ADDITIONAL INFORMATION: Contact: Dey Mansion, 199 Totowa Road, Wayne, New Jersey 07470; 973-696-1776.

Figure 98. The location of Dey Mansion, Wayne, New Jersey.

96. COLONIAL NATIONAL HISTORICAL PARK

YORKTOWN, VIRGINIA

On October 19, 1781, British General Lord Cornwallis, who claimed illness, dispatched his second-in-command to surrender the Yorktown garrison to a combined American and French force that had surrounded the British by land and sea. The Siege of Yorktown was not the last confrontation of the Revolutionary War, but the loss of Yorktown was, in effect, the straw that broke the camel's back in the minds, hearts, and pocketbooks of the British public. His Majesty's Government, beset by

293

other global conflicts and severe economic problems, soon sued for peace.

Cornwallis had begun his march to entrapment in South Carolina. He encountered military success as he swept across the Carolinas, but in the process over-extended his army. Lack of supplies and determined colonial resistance began to decimate his troops and forced him to seek shorter supply lines and the protection of a British fleet which he believed was near Chesapeake Bay. He marched his army to Yorktown, Virginia — only to experience entrapment and disaster. The vaunted British fleet did not appear and an American force led by the Marquis de Lafayette hemmed him in by land. A French fleet, however, did appear, and Cornwallis was effectively trapped between land and sea. When the combined armies of generals Washington and Rochambeau marched in from the north to join Lafayette, the Siege of Yorktown began.

The British surrender at Yorktown symbolized the end of eight long years of revolutionary military activity. American hopes could now turn to thoughts of peace, formation of a representative government, and prosperity based on freedom of opportunity. Therefore, a visit to Yorktown and Colonial National Historical Park is a special experience, for it was here that the dream of political freedom in America began to become reality. The British oppressors were sent packing, and the stage for a negotiated peace was set.

Colonial National Historical Park, lying on the peninsula between the York and James rivers, covers 9000 acres that encompass the Village of Yorktown, Yorktown Battlefield, and Colonial Parkway that transverses the peninsula from Yorktown through Williamsburg to Jamestown Island. Yorktown was founded in 1691 as a tobacco shipping port and a few surviving eighteenth-century buildings located within the park are open for public visitation. The National Park Service, which maintains Colonial National Historical Park, sums up a visit:

> *You will have the feeling of 'belonging' as you view the battlefield from the Visitor Center or drive the marked route through that scene of the defeat of Cornwallis. In the eye of the mind, you look back over the long past. You even feel, as part of your history, the great triangular contest between England, Spain and France of the possession of the New World. All that you see flowed from that source. And it is your history — you are a droplet in that stream.[89]*

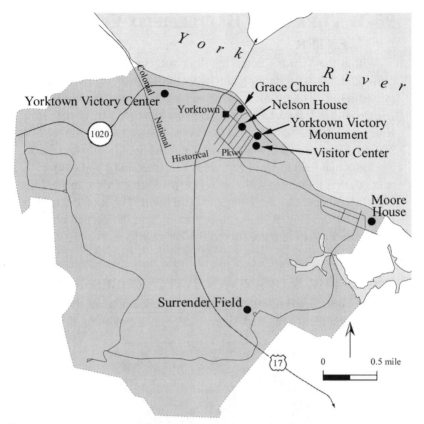

Figure 99. The location of featured sites within Yorktown Battlefield unit of Colonial National Historical Park, including Yorktown Victory Center.

DIRECTIONS: Colonial National Historical Park lies astride US 17 in Yorktown. The Visitor Center is located at the eastern end of Colonial National Historical Parkway, 0.5 mile east of US 17 in Yorktown (Figure 99).

PUBLIC USE: Season and hours: 8:30 AM–5 PM daily, with extended hours in spring, summer, and fall. Closed Christmas Day. **Admission fee. Visitor center. Gift shop. For people with disabilities:** Partially accessible. Please call ahead for assistance.

FOR ADDITIONAL INFORMATION: Contact: Colonial National Historical Park, Box 210, Yorktown, Virginia 23690-0210; 757-898-3400; **Web site:** *www.nps.gov/colo.* **Read:** (1) Burke Davis. 1970. *The Campaign that Won America.* (2) Charles E. Hatch. 1980. *Colonial Yorktown's Main Street and Military Entrenchment.*

96-1. YORKTOWN BATTLEFIELD VISITOR CENTER

Within the Visitor Center, the dramatic events of Yorktown are presented in an entertaining and educational theater program and a museum that displays military tents, part of a reconstructed British frigate, other treasures such as objects retrieved from the York River, and dramatic dioramas that depict aspects of the siege. The National Park Service sponsors self-guided automobile and walking tours that lead to various points of interest and a walkway connects the visitor center with the Yorktown Victory Monument (Figure 100) adjacent to the village of Yorktown. The monument was erected by the United States to commemorate the French alliance and victory over the beleaguered British garrison.

96-2. THE YORKTOWN BATTLEFIELD

The Yorktown Battlefield (Figure 101) encompasses the American encampment area and siege works with positions, fortifica-

Figure 100. The Yorktown Victory Monument, Yorktown, Virginia. (Photograph courtesy of National Park Service)

Figure 101. Colonial National Historical Park, Yorktown, Virginia. (Photograph courtesy of National Park Service)

tions, and the surrender field well marked for visitors. Of particular interest are the remains of British redoubts 9 and 10. Their capture by the French and Americans tightened the noose around the town and definitively persuaded Cornwallis to surrender. Parts of the French and American lines have been reconstructed.

96-3. MOORE HOUSE

Commissioners from the combined allied forces met with British representatives in the home of Augustine Moore on October 18, 1781 to finalize the surrender terms. The completed Articles of Capitulation required the British to surrender with less than full military honors, which they did the following day.

96-4. SURRENDER FIELD

On October 19, 1781, British and Hessian troops laid down their arms. Within a few days they marched off to prisoner of war camps while Cornwallis, who was paroled, sailed for New York and on to England. At a pavilion overlooking Surrender Field, today's visitors may listen to an account of the formal surrender ceremony. Surrender Field is part of an automobile tour that includes stops at the sites of Washington's headquarters, the American Artillery Park, and the French encampments.

96-5. NELSON HOUSE

The Nelson house within the village of Yorktown was the ancestral home of American General Thomas Nelson, Jr., Yorktown's most famous son and signer of the Declaration of Independence. During the siege, Nelson directed artillery fire on his own home in the belief that Lord Cornwallis was using it as headquarters. The Nelson House is at the corner of Main and Nelson streets.

96-7. GRACE EPISCOPAL CHURCH

Grace Church, at Church and Water streets in Yorktown, was built of native marl in 1697. During the siege the British used the building as an ammunition magazine. Communion silver dating to 1649 is still used in worship services.

97. YORKTOWN VICTORY CENTER

YORKTOWN, VIRGINIA

The Yorktown Victory Center, lying within Colonial National Historical Park, is an independently owned museum of the American Revolution, operated by the Jamestown-Yorktown Foundation, an educational agency of the Commonwealth of Virginia. The drama of the Revolution and the birth of our nation come alive in provocative indoor galleries where visitors witness the conflict through the eyes of those who were there — soldiers on the battlefield and women on the home front. An evocative film, *A Time of Revolution,* places one in an encampment where soldiers reminisce about their lives and war experiences. Outdoors, the sights and sounds of the war are found in a recreated Continental Army encampment. There is also a re-created colonial farm where costumed interpreters in the garden, tobacco barn, and farmhouse introduce visitors to life in 1780s colonial Tidewater Virginia. The stated mission of the Jamestown-Yorktown Foundation is to educate and promote understanding and awareness of Virginia's role in the creation of the United States of America. In addition to the Victory Center Museum, they sponsor many special events and educational activities through the year.

DIRECTIONS: The Yorktown Victory Center is located on the south side of SR 1020 in Yorktown immediately east of the intersection of Colonial National Historical Parkway and SR 1020 (Figure 99).

PUBLIC USE: Season and hours: June 15–August 15, 9 AM–7 PM daily. August 16–June 14, 9 AM–5 PM daily. Closed Christmas Day and New Year's Day. **Admission fee. Gift shop. For people with disabilities:** Accessible.

FOR ADDITIONAL INFORMATION: Contact: Yorktown Victory Center, Department BC, Box 1607, Williamsburg, Virginia 23187; 757-253-4838, or 888-593-4682. **Web site:** *www.historyisfun.org.* **Read:** Franklin Wickwire and MaryWickwire. 1970. *Cornwallis: The American Adventure.*

98. BETHLEHEM MORAVIAN COMMUNITY

BETHLEHEM, PENNSYLVANIA

In July, 1782, General George Washington visited Bethlehem to thank the Moravian community for its humanitarian efforts during the Revolutionary War. While the Moravians were opposed to the war, they supplied grain to the Continental Army at Morristown, and the Brethren's House was utilized twice as an official army hospital.

Bethlehem was the first securely established Moravian settlement in the British North American colonies. Founded in 1741 by missionaries, it was a planned community in which property, privacy, and personal relationships were subordinated to a common effort to achieve a spiritual ideal. The Moravian Church remained the official authority in local affairs until 1845 when the town was incorporated.

Today, Bethlehem is a unique blend of the old and new where buildings of glass and steel are mixed with 250-year-old structures of hand-hewn logs and limestone block. Bethlehem sponsors a "Walk into History" that describes twenty-seven sites important to the town's history, including some buildings that have been in continuous use for over 250 years.

The Brethren's House is a four-story structure that served as a dormitory and workshop for the young men of Bethlehem until they married and moved into their own homes. The Old Chapel on Heckewelder Place was Bethlehem's second place of worship. Among the people who attended services were generals Lafayette and Washington. The Geimeinhaus at Church Street and Heckwelder Place is Bethlehem's oldest building, a five-story log structure that was the gathering place and focal point of life in the early community. It is the largest log structure in the nation and currently houses the Moravian Museum of Bethlehem.

98-1. Sun Inn

564 Main Street

The Sun Inn, "…where history and hospitality live on," is a handsome jewel of eighteenth-century Moravian architecture that was established in 1758 as an extraordinary "ordinary" offering colonial travelers gracious service, food, drink, and comfortable rooms. In colonial days, the inn lay on Bethlehem's northern boundary, with its distinctive mansard tile roof "a visible and welcoming site from all directions." Today's inn is an authentic restoration of the building that hosted many prominent people, including George and Martha Washington, Benjamin Franklin, the Marquis de Lafayette, and John Adams, who wrote to his wife that the Sun Inn was the best inn he had ever seen. The first floor is a living history museum, the second houses dining and meeting rooms, and a landscaped courtyard adds to the colonial ambience for outdoor dining in season.

Figure 102. The location of the Bethlehem Area Chamber of Commerce and Sun Inn, Bethlehem, Pennsylvania.

DIRECTIONS: From I 78, take Exit 20 onto SR 378 northbound to the "Center City-Historic Bethlehem" Exit, go eastbound on Broad Street to Main Street, then go south on Main to the Chamber of Commerce on the west side of the street at #509 and the Sun Inn on the east side of the street at #564 (Figure 102).

PUBLIC USE: Season and hours: *Sun Inn:* Guided tours are conducted Tuesday–Thursday, 12:30 –4 PM; Friday, 12:30–9 PM; Saturday, 10 AM–9 PM. **Admission fee. Food service. For people with disabilities:** Partially accessible.

FOR ADDITIONAL INFORMATION: Contact: Bethlehem Area Chamber of Commerce, 509 Main Street, Bethlehem, Pennsylvania 18018; 610-867-3788. *Sun Inn:* **Contact:** Sun Inn, 564 Main Street, Bethlehem, Pennsylvania 18018; 215-866-1758.

99. VAN WYCK HOMESTEAD MUSEUM

FISHKILL, NEW YORK

Fishkill was a small crossroads village located on the main north-south road from Westchester to northern forts, and the east-west road between industrial New England and the forts of West Point and Fort

Montgomery. Due to its strategic location, Fishkill became the site of an important American supply depot and military encampment during the Revolutionary War.

Early in the conflict, Continental Army officers requisitioned the wood-frame house of Cornelius Van Wyck as headquarters. For some time, the house was used by General Israel Putnam who was visited by Lafayette, von Steuben, and George Washington. After the war, the house reverted to the Van Wyck family whose members resided there for another 150 years. The Van Wyck House is now a house museum managed by the Fishkill Historical Society.

An interesting sidelight is that the house is reputed to have been the setting for James Fenimore Cooper's novel, *The Spy.* The inspiration may have been a real-life American spy whose mock trial, held to protect his real activities, was conducted in the Van Wyck House. Whoever he was, he was imprisoned at the Dutch Reformed Church in Fishkill and allowed to escape under secret orders, perhaps from General Washington himself. After publication of *The Spy* in the 1820s, several professed double agents stepped forward, each claiming to be the real-life spy. James Fenimore Cooper, however, proclaimed that the character was a synthesis of a vast number of Revolutionary War spies.

DIRECTIONS: The Van Wyck Homestead Museum is at the intersection of US 9 and I 84, 1 mile south of the Village of Fishkill (Figure 103).

PUBLIC USE: Season and hours: Memorial Day–Labor Day, Saturday–Sunday, 1–5 PM, or by appointment. **For people with disabilities:** Accessible.

FOR ADDITIONAL INFORMATION: Contact: Van Wyck Homestead Museum, US 9 and I 84, Box 133, Fishkill, New York 12524; 845-896-9560.

100. New Windsor Cantonment State Historic Site

VAILS GATE, NEW YORK

New Windsor was the site of the last winter encampment of the Continental Army, the winter of 1782–1783. Seven thousand troops trans-

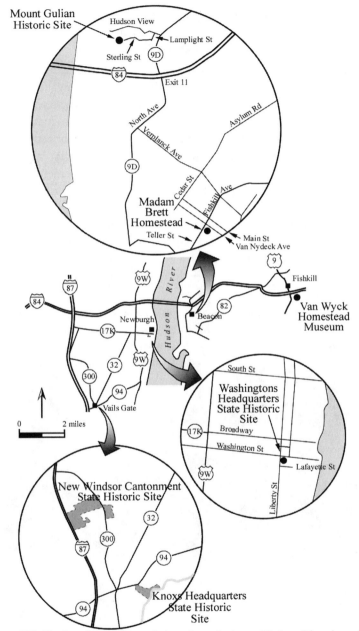

Figure 103. The location of featured sites along the lower Hudson River in and near Newburgh, New York.

formed 1600 acres of forests and fields into a military city of 600 huts, guardhouses, kitchens, and a large church called the Temple of Virtue where, on March 15, 1783, General Washington delivered an emotional oration that averted a serious uprising by disillusioned officers.

Today the Temple of Virtue and other camp buildings (Figure 104) have been accurately reconstructed, and costumed interpreters demonstrate aspects of colonial military life that include musket and artillery drills, woodworking, and blacksmithing. A modern visitor center houses a museum that features Revolutionary War exhibits, with emphasis on the Hudson Valley campaigns. The visitor center also screens a twenty-minute audio-visual show that dramatizes the final phases of the Revolutionary War.

A prominent artifact that always draws interest is an original Badge of Military Merit, an award established by General Washington to honor soldiers and non-commissioned officers for outstanding valor. It was the forerunner of today's Purple Heart, the medal awarded to all armed forces personnel wounded in action.

The New York State Office of Parks, Recreation and Historic Preservation operates the Cantonment as part of New Windsor Historic Parklands.

Figure 104. Temple of Virtue, New Windsor Cantonment, Vails Gate, New York. (Photograph by William G. Clotworthy)

DIRECTIONS: New Windsor Cantonment lies astride SR 300 about 1 mile north of Vails Gate (Figure 103).

PUBLIC USE: Season and hours: April 15–October 31, Wednesday– Saturday, 10 AM–5 PM; Sunday, 1–5 PM. **Admission fee. Visitor center. For people with disabilities:** The visitor center is accessible. Most of the interiors are accessible to people with mobility limitations.

FOR ADDITIONAL INFORMATION: Contact: New Windsor Cantonment State Historic Site, Temple Hill Road, Box 207, Vails Gate, New York 12584; 845-561-1765. **Web site:** *www.nysparks.state.ny.us.* **Read:** Janet Dempsey. 1987. *Washington's Last Cantonment: High Time for a Peace.*

101. WASHINGTONS HEADQUARTERS STATE HISTORIC SITE

NEWBURGH, NEW YORK

Many believe that the Revolutionary War ended with the British surrender at Yorktown. In reality it dragged on for another eighteen months while the antagonists negotiated a peace treaty in Paris. While the negotiations took place, more than half of George Washington's troops marched from Yorktown to the Hudson Highlands to counter threats from thousands of British troops that still occupied New York City.

While his troops bivouacked in New Windsor, George Washington resided in Jonathan Hasbrouck's house in nearby Newburgh. The General is quoted as saying, ". . . time will pass heavily in this dreary mansion in which we are fast locked by frost and snow."[90] There is no record of any comment by Mrs. Hasbrouck, forced to leave her home to make room for General and Mrs. Washington and the military staff.

On April 13, 1783, Washington issued a proclamation ordering the end of hostilities although a peace treaty had not been officially signed. As the army began to dissolve, Washington remained in Newburgh for another several months. The historic headquarters building has been preserved and a six-acre park that surrounds the house includes the imposing Tower of Victory Monument, dedicated in 1887. Above the gates and arches of the monument are bronze statues of soldiers and officers of the Continental Army, with a representation of Washington dominating the center.

The New York State Office of Parks, Recreation and Historic Preservation operates Washingtons Headquarters.

DIRECTIONS: From US 9W, turn eastbound at the intersection with Washington Street and go to Liberty Street, then go south on Liberty to Washingtons Headquarters on the east side of the street (Figure 103).

PUBLIC USE: Season and hours: Mid-April–October, Wednesday–Saturday, 10 AM–5 PM; Sunday, 1–5 PM. Also open Presidents' Day, Memorial Day, Independence Day, Labor Day, and Columbus Day. **Admission fee. For people with disabilities:** Partially accessible.

FOR ADDITIONAL INFORMATION: Contact: Washingtons Headquarters State Historic Site, 84 Liberty Street, Newburgh, New York 12551-1476; 845-562-1195. **Web site:** *www.nysparks.state.ny.us.*

102. KNOXS HEADQUARTERS STATE HISTORIC SITE

VAILS GATE, NEW YORK

Colonel Thomas Ellison, a veteran of the French and Indian War, returned home in 1754 to build a sturdy stone farmhouse. For the remainder of the eighteenth century and into the nineteenth, the Ellison family conducted important commercial dealings in milling, shipping their flour to New York City and the West Indies. During the Revolutionary War, Ellison's house was used as headquarters for high-ranking American officers that included generals Henry Knox and Horatio Gates. Gates, the hero of Saratoga, used the house when commanding the New Windsor Cantonment garrison.

Although George Washington found his quarters in nearby Newburgh "dreary and confined," it is certain that he visited the more comfortable Ellison house that became a social center for his staff. Oral traditions include a story that the staid general opened a ball held at the house, with Lucy Knox as his partner. The Jane Colden Native Plant Sanctuary, featuring over 100 kinds of wildflowers, is part of the forty-nine-acre site, as are the remains of the Ellison mill. Tours and workshops offer hands-on and interactive experiences that enable visitors to discover how the Ellisons and other families of the middle Hudson Valley lived over 200 years ago.

DIRECTIONS: From Vails Gate, go east on SR 94 to Forge Hill Road, and go south on Forge Hill to Knoxs Headquarters (Figure 103).

PUBLIC USE: Season and hours: Memorial Day–Labor Day; Wednesday–Saturday, 10 AM–5 PM; Sunday, 10 AM–5 PM; or by appointment. **Admission fee. For people with disabilities:** Not accessible.

FOR ADDITIONAL INFORMATION: Contact: Knoxs Headquarters State Historic Site, Box 207, Vails Gate, New York 12584; 845-561-5498. **Web site:** *www.nysparks.state.ny.us.* **Read:** North Callahan. 1958. *Henry Knox, General Washington's General.*

103. MOUNT GULIAN HISTORIC SITE

BEACON, NEW YORK

On May 13, 1783, a group of military officers gathered in the headquarters of General Baron von Steuben to form the nation's first fraternal organization, The Society of Cincinnati, named in honor of the Roman farmer-general who led an army to victory, only to return home rather than assume the mantle of dictator. The society's first president was, appropriately, George Washington, who emulated the Roman hero when he returned to Mount Vernon after the Revolutionary War.

Von Steuben's headquarters was in Mount Gulian, a significant example of early Dutch architecture in the Hudson Valley. Its gambrel roof sloped downward in a bell-like curve, and there were four capped chimneys, a huge cooking fireplace, and beehive oven. A disastrous fire destroyed the house in 1931, but it was reconstructed on the original foundation through the efforts of the Mount Gulian Society, a non-profit, private organization which promotes the site as an important historical, educational, and cultural facility.

DIRECTIONS: From I 84, take Exit 11 (Wappingers Falls/Beacon) northbound on SR 9D for 0.3 mile, go west through the gate of the Hudson View Park Apartments, then go south onto Lamplight Street that becomes Sterling Street. Mount Gulian is at the west end of Sterling Street (Figure 103).

PUBLIC USE: Season and hours: Mid-April–December, Wednesdays and Sundays, 1–5 PM; other times by appointment. **Admission fee. Gift shop. For people with disabilities:** Accessible.

FOR ADDITIONAL INFORMATION: Contact: Mount Gulian Historic Site, 145 Sterling Street, Beacon, New York 12508; 845-831-8172.

104. MADAM BRETT HOMESTEAD
BEACON, NEW YORK

Catheryna and Roger Brett built a homestead in 1709. Widowed shortly thereafter, Mrs. Brett remained in the "wilderness" of the Hudson Valley to raise three sons, operate a mill, and form a trading cooperative. During the Revolution the house was occupied by Madam Brett's granddaughter, Hannah Brett Schenck, whose husband was the purchasing agent for the Commissary Department of the Continental Army. As a leading area family, there is little doubt that the Schencks entertained George Washington, Lafayette, and von Steuben.

The Madam Brett Homestead is considered Dutchess County's oldest home, an architectural gem with handmade scalloped red cedar shingles, sloped dormers, and a native stone foundation. Some of the furnishings are original, or owned by the family, and include a large China Trade porcelain collection plus eighteenth- and nineteenth-century furniture. The exterior is graced by a large formal garden.

In 1954, the property, in danger of demolition, was saved through the efforts of the Melzingah Chapter of the Daughters of the American Revolution who maintain it as a vital part of Hudson Valley and Revolutionary War history.

DIRECTIONS: From I 84, take Exit 11 onto SR 9D southbound to Verplanck Avenue, go south on Verplanck to Fishkill Avenue, then go south on Fishkill to Van Nydeck Avenue and the Brett Homestead on the southeast corner of the intersection (Figure 103).

PUBLIC USE: Season and hours: First Sunday of each month, 1–4 PM; other times by appointment. **Admission fee. For people with disabilities:** Not accessible.

FOR ADDITIONAL INFORMATION: Contact: Madam Brett Homestead, 50 Van Nydeck Avenue, Beacon, New York 12508; 845-831-6533.

105. MANDEVILLE HOUSE

GARRISON-ON-HUDSON, NEW YORK

The main portion of the Mandeville House was built by tenant farmer Jacob Mandeville in 1737, with a kitchen wing, parlor, and bedroom added sometime before the Revolution. During the conflict the Dutch-English house served as headquarters for General Israel Putnam and there is documentation that George Washington visited the house on July 26, 1779, as his expense account entry reads, "to cash paid at Mandeville's for house, rooms, etc. £2:5:"[91]

Local legend relates that Major John Andre was paraded past the Mandeville House on the way to his incarceration, trial, and execution in Tappan, New York. A black walnut tree from that period still stands in front of the house. The Mandeville House is owned and maintained by the Perry-Gething Foundation, a private organization dedicated to the preservation of Victorian and early American history of the Hudson Valley. The Mandeville House is open on a limited basis for group tours by appointment.

DIRECTIONS: The Mandeville House is at the northwest corner of the intersection of SR 9D and CR 403 (Lower Station Road) in Garrison-on-Hudson (Figure 90).

FOR ADDITIONAL INFORMATION: Contact: The Perry-Gething Foundation, c/o Mandeville House, Route 9D, Box 214, Garrison-on-Hudson, New York 10524; 845-424-3626.

106. BEEKMAN ARMS HOTEL

RHINEBECK, NEW YORK

The Beekman Arms, "America's oldest Inn," has long been a place for rest and refreshment for travelers. The original tavern, built in

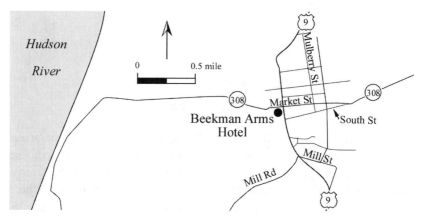

Figure 105. The location of Beekman Arms Hotel, Rhinebeck, New York.

1700, was a two-room stone building built on the Sepasco Indian Trail as a combination inn and shelter for local residents against Indian attacks. By mid-century, it had become an important stagecoach stop on the Albany Post Road, which ran between New York and Albany. General Washington often watched his troops drilling in the square while he waited for couriers to arrive with news.

The Beekman Arms has evolved over the years into a splendid modern facility of fifty-five rooms, and has retained the welcoming spirit and authentic atmosphere of colonial days. The taproom, with its original strong oak beams and broad planks in the ceiling, contains muskets, powder horns, and other artifacts of the colonial period.

DIRECTIONS: Beekman Arms Hotel is located on the southwest corner of the intersection of US 9 and SR 38 (Market Street) in Rhinebeck (Figure 105).

FOR ADDITIONAL INFORMATION: Contact: The Beekman Arms Hotel, Route 9, Rhinebeck, New York 12572; 845-876-7077.

107. OLD FORT HOUSE MUSEUM

FORT EDWARD, NEW YORK

The Old Fort House, built around 1772, is one of the oldest frame houses in New York, constructed with timbers taken from nearby Fort Edward, a facility that dated to the French and Indian War. During the Revolution, the Old Fort House served as both a tavern and courthouse under British occupation and, at various times, as headquarters for American generals Benedict Arnold and Philip Schuyler and British generals John Burgoyne and John Stark. In 1783, General George Washington dined at the house, as attested to by a copy of his handwritten bill on display.

Old Fort House Museum, maintained by the Fort Edward Historical Association, features a collection of photographs and furniture that provides visitors with an instructive glimpse of daily life in rural New York from the mid-eighteenth to the early-twentieth century. The museum is the center of a five-building campus complex; the others are an 1840s tollhouse, an 1853 law office, the Riverside one-room schoolhouse, and a late nineteenth century Washington County Fairgrounds building. All are open for visitation.

DIRECTIONS: Old Fort House Museum is located along US 4 about 1 mile south of Fort Edward (Figure 106).

PUBLIC USE: Season and hours: June 1–August 30, 1–5 PM; September 1–October 13, Saturday–Sunday, 1–5 PM. Other times by appointment. **Admission fee. Gift shop. For people with disabilities:** The Old Fort House is accessible.

FOR ADDITIONAL INFORMATION: Contact: Old Fort House Museum, 27 Lower Broadway, Box 106, Fort Edward, New York 12828; 518-747-9600.

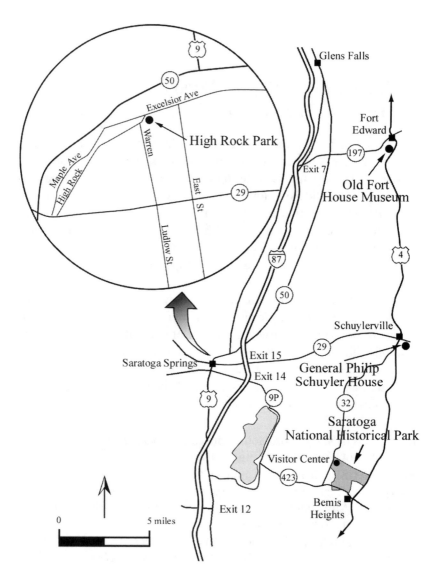

Figure 106. The location of featured sites in and near Saratoga Springs, New York.

108. SARATOGA NATIONAL HISTORICAL PARK AND GENERAL PHILIP SCHUYLER HOUSE

STILLWATER, NEW YORK

Saratoga National Historical Park is a 2800-acre site commemorating the battles fought on September 19 and October 7, 1777, when American forces defeated General John Burgoyne's British army advancing south from Canada. The American victory is considered by many to be the turning point of the Revolution as it not only prevented the British from bisecting the colonies along the Hudson, but was instrumental, along with Brandywine, in convincing France to enter the conflict as America's ally.

The National Park Service maintains and operates Saratoga National Historical Park, where a nine-mile, self-guided automobile tour covers ten stops at critical battlefield sites. For example, the Freeman Farm Overlook looks down on open fields where major fighting on September 19ᵗʰ took place — when Daniel Morgan's Virginia riflemen opened the battle by firing on Burgoyne's advance guard.

The country home of General Philip Schuyler at Saratoga was burned by the British to keep patriots from using it for cover, but the government approved of its replacement after the Revolutionary War. The new house became the center of Schuyler's extensive milling and farming operations. The Schuyler House is administered as part of Saratoga National Historical Park.

George Washington honored the victory by visiting Saratoga on his "vacation" trip from Newburgh in 1783.

DIRECTIONS: Saratoga National Historical Park is cradled within an area bounded by US 4, SR 423, and SR 32, with the primary access being from SR 32 about 2 miles north of SR 423. The General Philip Schuyler House is located in the southeastern corner of the intersection of US 4 and SR 29 in Schuylerville (Figure 106).

PUBLIC USE: Season and hours: *Visitor center:* 9 AM–5 PM daily. Closed Thanksgiving Day, Christmas Day, and New Year's Day. *The

Tour Road: April 1–mid-November, dawn–dusk, daily. ***Schuyler House:*** Guided tours available from June 1–Labor Day, Friday–Sunday, 10 AM–4 PM. **Admission fee. Gift shop. For people with disabilities:** The visitor center is accessible, the Schuyler House is partially accessible.

FOR ADDITIONAL INFORMATION: Contact: Saratoga National Historical Park, 648 Route 32, Stillwater, New York 12170-1604; 518-664-9821. **Web site:** *www.nps.gov/sara.* **Read:** (1) Max M. Mintz. 1991. *The Generals of Saratoga.* (2) Richard Ketchum. 1997. *Saratoga: Turning Point of the Revolution.*

109. SCHUYLER MANSION STATE HISTORIC SITE

ALBANY, NEW YORK

Philip Schuyler served in the French and Indian War as a captain of militia before he returned home to carry on family interests in land speculation, trading, politics, and Indian relationships. In 1760, he initiated construction of a Georgian home on a bluff in the southern part of Albany. The interior of the house was decorated in high style as befitted Schuyler's social and economic standing. He purchased wallpaper from London, with flock enough for seven rooms and hand-painted classical scenes for others.

The sitting room's furniture arrangement is brilliant due to an ongoing process that has recreated the interior much as it was when the Schuyler family was in residence. A New York upholsterer prepared two large settees and ten chair seats with yellow worsted damask, and analysis of the woodwork enabled refurbishers to paint the walls in the same colors chosen by Schuyler in the 1790s.

At the outbreak of the Revolution, Schuyler was named a delegate to the Continental Congress that commissioned him major general in command of the Northern Department. His home became the center of military activities wherein Benjamin Franklin and Benedict Arnold were among his visitors. Alexander Hamilton, who married Schuyler's daughter Elizabeth in 1780, visited frequently, and General George Washington visited near the end of the war.

Figure 107. The location of Schuyler Mansion State Historic Site, Albany, New York.

Following Schuyler's death, the mansion was sold as a private residence. In 1910, the mansion was sold to a consortium of patriotic societies and individuals. Restoration efforts began in 1914 and the mansion was dedicated as an historic site on October 17, 1917, the 140th anniversary of Burgoyne's defeat at Saratoga.

DIRECTIONS: From US 20 in Albany, go south on South Pearl Street to Morton Avenue, then west on Morton to Clinton Street, then south on Clinton to Catherine Street, then west on Catherine to Schuyler Mansion (Figure 107).

PUBLIC USE: Season and hours: Mid-April–October, Wednesday–Saturday, 10 AM–5 PM; Sunday, 1–5 PM. Groups year-round by appointment. **Admission fee. Gift shop. For people with disabilities:** The first floor is accessible, the second is not. There is a visual aid for picturing the second floor.

FOR ADDITIONAL INFORMATION: Contact: Schuyler Mansion State Historic Site, 32 Catherine Street, Albany, New York 12202; 518-434-0834. **Read:** George Waller. 1966. *Saratoga, Saga of an Impious Era.*

110. HIGH ROCK PARK

SARATOGA SPRINGS, NEW YORK

In 1783, General Philip Schuyler cut a road through the wilderness of central New York to High Rock Springs, the site of natural mineral waters with reported medicinal qualities and curative powers. He constructed a small frame house for summer use. In that same year, General Washington journeyed to the springs on his vacation trip. Impressed by the area, he tried to purchase land, but was disappointed to discover the parcel he wanted had already been taken. Washington's taste and vision, however, were wise, as High Rock Springs became Saratoga Springs, one of America's premier resorts. A commemorative plaque in High Rock Park marks the spot where George Washington stood to admire the view — and recognize a smart investment opportunity.

DIRECTIONS: Saratoga Springs is just off of I 87, 30 miles north of Albany, New York. Take Exit 15 to SR 50 southbound that merges with US 9 just north of the park. From the intersection of SR 50 and SR 29, go east on SR 29 2 blocks to High Rock Road, then go north on High Rock Road to High Rock Park (Figure 106).

111. FORT TICONDEROGA

TICONDEROGA, NEW YORK

Three weeks after the battles in Lexington and Concord in 1775, American military officers Ethan Allen and Benedict Arnold led a daunting raid on the British fort at Ticonderoga, the first American victory of the nascent war. Later in the year, Colonel Henry Knox hauled Fort Ticonderoga's captured ordnance to Boston, shepherding the "noble train of artillery"[92] across lakes and rivers, through the snow and trackless forests in one of the most remarkable logistical feats in military history.

The cannons were put into place on Dorchester Heights overlooking Boston, a maneuver that enabled the colonials to effect the siege that forced the British to evacuate the city.

Fort Ticonderoga, situated between Lake Champlain and Lake George in upstate New York, was built by the French in 1755 to protect their commercial interests in the American wilderness. Its strategic location made it one of the most important bastions of the French during the French and Indian War. The star-shaped fortress was the ultimate defensive structure of the eighteenth century.

Fort Ticonderoga traded masters over the next few decades and was eventually abandoned until a building project in 1908 restored the fort to its original eminence, standing proudly as one of America's most prominent military reconstructions. The Fort Ticonderoga Museum houses an outstanding collection of eighteenth-century military artifacts and memorabilia. The Fort Ticonderoga research collection is preserved in the Thompson-Pell Research Center and consists of 12,000 volumes including definitive collections of eighteenth-century French, English, German, and American military manuals and published documents relating to the Seven Years War and the American Revolution.

DIRECTIONS: From the intersection of SR 74 and SR 22 in Ticonderoga, go east on SR 74 0.5 mile to the entrance to Fort Ticonderoga (Figure 108).

PUBLIC USE: Season and hours: May–October, 9 AM–5 PM; July–August, 9 AM–6 PM. **Admission fee. Visitor center. Gift shop. For people with disabilities:** Accessible except for the upper floor.

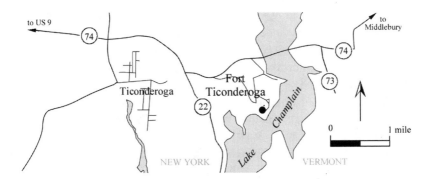

Figure 108. The location of Fort Ticonderoga, Ticonderoga, New York.

FOR ADDITIONAL INFORMATION: Contact: Fort Ticonderoga, Box 390B, Ticonderoga, New York 12883; 518-585-2821. **Web site:** *www.fort-ticonderoga.org.* **Read:** Benson Bobrick. 1997. *Angel in the Whirlwind.*

112. ROCKINGHAM STATE HISTORIC SITE

PRINCETON, NEW JERSEY

While attending a Continental Congress in 1783, George and Martha Washington resided in the Berrien House where news was received that the Treaty of Paris had been signed. The War for Independence was officially over. General Washington sat down to write his famous "Farewell to the Armies" in which he stated, "Before the Cmdr in Chief takes his final leave of those he holds most dear he wishes to indulge himself a few moments in calling to mind a slight review of the past . . . ."[93]

A visit to Rockingham encourages us to reflect on the past and our noble heritage — to take a moment to consider the deeds of our patriot ancestors and how much we owe to their vision, wisdom, and courage. The Berrien's two-story white clapboard house has been preserved by the State of New Jersey as a repository of historical treasures — real ones embodied in original furnishings and ethereal ones represented in the ideas and ideals of our patriot ancestors whose presence may be felt within its walls. The general's desk is prepared with a quill, writing box, and whale oil lamp and the parlor tea table glistens in anticipation of an afternoon visit by Alexander Hamilton, John Adams, or Thomas Jefferson.

DIRECTIONS: From US 1 north of Princeton, go north on CR 522 to Kingston, then go north on CR 603 1 mile to the site on the west side of the road (Figure 68).

PUBLIC USE: Rockingham State Historic Park is currently (2002) closed while the site undergoes extensive renovation. The schedule for completion is not available at this time.

FOR ADDITIONAL INFORMATION: Contact: Rockingham State Historic Site, P. O. Box 496, Kingston, New Jersey 08528; 609-921-8835. **Web site:** *www.rockingham.net.*

113. FRAUNCES TAVERN MUSEUM

NEW YORK, NEW YORK

As the last English soldier embarked to the waiting fleet in December, 1783, British occupation of New York ended, and General Washington led triumphant troops into the city. He remained for a week of honors and festivities before he hosted a private luncheon at Fraunces Tavern where he bid an emotional farewell to some of the officers who had served under him throughout the Revolution.

> *With a heart full of love and gratitude, I now take leave of you. I most devoutly wish that your later days may be as prosperous and happy as your former ones have been glorious and honorable.*[94]

With that, he embraced each man and took leave. He passed silently through a double line of light infantry, then walked to Whitehall, where a barge ferried him across the Hudson River to New Jersey and the beginning of the journey home.

Fraunces Tavern was built as a private residence in 1719 but was converted to a tavern by Samuel Fraunces, a West Indian émigré and innkeeper par excellence. Conveniently situated at the crossroads of trade and travel, the establishment became a great success as taverns, inns, and "ordinaries" were gathering places for influential colonials. Fraunces's reputation for high quality service and his maintenance of a balance between dignified elegance and democratic cordiality assured the patronage of an important and distinguished clientele. Fraunces was also a meeting place for those who opposed the crown, which made life difficult for owner Fraunces during the long British occupation of New York, but the establishment regained its reputation and clientele following the war. Fraunces sold the tavern in 1785 and slipped into a short-lived retirement before President Washington persuaded him to become steward at the Executive Mansion on Cherry Street.

Very little of the original tavern remains although a portion was reconstructed by a patriotic group, Sons of the Revolution, in the early part of the twentieth century. The first floor is an active restaurant furnished in colonial style and the second and third floors have been converted to a museum devoted to Washington and his famous farewell luncheon. Based on extensive research of inventories and estates of many tavern keepers, "The Long Room" is an accurate re-creation of an eighteenth-century public room, with tables set as they may have been for Washington and his guests in 1783.

DIRECTIONS: Fraunces Tavern is located in lower Manhattan at the corner of Pearl and Broad streets (Figure 60).

PUBLIC USE: Season and hours: *Tavern:* Monday–Friday, open for breakfast, lunch, and dinner. *Museum:* Monday–Friday, 10 AM–4:45 PM; Sunday, 12 N–4 PM. **Admission fee. Gift shop. For people with disabilities:** Accessible.

FOR ADDITIONAL INFORMATION: Contact: Fraunces Tavern Museum, 54 Pearl Street, New York, New York 10004; 212-269-0144 (Tavern), 212-425-1778 (Museum). **Web site:** *www.frauncestavern.org.*

114. ANNAPOLIS CITY HALL

ANNAPOLIS, MARYLAND

George Washington was a regular social visitor to Annapolis where he attended the races, visited friends, or over-nighted on his innumerable trips between Mount Vernon and the north. His most memorable visit was in December, 1783, when he appeared before the Continental Congress to resign his commission as Commander-in-Chief.

On the 22nd of December, the Maryland General Assembly honored him at a ball. James Tilton wrote of the colorful event, "the General danced every set, that all ladies might have the pleasure of dancing with him, or as it has since been handsomely expressed, get a touch of him."[95]

The social hall has been greatly expanded through the years and is currently utilized as Annapolis City Hall where the ballroom serves as the City Council Chamber.

DIRECTIONS: Annapolis City Hall is located at #150 Duke of Gloucester Street (Figure 43).

PUBLIC USE: Season and hours: 9 AM–5 PM daily.
FOR ADDITIONAL INFORMATION: Contact: Annapolis City Hall,
150 Duke of Gloucester Street, Annapolis, Maryland 21401; 410-263-
7942. **Web site:** *www.ci.annapolis.md.us*. **Read:** William L. Lebovich.
1984. *America's City Halls.*

115. MARYLAND STATE HOUSE

ANNAPOLIS, MARYLAND

The Maryland State House, the oldest state house in the nation still
in use, was the capitol of the fledgling United States from November 11,
1783 until August 13, 1784, when Congress and the administration moved
to Philadelphia. On December 23, 1783, General George Washington
appeared before Congress in the Old Senate Chamber to deliver an emotional speech of resignation as Commander-in-Chief of the Continental
Army. Today, a life-sized wax figure of the general stands on the exact
spot to commemorate his appearance (Figure 109).

Figure 109. Wax figure of General Washington in the Old Senate Chamber, Maryland
State House, Annapolis, Maryland. (Photograph by William G. Clotworthy)

Construction of the State House was begun in 1772, but progress was delayed by the outbreak of the Revolutionary War and it was not completed until 1779. The interior of the original section of the State House is of wood and plaster and the dome is the largest wooden dome in the United States. A colonial revival section installed between 1902 and 1905 has matching Italian marble walls and columns. A broad, black line across the floor of the center hall marks the line between the old and new sections of the building.

DIRECTIONS: The Maryland State House is located at the center of Capitol Circle (Figure 43).

PUBLIC USE: Season and hours: 9 AM–5 PM daily. Guided tours are conducted at 11 AM and 3 PM. Closed Christmas Day. **Visitor center. For people with disabilities:** Accessible.

FOR ADDITIONAL INFORMATION: Contact: Maryland State House, State Circle, Annapolis, Maryland 21401; 410-974-3400. **Web site:** *www.ci.annapolis.md.us.* **Read:** Morris L. Radoff. 1972. *The State House at Annapolis.*

~

VICTORY AND THE PRESIDENCY

After he resigned his command of the Continental Army, George Washington returned to Mount Vernon with plans to resume life as a Virginia planter. During the war, however, significant alterations to the mansion had been effected, and some were unsatisfactory. Skilled labor was hard to find, the grounds needed to be upgraded, and salaries and taxes had to be paid. Washington found himself in financial difficulty as Mount Vernon had not been profitable during his absence and he had served for eight years as commander-in-chief without compensation save reimbursement of his personal expenses.

A lavish life-style resumed, however, and he even expanded his outside commitments. He remained interested in the Great Dismal Swamp project and became president of the Patowmack Canal Company, a speculative enterprise that undertook to build a canal that would link Alexandria, Virginia, with the Ohio Valley.

Although George Washington was a man of character and honesty, and sincere in his desire to remain at Mount Vernon as a gentleman farmer, that was not to be, as he had, above all else, a sense of duty and commitment to the confederation of states he had so nobly served. It became clear that the confederation system was not working. There were trade problems with other nations and the government was too weak to solve problems. It seemed impossible to remove the British from royal forts in the wilderness and, on a personal basis, jealousy between the states and other sectional rivalries posed a menace to his plans for the Potomac. It became obvious to Washington and others that a national government with a viable constitution was essential if the nation were to survive.

With reluctance, he laid down the plowshare in 1789. He returned to Philadelphia to preside over a Constitutional Congress, where a constitution for the United States was debated, written, and approved by the delegates, then distributed to the states for ratification.

Washington rode home from the Congress with misgivings — it was obvious that the section regarding the office of chief executive of the proposed new government had been written with him, and only him, in mind. Once again, he would be called to service and, predictably, he knew he would answer it.

On April 30, 1789, George Washington was sworn in as President of the United States in New York City (Figure 1), then the capital of the fledgling nation. The government would later move to Philadelphia before it found a permanent home in The Federal City (Washington) in 1800. The Residency Act had provided for such a capital city and President Washington was instrumental in choosing the site and the architect and remained vitally interested in its development. He made numerous trips from Philadelphia and Mount Vernon to check on its progress.

Washington believed strongly in inclusion and made two important presidential tours during his first term in office. In a letter to his sister, President Washington wrote of his reason for making the first tour — "by way of relaxation from business and re-establishment of my health."[96] To government officials, however, he stated that he wished to acquire knowledge of the country and its attitude toward the new government. Author Thomas Flexner commented, "If he also believed that his presence would cement allegiance, he was too modest to say so."[97]

The first trip was to New England where he visited Connecticut, Massachusetts, and New Hampshire (Rhode Island had not ratified the

Constitution at this time). He was received everywhere with honors and patriotic outpourings of great joy and respect. Later on, he made a special trip to Rhode Island, once that tiny state ratified the Constitution.

Following the success of the New England tour, and in an effort to further his policy of inclusion, President Washington announced plans to tour the southern states of North Carolina, South Carolina, and Georgia, none of which he had previously visited. In a letter to Edward Rutledge of South Carolina on June 16, 1791, he wrote:

> *It was among my first determinations when I entered upon the duties of my present station to visit every part of the United States in the course of my administration of the government, provided my health and other circumstances would admit of it . . . .* [98]

In the spring of 1791, the president embarked on a journey of almost 2000 miles that began in Philadelphia, Pennsylvania, and extended as far south as Savannah, Georgia, before he turned back north to end it at his sister's home in Fredericksburg, Virginia. The trip was a tremendous success, although from today's perspective it is difficult to visualize such an arduous journey — by carriage or on horseback over sometimes non-existent roads and across rushing rivers.

Early on, Washington toyed with resignation once a working national government was established, an idea that died a-borning and he was unanimously re-elected in 1793. In 1796, he made a final decision to retire at the end of that term, thus setting a precedent of two-term service broken only by Franklin Roosevelt in the 1940s.

The sites identified in this section are places he visited from after the end of the Revolutionary War until he left the presidency in 1797 (Figure 110, Table 6).

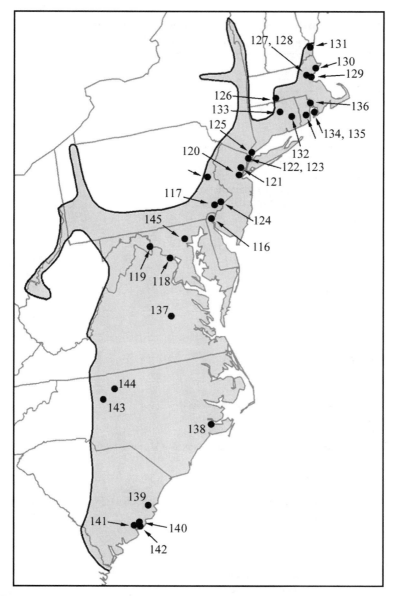

Figure 110. George Washington traveled widely throughout the new United States between the years 1783 and 1797. Most of this travel took place while he was president, and was a deliberate expression of his belief that he should visit all states of the new country. The names and page numbers for descriptions of the numbered sites shown here are given in Table 6.

Table 6. Publicly accessible sites identified with George Washington's travels during the period 1783-1799.

116. AMSTEL HOUSE

NEW CASTLE, DELAWARE

Amstel House, built in 1730, was rented by Nicholas Van Dyke who became president (governor) of the State of Delaware. In 1784, George Washington attended a reception at the house to celebrate the marriage of Van Dyke's daughter Ann to Kensey Johns, Sr., who became chancellor of the Supreme Court of Delaware. Portraits of the couple are displayed in the handsome Georgian house, along with colonial furniture and artifacts.

The house is named for the Dutch community of New Amstel, established at this location in the 1650s by the Dutch governor of New York, Peter Stuyvesant, in an attempt to take control of Chesapeake Bay from the Swedes. The area changed hands twice again before the English took possession in 1664 and changed the name of the community to New Castle. In 1682, Willliam Penn took it over as part of his Pennsylvania domain, and in 1776 it became part of the new State of Delaware. A number of homes from the eighteenth and nineteenth centuries surround a town green believed to have been laid out by Stuyvesant.

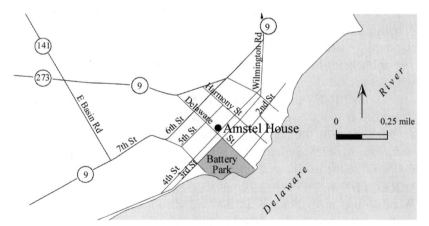

Figure 111. The location of Amstel House, New Castle, Delaware.

Amstel House is maintained as a house-museum by the New Castle Historic Society.

DIRECTIONS: From SR 9, exit onto Wilmington Road (becoming 3rd St, one-way traffic) southbound 0.25 mile to Delaware Street, then go north on Delaware 1 block to 4th Street and the Amstel House on the north corner of the intersection (Figure 111).

PUBLIC USE: Season and hours: March–December, Tuesday–Saturday, 11 AM–4 PM; Sunday, 1–4 PM. Other times by appointment. Closed major holidays. **Admission fee. For people with disabilities:** The first floor is accessible.

FOR ADDITIONAL INFORMATION: Contact: Amstel House, 2 East 4th Street, New Castle, Delaware, 19720; 302-322-2794. **Web site:** *www.newcastlecity.net/visitors/bldgs.html.*

117. WOODLANDS

PHILADELPHIA, PENNSYLVANIA

Washington's diary for May 23, 1787, reads, ". . . in company with Mr. Madison, Mr. Rutledge and others, I crossed the Schuylkill above the falls — visited Mr. Peters and Mr. Wm. Hamilton."[99]

William Hamilton inherited land holdings in 1747 and proceeded to indulge his passions for architecture, botany, and landscape design by planning and building an estate named Woodlands. The house set a new standard for Classical Revival architecture and was described by British visitor Nicholas Pickford: "I know of no house in England of like Estate where a greater degree of Elegancy and Comfort can be found."[100]

Since 1840, Woodlands has been the centerpiece of the Woodlands Cemetery, one of the first rural cemeteries in America and a precursor to the public parks of the nineteenth century. The mansion is currently (2002) under extensive renovation, but the Woodlands Cemetery Company hopes to open it to the public in the near future.

DIRECTIONS: From US 13 west of the Schuylkill River, go south onto Woodland Avenue, then go east into Woodlands Cemetery (Figure 47).

FOR ADDITIONAL INFORMATION: Contact: Woodlands, 4000 Woodland Avenue, Philadelphia, Pennsylvania 19104; 215-386-2181.

118. GREAT FALLS PARK

GREAT FALLS, VIRGINIA

George Washington developed an interest in the west at an early age and it remained with him throughout his life. One personal expression of this interest was his investment in thousands of acres of land, some as far west as the mouth of the Kanawha River in what is now West Virginia. As businessman and politician, he recognized both the commercial potential and political importance of integration of the western lands, especially those of the Ohio River Valley with the Atlantic Seaboard. One way to accomplish these commercial and political objectives, he thought, would be to connect the upper Ohio Valley and the Tidewater portion of the Potomac River by a commercially viable waterway.

As early as 1754, Washington canoed the Potomac between Cumberland and Great Falls and became familiar with the topography of the area. In 1769, he drew plans for a privately financed system of canal locks to be placed at strategic points along the river between Georgetown and Cumberland, locks that would allow riverboats to negotiate changes of elevation along the river. The integration of locks that by-passed rapids and falls, and segments of open, navigable river, would create a continuous waterway between the Tidewater and Cumberland. The Forks of the Ohio region, where the Alleghany and Monongahela rivers come together to form the Ohio River (and the site of today's Pittsburgh), might then be reached by an overland trail from Cumberland.

In May, 1785, the Patowmack Canal Company was formed, with Washington as its first president, its purpose to implement his idea of an improved waterway along and astride the Potomac. Inexperienced engineers and laborers faced a difficult challenge made all the more daunting by the myriad problems presented by the river, in particular the seasonal ranges in water flow, shallow areas that needed to be dredged and re-dredged, and the rapids and falls that needed to be bypassed with locks. The Potomac dropped some 600 feet from Cumberland to Tidewater, and nowhere was the change in elevation more pronounced than at Great

Falls, the spot where the river plunged almost eighty feet in less than a mile as it cascaded down the Fall Line from the Piedmont to the Tidewater (Plate 11).

Construction of the canal and locks at Great Falls began in 1786 and continued for sixteen years, not completed until three years after Washington's death. The system at Great Falls consisted of a segment of canal on the upstream end and five locks on the lower end. The two upper locks were built of hewn stone and timbers on the relatively level surface of the Piedmont, while the lower three locks were blasted out of solid rock into the face of the Fall Line itself. The headquarters of the Patowmack Canal Company was located in the village of Matildaville, which developed at the upper end of the Great Falls canal system. When the canal worked, Matildaville provided travelers and laborers alike with goods and services, but, unfortunately, frequently low water and the high debt of the company combined to bring the venture to an end. In 1828, the new Chesapeake and Ohio Canal Company acquired the assets of the Patowmack Canal Company, and by 1830 water transport along the Potomac had shifted to the new canal on the north side of the river.

Great Falls Park is an 800-acre unit of the National Park Service located along the Potomac River fourteen miles west of Washington, DC. The park takes its name from the Great Falls of the Potomac, one of the most beautiful, dynamic, and moody segments of river along the Fall Line of the Middle Atlantic region. These falls change regularly as the water level in the river waxes and wanes. Several observation areas allow comprehensive views of the site.

Great Falls Park also contains and interprets the remains of Matildaville and the canal and locks that were built to allow river boats to by-pass Great Falls. These works represent one of the most significant engineering accomplishments of the United States at the end of the eighteenth century. A walk through the former site of Matildaville will allow the visitor to see imprints of buildings, sluices, and other features and to comprehend the location, size, and shape of much of the village — both individual structures and the community collectively. The Patowmack Canal Interpretive Trail leads alongside the canal and the upper locks through the deep cut in the face of the region's bedrock to the banks of the Potomac downstream from the Fall Line, the very spot at which riverboats entered and left the locks 200 years ago.

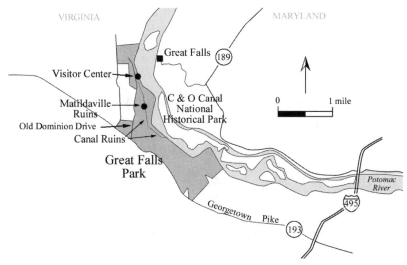

Figure 112. The location of Great Falls Parkin northern Virginia.

DIRECTIONS: From I 495 (Capital Beltway), take Exit 13 onto SR 193 (Georgetown Pike) westbound 4 miles to Old Dominion Drive, then go north on Old Dominion Drive to the park entrance (Figure 112).

PUBLIC USE: Season and hours: *Grounds:* Dawn to dusk, daily. Closed Christmas Day. *Visitor Center:* April 15–October 15, Monday–Friday, 10 AM–5 PM; Saturday–Sunday, 10 AM–6 PM. October 16–April 14, daily, 10 AM–4 PM. **Admission fee. Visitor center. Gift shop. Food service:** Available April–November only. **For people with disabilities:** The visitor center and overlook #2 are accessible.

FOR ADDITIONAL INFORMATION: Contact: Great Falls Park, c/o George Washington Memorial Parkway, Turkey Run Park, McLean, Virginia 22101; 703-285-2965. **Web site:** *www.nps.gov/gwmp/grfa.* **Read:** Wilbur E. Garrett. 1987. "George Washington's Patowmack Canal."

119. HARPERS FERRY NATIONAL HISTORICAL PARK

HARPERS FERRY, WEST VIRGINIA

Harpers Ferry (Plate 12) often is thought of as the place where abolitionist John Brown attempted to seize the federal arsenal in 1859, an action that resulted in his capture, execution and, unfortunately, further division of the nation over the issue of slavery. The history of Harpers Ferry, however, goes back a century before John Brown to a time when intrepid explorers such as surveyor George Washington traversed the area before any town existed. In 1783, Thomas Jefferson visited the Harpers Ferry area and declared the view of the crashing Potomac and Shenandoah rivers as "one of the most stupendous scenes in nature."[101]

In 1785, Washington returned to Harpers Ferry on an inspection tour with other directors of the Patowmack Canal Company, and again later when he was President of the United States. George Washington recognized Harpers Ferry as an essential link in his vision of a transportation system connecting the west with the Atlantic seaboard, and he further recognized the potential for harnessing the power of the rivers, an important factor that led to the choice of Harpers Ferry as the site for a federal armory and arsenal. As president, Washington worked to establish a federal armory and arsenal as a contribution to the industrial and commercial development, and the security, of the fledgling republic. Between the time the first buildings were constructed in 1799 and the Civil War, the armory produced more than 600,000 muskets, rifles, and pistols and employed over 400 people. Today only ruins remain of Harpers Ferry's nineteenth-century industrial heyday.

The history of Harpers Ferry is complex, and to understand its past, the National Park Service, which maintains Harpers Ferry as a National Historical Park, has identified six themes running through its history — Industry, Transportation, Environment, John Brown, the Civil

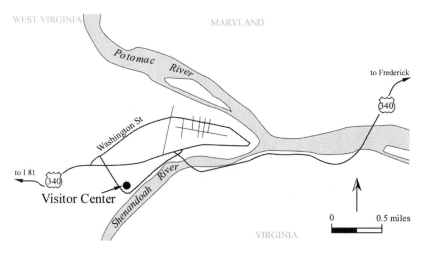

Figure 113. The location of Harpers Ferry National Historical Park in easternmost West Virginia.

War, and Black History. Each is interpreted in displays and reconstructed sites that bring this important American scene into dramatic focus. Harpers Ferry National Historical Park conducts a program, "Path through History," that delineates the various historic and environmental aspects of the park. There are special events held throughout the year such as February's Black History Month, a nineteenth-century July 4th celebration, and others. Ranger-conducted tours are available except during the winter months when park activities are limited.

DIRECTIONS: Harpers Ferry National Historical Park Visitor Center is located immediately south of US 340 in Harpers Ferry (Figure 113).

PUBLIC USE: Season and hours: Summer, 8 AM–6 PM; Winter, 8 AM–5 PM. Closed Christmas Day. **Admission fee. Visitor center. Gift shop. Food service. For people with disabilities:** Accessible, with a special van service available for transportation to the historic site.

FOR ADDITIONAL INFORMATION: Contact: Harpers Ferry National Historical Park, Box 65, Harpers Ferry, West Virginia 25425; 304-535-6298. **Web site:** *www.nps.gov/hafe.* **Read:** (1) James V. Murfin. 1989. *From the Riot and Tumult.* (2) David T. Gilbert. 1995. *A Walker's Guide to Harpers Ferry, West Virginia.*

120. BUCCLEUCH MANSION AND PARK

NEW BRUNSWICK, NEW JERSEY

Buccleuch (Buck-clue) Mansion was named White House Farm when it was built by Anthony White in 1739. White's son was a gallant patriot who donated his fortune to the revolutionary cause and became an aide to George Washington. During the war the house was occupied twice by the British; saber cuts and spur marks dating from their occupancy are still visible in the floorboards. In 1783, General George Washington visited Buccleuch when his Commissary General, Charles Stewart, owned it, and it is probable that he stopped for lunch at the house on his journey to the presidential inauguration in 1789. After the war, the property was named Buccleuch by then-owner Colonel Joseph Warren Scott in honor of his Scottish ancestor, the Duke of Buccleuch. The house and grounds were donated by Colonel Scott's descendants to the city of New Brunswick in 1911, and the local chapter of the Daughters of the American Revolution assumed responsibility for furnishing and main-

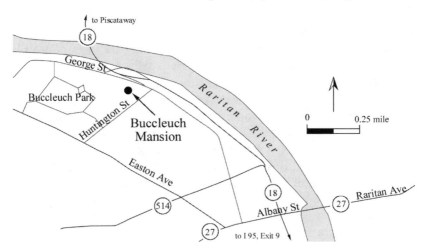

Figure 114. The location of Buccleuch Mansion, New Brunswick, New Jersey.

taining the interior as a house museum. The parlor, dining room, office, and other bedrooms have been carefully restored to reflect various periods of the home's occupancy. Historic mural wallpaper in the lower and upper halls, for example, dates to 1815. In 1783, Washington slept in the "Early Bedroom" that features furnishings from 1700. Buccleuch Mansion is the centerpiece of Buccleuch Park, seventy-eight acres of public space in New Brunswick.

DIRECTIONS: From SR 27 (Albany Street), go west on Easton Avenue for about 0.75 mile, then go north into Buccleuch Park. The mansion overlooks the Raritan River at the north end of the park (Figure 114).

PUBLIC USE: Season and hours: June–October 1; Sundays, 2–4 PM. For people with disabilities: Accessible.

FOR ADDITIONAL INFORMATION: Contact: Buccleuch Mansion, College Road, New Brunswick, New Jersey 08901; 732-745-5094.

121. BOXWOOD HALL STATE HISTORIC SITE

ELIZABETH, NEW JERSEY

Elias Boudinot was a president of the Continental Congress and signer of the Treaty of Paris. Mr. Boudinot had been selected by Congress to serve as chairman of a committee to conduct President-elect George Washington from Philadelphia across New Jersey to his inauguration in New York City. Boudinot offered his home as a stopping place and Washington and the committee lunched and rested there on April 23, 1789, before continuing their journey.

The red clapboard house, built in 1750, has been restored as an historic house museum maintained by the New Jersey Department of Environmental Protection.

DIRECTIONS: From US 1/9, go west on Jersey Street 1½ blocks to the house on the north side of the street (Figure 115).

PUBLIC USE: Season and hours: Wednesday–Saturday, 10 AM–12 N, 1–5 PM. Closed major holidays. **For people with disabilities:** Call ahead for assistance.

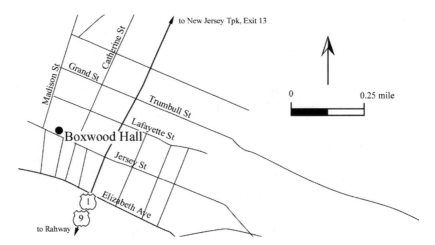

Figure 115. The location of Boxwood Hall, Elizabeth, New Jersey.

FOR ADDITIONAL INFORMATION: Contact: Boxwood Hall, 1073 East Jersey Street, Elizabeth, New Jersey 07201; 201-648-4540. **Read:** Elias Boudinot. 1968. *Journal or Historical Recollections of American Events During the Revolutionary War.*

122. FEDERAL HALL NATIONAL MEMORIAL

NEW YORK, NEW YORK

Federal Hall, the first US Capitol, was the location of the trial of John Peter Zenger in 1735, the Convention of the Stamp Act Congress in 1765, and the inauguration of George Washington as first President of the United States on April 30, 1789. The present building dates to 1842 when it was designed as a federal customs house. A dignified statue of Washington executed by John Quincy Adams Ward dominates the entrance to Federal Hall, now a museum of early American political history. Federal Hall is a National Park Service site.

DIRECTIONS: Federal Hall is located at the intersection of Wall and Nassau streets (Figure 60).

PUBLIC USE: Season and hours: Monday-Friday, 9 AM-5 PM. Open weekends and holidays in July and August. Closed national holidays. **Gift Shop. For people with disabilities:** Accessible.

FOR ADDITIONAL INFORMATION: Contact: Federal Hall National Memorial, 26 Wall Street, New York, New York 10005; 212-825-6888. **Web site:** *www.nps.gov/feha.*

123. Saint Pauls Chapel of Trinity Church (Episcopal)

New York, New York

Saint Pauls Chapel, Trinity Parish, the oldest church building in Manhattan, was dedicated in 1766 (Figure 116). Immediately upon his inauguration as president in 1789, George Washington led worshipers the few blocks from Federal Hall to a special service of thanksgiving at Saint Pauls and he continued regular worship there during his time in New York. Washington's pew remains in the chapel as does the oldest known representation of the Great Seal of the United States.

Saint Pauls Chapel is located only a few short blocks from the site of the World Trade Center. In one of the few miracles of September 11, 2001, Trinity Church, covered with ashes and soot, remained standing, with no structural damage, not even a broken window. Its presence, which has brought comfort and solace to American citizens for almost 250 years, continues to be a symbol of temporal and spiritual strength in the midst of great national peril. It represents the spirit and vision of George Washington and other founding fathers who prayed, as we do today, for the future of our nation.

DIRECTIONS: Saint Pauls Chapel is located at the corner of Broadway and Fulton Street (Figure 60).

PUBLIC USE: Season and hours: Monday–Friday, 9 AM–3 PM; Sunday, 7 AM–3 PM. Closed holidays. **Gift shop.**

FOR ADDITIONAL INFORMATION: Contact: Saint Pauls Chapel of Trinity Church, Fulton and Broadway, New York, New York 10006; 212-732-5564.

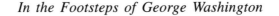

Figure 116. Interior of Saint Pauls Chapel of Trinity Church, New York, New York. (Print courtesy Parish of Trinity Church in the City of New York)

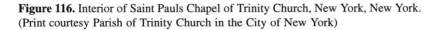

124. DESHLER-MORRIS HOUSE

PHILADELPHIA, PENNSYLVANIA

A yellow fever epidemic that swept Philadelphia in 1793 forced President Washington to flee the city for the more salubrious atmosphere of Germantown where he took up residence and conducted the business of government in the Deshler-Morris House, a magnificent Georgian mansion. The setting was so pleasant and restful that the president returned the next year, thus the house may be considered the first "vacation White House." The house is furnished in period and a gingko tree in the garden dates to the residency of Washington. Deshler-Morris is administered as part of Independence National Historical Park and maintained in association with the Deshler-Morris House Committee, Inc.

DIRECTIONS: From US 1 (Roosevelt Boulevard), take Wissahickon Avenue westbound to West Coulter Street, then go north on West Coulter to Germantown Avenue, then go west to the Deshler-Morris House immediately ahead on the south side of the street (Figure 81).

PUBLIC USE: Season and hours: April–mid-December, Tuesday–Sunday, 1–4 PM. Other times by appointment. **Gift shop. For people with disabilities:** The first floor is accessible after climbing three steps into the house.

FOR ADDITIONAL INFORMATION: Superintendent, Independence National Historical Park, 313 Walnut Street, Philadelphia, Pennsylvania 19106; 215-597-8974. **Read:** J. M. Powell. 1993. *Bring Out Your Dead.*

THE NEW ENGLAND TOUR

125. THE SQUARE HOUSE
RYE, NEW YORK

The Square House is a two-story house with hand-split fishscale shingles and wooden beams that was built as a private home around 1730, then operated as an "ordinary" between 1760 and 1830 (Figure 117). George Washington and John Adams were among the guests who stayed at this ordinary when they traveled to and from New England. Washington's diary for October 15, 1789, as he began his tour of New England, describes it as ". . . a very neat and decent inn."[102] The Square House, owned by the City of Rye, has been restored and is operated as a house museum by the Rye Historical Society.

DIRECTIONS: From I 95 (New England Thruway), take Exit 20 onto US 1 (Boston Post Road) southbound to SR 120 (Purchase Street), then go north onto SR 120 to the Square House immediately to the west on the Village Green (Figure 64).

PUBLIC USE: Season and hours: Tuesday and Saturday, 12:30–4:30 PM; Wednesday, Thursday, Friday, and Sunday, 2:30–4:30 PM. Closed holidays. **For people with disabilities:** Partially accessible.

Figure 117. The Square House, Rye, New York. (Photograph by William G. Clotworthy)

FOR ADDITIONAL INFORMATION: Contact: The Square House, 1 Purchase Street, Rye, New York 10580; 914-967-7588.

126. SPRINGFIELD ARMORY NATIONAL HISTORIC SITE

SPRINGFIELD, MASSACHUSETTS

In 1777, General George Washington and his Chief of Artillery, General Henry Knox, chose Springfield as the site of a military arsenal as it was centrally located, within reach of American troops, and safe from the British. In 1794, the newly-formed federal government decided to manufacture its own weaponry so that it would not be dependent on foreign arms. President Washington knew of Springfield first hand, as he had inspected it personally in 1789, so Springfield was chosen as the site of the factory that became operative in 1795. Over the next 190 years, the armory grew into the most important facility in the world for the design, development, and manufacture of military small arms.

In 1968, the research, development, and manufacturing installation was closed for economic reasons and replaced by an imposing military museum. The Armory encompasses over fifty acres of historic buildings, including the Master Armorer's House, the Main Arsenal, and the Commanding Officer's Quarters. An Historic Museum contains the larg-

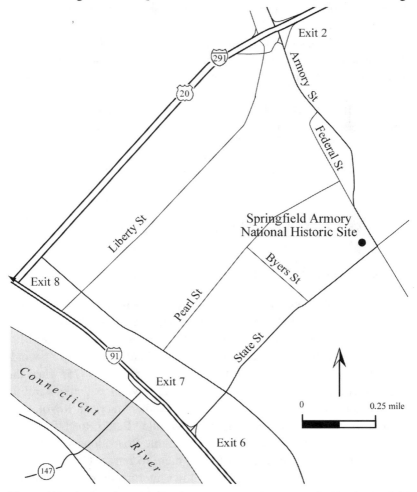

Figure 118. The location of Springfield Armory National Historic Site, Springfield, Massachusetts.

est array of military small arms in the world, from the sleek, long-barreled muskets of 1785 to the famous Springfield rifle to the M-1 of World War II and today's M-16. The museum houses personal firearms collections donated by presidents John F. Kennedy, Dwight D. Eisenhower, Franklin D. Roosevelt, and Woodrow Wilson.

DIRECTIONS: From I 291, take Exit 2 onto Armory Street eastbound about 0.75 mile to Federal Street, continue eastbound on Federal to the campus of Springfield Technical Community College, then go south onto the campus and follow signs to the museum at the corner of Federal and State streets (Figure 118).

PUBLIC USE: Season and hours: Wednesday–Sunday, 10 AM–4:30 PM. Closed Thanksgiving Day, Christmas Day, and New Year's Day. **Visitor center. Gift shop. For people with disabilities:** Fully accessible.

FOR ADDITIONAL INFORMATION: Contact: Springfield Armory National Historic Site, One Armory Square, Springfield, Massachusetts 01105-1299; 413-734-8551. **Web site:** *www.nps.gov/spar.*

127. MINUTE MAN NATIONAL HISTORICAL PARK

CONCORD, MASSACHUSETTS

During his New England tour, President Washington visited Lexington and Concord to "view the spot on which the first blood was spilt in the dispute with Great Britain."[103] That spot is today's Minute Man Historical Park that encompasses a narrow, twenty-mile strip of winding, hilly land commemorating the events of April 19, 1775, when the forces of British General Thomas Gage clashed with local citizen militia in a series of running skirmishes that ignited the American Revolution. Today's visitors may meander down a 5½-mile "Battle Road Trail," an educational project covering remnants of Battle Road along which Militiamen harassed the British and forced them to retreat to Boston. The trail, open to walkers and bicyclists, allows interpretation of natural history and the broader human story of the gallant fight by a determined band of local militia against the might of the British army.

The trail begins at Lexington Green and North Bridge, continues past the historic Meriam House that overlooked some of the bloodiest fighting, then goes on to the "Bloody Angle" where the militia set up an ambush that caught the British in a devastating crossfire. Captain William Smith was commander of the Lincoln Minute Men and his home on the Battle Road Trail has been restored, as has historic Hartwell Tavern. A stone monument marks the approximate site where Paul Revere was captured on his famous "Midnight Ride." Although he was detained, his companion, Dr. Samuel Prescott, escaped to carry the alarm on to Concord.

Minute Man National Historical Park is a National Park Service site where nearly a million visitors a year cross the famous North Bridge to view the Minute Man Statue sculpted by Daniel Chester French and to explore the places where shots were exchanged between the British and colonial militia.

North Bridge Visitor Center offers exhibits and a video program, *April Fire,* that explains the Lexington-Concord battle. "Two Revolutions" is a ranger-conducted interpretive program that focuses on the area's two historical revolutions, the American revolution of April 19, 1775, and the 19th-century American Literary Renaissance. A summer weekend program, "In the Footsteps of the Minute Men," features a leisurely ranger-led walk to places where the colonial militia clashed with the British regulars.

Minute Man Visitor Center features *The Road to Revolution,* a 25-minute multimedia theater presentation detailing the events of April 18 and 19, 1775.

DIRECTIONS: *North Bridge Visitor Center:* From I 95 (SR 128-Boston Beltway) take Exit 30B to SR 2A westbound to Concord Center. At the monument, turn right 0.25 mile to the parking area for the visitor center. *Minute Man Visitor Center:* From I 95 (SR 128-Boston Beltway), take Exit 30A or 30B and go west on North Great Road 1 mile to the visitor center (Figure 119).

PUBLIC USE: Season and hours: *Grounds:* Dawn–dusk daily. *North Bridge Visitor Center:* 9 AM–5:30 PM daily. November through March, 9 AM–4 PM daily. Closed Christmas Day, New Year's Day. **Gift shop. For people with disabilities:** Accessible. *Minute Man Visitor Center:* 9 AM–5 PM daily. November through March, 9 AM–4 PM daily. Closed Christmas Day, New Year's Day. **Book store. For people with disabilities.** Accessible.

Figure 119. The location of Minute Man National Historical Park and Munroe Tavern near Lexington, Massachusetts.

FOR ADDITIONAL INFORMATION: Contact: Minute Man National Historical Park, 174 Liberty Street, Concord, Massachusetts 01742; 978-369-6993. **Web site:** *www.nps.gov/mima.* **Read:** (1) Jean Poindexter Colby. 1975. *Lexington and Concord: What Really Happened.* (2) Neil Johnson. 1992. *The Battle of Lexington and Concord.* (3) David Hackett Fischer. 1994. *Paul Revere's Ride.*

128. MUNROE TAVERN

LEXINGTON, MASSACHUSETTS

On the afternoon of April 19, 1775, Munroe Tavern (Figure 120) was headquarters for British Brigadier General Earl Percy when his troops began a running battle with the American militiamen. Harassed by patriots fighting "Indian-style" behind walls and trees, only the timely arrival of British reinforcements turned the tide which enabled Percy's troops to retreat to Boston safely.

The tavern, a plain red clapboard building with a foundation arch of hand-made brick and stone, was named for Minute Man William Munroe, its owner from 1770 to 1827. On November 5, 1789, President George Washington dined at the Munroe where an upstairs room contains his dining table and displays documents relating to his New England trip.

Figure 120. Munroe Tavern, Lexington, Massachusetts. (Photograph by William G. Clotworthy)

Munroe Tavern is noted for an outstanding wildflower garden that features plants that grew in the Boston area during the colonial era.

Munroe Tavern is one of three historical homes owned and maintained as house museums by the Lexington Historical Society — the others are the Hancock-Clarke House where Samuel Adams was sleeping when aroused by Paul Revere's midnight ride, and Buckman Tavern, a rendezvous point for the militiamen before the battle at Lexington Green.

DIRECTIONS: Munroe Tavern is on the south side of SR 225 1 mile east of the Lexington Common (Figure 119).

PUBLIC USE: Season and hours: Mid-April–October 31, Monday–Saturday, 10 AM–5 PM; Sunday, 12 N–5 PM. **Admission fee. Museum shop. For people with disabilities:** Partially accessible. There are three steps to the first floor.

FOR ADDITIONAL INFORMATION: Contact: Munroe Tavern, 1332 Massachusetts Avenue, Lexington, Massachusetts 02173; 617-862-1703.

129. WARREN TAVERN

CHARLESTOWN, MASSACHUSETTS

Warren Tavern, named for General Joseph Warren, is the oldest tavern in the Boston area. It was one of the first buildings to be rebuilt in Charlestown after a devastating conflagration was set by the British in a vain effort to exterminate the patriot menace. Paul Revere referred to the Warren as his "favorite place" when he presided over meetings of his Masonic Lodge. President Washington crossed from Boston to Charlestown in the autumn of 1789 to see his old friend Major Benjamin Frothingham, and stopped at the Warren for "refreshments." The Warren Tavern continues to operate as a popular restaurant, open to the public for lunch and dinner.

DIRECTIONS: The Warren Tavern is at the west end of Pleasant Street (Figure 55).

FOR ADDITIONAL INFORMATION: Contact: Warren Tavern, 2 Pleasant Street, Charlestown, Massachusetts 02129; 617-241-8142.

130. LEE HOUSE NATIONAL HISTORIC LANDMARK

MARBLEHEAD, MASSACHUSETTS

In 1768, Colonel Jeremiah Lee, a well-to-do ship owner and patriot, built a magnificent Georgian townhouse in Marblehead, considered one of the most beautiful colonial mansions in the nation. Its most outstanding feature — unique in the country — is the hand-painted classical tempera wallpaper depicting Roman ruins. The mansion's twelve rooms are filled with priceless American furniture, textiles, needlework, porcelain, china, silverware, and portraiture of the colonial period (Plate 13). The exterior is noble in appearance, with classical columns and carved pediments that set off period gardens of rare beauty.

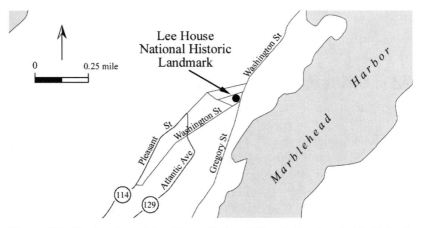

Figure 121. The location of Lee House National Historic Landmark, Marblehead, Massachusetts.

Colonel Lee, a patriot devoted to the cause of liberty, did not live to enjoy the fruits of his commercial success. He carried ammunition to the 1775 Lexington/Concord battle, and in an attempt to avoid capture by the British, suffered exposure and died of fever within a month. His widow entertained President Washington with a reception at the mansion during the President's New England tour in 1789.

Since 1909, the Lee Mansion has been the home of the Marblehead Historical Society which has meticulously preserved one of America's architectural and historical treasures.

DIRECTIONS: From SR 129 or SR 114, go north on Washington Street to the Lee Mansion on the north side of the street near the intersection of Washington and Gregory streets (Figure 121).

PUBLIC USE: Season and hours: Tuesday–Saturday, 10 AM–4 PM; Sunday, 1–4 PM. Closed holidays. **Admission fee. For people with disabilities:** Partially accessible. There are four steps into the house.

FOR ADDITIONAL INFORMATION: Contact: Lee House National Historic Landmark, 161 Washington Street, Box 1048, Marblehead, Massachusetts 01945; 781-631-1768. **Web site:** *www.essexheritage.org/ jeremiah_lee.htm.* **Read:** Priscilla Sawyer Lord and Virginia Clegg Gamage. 1972. *Marblehead: The Spirit of '76 Lives Here.*

131. GOVERNOR JOHN LANGDON HOUSE

PORTSMOUTH, NEW HAMPSHIRE

John Langdon, one of New Hampshire's most prominent citizens, was twice governor of the state and later served as a United States Senator. He made a fortune in shipbuilding and privateering during the Revolution and financed several military campaigns with funds from his own deep pockets. In 1783, he began construction of a grand mansion with a monumental exterior and an interior featuring exquisite carved woodwork in the rococo style. George Washington, a guest in 1789, compared the house to others in which he'd been a guest: "Col. Langdon's may be esteemed the first."[104]

In 1905, descendant Elizabeth Langdon added a formal dining room that leads to a rear garden, rose arbor, and evergreen glade, and other family members have furnished the house with period antiques. The

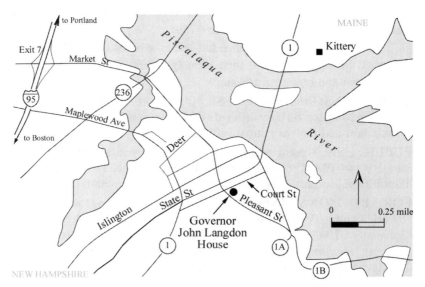

Figure 122. The location of Governor John Langdon House, Portsmouth, New Hampshire.

Langdon House is a museum property of the Society for the Preservation of New England Antiquities.

DIRECTIONS: From I 95, take Exit 7 onto Market Street (which becomes Pleasant Street) eastbound to the intersection of Court Street and the house on the northeast corner (Figure 122).

PUBLIC USE: Season and hours: June–mid-October, Wednesday–Sunday, 11 AM–5 PM. **Admission fee. Gift shop. For people with disabilities:** Only the first floor is accessible.

FOR ADDITIONAL INFORMATION: Contact: Governor John Langdon House, 143 Pleasant Street, Portsmouth, New Hampshire 03801; 603-436-3205. **Web site:** *www.spnea.org.*

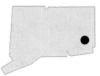

132. LEFFINGWELL INN

NORWICH, CONNECTICUT

Thomas Leffingwell purchased a private home, built in 1665, and converted it to a public inn that served the Norwich community as a post office and gathering place for patriots throughout the eighteenth century. Norwich, then one of the twelve largest towns in the colonies, became an essential source of military supplies during the Revolutionary War. Leffingwell's grandson Christopher was a Commissioner of Correspondence, financier to the Revolution and a friend to George Washington, who stopped at Leffingwell's on trips to New England. The two-story clapboard house, actually two attached saltboxes, has been restored by the Society for the Founders of Norwich as a colonial museum featuring period furniture pieces and a collection of Norwich silver. The house is unique as it illustrates development from simple seventeenth-century beginnings to its mid-eighteenth-century position as an important town house.

DIRECTIONS: From I 395, take Exit 81 onto SR 2 eastbound, go 1 mile to SR 169, then go north of SR 169 and immediately north again onto Washington Street to the inn on the west side of the road (Figure 123).

PUBLIC USE: Season and hours: Mid-May–mid-October, Tuesday–Sunday, 1–4 PM. **Admission fee. Gift shop. For people with disabilities:** Accessible.

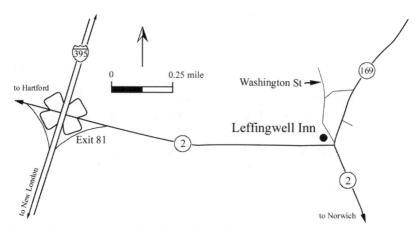

Figure 123. The location of Leffingwell Inn, Norwich, Connecticut.

FOR ADDITIONAL INFORMATION: Contact: Leffingwell Inn, 348 Washington Street, Norwich, Connecticut 06360; 860-889-9440.

133. OLIVER ELLSWORTH HOUSE

WINDSOR, CONNECTICUT

Oliver Ellsworth was one of the five men who drafted the Constitution of the United States. He later served as a United States Senator from Connecticut before his appointment as Chief Justice of the United States Supreme Court. George Washington, John Adams, and other patriots were recipients of Ellsworth's hospitality in the home that has been restored to its colonial condition. The house is a white clapboard structure of distinctive beauty, with eleven rooms that contain many original family heirlooms including a letter from George Washington and a square of Gobelin tapestry presented to Ellsworth by Napoleon. The Ellsworth House is owned and maintained by the Connecticut Daughters of the American Revolution.

DIRECTIONS: From I 91, take Exit 39 onto Kennedy Road. Proceed eastbound, turning northbound onto Basswood Road (that becomes

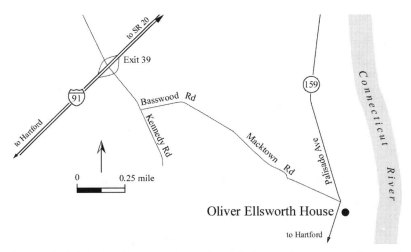

Figure 124. The location of Oliver Ellsworth House in Windsor, Connecticut.

Macktown Road) and follow it to the end, turning right on Palisado Avenue. The Homestead is the first house on the left (Figure 124).

PUBLIC USE: Season and hours: Mid-May–mid-October, Tuesday, Wednesday, and Saturday, 12 N–4:30 PM. **Gift shop. For people with disabilities:** The first floor is accessible with thresholds to maneuver between rooms.

FOR ADDITIONAL INFORMATION: Contact: Oliver Ellsworth Homestead, 778 Palisado Avenue, Windsor, Connecticut 06095; 860-688-8717. **Web site:** *www.ctssar.org.*

END OF NEW ENGLAND TOUR

134. TRINITY CHURCH

NEWPORT, RHODE ISLAND

Trinity was the first Anglican Church in Rhode Island (Figure 125) and has served the Newport community since 1726. Its slim spire is tipped with a golden bishop's mitre of the Church of England, and a three-tiered wineglass pulpit, Tiffany windows, and an organ tested by

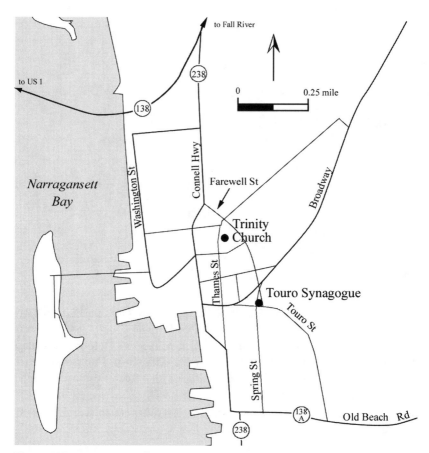

Figure 125. The location of Trinity Church and Touro Synagogue in Newport, Rhode Island.

George Frederick Handel grace the interior where original chandeliers hang from ropes extending to ceiling medallions as when they were installed. George Washington was a communicant of Trinity when in Newport, and his pew is marked.

DIRECTIONS: From SR 138 (Newport Bridge), take SR 238 southbound to Farewell Street, go south on Farewell to Thames Street, go south on Thames to Trinity Church, opposite Long Wharf Mall (Figure 125).

PUBLIC USE: Season and hours: May 1–mid-June, Monday–Saturday, 10 AM–4 PM; Sunday, 12 N–4 PM. Mid-June–Labor Day, Monday–Saturday, 10 AM–4 PM; Sunday, after services–4 PM. Day after Labor Day–mid-October, 1–4 PM. **For people with disabilities:** Accessible.

FOR ADDITIONAL INFORMATION: Contact: Trinity Church, Queen Anne Square, Newport, Rhode Island 02840; 401-846-0660. **Web site:** *www.trinitynewport.org.* **Read:** Desmond Guiness. 1982. *Newport Preserved: Architecture of the 18ᵗʰ Century.*

135. TOURO SYNAGOGUE

NEWPORT, RHODE ISLAND

Inspired by the beliefs of founder Roger Williams, Rhode Island was a beacon of religious tolerance, its 1647 Code of Laws proclaiming:

> *These are the lawes that concerne all men . . . and otherwise than . . . what is herein forbidden, all men may walk as their consciences persuade them, everyone in the name of God.*[105]

Spanish and Portuguese Sephardim, seeking escape from religious persecution in Europe, established a congregation in New Port in 1658 and founded their own house of worship, Touro Synagogue, in 1763. Touro was designed by Peter Harrison, the most notable architect of the day, and it is considered an architectural masterpiece, its delicate and ornate interior contrasting sharply with exterior simplicity. President Washington visited the synagogue during his Rhode Island tour, and in reply to an address of thanks from the congregation, wrote a famous letter guaranteeing religious freedom in the brand-new nation:

> *. . . it is no more that toleration is spoken of, as if it was by the indulgence of one class of people, that another enjoyed the exercise of their inherent natural rights. For happily the Government of the United States, which gives to bigotry no sanction, to persecution no assistance requires only that they who live under its protection should demean themselves as good citizens, in giving it on all occasion their effectual support.*[106]

Touro Synagogue proudly displays a copy of the letter within the sanctuary. The original is owned by the Morgan Stern Foundation of Washington, DC.

DIRECTIONS: From SR 138 (Newport Bridge), take SR 238 southbound to Farewell Street, go south on Farewell to Thames Street, go south on Thames to Touro Street, then go east on Touro 1½ blocks to the synagogue on the north side of the street (Figure 126).

PUBLIC USE: Season and hours: May 1–June 30, Monday–Friday, 1 PM–3 PM; Sunday, 11 AM–3 PM. July–August, Sunday–Friday, 10 AM–5 PM; September–October 30, Monday–Friday, 1–3 PM; Sunday, 11 AM–3 PM. No tours on High Holidays. Closed Holy Days except for services. Allow one hour to enjoy Touro Synagogue. **For people with disabilities:** Please call ahead for assistance.

FOR ADDITIONAL INFORMATION: Contact: Touro Synagogue National Historic Site, 85 Touro Street, Newport, Rhode Island 02840; 401-847-4794. **Web site:** *www.tourosynagogue.org.*

136. JOHN BROWN HOUSE

PROVIDENCE, RHODE ISLAND

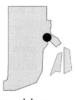

John Brown was one of Rhode Island's most prominent citizens, best known for initiating the China Trade. His mansion, built around 1786, has been handsomely refurbished and filled with an outstanding collection of colonial furniture and artifacts. John Quincy Adams, after a visit, pronounced the house "the most magnificent and elegant private mansion that I have ever seen on this continent."[107] Mr. Brown entertained George Washington during the president's visit to Providence in 1790.

DIRECTIONS: From I 95, take Exit 2 to Benefit Street northbound and go about 0.5 mile to Power Street, then go east on Power to the house immediately ahead on the north side of the street (Figure 57).

PUBLIC USE: Season and hours: Mid-May–mid-October; Tuesday, Wednesday, and Saturday; 10 AM–5 PM. **Gift shop. For people with disabilities:** The first floor is accessible with some thresholds to maneuver between rooms.

FOR ADDITIONAL INFORMATION: Contact: John Brown House, 52 Power Street, Providence, Rhode Island 02906; 401-331-8575.

137. JAMES RIVER AND KANAWHA CANAL LOCKS

RICHMOND, VIRGINIA

On the night of April 11, 1791, the city of Richmond was illuminated in honor of the visiting President who took time to inspect the sluices and locks of the James River Canal Company, involved with construction of a canal between Richmond and the town of Buchanan in the Shenandoah Valley, with the intention of opening an important commercial artery to the west.

The visit to Richmond was one of the first stops on Washington's tour of the south, a month-long trip of almost 2000 miles. Washington had not visited the Richmond area since 1784 when he made a presentation to the Virginia Assembly regarding the Great Dismal Swamp project, so it was with great satisfaction that he toured the canal terminus as President of the United States. In appreciation of his pioneer efforts, the directors of the Patowmack and James River companies presented him with shares in the two companies. Embarrassed, he had the gifts earmarked for educational purposes and, at his death, the James River shares were bequeathed to the institution that became Washington and Lee University.

Remnants of the original canal are still visible in Richmond. An arch stands at the foot of Byrd Park, some pieces of locks may be seen in Hollywood Cemetery, and original locks have been restored in a city park at 5th and Byrd streets.

DIRECTIONS: From I 95 southbound, take Exit 74B onto Franklin Street westbound for 2 blocks to 12th Street, then go south on 12th to the canal locks. From I 95 northbound, take Exit 74C, onto 17th Street, then turn west on Main Street and go to 12th, then go south on 12th (Figure 40).

FOR ADDITIONAL INFORMATION: Read: Wayland Dunaway. 1969. *History of the James River and Kanawha Company.*

355

THE SOUTHERN TOUR

138. TRYON PALACE RESTORATION AND GARDENS

NEW BERN, NORTH CAROLINA

In 1764, Royal Governor William Tryon arrived in North Carolina, determined to establish a permanent capital for the colony. Tryon persuaded the assembly to select coastal New Bern as the site and to appropriate funds for a royal mansion which was completed in 1770 — acclaimed as the finest government building in the colonies, although it served only Tryon and successor Josiah Martin, before the Revolutionary War began.

The palace, named for Governor Tryon, was praised for its elegance and beauty, a Georgian mansion of classic proportions. The central building contained public rooms for government functions on the

Figure 126. Tryon Palace Restoration and Gardens, New Bern, North Carolina. (Photograph courtesy Tryon Palace Restoration and Gardens)

ground floor, with living quarters upstairs. Cooking and laundry facilities were in a wing to the left and stables to the right. The landscaping was in the geometric style typical of eighteenth-century Europe.

After the Revolution the palace was used for meetings of the General Assembly and served as residence for governors of the State of North Carolina. During his southern tour, George Washington stopped in New Bern where he was entertained at a public dinner and dance at the palace.

In 1798, a disastrous fire destroyed Tryon Palace, but interest in its value as an historic site did not die and in 1944 a trust fund was established as the first step in re-creating the Palace. By 1959, the manor house had been reconstructed, using the original architectural plans. The gardens feature many of the plants and varieties available in the glory days of Tryon Palace.

John Wright Stanly's House, where Washington slept, is an elegant Georgian reflecting the wealth of Mr. Stanly, a powerful citizen of New Bern whose merchant ships raided British vessels to aid the revolutionary cause. The house is part of the Tryon Palace complex, a truly noteworthy example of historic reconstruction (Figure 126).

According to the museum brochure, "Tryon Palace — Where Governors Ruled, Legislators Debated, Patriots Gathered, and George Washington Danced."[108]

DIRECTIONS: From US 17, go south on George Street, then west ½ block on Pollock Street, then south onto the grounds of Tryon Palace (Figure 127).

PUBLIC USE: Season and hours: Monday–Saturday, 9 AM–5 PM; Sunday, 1–5 PM; summer hours extended to 7 PM. Closed Thanksgiving Day, December 24–26, and New Year's Day. **Admission fee. Visitor center. Gift shop. For people with disabilities:** The Visitor center and first floor of the Palace are accessible. The John Wright Stanly House is not accessible.

FOR ADDITIONAL INFORMATION: Contact: Tryon Palace Restoration, 610 Pollock Street, Box 1007, New Bern, North Carolina 28560; 252-638-1560, 800-767-1560. **Web site:** *www.tryonpalace.org.* **Read:** Joseph D. Henry. 1960. *Historic Tryon Palace: First Permanent Capital of North Carolina, New Bern, N. C.*

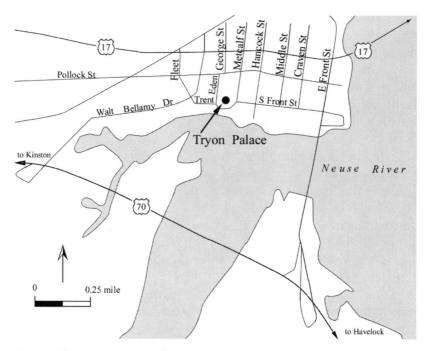

Figure 127. The location of Tryon Palace Restoration and Gardens, New Bern, North Carolina.

139. HAMPTON PLANTATION STATE PARK
MCCLELLANSVILLE, SOUTH CAROLINA

Hampton Plantation contains one of the most impressive homes in the South Carolina Low Country, a monument to South Carolina's age of rice. A colossal Adams-style portico at the entrance of the manor house is a fine example of its type and extensive grounds offer an opportunity to examine wildlife of the Low Country. Hampton was built around 1750 as a modest six-room farmhouse but by the mid-1780s had been transformed to a mansion — at least six rooms were added, including a stately ballroom. President Washington breakfasted with owner Harriott Pinckney Horry during his tour of the south.

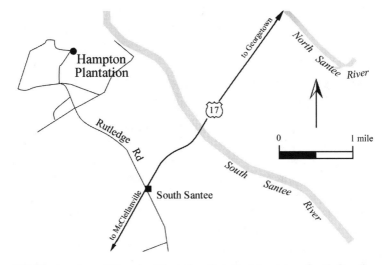

Figure 128. The location of Hampton Plantation State Park in eastern South Carolina.

The state of South Carolina purchased Hampton in 1971 to preserve the plantation as a state park interpreting Hampton's natural and cultural history. The mansion's interior has been left unfinished, spotlighting the structure's architectural and construction details. Cutaway sections of walls and ceilings show the building's evolution by exposing timber framing and hardware of the eighteenth-century building craft. Tours of the mansion depart on the hour when the mansion is open to visitors.

DIRECTIONS: From US 17, 1 mile south of the South Santee River, go north on Rutledge Road 2 miles to the mansion (Figure 128).

PUBLIC USE: Season and hours: *Park:* Daily, 9 AM–6 PM. *Mansion:* Labor Day–Memorial Day, daily, 1–4 PM; Memorial Day–Labor Day, daily, 11 AM–4 PM. Closed Thanksgiving Day and Christmas Day. **Admission fee. Gift shop. For people with disabilities:** Partially accessible.

FOR ADDITIONAL INFORMATION: Contact: Hampton Plantation State Park, 1950 Rutledge Road, McClellansville, South Carolina 29458; 843-546-9361. **Web site:** *www.southcarolinaparks.com.* **Read:** Gerald Gutek and Virginia Gutek. 1996. *Plantations and Outdoor Museums in America's Historic South.*

140. SNEE FARM AND CHARLES PINCKNEY NATIONAL HISTORIC SITE

MOUNT PLEASANT, SOUTH CAROLINA

Snee Farm was the country seat of patriot and South Carolina Governor Charles Pinckney, and where President Washington dined under the trees on his way to Charleston on May 2, 1791. Snee Farm, part of a royal grant, remained a working plantation for over 200 years when indigo and rice were its principal crops. Over the years, Snee Farm acreage was gradually sold off and its buildings began to disintegrate. Recent archaeological surveys conducted by the National Park Service have uncovered important remains that date from the eighteenth century, including a brick foundation and piers that may represent the original plantation house. The ongoing studies will surely reveal more about southern plantation life from the viewpoint of plantation owners and their slaves.

The historic site was established to interpret Charles Pinckney's part in the development of the United States Constitution as one of South Carolina's four representatives at the Constitutional Convention, and to commemorate his unparalleled contributions to the state and the nation as governor, United States Senator, and, finally, United States Ambassador to Spain. Twenty-eight of the plantation's original 715 acres remain, as does an 1827 house that has been converted to a museum that features panels describing the Pinckney family's contributions to American political life.

DIRECTIONS: From US 17, go west on Long Point Road 0.5 mile to the Charles Pinckney National Historic Site on the south side of the road (Figure 129).

PUBLIC USE: Season and hours: 9 AM–5 PM daily, with extended summer hours. Closed Christmas Day. **Visitor center. Gift shop. For people with disabilities:** Accessible.

FOR ADDITIONAL INFORMATION: Contact: Charles Pinckney National Historic Site, 1214 Middle Street, Sullivan's Island, South Carolina 29462-9748; 843-881-5516. **Web site:** *www.nps.gov/chpi.* **Read:** Samuel Gaillard Stoney. 1964. *Plantations of the Carolina Low Country.*

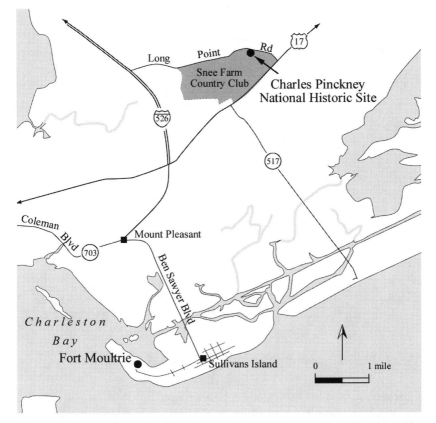

Figure 129. The location of Charles Pinckney National Historic Site and Fort Moultrie, near Charleston, South Carolina.

141. CHARLESTON, SOUTH CAROLINA

After his visit to Snee Farm, President Washington was transported across the Cooper River to Charleston in a ceremonial barge manned by thirteen sea captains, accompanied by a flotilla of other craft — a nautical welcome reminiscent of his Hudson River welcome to New York as president-elect. He stayed in Charleston for a week, a week filled with sightseeing, galas, balls, dinners, church services, and military inspections. A number of places dating to Washington's visit remain within

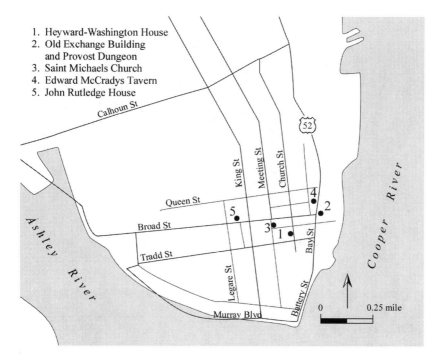

1. Heyward-Washington House
2. Old Exchange Building
   and Provost Dungeon
3. Saint Michaels Church
4. Edward McCradys Tavern
5. John Rutledge House

Figure 130. The location of featured sites in Charleston, South Carolina.

Charleton's Historic District, and are open for public visitation (Figure 130).

Preservation is a way of life in Charleston, a 300-year-old city renowned for its architecture and splendid gardens. Charleston's Historic District encompasses more than 2000 buildings, of which 73 predate the Revolutionary War and 136 date from the late 1700s. The character of the city is genteel, its pace is leisurely, and the residents are friendly and hospitable.

Charleston was a reluctant participant in the Revolutionary War, although it repulsed a British attack by sea in 1776 and another by land in 1778 before it was captured in 1782. Its most famous existing landmark is, of course, Fort Sumter, the harbor fortress shelled by South Carolinians in April, 1861, an action that initiated the Civil War.

It is suggested that visitors stop at the Charleston Visitor Center for maps, brochures, and information on walking and carriage tours, boat trips to Fort Sumter, restaurants, and hotel accommodations within the Historic District. The center also features a 24-minute multimedia presentation, *Forever Charleston,* that focuses on the history and essence of Charleston and comprises more than 2400 projected images revealing the beauty of Charleston and the heritage of its people.

FOR ADDITIONAL INFORMATION: Contact: Charleston Visitor Center, 375 Meeting Street, Charleston, South Carolina 29402; 800-774-0006.

141-1. HEYWARD-WASHINGTON HOUSE
87 CHURCH STREET

The Heyward-Washington House takes its name from its wealthy rice planter-owner, Thomas Heyward, Jr., and his most famous guest, President George Washington, who leased the house for eight days during his southern tour. The architectural scale and interior of the brick double house are a reflection of the prosperity and social prominence of the Heyward family. The historic house museum is owned and maintained by the Charleston Museum which has filled it with a magnificent collection of eighteenth-century Charleston-manufactured furniture, the quality of which reflects the wealth and sophistication of that colonial city. A separate kitchen building, servant's quarters, and garden are behind the main house.

PUBLIC USE: Season and hours: Guided tours are conducted Monday–Saturday, 10 AM–5 PM; Sunday, 1–5 PM. Closed major holidays. **Admission fee.**

FOR ADDITIONAL INFORMATION: Contact: Heyward-Washington House, 87 Church Street, Charleston, South Carolina 29401; 843-722-0354. **Web site:** *www.charlestonmuseum.com.* **Read:** Thomas Petigru Lesesne. 1939. *Landmarks of Charleston.*

141-2. THE OLD EXCHANGE BUILDING AND PROVOST DUNGEON
122 EAST BAY BOULEVARD

In the 1760s, Charles Town was a thriving shipping terminus; the social, political, and economic center of the Royal Colony of

South Carolina and one of the intellectual centers of Britain's American colonies. Reflecting its importance, an exchange and custom house was built on the site of a former council hall and basement dungeon. With its striking Palladian architecture and dramatic location, the Exchange Building (Plate 14) dominated the harbor and became the hub of a bustling eighteenth century port where up to 300 ships could be seen in port at any one time.

The first floor of the new building was an open arcade while the second floor housed the customs offices and a Great Hall. The Great Hall, an elegant assembly room, was referred to as "The Independence Hall of South Carolina" as it was there that the South Carolina Colony declared its independence from England, and as a state, ratified the Constitution of the United States. It is also where President George Washington was entertained during his southern tour.

In 1981, the Great Hall, with the aid of original blueprints, was restored to its 1771 appearance. The Old Exchange Building, and particularly the Great Hall, is a popular site for social gatherings, its grandeur and opulence a beacon for visitors. The Provost Dungeon below the Old Exchange Building represents an unpleasant part of pre-colonial life, but visitors to the dungeons are impressed when they realize they are viewing portions of Charleton's original fortified walls that date to 1680. The Old Exchange Building and Provost Dungeon is owned and maintained by the Daughters of the American Revolution.

PUBLIC USE: Season and hours: 9 AM–5 PM daily. Closed major holidays. **Admission fee. Gift shop. For people with disabilities:** Accessible.

FOR ADDITIONAL INFORMATION: Contact: Old Exchange Building and Provost Dungeon, 122 East Bay Boulevard, Charleston, South Carolina 29401; 843-727-2165. **Web site:** *www.oldexchange.com.* **Read:** Carl Julien. 1948. *Beneath So Kind a Sky.*

141-3. SAINT MICHAELS EPISCOPAL CHURCH

80 MEETING STREET

Saint Michaels is considered a notable architectural achievement as it is based on the design of Saint Martins-in-the-Fields Church in London. Saint Michaels (Figure 131) features a Palladian Doric portico, a steeple rising 186 feet above the street, and a tower clock that has marked time since 1764. The richly ornamented interior includes old-fashioned pew boxes and the church's original pulpit. President Washington worshipped at Saint Michaels (his pew is marked), then climbed the steeple to enjoy an unparalleled view of the city. Showing no favoritism, he attended services later that day at nearby Saint Philips Episcopal Church, a building that has been replaced with a more modern structure.

PUBLIC USE: Season and hours: Monday–Friday, 9 AM–4:45 PM; Saturday, 9 AM–12 N. **For people with disabilities:** Accessible.

FOR ADDITIONAL INFORMATION: Contact: Saint Michaels Church, 80 Meeting Street, Charleston, South Carolina 29401; 843-723-0603. **Read:** Charles Norbury Beesley. 1906. *Saint Michael's Church.*

Figure 131. The steeple of Saint Michaels Church, Charleston, South Carolina. (Photograph by William G. Clotworthy)

141-4. John Rutledge House Inn
116 Broad Street

John Rutledge was one of the fifty-five men who signed the Constitution of the United States. His home (Plate 15), built around 1763, is one of only fifteen houses belonging to members of that group that has survived. It has been restored and visitors marvel at many of its interior details — elaborately-carved Italian marble fireplaces, original plaster moldings, inlaid floors, and graceful ironwork. Judge Rutledge's diary tells us that President Washington breakfasted with Mrs. Rutledge during the southern tour while Rutledge, then Chief Justice of the South Carolina Supreme Court, was "on the circuit." The Rutledge House is currently operated as a Bed and Breakfast Inn although visitors are encouraged to call at the house where the lobby, second floor ballroom, and courtyard are open for public visitation.

PUBLIC USE: Season and hours: Daily, open to drop-in visitors during normal business hours. **Gift shop. For people with disabilities:** Not accessible.

FOR ADDITIONAL INFORMATION: Contact: John Rutledge House Inn, 116 Broad Street, Charleston, South Carolina 29401; 843-723-7999, 800-476-9741. **Web site:** *www.innbook.com/johnr.html.*

141-5. Edward McCradys Tavern
2 Unity Alley

The "Long Room" of Edward McCradys Tavern was the scene of a dinner held in honor of George Washington by the Society of Cincinnati on May 4, 1791. Historians believed the second-story tavern, located above a stable, had been razed, but preservationists unearthed it from behind a warehouse in 1972 — intact! Restored to its original condition, the Long Room is now utilized as a meeting room and banquet facility for a modern four-star McCrady's restaurant that has replaced the stable on the ground floor (no horses allowed).

FOR ADDITIONAL INFORMATION: Contact: McCradys, 2 Unity Alley, Charleston, South Carolina 29401; 843-577-0025. **Web site:** *www.restaurant.com/mccradys.*

142. Fort Johnson and Fort Moultrie
Sullivans Island, South Carolina

On May 5, 1791, President Washington visited forts Johnson and Moultrie, part of Charleston's harbor defenses during the Revolutionary War. Fort Moultrie was the scene of South Carolina's first bloodshed when it repulsed a British naval attack on June 28, 1776, and it continued to defend Charleston until it succumbed to enemy pressure in 1780. The British occupied Fort Johnson on James Island the same year. Fort Johnson has been destroyed, although its location is visible from tour boats.

Fort Moultrie remains, rebuilt and improved several different times as national defense has required, military technology changed, and harbor defense became more complex. For example, World Wars I and II brought submarine threats and the possibility of aerial attack, each requiring new means of defense. Those armaments became obsolete as nuclear weapons and guided missiles altered the entire concept of national defense. Fort Moultrie has been restored to portray the major periods of its history with displays moving chronologically backward, from the World War II Harbor Entrance Control post to a reconstructed section of the palmetto-log fort of 1776.

DIRECTIONS: From I 526 in Mt. Pleasant go south on SR 703 3 miles to Sullivans Island, then go west on Middle Street 1½ miles to the fort (Figure 129).

PUBLIC USE: Season and hours: 9 AM–5 PM daily. Closed Christmas Day. **Admission fee. Visitor center. Gift shop. For people with disabilities:** The visitor center is accessible, as is most of the fort.

FOR ADDITIONAL INFORMATION: Contact: Fort Sumter National Monument, 1214 Middle Street, Sullivans Island, South Carolina 29482; 843-883-3123. **Web site:** *www.nps.gov/fomo.*

143. OLD SALEM

WINSTON-SALEM, NORTH CAROLINA

In 1735, Moravian missionaries emigrated from Europe to settle in Savannah, Georgia. Five years later, they moved north, to Pennsylvania and New Jersey and, in the early 1760s, founded Salem, North Carolina. The Moravians, a protestant denomination, created towns they considered refuges for mission work and havens from despair — meticulously planned and organized communities where church members could lead secure and productive lives while seeking personal salvation. Today's Old Salem is a restoration of a 1766 Moravian village, one of the most authentic living-history towns in the United States. Many buildings have been restored or reconstructed on their original foundations and costumed interpreters carry on the work as the Moravians would have in what was a backcountry congregation town.

President Washington was in Salem for two days near the end of his southern tour. He stayed at the Salem Tavern at 600 Main Street — a building currently housing a Moravian Museum where visitors have an opportunity to become acquainted with Moravian history. The quality of life in Salem was the envy of travelers and neighbors alike, and Old Salem remains an oasis in our modern culture where visitors experience the tranquility of less stressful times as they visit buildings two centuries old. Crafts, cooking, and many other demonstrations enable one to learn something of the life of the settlers who cherished music, valued education, and built a backwoods community into an important trading center. Thanks to meticulous records kept by the church fathers, the lifestyle of these pioneers has been authentically recreated, making Old Salem a living restoration.

DIRECTIONS: From US 52, take Exit 108C onto Stadium Drive westbound and follow signs 1 mile to Old Salem. The visitor center is located at the corner of Academy and Old Salem Road (Figure 132).

PUBLIC USE: Season and hours: Monday–Saturday, 9 AM–5 PM; Sunday, 12:30 PM–5 PM. Closed Thanksgiving Day, Christmas Eve Day, and Christmas Day. **Admission fee. Visitor center. Gift shop. Food**

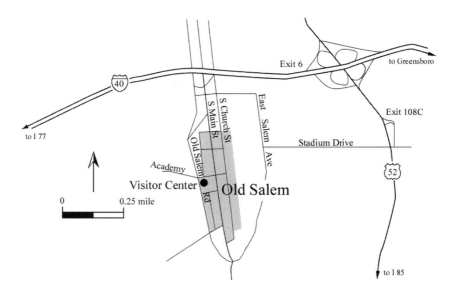

Figure 132. The location of Old Salem, Salem, North Carolina.

service: The modern Salem Tavern Dining Room, next door to the museum, is open for lunch and dinner. **For people with disabilities:** Most historic houses are accessible on the first floor after navigating a curb or single step.

FOR ADDITIONAL INFORMATION: Contact: Old Salem, Inc., Box F, Salem Station, Winston-Salem, North Carolina 27108; 336-721-7300, 888-653-7253. **Web site:** *www.oldsalem.org.* **Read:** Bruce Roberts, with text by Frances Griffin. 1986. *Old Salem in Pictures.*

144. GUILFORD COURTHOUSE NATIONAL MILITARY PARK

GREENSBORO, NORTH CAROLINA

The Battle of Guilford Courthouse, one of the final engagements of the Revolutionary War, pitted American General Nathanael Greene's mixed Continental and militia army against Lord Cornwallis's smaller but vet-

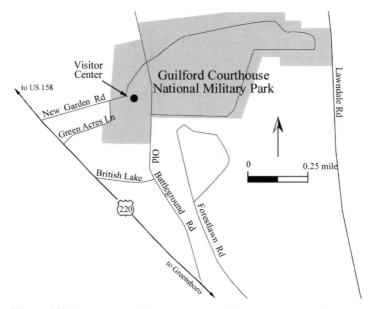

Figure 133. The location of Guilford Courthouse National Military Park, Greensboro, North Carolina.

eran British force on March 15, 1781. Cornwallis won the battle, but suffered irreplaceable losses and failed to destroy his enemy. With supplies cut off, he retreated to eastern Virginia where he hoped to reach the protection of the British fleet at Yorktown.

President Washington, on the final leg of his southern tour, stopped to honor the Continental soldiers and militiamen who fought at Guilford. Guilford Courthouse is a 220-acre National Park Service site that includes wayside exhibits, a modern visitor center, and a 2½-mile automobile tour which transverses battle sites and monuments. The most impressive is a large equestrian statue of General Nathanael Greene, strategist of the Southern Campaign. "We fight, get beat, rise, and fight again," said Greene of that war within a war.[109]

DIRECTIONS: From US 220, go east on New Garden Road 0.5 mile to Old Battleground Road and the Guilford Courthouse National Military Park Visitor Center (Figure 133).

PUBLIC USE: Season and hours: 8:30 AM–5 PM daily. Closed Christmas Day and New Year's Day. **Visitor center. Gift shop. For people with disabilities:** The visitor center is accessible as is most of the park.

370

FOR ADDITIONAL INFORMATION: Contact: Guilford Courthouse National Military Park, 2332 New Garden Road, Greensboro, North Carolina 27410-2335; 336-288-1776. **Web site:** *www.nps.gov/guco.* **Read:** (1) John Buchanan. 1997. *The Road to Guilford Courthouse.* (2) Thomas E. Baker. 1981. *Another Such Victory.*

END OF SOUTHERN TOUR

145. HAMPTON NATIONAL HISTORIC SITE

TOWSON, MARYLAND

Hampton is a glorious Georgian-style mansion representative of the opulence of the post-revolutionary period — constructed between 1783 and 1790 by Captain Charles Ridgely who made his fortune in iron-making, shipping, trading, and agriculture. Captain Ridgely was a confidante of George Washington and it is probable that Washington visited Hampton on many occasions. The mansion reflects classic Georgian symmetry; a large three-story structure connected to smaller wings on either side by hallways. The exterior is of stone quarried on Ridgeley property and is stuccoed over to resemble blocks of limestone. Hampton is the largest eighteenth-century Georgian house extant and dominates sixty acres of formal gardens and sculptured lawns. The Great Terrace once provided a level green for bowling and the garden provided herbs for cooking and medicine. Greenhouses sheltered colorful plants and flowers and an orangery contained citrus trees and other tropical plants.

The rooms at Hampton are decorated in various styles popular during the long occupancy of the Ridgely family. The parlor reflects the earliest period, 1790 to 1830, while others represent the Victorian, Rococo, Revival, and early-American eras. The thirty-three-room house with its twenty-seven dependencies (ice house, smokehouse, dairy, slave quarters, and others) was once the hub of a 25,000-acre estate that remained in the Ridgely family until 1948 when Hampton was acquired by the National Park Service for maintenance as a home of historic and architectural importance. A visit to Hampton provides an opportunity to

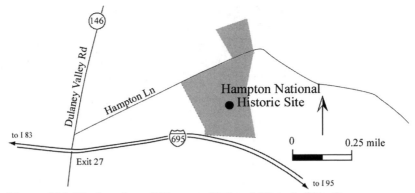

Figure 134. The location of Hampton National Historic Site, Towson, Maryland.

experience a way of life that flourished 200 years ago.

DIRECTIONS: From I 695 (Baltimore Beltway), take Exit 27 onto SR 146 (Dulaney Valley Road) northbound, then immediately go east on Hampton Lane to Hampton National Historic Site (Figure 134).

PUBLIC USE: Season and hours: 9 AM–5 PM daily, with the last hourly mansion tour at 4 PM. Closed Thanksgiving Day, Christmas Day, and New Year's Day. **Admission fee. Visitor center. Gift shop. Food service:** A tearoom is open Tuesday–Saturday, 11:30 AM–3 PM. **For people with disabilities:** Accessible.

FOR ADDITIONAL INFORMATION: Contact: Hampton National Historic Site, 535 Hampton Lane, Towson, Maryland 21286-1397; 410-823-1309. **Web site:** *www.nps.gov/hamp.* **Read:** Lynne Dakin Hastings. 1986. *A Guidebook to Hampton National Historic Site.*

～

THE FINAL YEARS

From March, 1797, when George Washington relinquished the presidency, until his death in December, 1799, he left the Mount Vernon area only once. A serious political disagreement with America's former ally, France, threatened to boil over into armed conflict. President John Adams persuaded Washington to leave the comfort of retirement to revitalize and expand the Continental armed forces in anticipation of possible war. Fortunately, further diplomatic efforts were successful, but only after General Washington spent thirty days in Philadelphia recruiting and organizing.

The rest of Washington's "retirement" was spent in the daily supervision and management of his estate, the continuation of voluminous correspondence, attendance on business interests in the Patowmack Canal Company, constant entertaining, and negotiating for the disposition of his property, especially the hundreds of acres he owned in the west.

Washington remained vitally interested in the progress of the Federal City. As president, he had attended the laying of the cornerstone of the President's House in 1792, although he never lived in it and, in 1793, he laid the cornerstone of the Capitol Building that, over 200 years later, still functions as the seat of our nation's government. Today, these two buildings are among the most important functional and symbolic structures in the nation's capital, and near them is situated one of the simplest and most conspicuous obelisks in the country that honors this man who gave so much to create a new nation (Figure 135).

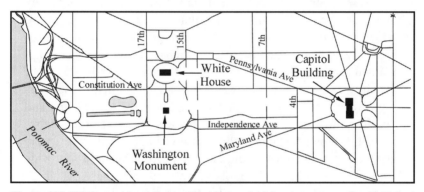

Figure 135. While president, George Washington laid the cornerstones for the United States Capitol Building and the Presidents House, and his cumulative contributions to United States History are commemorated by the Washington Monument, one of the simplest but most conspicuous monuments in the city that bears his name.

Table 7. Major publicly accessible sites in Washington, DC, directly related to George Washington.

MAP NUMBER	SITE NAME	PAGE NUMBER FOR SITE ACCOUNT
146.	Washington, DC	374
	United States Capitol Building	375
	White House	375
	Washington Monument	376

The Federal City was a dream close to George Washington's heart and as author John Ferling concluded in a biography of Washington:

> *George Washington had always enjoyed success as a dreamer. Seldom do people dream on the grandiose scale that typified his vision. Even more rarely do such dreamers have the opportunity to realize even the least of their longings. In fact, almost never in history has a major leader been able to look back at the end of his life and acknowledge that virtually every grand design he had ever conceived had been realized.*
> *But George Washington would have done just that.*[110]

146. WASHINGTON, DC

It is sometimes overlooked that our nation's capital is not merely named for George Washington, but that he was intimately involved with its planning. It was President George Washington who approved of the site, supervised the purchase of the land, then appointed (and controlled) a committee to coordinate the design of the city and its major buildings with the architect, French engineering officer Charles L'Enfant. Washington used his personal and political powers of persuasion to convince the public of the viability of L'Enfant's inspired architectural vision — a city with broad avenues, spacious squares, and a mile-long, four-hundred-foot-wide mall to extend from the Capitol to the President's House. Although George Washington never lived in the President's House, his presence is everywhere — from the statuary in the Capitol building to those in the parks, from his portraits within the White House to those in the National Portrait Gallery, from the grandeur and inspiration of the Washington Monument to the George Washington Memorial Parkway. It is his city — his vibrant living memorial — the representation of his legacy to the nation and to the system of government he fought for and nurtured so selflessly.

FOR ADDITIONAL INFORMATION: Contact: Washington, DC Visitor Center, 1455 Pennsylvania Avenue, NW, Washington, DC 20005, 202-789-7038 *or* Washington, DC Convention and Visitors Association, 1212 New York Avenue NW, Washington, DC

The Final Years

20005, 202-789-7000. **Web site:** *www.washington.org.* **Read:** Patricia Gallagher, ed. 1992. *A Smithsonian Book of the Nation's Capital.*

146-1. UNITED STATES CAPITOL BUILDING

The United States Capitol Building, located on a high point overlooking the city, has been the seat of government since 1800. The building underwent many architectural modifications before construction began and has been expanded more than once as America's population and government have grown. The original design is attributed to Dr. William Thornton, a West Indian physician with little architectural experience. The cornerstone was laid in 1793 by President Washington, bedecked in full Masonic regalia. The ceremonial cement trowel used by Washington was also used to lay the cornerstone of the Washington Monument fifty years later.

DIRECTIONS: The Capitol is located on Capitol Hill at the east end of the National Mall.

PUBLIC USE: Season and hours: Monday–Saturday, 9 AM-4:30 PM. Closed Thanksgiving Day and Christmas Day. The Capitol is open for guided tours only. Free tour tickets are available on a first-come, first-served basis at the East Front Screening Facility, located near the fountains on the East Front plaza of the Capitol.

FOR ADDITIONAL INFORMATION: Contact: Capitol Guide Service, United States Capitol, Washington, DC 20515; 202-225-6827. **Web site:** *www.aoc.gov.* **Read:** United States Capitol Historical Society. 1991. *We, the People: The Story of the United States Capitol.*

146-2. THE WHITE HOUSE

One of the enduring symbols of our government is The White House, the oldest public building in the District of Columbia — the official office and residence of the president since November 1, 1800, when John and Abigail Adams moved into the still-unfinished building. The design was chosen by a competition won by Irish-born James Hoban whose entry was loosely based on Leinster House near Dublin. The Freemasons of the District of Columbia laid the cornerstone on October 13, 1792, with President Washington in attendance. Known as The President's House, the residence was not called The White House until the administration of Theodore Roosevelt a century later.

DIRECTIONS: The White House is on Pennsylvania Avenue, between 15th and 16th Streets.

PUBLIC USE: Season and hours: Tuesday through Saturday, 10 AM-12N, with extended hours during the summer. **For people with disabilities:** Accessible.

FOR ADDITIONAL INFORMATION: Contact: The White House Visitors Office, 1600 Pennsylvania Avenue, Washington, DC 20005; 202-456-7041. **Web site:** *www.whitehouse.gov.* **Read:** The White House Historical Association. 1991. *The White House: An Historic Guide.*

146-3. WASHINGTON MONUMENT

The most distinctive landmark in the nation's capital is the famous 555-foot obelisk on the National Mall that memorializes our nation's most distinguished citizen and his unparalleled contributions to our history. The Washington Monument was designed by Robert Mills and the cornerstone was laid in 1848 in a ceremony presided over by President James K. Polk. The monument rose steadily to a height of 152 feet until funding expired in 1854. The monument stood in an unfinished state for nearly twenty-five years until President Grant signed an act authorizing completion of the project. In December, 1884, a 3300-pound capstone was put in place and topped with a nine-inch pyramid of cast aluminum. The Washington Monument was finished at last.

Time and the elements took their toll on the structure, and a major overhaul was completed in 2000. The elevator was refurbished, cracks in the masonry filled, some stones were replaced, and the exterior was chiseled, washed, and buffed. The elevator carries visitors to the 500-foot observation level to enjoy a spectacular view of Washington and its environs. From there, if desired, park rangers lead tours to descend the 897 steps, past 192 memorial stones donated by individuals, societies, cities, states, and nations. Each reminds us of our heritage and the one man most responsible for the freedom we enjoy today.

PUBLIC USE: Season and hours: Memorial Day through Labor Day, 8 AM–11:45 PM daily. Rest of year, 9 AM–4:45 PM daily. Closed Christmas Day. **Admission fee:** Free tickets are available at the monument ticket kiosk at 15th Street and Madison Drive on a first-come, first-served basis. Reservations may be made at 1-800-967-2283 *or* over the Internet at *http://reservations.nps.gov.* There is a charge for the service.

FOR ADDITIONAL INFORMATION: Contact: Washington Monument, c/o National Capitol Parks-Central, 900 Ohio Drive, SW, Washington, DC 20024; 202-6426-6841. **Web site:** *www.nps.gov/wamo.* **Read:** Frank Freidel and Lonnelle Aikman. 1998. *George Washington: Man and Monument.*

SECTION III

OTHER SITES RELATED TO GEORGE WASHINGTON

Museums with Washington-Related Exhibits

There are numerous places that George Washington never visited but which, through formal exhibits and other methods, honor him, his life, and his legacy. Here we provide a selection of museums and related educational enterprises which offer perspectives on the life or times of George Washington. These entities are arranged in alphabetical order.

THE AMERICAN VILLAGE, MONTEVALLO, ALABAMA

The American Village is a 113-acre replicated colonial village managed by the Citizenship Trust, a public education corporation of the State of Alabama, its mission to enhance understanding and appreciation of the American republic and encourage the application of good citizenship in everyday life.

The village opened in 1999 as a unique educational center and historical park. In the belief that the essence of the American civic system is participation, visitors do so by reliving the drama and pageantry of the nation's journey to independence and self-government. Hands-on activities might include a drill with the Continental Army, participation in the Siege of Yorktown, or rallying with the Sons and Daughters of Liberty as they protest the Stamp Act and other indignities. There are reenacted debates at the Virginia Convention of 1775 and face-to-face chats with George Washington and other patriots attending the Constitutional Convention of 1787.

The centerpiece of the Village is Washington Hall, inspired by the design of Mount Vernon. Its Grand Foyer displays a replica of Jean Antoine Houdon's life-size sculpture of George Washington from the original in Virginia's State Capitol, and the Assembly Room is really a classroom designed to appear as the chamber in Independence Hall in Philadelphia where the Declaration of Independence and the Constitution were debated and adopted. The room features an exact replica of the famous "Rising Sun" chair used by George Washington when he chaired the Constitutional Convention.

Constitution Green is an authentic colonial green centering a post office, print shop, trade shops, and other buildings such as the Colonial Courthouse, where students and other visitors serve as justices, jurors, and defendants in mock cases. A Visitor Center is patterned after the Yorktown home of Dudley Digges, a member of the Virginia House of Burgesses. The rest of the grounds contain a military encampment, monuments, and a Southern Living colonial garden that evokes eighteenth-century formal gardens.

The emphasis at the American Village is educational, particularly as it pertains to K–12 students, yet all visitors, no matter their age, are encouraged to step back in time to refresh their minds and hearts with the ideas and ideals that guided their ancestors as they formed a new nation. **FOR ADDITIONAL INFORMATION: Contact:** American Village, PO Box 6, Montevallo, Alabama 35115; 205-665-3535, *or* 877-811-1776. **Web site:** *www.americanvillage.org.*

ANDERSON HOUSE MUSEUM, WASHINGTON, DC

Anderson House is a magnificent mansion built by Captain and Mrs. Larz Anderson in 1905. One of the few palatial residences in Washington open to the public, it features decorative art of Asia and Europe, Revolutionary War artifacts, and colonial portraiture. Anderson House houses the headquarters, library, and museum of the Society of Cincinnati, the patriotic organization founded by Continental Army officers in 1783 with George Washington as its first president. **FOR ADDITIONAL INFORMATION: Contact:** Anderson House Museum, 2118 Massachusetts Avenue, NW, Washington, DC 20008; 202-785-2040. **Web site:** *www.thesocietyofthecincinnati.addr.com.* **Read:** Garry Wills.1984. *Cincinnatus: George Washington and the Enlightenment.*

DAR MUSEUM, WASHINGTON, DC

The DAR Museum has been collecting historical objects for over a century and displays over 33,000 examples of decorative and fine arts including many objects made in America prior to the Industrial Revolution. There are thirty-three period rooms representing a range of historical themes. J. Carter Brown, Chairman Emeritus of the National Gallery has called the DAR Museum "one of Washington DC's undiscovered gems."[111]

The Daughters of the American Revolution sponsors a complete research facility devoted to the genealogy of the colonial and revolutionary periods as part of the museum complex. **FOR ADDITIONAL INFORMATION: Contact:** DAR Museum, 1776 D Street, Washington, DC 20006-5392; 202-879-3241. **Web site:** *www.dar.org.*

Museums

GENEALOGICAL LIBRARY AND HISTORIC MUSEUM, LOUISVILLE, KENTUCKY

The Genealogical Library and Historic Museum of the Sons of the American Revolution contains a reference collection of 40,000 volumes and manuscripts concerning genealogy, the American Revolution era, and local, county, regional, and state histories. There are 7500 family genealogies, over 2600 volumes of historical journals, 1200 volumes on George Washington, and 365 indexes to the US Census, 1790–1880.

An exhibit area of art and artifacts from the colonial and revolutionary periods provides a rich experience delineating the patriotic, historical, and educational aims of the SAR. **FOR ADDITIONAL INFORMATION: Contact:** National Society of the Sons of the American Revolution, 1000 South 4th Street, Louisville, Kentucky 40203; 502-589-1776. **Web site:** *www.sar.org.*

HALL OF FAME FOR GREAT AMERICANS, BRONX, NEW YORK

George Washington was the first of thirteen presidents to be enshrined in the Hall of Fame for Great Americans, founded by New York University to encourage deeper appreciation of many of the illustrious men and women who have contributed to the American experience. Ninety-eight portrait busts executed by noted sculptors (Washington's is a replica of the Houdon bust) are housed in a magnificent granite colonnade that winds gracefully around three neoclassic buildings designed by renowned architect Stanford White. In 1973, New York University transferred stewardship of the Hall to Bronx Community College which describes the pantheon as:

> . . . *a national treasure, standing as a constant reminder that America's strength is derived ultimately from the vitality, strength and intellect of its people. Our country has not only been a land of opportunity, but also one of accomplishment. Uniquely American, this is a democratic historical institution appealing to a broad public seeking to celebrate not merely the exploits of rulers and soldiers, but to honor the achievements of scientists, artists and humanitarians.* [112]

FOR ADDITIONAL INFORMATION: Contact: Hall of Fame for Great Americans, *c/o* Bronx Community College, University Avenue at West 181st Street, Bronx, New York 10453; 718-289-5100. **Web site:** *www.bcc.cuny.edu/halloffame/halloffame.htm.*

HALL OF PRESIDENTS, WALT DISNEY WORLD, LAKE BUENA VISTA, FLORIDA

The Hall of Presidents is a collection of audio-animatronic figures of all the presidents of the United States. The assembled presidents interact by expressing thoughts taken from their speeches and writings. **FOR ADDITIONAL INFORMATION: Contact:** Walt Disney World, Lake Buena Vista, Florida 32830; 407-824-2222. **Web site:** *www.disneyworld.com.*

HALL OF PRESIDENTS AND THEIR FIRST LADIES, GETTYSBURG, PENNSYLVANIA

Using simulated voices and stirring music, "The Story of Your Land" is dramatized by our chief executives, meticulously reproduced in wax. A second-floor gallery is devoted to figures of the first ladies dressed in authentic reproductions of the Smithsonian collection of their inaugural gowns. **FOR ADDITIONAL INFORMATION: Contact:** Hall of Presidents and their First Ladies, 789 Baltimore Street, Gettysburg, Pennsylvania 17325; 717-334-5717.

HENRY FORD MUSEUM AND GREENFIELD VILLAGE, DEARBORN, MICHIGAN

The Henry Ford Museum and Greenfield Village is devoted to the 300 years of technological changes that transformed America from an agrarian to industrial society. Benefactor-industrialist Henry Ford attempted to collect one example of everything ever made in America to prove his point that "As a nation we have not depended so much on rare or occasional genius as on the general resourcefulness of our people."[113]

The displays contain items such as George Washington's folding camp bed, Abraham Lincoln's rocker from Ford's Theatre, the entire Postville, Illinois Courthouse where Lincoln "rode the circuit," Theodore Roosevelt's horse drawn 1902 brougham, four modern presidential limousines, and inventions of such pioneer innovators as Charles Lindbergh, Thomas A. Edison, George Washington Carver, and Wilbur and Orville Wright. **FOR ADDITIONAL INFORMATION: Contact:** Henry Ford Museum and Greenfield Village, 20900 Oakwood Boulevard, Dearborn, Michigan 48121-1970; 313-271-1620. **Web site:** *www.hfmgv.org.*

HOUSE OF PRESIDENTS, CLERMONT, FLORIDA

The House of Presidents is a multi-layered exhibition hall of presidential history. There is a wax museum with life-size figures of all US presidents, a gallery of presidential memorabilia, china and *objets d'art,* replicas of the inaugural gowns of the first ladies, and a large diorama delineating the construction of the White House during the administration of George Washington.

The most remarkable exhibit is the famed "White House Replica" as envisioned and constructed by John Zweifel and friends over a thirty-seven-year period — a 1:12 scale model "dollhouse" sixty feet long and twenty feet wide that contains authentic and detailed reproductions of each room in the actual White House. Every piece is handmade to duplicate the original — rugs recreated by painstaking needlework and miniature furniture whittled by hand. The replica includes 1600 feet of electrical wiring, 548 tiny light bulbs, and six working television sets.

Mr. Zweifel's near life-long project is a "gift to the people. This is not just a dollhouse. It's a history of the past and a project working toward the future."[114] **FOR ADDITIONAL INFORMATION: Contact:** The House of Presidents, 123 N. Highway 27, Clermont, Florida 34712; 352-394-2836.

JOSEPHINE TUSSAUD WAX MUSEUM, HOT SPRINGS, ARKANSAS

Josephine Tussaud is the great-granddaughter of Madame Tussaud who established the famous wax museum in London in 1833. Josephine has continued the family heritage by establishing a museum in Hot Springs where historical figures ranging from Marie Antoinette to Pope John Paul II to United States President George Washington are presented in lifelike settings. **FOR ADDITIONAL INFORMATION: Contact:** Josephine Tussaud Wax Museum, 250 Central Avenue, Hot Springs, Arkansas 71901; 501-623-5836.

LOUDOUN MUSEUM, LEESBURG, VIRGINIA

Leesburg is nestled in the foothills of the Blue Ridge Mountains, west of Washington, DC. George Washington spent a great deal of time in this area as explorer, landowner, and executive of the Patowmack Canal Company, and may have surveyed some of Leesburg's home sites. The Loudoun Museum conducts a guided walking tour of the city that includes what may be a building used by Washington as one of his headquarters during the French and Indian War.

The Loudoun Museum is a repository of over 200 years of Loudoun County history. Much of its heritage and beauty is shown in a video presentation, and a hands-on display of Indian artifacts and tool manufacturing methods dramatizes its earliest period. A colonial era exhibit covers the original plan of Leesburg and nineteenth century agriculture is represented by farming and milling artifacts. The Civil War is brought to light with the story of the battle of nearby Ball's Bluff, and twentieth-century exhibits illustrate the area's modern growth and prosperity. **FOR ADDITIONAL INFORMATION: Contact:** Loudoun Museum, 16 Loudoun Street, SW, Leesburg, Virginia 22075; 703-777-7427.

In the Footsteps of George Washington

MARY BALL WASHINGTON MUSEUM, LANCASTER, VIRGINIA

George Washington's life journeys led him to the west, north, and south, but there is no indication that he traveled very far to the east of his birthplace at Popes Creek on the Northern Neck. There are, however, places of historical interest in the eastern part of the Northern Neck that relate to his life and legacy. Following US 3 eastward 50 miles from Popes Creek, for example, brings one to the town of Lancaster that boasts The Mary Ball Washington Museum, a five-building complex that honors George Washington's mother who was born nearby. Also in Lancaster are Lancaster House, a museum with Washington family artifacts; the Old Jail which houses historical archives; the Stewart-Blakemore Building containing a genealogical library that includes Washington family records; the Old Clerk's Office which displays memorabilia from Lancaster County; and a small brick house that serves as a history research library. Beyond the town green the museum staff has planted a boxwood garden, tobacco plot, and a Ladies' Kitchen Herb Garden that reflects the agricultural nature of Lancaster in the eighteenth century. **FOR ADDITIONAL INFORMATION: Contact:** Mary Washington Museum, Courthouse Green, Lancaster, Virginia 22503-0097; 804-462-7280. **Web site:** *www.mbwm.org.*

MUSEUM OF AMERICAN POLITICAL LIFE, WEST HARTFORD, CONNECTICUT

The Museum of American Political Life concentrates on the examination of different movements that have affected American political attitudes — women's rights, temperance, prohibition, and the like. It also features a wonderful display of rare presidential artifacts from the campaigns of George Washington to those of George W. Bush. **FOR ADDITIONAL INFORMATION: Contact:** Museum of American Political Life, University of Hartford, 20 Bloomfield Avenue, West Hartford, Connecticut 06117; 860-768-4090. **Web site:** *www.hartford.edu/mapl/.*

MUSEUM OF AMERICAN PRESIDENTS, STRASBURG, VIRGINIA

The Museum of American Presidents, located in the historic town of Strasburg, Virginia, contains the private presidential collection of Mr. Leo Bernstein. Prominent among the items are James Madison's writing desk and a handsome chandelier from Montpelier. The museum conducts regular presentations and seminars "dedicated to helping Americans, especially our youth, understand the principles upon which this nation was founded."[115] **FOR ADDITIONAL INFORMATION: Contact:** Museum of American Presidents, 130 N. Massanutten Street, Strasburg, Virginia 22657; 540-465-5999. **Web site:** *www.waysideofva.com/presidents/.*

Museums

PARADE OF PRESIDENTS WAX MUSEUM, KEYSTONE, SOUTH DAKOTA

The Parade of Presidents Wax Museum, located 2½-miles from Mount Rushmore, displays wax figures of every president, along with the likenesses of other famous personages, in life-like settings representing memorable historic events — drafting of the Declaration of Independence, George Washington's acceptance of the first American flag from Betsy Ross, a Lincoln-Douglas debate, the Yalta Conference, a meeting between Reagan and Gorbachev, and many others. **FOR ADDITIONAL INFORMATION: Contact:** Parade of Presidents Wax Museum, Highway 16A South, Keystone, South Dakota 57751; 605-666-4455. **Web site:** *www.presidentialmuseum.org.*

THE PRESIDENTIAL MUSEUM, ODESSA, TEXAS

The Presidential Museum is dedicated to the study of the office of president, with exhibits and educational programs about the people who have held — or who have run for — the presidency. The displays include campaign paraphernalia, signatures, cartoons, and the famous Dishong Collection of First Lady miniature dolls dressed in inaugural finery. A separate library contains more than 4500 volumes on subjects relating to the presidency, and the museum conducts regular educational programs and tours. **FOR ADDITIONAL INFORMATION: Contact:** The Presidential Museum, 622 North Lee Avenue, Odessa, Texas 79761; 915-322-7123.

TUDOR PLACE, WASHINGTON, DC

Tudor Place is considered the finest mansion in the Georgetown section of Washington. It is one of the five most important houses in the city, a neoclassical masterpiece designed by Architect William Thornton in 1805 for Thomas Peter and his wife, Martha Parke Custis, Martha Washington's granddaughter. The House was donated to a private foundation by Peter descendants in 1988 and opened as an important house museum featuring original furniture and some Washington artifacts from Mount Vernon. The mansion is surrounded by a 5½-acre historic garden of exquisite beauty. **FOR ADDITIONAL INFORMATION: Contact:** Tudor Place, 1644 31st Street NW, Washington, DC 20007; 202-965-0400. **Web site:** *www.tudorplace.org.*

VERMONT MARBLE EXHIBIT MUSEUM, PROCTOR, VERMONT

The Washington Monument and the Lincoln Memorial are two of the distinguished edifices built with Vermont Marble. This museum memorializes marble by illustrating the origin, quarrying, and finishing of the beautiful stone. Visitors may watch a sculptor at work and visit a Hall of Presidents which displays white marble relief carvings of all presidents from Washington to George W. Bush. **FOR ADDITIONAL INFORMATION: Contact:** Vermont Marble Museum, 62 Main Street, Proctor, Vermont 05765; 802-459-2300.

VIRGINIA HISTORICAL SOCIETY, RICHMOND, VIRGINIA

The mission statement of the Virginia Historical Society proclaims it as "The Center for Virginia History, collecting, preserving, and interpreting the commonwealth's past for the education and enjoyment of present and future generations."[116] And what a glorious history it is, if only for the fact that Virginia is the birthplace of eight presidents of the United States.

Within the society's magnificent building is a Museum of Virginia History that delineates four hundred years of Virginia's past in a 10,000-square-foot permanent exhibit called "The Story of Virginia, an American Experience." Performances by living history reenactors and hands-on exhibits enable visitors to experience the challenges and hardships of the first arrivals to our shores and the trials faced by explorers such as George Washington on their journeys to the western wilderness. Memorabilia on display includes gold buttons from Pocahontas's hat and the original copy of George Washington's diary from his first year as president (1790–1791). **FOR ADDITIONAL INFORMATION: Contact:** Virginia Historical Society, 428 North Boulevard, Richmond, Virginia 23220; 804-348-4901. **Web site:** *www.vahistorical.org.*

WEEMS-BOTTS MUSEUM, DUMFRIES, VIRGINIA

Parson Weems was the famous biographer of George Washington, best known for his apocryphal stories about Washington's cherry-tree-chopping and tossing dollars across the Rappahannock River. Weems used his home as a bookstore that has been converted to a museum of Dumfries-area history, including Weems and Dumfries's association with George Washington. Dumfries was a thriving river port and transit point for travelers to Fredericksburg and Williamsburg and Washington visited many times. **FOR ADDITIONAL INFORMATION: Contact:** Weems-Botts Museum, Merchant Park, 300 Duke Street, Dumfries, Virginia 22026; 703-221-3346.

Monuments and Memorials

The image and name of George Washington will forever be before us. His presence is everywhere — the magnificent Houdon statue in Richmond, breathtaking Mount Rushmore, an impressive 164-foot monument in Baltimore, the Masonic Memorial in Alexandria and, of course, on the simple quarter and the dollar bill. The 555-foot-tall Washington Monument graces our nation's capital and his name has been applied to one state and at least 32 counties, 257 townships, 121 cities and other municipalities, 10 lakes, 9 streams, and 3 mountains — as well as uncounted streets, buildings, schools, and other monuments in the United States.

Surprisingly, there are over 125 features named for Washington outside the continental United States — at least 22 mountains, rivers, islands, capes, and arms of the sea; 16 statues or monuments; 96 streets, plazas, and villages — commemorations that range from the application of his name to the Washington Straits in the Orkney Islands to Washington Island in the Marquesas. There are remembrances in Brazil, Venezuela, Argentina, Mexico, Greenland, Belgium, Ireland, Germany, Sweden, Portugal, Spain, Morocco, Latvia, Hungary, Romania, Albania, Italy, Korea, Philippines, Australia, Fiji, and New Zealand as well as other countries. It is no surprise to find twenty-eight remembrances in France, the most distinguished being the Lafayette-Washington monument in Paris, but it is a surprise to discover seventeen in England and Scotland, including two statues in London. Somehow Washington's accomplishments and greatness transcended the bitterness of the defeat and loss of the colonies.

If a monument is defined in Webster's Dictionary as "a lasting evidence, reminder or example of someone or something notable or great,"[117] then, for having left such a legacy, these monuments are a proper tribute to George Washington, who earned all of the honor and approbation that has been bestowed upon him by a grateful nation and those elsewhere who have recognized and appreciated his accomplishments. A selection of some notable monuments and memorials is given below; except for the first two, perhaps the most impressive of the group, the sites are arranged alphabetically by state.

MOUNT RUSHMORE NATIONAL MEMORIAL, KEYSTONE, SOUTH DAKOTA

Mount Rushmore (Plate 16) is the breathtaking sculpture of George Washington, Thomas Jefferson, Abraham Lincoln, and Theodore Roosevelt carved by Gutzon Borglum into the granite face of a mountain in South Dakota's Black Hills. The four figures symbolize the major achievements of the great leaders: Washington and the founding of the nation; Jefferson and the Declaration of Independence and the Louisiana Purchase; Lincoln and the preservation of the Union; and Roosevelt and the expansion of the country and the conservation of its natural resources.

A viewing platform called Grandview Terrace offers visitors an unobstructed look at the faces and an interactive museum at the visitor center contains interesting exhibits on the sculpting operation by Gutzon Borglum and the 392 workers who worked on it from 1927 until its completion in 1941. **FOR ADDITIONAL INFORMATION: Contact:** Mount Rushmore National Memorial, Box 268, Keystone, South Dakota 57751; 605-574-2523. **Web site:** *www.nps.gov/moru.* **Read:** Rex Alan Smith. 1985. The Carving of Mount Rushmore.

GEORGE WASHINGTON MASONIC NATIONAL MEMORIAL, ALEXANDRIA, VIRGINIA

The Masonic Order, to honor its most famous American member, constructed the George Washington Masonic National Memorial (Figure 136), a dramatic 333-foot-high building dedicated to: "George Washington — Patriot, President, Mason — as an expression of the Masonic Fraternity's faith in the principles of civil and religious liberty and orderly government which were portrayed in the life and character of our country's first President."[118] The memorial was dedicated on May 12, 1932.

A larger-than-life statue of Washington sculpted by Bryant Baker dominates the magnificent lobby of the memorial and a Masonic museum contains the Washington family bible, large murals, stained glass windows, dioramas, and other displays depicting important events in Washington's life. Guided tours of the facility end on a sixth-floor observation deck that has an unparalleled view of downtown Alexandria and Washington, DC. **FOR ADDITIONAL INFORMATION: Contact:** George Washington Masonic National Memorial, 101 Callahan Street, Alexandria, Virginia 22301; 703-683-2007. **Web site:** *www.georgewashington.org.* **Read:** Allen E. Roberts. 1976. *George Washington: Master Mason.*

Monuments and Memorials

Figure 136. George Washington Masonic National Memorial, Alexandria, Virginia. (Photograph courtesy of George Washington Masonic National Memorial)

FOREST LAWN – MEMORIAL PARK, LOS ANGELES, CALIFORNIA

Forest Lawn – Memorial Park in the Hollywood Hills of Los Angeles is a 340-acre cemetery with several areas dedicated to America's heritage — a full-sized replica of Boston's Old North Church and a fifteen-acre Court of Liberty that contains a reproduction of the Liberty Bell. The exterior of the Court of Liberty features a 30x165-foot mosaic, "The Birth of Liberty," that depicts epic moments in our nation's history. There is also a sixty-foot bronze and marble memorial to George Washington, a powerful bronze statue of Thomas Jefferson, and a sculpture of Abraham Lincoln executed by Augustus Saint-Gaudens. **FOR ADDITIONAL INFORMATION: Contact:** Forest Lawn – Memorial Park, 6300 Forest Lawn Drive, Los Angeles, California 90068; 213-254-7251. **Web site:** *www.forestlawn.com.*

FOREST LAWN-MEMORIAL PARK, GLENDALE, CALIFORNIA

Forest Lawn's Glendale branch contains its own pieces of Americana — a reproduction of the "Church of the Hills," the New England meeting house where Henry Wadsworth Longfellow worshipped, and a dramatic "Court of Freedom," its centerpiece one of the most inspiring sculptural representations of George Washington ever executed, the second casting made from the mold of the statue standing at Federal Hall in New York City.

FOR ADDITIONAL INFORMATION: Contact: Forest Lawn-Memorial Park, 1712 South Glendale Avenue, Glendale, California 91209; 213-254-3131. **Web site:** *www.forestlawn.com.*

BALTIMORE WASHINGTON MONUMENT, BALTIMORE, MARYLAND

A slim, handsome 164-foot column topped by a sixteen-foot statue of the first president, is considered an architectural masterpiece. Construction under the direction of sculptor Robert Mills began in 1815, but it was not until 1829 that a figure of President Washington holding his scroll of resignation was mounted atop the spire. The monument is located at the intersection of Charles and Monument streets in downtown Baltimore.

WASHINGTON MONUMENT STATE PARK, BOONSBORO, MARYLAND

The first substantial monument in the nation to honor George Washington is a rough-stone, thirty-four-foot-high shaft dedicated on July 4, 1827. The monument was damaged during the Civil War but was rebuilt in 1882. **FOR ADDITIONAL INFORMATION: Contact:** Washington Monument State Park, Boonsboro, Maryland 21713; 301-432-8065.

WASHINGTON COLLEGE, CHESTERTOWN, MARYLAND

Washington College, founded in 1782, was the first institution of higher learning named for George Washington. Washington visited the college in 1794, at which time the students presented the play *Gustavus Vasa,* a celebration of Sweden's hero, in which a few lines were added to compare him to America's own great hero seated in the audience. Washington was also presented with an honorary Doctor of Laws degree.

GEORGE WASHINGTON STATUE, MANHATTAN AVENUE AT 114TH STREET, NEW YORK, NEW YORK

A statue of Washington, standing with the Marquis de Lafayette, dominates a corner of Morningside Park in northwestern Manhattan, two blocks east of Columbia University. Frederick Bartholdi was the sculptor.

GEORGE WASHINGTON STATUE, MASONIC HALL, NEW YORK, NEW YORK

A massive statue of Washington dominates the Hollender Room of the recently renovated Masonic Hall. It is from the same casting as the statue in the George Washington Masonic Memorial in Alexandria, Virginia. Masonic Hall is on 23rd Street in mid-Manhattan, between Broadway and Avenue of the Americas. **FOR ADDITIONAL INFORMATION: Contact:** Masonic Hall, 71 West 23rd Street, New York, New York 10010; 212-741-1323.

Monuments and Memorials

GEORGE WASHINGTON STATUE, UNION SQUARE, NEW YORK, NEW YORK

Union Square features a bronze equestrian statue of George Washington executed by Henry Kirke Brown. Union Square is in downtown New York at the intersection of Broadway and 14th Street.

GEORGE WASHINGTON STATUE, PHILADELPHIA, PENNSYLVANIA

In 1897, the Society of Cincinnati presented the city of Philadelphia with a larger-than-life equestrian representation of George Washington which stands in front of the Philadelphia Museum of Art on Eakins Oval. The sculptor was Rudolph Siemering.

WASHINGTON STATUE, CHARLESTON, SOUTH CAROLINA

The most recent rendering of George Washington was unveiled in Charleston's Washington Square on December 14, 1999, the statue honoring President Washington's visit to Charleston in 1791. According to sculptor John Michel, the nine-foot bronze statue represents Washington "standing as if in the moment of applause from enthusiastic and adoring Charlestonians."[119]

GEORGE WASHINGTON MEMORIAL PARKWAY, McLEAN, VIRGINIA

The George Washington Memorial Parkway is more than a road, as it preserves the natural scenery along the Potomac River and links historic sites along its path — from George Washington's Mount Vernon, past the nation's capital, and on to the Great Falls area where Washington demonstrated his engineering skill and vision for the future. Washington's hometown, Alexandria, lies on the parkway, as does Arlington National Cemetery and Arlington House, the home of Robert E. Lee. Theodore Roosevelt Island, Clara Barton National Historic Site, Glen Echo Park, and the Lyndon B. Johnson Grove are all located on or near the parkway that features scenic overlooks where visitors may stop to rest, or perhaps to merely enjoy the magnificent river and lush natural environment. **FOR ADDITIONAL INFORMATION: Contact:** George Washington Memorial Parkway, Turkey Run Park, McLean, VA 22101; 703-289-2500. **Web site:** *www.nps.gov/gwmp.*

GEORGE WASHINGTON STATUARY, CAPITOL SQUARE, RICHMOND, VIRGINIA

In 1785, renowned sculptor Jean Antoine Houdon appeared at Mount Vernon to make preliminary sketches before sculpting a life size statue of George Washington, as commissioned by the State of Virginia. The resulting figure is the only statue for which the President posed. The general even subjected himself to the molding of a life mask. In addition to two

Figure 137. George Washington Statue, Virginia Capitol Building, Richmond, Virginia. (Photograph by William G. Clotworthy)

busts and the classic statue that stands in the rotunda of the Virginia Capitol (Figure 137), two other castings were made — one is prominently displayed on the campus of the University of Virginia and the other stands on the steps of the South Carolina State House in Columbia.

A park area just outside the main entrance of the capitol building features an equestrian statue of Washington encircled by heroic figures of Thomas Jefferson, Patrick Henry, John Marshall, and other distinguished Virginians. **FOR ADDITIONAL INFORMATION: Contact:** Virginia State Capitol, Capitol Square, Richmond, Virginia 23219; 804-786-4344.

WASHINGTON AND LEE UNIVERSITY, LEXINGTON, VIRGINIA

Washington and Lee is a distinguished university housed in white colonnaded buildings within a tree-filled campus of rare beauty. The school was founded in 1749 as Augusta Academy — renamed Liberty Hall in 1776. Liberty Hall received a posthumous endowment from George Washington and the school took his name as a gesture of thanks and respect. Confederate General Robert E. Lee became president of the university following the Civil War and after his death the name was again changed — to Washington and Lee.

Monuments and Memorials

GEORGE WASHINGTON STATUE, WASHINGTON, DC

In 1860, President James Buchanan dedicated a bronze equestrian statue of George Washington as rendered by sculptor Clark Mills. The statue is located in Washington Circle at the intersection of Massachusetts and New Hampshire avenues.

WASHINGTON STATUE, NATIONAL MUSEUM OF AMERICAN HISTORY, WASHINGTON, DC

To commemorate the centennial of Washington's birth in 1832, Congress commissioned Horatio Greenough to sculpt a statue of George Washington to be placed in the rotunda of the capitol building. Greenough did not provide preliminary sketches and insisted on working in Italy. It was not until 1841 that, sight unseen, the fourteen-ton work was delivered. When unveiled, Congress was shocked to see Washington portrayed as a half-naked figure wearing only a toga resembling a bath towel to cover his nudity — the work was based on a classic statue of the god Zeus done by the Greek sculptor Phisias. The work, deemed inappropriate by the Senate, was moved to a shed on the east side of the Capitol before it was removed to the cellar of the Smithsonian Institution. Years later it was placed in the lobby of the Smithsonian's National Museum of American History. **FOR ADDITIONAL INFORMATION: Contact:** Smithsonian Information, SI Building, Room 153, Washington, DC 20560; 202-357-2700. **Web site:** *www.smithsonian.org.*

Other Sites of Interest

Many sites in the United States associated with George Washington are privately owned or otherwise closed to public visitation. In almost every case, the owners or caretakers take great pains to maintain the integrity of the house, park, or garden. We owe them our gratitude.

The following is a listing of these sites in an order that more or less corresponds to the chronology experienced by George Washington. Again, we emphasize the fact that these properties are privately owned and, unless specifically indicated, are not open to public visitation.

George Washingtons Surveying Office, White Post, Virginia

In 1749, Lord Fairfax built a wilderness home called Greenway Court as a personal retreat and headquarters for his extensive landholdings. Much of Greenway Court was destroyed by fire in the mid 1800s; the only buildings that survived were a porter's lodge, an arsenal, and a small stone structure that had been used as an office by the surveying staff that included George Washington.

Washington, Virginia

The town of Washington, lying in the picturesque western hills of the Virginia Piedmont, is a residential community of 700 structures — a well-preserved example of a nineteenth-century county seat, said to have been built on a grid plan laid out by surveyor George Washington in 1749. It is the oldest of the many American towns or cities named for him.

George Washington House, Barbados, St. Michael, Barbados, West Indies

In a search for relief for brother Lawrence's tuberculosis, George Washington accompanied him to Barbados in 1751, the only time George left the North American mainland. On Barbados, George was stricken with smallpox, but recovered and was therefore immune to the disease that killed much of his army during the Revolutionary War. The house where the brothers lived was definitively identified a few years ago and is currently (2002) undergoing study and restoration by the Barbados National Trust. Visitors may visit the site to witness restoration efforts in progress, although the house is not yet open for visitation. Additional contact information: 246-228-4772.

CHARLES DICK HOUSE, FREDERICKSBURG, VIRGINIA

Charles Dick was a popular storeowner and civic leader in Fredericksburg whose home is one of the town's oldest buildings. The house, built in 1750, lies on a hill facing the Rappahannock River, with steps hewn in the steep hill which gave Mr. Dick access to Caroline Street and his store. George Washington's diaries indicate many visits to Mr. Dick's. The Charles Dick House currently is managed as a bed and breakfast inn (540-372-6625).

THE SENTRY BOX, FREDERICKSBURG, VIRGINIA

The Sentry Box is a simple gray clapboard house built in 1784 by General George Weedon, a member of George Washington's military staff and owner of Weedon's Tavern, George Washington's favorite. The tavern has been lost to fire, but Weedon's home, host to every US President from Washington through James Buchanan, still stands.

MORTIMER HOUSE, FREDERICKSBURG, VIRGINIA

Mortimer House is a white brick structure built by Dr. Charles Mortimer in 1764. Twice mayor of Fredericksburg, Dr. Mortimer was known for his gracious hospitality, especially as host of a lavish Peace Ball in 1784. Among his distinguished guests were George Washington, the Marquis de Lafayette, and Compte de Rochambeau.

THE LEWIS STORE, FREDERICKSBURG, VIRGINIA

The Historic Fredericksburg Foundation is restoring (2002) the two-story brick Lewis Store, built by Fielding Lewis's father in 1749. The intention is to recreate the ambience of a colonial retail establishment, with costumed interpreters selling colonial-style artifacts and reproduction products of the eighteenth century. Plans call for the store to open to the public in the spring of 2003.

YEW HILL, DELAPLANE, VIRGINIA

A Potomac-style wooden frame farmhouse called Yew Hill was the home of pioneer Thomas Ashby for whom Ashby's Bent in the Blue Ridge was named. His son Robert, a marker for surveyor George Washington in 1748, inherited Yew Hill where his friend Washington spent several days in March, 1769. Washington's diary reads, "Set out for Robt. Ashby's, and after dining by the way, reachd it a little after dark."[120]

THORNTON HILL, SPERRYVILLE, VIRGINIA

The manor house at Thornton Hill, still a working farm, was constructed between 1740 and 1750 by wealthy landowner Francis Thornton as the centerpiece of a 30,000-acre farm. Young surveyor George Washington stayed at Thornton Hill, and visited again when the house became the residence of his aunt. Thornton Hill is a 2½-story, sixteen-room mansion with a formal dining room.

MONTPELIER, SPERRYVILLE, VIRGINIA

Montpelier, unrelated to James Madison's estate home, is similar to Thornton Hill in both architecture and history as it was also built by Francis Thornton as a manor house for a separate Thornton landholding.

BEL AIR, MINNIEVILLE, VIRGINIA

In 1740, Major Charles Ewell, married to Sarah Ball, a relative of George Washington's mother, built a 2½-story, fourteen-room country house in the traditional colonial style. George and Martha Washington were overnight guests at Bel Air on their honeymoon journey from Williamsburg to Mount Vernon. By coincidence, the house was later owned by Parson Weems, the cleric who wrote the first biography of George Washington, the book that included the famous cherry-tree and dollar-tossing anecdotes. Today Bel Air is the heart of a working farm.

THE COCKS RESIDENCE, WINCHESTER, VIRGINIA

When visiting Winchester after the Revolutionary War, George Washington stayed at this home of a friend.

Other Sites

HAPPY RETREAT, CHARLES TOWN, WEST VIRGINIA

George Washington's brother Charles founded Charles Town around 1780 and began to construct a fine home, the two wings of which were connected by an open breezeway. Charles wanted to build a middle section but may have run out of money, or was perhaps too obsessed with building the entire town to complete the project. After his death, the house had several owners, including Judge Isaac Douglas who finished it by constructing a three-story middle section in 1857.

HAREWOOD, CHARLES TOWN, WEST VIRGINIA

George Washington's brother Samuel inherited land in the Charles Town area and built a house called Harewood, the English word for sycamore. There is evidence that the architect was John Ariss, the designer of Kenmore Plantation, as the proportions, grace of design, and sense of space reflect the taste and majesty of Kenmore, which follows the Virginia style of two large rooms off a center hallway, with end chimneys and an outside kitchen.

There is little question that brother George visited Harewood although its major claim to fame was as the site of the wedding of Dolley Payne Todd to James Madison. Harewood is owned and occupied by a direct descendant of Samuel Washington.

SNODGRASS TAVERN, HEDGESVILLE, WEST VIRGINIA

Snodgrass Tavern is one of the oldest buildings in West Virginia; parts of the log house and outbuildings date from the 1740s. During its 100-year life as a tavern, many famous people visited, including George Washington whose diary for September 5, 1784, noted, "...despatched my wagon at daylight and at 7 o'clock followed it. Bated at one Snodgrasses on Back Creek and dined there."[121] An early slave cemetery is just west of the house.

THE OLD MANSION, BOWLING GREEN, VIRGINIA

In 1669, Major Thomas Hoomes constructed a fine home on the Colonial Highway between Philadelphia and Williamsburg. It is a pre-Georgian, 1½-story brick house, the second oldest surviving house in Virginia and the oldest continuously inhabited home in the Commonwealth — and probably the only one with a horse racing track encircling the front lawn. The center hall is flanked by two rooms on either side with a washroom and three bedrooms above. The Hoomeses were close friends of George Washington and he frequently stayed with them on his trips to and from Williamsburg. During the Revolutionary War the house was host to British Lord Cornwallis, French General Lafayette and to Washington and Rochambeau as they made their way to and from Yorktown. As president, Washington was "wined and dined" by the Hoomes family on April 10, 1791. The Old Mansion is open to the public during Virginia Garden Week.

THE WILLIAM FOX TAVERN, PORT ROYAL, VIRGINIA

In 1755, Captain William Fox obtained a license to operate a tavern in his home. When Captain Fox was away at sea, his wife, Ann Roy Fox, managed the establishment that became the most renowned in Port Royal. George Washington first stayed at the Fox Tavern on January 14, 1760, the bill for his lodgings coming to five shillings (about $1.20).

HUBBARDS TAVERN, SPARTA, VIRGINIA

The Old Colonial Highway between Fredericksburg and Williamsburg was filled with "ordinaries," where weary travelers could obtain a good meal, drink, a comfortable bed for a few shillings, and oats and a straw bed for one's horse. Todd's, Coleman's, Buckner's — all were popular, and all are gone. An exception is Hubbard's, apparently one of George Washington's favorites, as he stayed there at least sixteen times on his journeys between Mount Vernon and the capital.

Unfortunately, Hubbards Tavern, a 1½-story frame house with two chimneys, has been neglected over the years. It stands forlornly empty, its roof sagging and walls overgrown with brush.

AMPTHILL, RICHMOND, VIRGINIA

Archibald Cary was a close friend of George Washington who sometimes stayed with the Carys when visiting Richmond. Cary's house, built in 1732, was somewhat modified and moved from its original location on the west side of town to a site near the James River.

RIPPON LODGE, WOODBRIDGE, VIRGINIA

The Potomac Path, or King's Highway, was a major transportation route linking the northern and southern colonies. Washington used it frequently on trips south of Mount Vernon, stopping at the Woodbridge estate of George Mason (Gunston Hall) or Rippon Lodge, the home of Colonel Richard Blackburn. Modern US 1 closely follows the Potomac Path.

GEORGE WASHINGTON TOWNHOUSE, ALEXANDRIA, VIRGINIA

The townhouse is a replica of a house built by George Washington in 1769 when he was heavily involved with civic affairs in Alexandria and he utilized it as an office and guest house to accommodate the overflow of visitors at Mount Vernon. The house was razed in 1855, then rebuilt in 1960 by Virginia Governor and Mrs. Lowe, who used some bricks and stones from the original structure. There is a commemorative plaque on the outside wall.

BANK OF ALEXANDRIA, ALEXANDRIA, VIRGINIA

The Bank of Alexandria was established in 1792, with George Washington as a charter stockholder. The building is the original, although a different banking institution is currently housed in it.

DOCTOR JAMES CRAIK HOUSE, ALEXANDRIA, VIRGINIA

Dr. James Craik, a Scottish émigré, met George Washington on a military mission to the west in 1754 and they remained close friends and compatriots. Craik ministered to the dying Braddock at Monongahela and saw General Hugh Mercer breathe his last at Princeton. Then, as the Washington family physician, he nursed Jacky Custis during his last hours, delivered Nelly Custis's first child, and was in attendance when his friend Washington passed away.

Craik bought the Duke Street house in 1795. Typical of Alexandria architecture, it is 3½-stories tall with dormer windows.

THE OLD CLUB, ALEXANDRIA, VIRGINIA

The oldest portion of this building, the front hall and living room, was built at Broomilaw Point on the Potomac as a gentlemen's club by a group that included George Washington and George Mason. In 1790, it was moved to its present site where the main portion of the existing house was added. The Old Club was used as a private residence for many years before it deteriorated and was abandoned. Current restoration efforts have been completed on the exterior but the interior remains unfinished.

DUVALLS TAVERN, ALEXANDRIA, VIRGINIA

George Washington attended a reception at Duvalls Tavern shortly after he resigned his commission as Commander-in-Chief of the Continental Army. Duvalls has been converted to an antique shop.

WISES TAVERN, ALEXANDRIA, VIRGINIA

George Washington and the directors of the Patowmack Canal Company met at Wises to plan a canal designed to connect Alexandria with the C&O Canal. He attended a dance at Wises to celebrate the ratification of the Constitution in 1788, and was honored at Birthday balls in 1792 and 1794. The building is now part of a residential and sales complex.

ALEXANDRIA ACADEMY, ALEXANDRIA, VIRGINIA

Alexandria Academy is a landmark in the history of public education and a tribute to George Washington's interest in education. Built by leading citizens of Alexandria around 1785, it was one of the first experiments in universal education, and as such included a free school for orphans and poor children. George Washington was vitally interested in fostering education; he not only funded the Academy but left a bequest in his will for that purpose. The three-story brick building, restored by the Historic Alexandria Foundation, was re-opened in 1999 to fulfill a continuing educational role as part of the private Remediation and Training Institute.

BOYHOOD HOME OF ROBERT E. LEE, ALEXANDRIA, VIRGINIA

When William Fitzhugh sold Chatham Plantation near Fredericksburg, he moved to Alexandria where he purchased an elegant red brick mansion. George Washington often dined with the Fitzhughs, and it was here that Washington's adopted grandson courted and married Mary Fitzhugh.

In 1812, the house was purchased by "Light Horse Harry" Lee who moved into the home with his family that included five-year-old

Robert E. Lee. The future Confederate general spent his boyhood in this house.

FALLS CHURCH, FALLS CHURCH, VIRGINIA

George Washington was a vestryman of Truro Parish at the time Falls Church, in desperate need of repair, was declared unsafe. Church records show that Washington attended a meeting to discuss the issue and advertised publicly for financial assistance for restoration efforts. Reconstruction was begun in 1769 to replace the original wood building with a brick edifice that was later destroyed by fire. The baptismal font in the sanctuary is the only souvenir that remains of the two early church buildings.

THE BRICE HOUSE, ANNAPOLIS, MARYLAND

James Brice was an ardent patriot who entertained early political leaders, including George Washington, John Adams, and James Madison. His estate home is owned by the National Masonry Institute.

MOUNT AIRY, ROSARYVILLE, MARYLAND

In 1774, George Washington's stepson, Jacky Custis, was married at the home of his bride's parents. The event was attended by then-Colonel Washington, although without enthusiasm, as he considered the couple too young to marry. The Calvert House is owned by the Maryland Department of Natural Resources.

SAINT JOHNS COLLEGE, ANNAPOLIS, MARYLAND

On the morning after the "ship grounding" debacle on Middleton's Ferry, President Washington began a tour of Annapolis by visiting a new seminary, Saint Johns College. The seminary later acknowledged his visit, to which he responded, "The satisfaction which I have derived from my visit to your infant seminary, is expressed with real pleasure, and my wishes for its progress to perfection are preferred with sincere regard."[122] He demonstrated his sincerity by installing his ward, George Washington Parke Custis, as a student, along with two nephews. McDowell Hall, one of the original buildings, is still used for classrooms. The campus is part of an Annapolis Historical Walking Tour.

In the Footsteps of George Washington

THE RECTORY OF SAINT ANNES PARISH, ANNAPOLIS, MARYLAND

Jonathan Boucher, Rector of Saint Annes, conducted a Boys' Academy in his home where George Washington's stepson Jacky boarded for a time. Washington befriended the Rector, dined at his home, and spent many hours in lively political discussions, but eventually terminated the relationship due to disagreements over Boucher's Tory views.

A nineteenth-century mansard roof and gallery porch serve to disguise the colonial brick residence that may be viewed from the street as part of an Annapolis Historical Walking Tour.

LA GRANGE, LA PLATA, MARYLAND

La Grange, a 2½-story Georgian mansion built around 1760, was the early home of Dr. James Craik, intimate friend and personal physician to George Washington. Craik served as Physician General of the Continental Army, accompanied Washington on his post-war trip to the west, and was present at the general's death in 1799. It is known that Washington visited Craik's home on numerous occasions.

THOMAS BOND HOUSE, PHILADELPHIA, PENNSYLVANIA

Dr. Thomas Bond was a celebrated physician and surgeon whose four-story home, built around 1769, is an example of a classic revival Georgian. South 2nd Street was a fashionable residential area of Philadelphia that boasted many prominent residents such as Samuel Morris, Robert Fulton, and Clement Biddle, George Washington's business agent. It is probable that Washington visited them, and Dr. Bond. The house, situated across the street from City Tavern, had many owners and uses through the years until it was restored as a bed and breakfast inn in 1988, operated by a concessionaire under lease from the National Park Service.

HOLLINGSWORTH TAVERN, ELKTON, MARYLAND

Elkton, once known as Head of Elk (River), was an important rest stop in Maryland in colonial times. George Washington's diary indicates that he stayed at the Hollingsworth Tavern, a 2½-story English brick structure with thick walls, and it is possible that he used it as his headquarters on August 25, 1777, preceding the Battle of Brandywine.

Other Sites

THE HERMITAGE, ELKTON, MARYLAND

Robert Alexander, a delegate to the Continental Congress in 1775, built the Hermitage in 1735. George Washington was entertained by Mr. Alexander on August 25, 1777. Only a few days later, the Hermitage was utilized as the headquarters of British General Howe.

WASHINGTONS FACTORS HOUSE, WARWICK, MARYLAND

Washington's "factor" was his agent, a commercial representative who sold a plantation owner's crops and collected his fees — an eighteenth-century commodities broker. A plaque on the outside of a one-room-wide brick house on Warwick's Main Street states, "George Washington visited Warwick Feby.1756. March 1756. Din'd and lodg'd at Mr. D'L Heaths May 1773. Passed through Sept. 3 and Oct. 28, 1774. Breakfasted March 23, 1791 and again in September 1793."

WORSELL MANOR, WARWICK, MARYLAND

Worsell Manor is one of the oldest and most distinguished homes in Maryland, the centerpiece of 1000 acres granted to Major Peter Sayer in 1685. Worsell Manor features ancient paneling, stairways, corner fireplaces, Dutch fireplace tiles, and other details evidencing the Charles II, pre-1700 architectural style rarely extant in America. One plaque in downtown Warwick and another on the road bypassing the house state, "Worsell Manor, 1000 acres. Established 1685 by Major Peter Sayer, a prominent Catholic. Later acquired by the Heath family. On the 14th of May, 1773, George Washington dined and lodged at Mr. D'L Heath's taking his stepson, Jacky Custis to King's College, [now Columbia University]."

ANCHOR AND HOPE FARMHOUSE, PORT DEPOSIT, MARYLAND

The Anchor and Hope, on the bank of the Susquehanna River, served colonial travelers as a stagecoach and ferry ticket office. It is believed that George Washington stopped at the Anchor and Hope on his way to the Continental Congress in 1775. Anchor and Hope is a pre-1700 Dutch Colonial featuring a twelve -foot ceiling with hand-hewn beams and two large fireplaces with original paneling.

GENERAL JEDIDIAH HUNTINGTON HOUSE, NORWICH, CONNECTICUT

General Huntington served in the Revolutionary War with great distinction. His house, built in 1765, was used to entertain General Washington and Connecticut Governor Trumbull on April 8, 1776, during the Continental Army's march from Boston to New York. Just across the street at Number 234 is the home of his brother, Governor Samuel Huntington, signer of the Declaration of Independence and President of the Continental Congress from 1779 to 1781 — and around the corner at 11 Huntington Lane is the house of Colonel Joshua Huntington. The three houses are similar in design, each 2½-storied frame and clapboard structures.

JOHN MACCURDY HOUSE, OLD LYME, CONNECTICUT

John MacCurdy was a prosperous shipping merchant and storeowner who bought a small four-room house that had been built in 1700. Through the years the house was enlarged by MacCurdy and others until it measured 90 feet in length. The house features eight gables and an unusual combination of architectural features, including Gothic Revival alterations — medieval chimneys and pointed arch windows. General George Washington spent the night of April 10, 1776, at the MacCurdy house during the Continental Army's march to New York.

ALEXANDER DOUGLASS HOUSE, TRENTON, NEW JERSEY

General Washington held a council of war in the Douglass home on January 2, 1777. The house, a simple frame building, was at 5 Broad Street, now the site of the Evangelical Lutheran Church. The house was moved to Mill Hill Park, close to the Assunpink River, at the intersection of Montgomery and Front streets.

OLIVER WOLCOTT HOUSE, LITCHFIELD, CONNECTICUT

Oliver Wolcott, member of the Continental Congress, signer of the Declaration of Independence, and Governor of Connecticut, built a large frame and clapboard house in 1753. Wolcott hosted General George Washington on September 23, 1780, as Washington made his way to a meeting with General Rochambeau in Newport.

OLD COLONY HOUSE, NEWPORT, RHODE ISLAND

The Declaration of Independence was read to Rhode Island citizens from the balcony, French General Rochambeau was greeted in its

Great Hall by George Washington, and the United States Constitution was ratified in the Old Colony House when it served as the capitol of Rhode Island.

In 1997, management of the deteriorating building was assumed by the Newport Historical Society which, in cooperation with the state of Rhode Island and the Historical Preservation and Heritage Commission, is formulating plans for the reconstruction and refurbishing of the building. There is no schedule for opening the Old Colony House for visitation.

VERNON HOUSE, NEWPORT, RHODE ISLAND

A simple, two-story clapboard home served as the headquarters of French General Rochambeau at the time he conferred with General Washington in 1780. Washington's trip to Newport was his first chance to review allied troops. The French formed an honor guard from the wharf to Vernon House, then held a ball in Washington's honor where it was reported that the Europeans were very impressed with the General's demeanor and presence.

RICHARD HOLCOMBE HOUSE, LAMBERTVILLE, NEW JERSEY

General Washington was Holcombe's guest during the Continental Army's retreat from Fort Lee to Pennsylvania. The Holcombe House is a two-story brick farmhouse.

MALIN HALL, MALVERN, PENNSYLVANIA

General Washington's expense account for September 16, 1777, shows an entry for "Cash paid Mr. Malin for sundrys used+his house and trouble+7& 10f."[123] The Malin House is a typical stone farmhouse of the revolutionary period.

FATLANDS, VALLEY FORGE, PENNSYLVANIA

This stone farmhouse was located just across the Schuylkill River from Valley Forge and was visited by Washington on September 21, 1777, during an inspection trip.

THE CASTLEBERRY HOUSE, EVANSBURG, PENNSYLVANIA

General Washington reputedly used this stone farmhouse as headquarters from September 19 through 22, 1777. The house was enlarged sometime in the nineteenth century as attested by a line of demarcation visible on the walls. A mansard roof was added, somewhat blemishing the original colonial lines.

DAWESFIELD, WHITEMARSH, PENNSYLVANIA

Washington visited the stone farmhouse of James Morris on October 21, 1777, during the Whitemarsh encampment.

EMLEN HOUSE, FORT WASHINGTON, PENNSYLVANIA

While his troops rested at Whitemarsh, General Washington headquartered in the home of George Emlen where he remained from November 2 to December 11, 1777, prior to the move to Valley Forge. Emlen's magnificent three-story colonial mansion is the centerpiece of a 100-acre estate.

RED LION INN AND QUAKER MEETING HOUSE, LIONVILLE, PENNSYLVANIA

To handle an overflow of sick and injured soldiers at Yellow Springs, the Continental Army requisitioned the Quaker Meeting House in Lionville. During visits to the patients, General Washington stayed at the Red Lion, a drover's inn across the street. A small stone building of 2½-stories, it has been converted to a private home with only part of the original remaining. The Meeting House is a large stone structure used as headquarters of the Uwchlan Conservation Trust that has renamed the building the Uwchlan Meeting House.

REDDING FURNACE FARM, EAST NANTMEAL, PENNSYLVANIA

As early as 1736, iron furnaces and foundries such as Reading, Warwick, and Hopewell had been established west of Valley Forge. Redding Furnace Farm, a stone farmhouse built by iron-master William Branson, is one of the surviving remnants of the business that supplied cannons to the Continental Army. It has been documented that General Washington inspected the forges and foundries during the Valley Forge encampment in 1777.

FELL HOUSE, DOYLESTOWN, PENNSYLVANIA

The Continental Army broke camp at Valley Forge on June 19, 1778, to follow the British army that had abandoned Philadelphia and withdrawn to the north. When the Americans reached Doylestown, General Washington set up headquarters in a tent on the property of Jonathan Fell, but took his meals inside Fell's small house.

VILLAGE INN, ENGLISHTOWN, NEW JERSEY

The Village Inn is where General Washington drew up plans for the Battle of Monmouth and later, unhappily, drafted charges against General Charles Lee for Lee's inept and cowardly behavior during the battle.

HUNT HOUSE FARM, HOPEWELL, NEW JERSEY

The Joseph Stout House, a 2½-story Georgian farmhouse, also served as headquarters for George Washington in June, 1778, preceding the Battle of Monmouth. The stone house has been slightly altered yet retains the architectural integrity and symmetry of the original.

FOWLER HOUSE, CARMEL, NEW YORK

Enroute to an encampment in Pawling, New York, General Washington stayed one night in the Fowler House, a 1½-story vernacular frame farmhouse that has been enlarged through the years.

DENNING HOUSE, SALISBURY MILLS, NEW YORK

Tory James Peters sold a 1½-story shingle and stone farmhouse to William Denning around 1770, probably to prevent its confiscation. Legend says that Peters hid in a secret recess, still visible in a bedroom, to escape arrest before fleeing to Canada.

New owner Denning, a member of the New York Provincial Congress, was an important revolutionary figure as his financial competence led to his assignment as Commissioner of the Board of Treasury and subsequent service with the Quartermaster Department. He was close to General Washington and documentation exists that the Washingtons visited the Denning home. The house is a fine example of gracious colonial living, with simple shingled walls over a stone foundation, broad stone chimneys, and small-paned windows with paneled shutters. The interior follows the common architectural pattern — a central hall with two rooms on each side and four bedrooms with sloping ceilings and small windows on the second floor. Many touches of elegance adorn the interior, from handsome paneling, moldings, and pilasters to authentic period pieces.

In the Footsteps of George Washington

DERICK BRINCKERHOFF HOUSE, FISHKILL, NEW YORK

Derick Brinckerhoff, a third-generation family farmer, was active in governmental affairs as a representative in the Colonial Legislature of New York, and later served as colonel of militia and as a member of the New York State Assembly.

Some time before the war, he modified his stone house by raising it to two stories and adding clapboards. During the war, the house was requisitioned as headquarters for General Alexander McDougall, military commander of the Highlands, whose guests included Governor George Clinton and generals Washington, Lafayette, Putnam, Knox, Arnold, and Gates.

At the conclusion of the war, George Washington, Aide Alexander Hamilton, and General von Steuben stood on the front porch to review thousands of British and Hessian prisoners being marched from Boston to Virginia for repatriation. The house is still owned by the Brinckerhoff family, and the current owner has initiated an unusual tradition to commemorate Washington's review of the prisoners. Each year fourth-graders from a nearby elementary school stand on the front porch to "take the salute" from "prisoners and guards" as they march past.

STORM-ADRIANCE-BRINCKERHOFF HOUSE, EAST FISHKILL, NEW YORK

A 1½-story frame building was built in 1759 by militia Captain Thomas Storm who resided there during the Revolutionary War, and it is thought that Tory and British prisoners were confined in the cellar. As the house was located on a major east-west route, Storm extended colonial hospitality to passing travelers that included George Washington and John Adams. The house is named for its three earliest owners.

JOHN BRINCKERHOFF HOUSE, FISHKILL, NEW YORK

In the west gable of the John Brinckerhoff House, black bricks inlaid among the red outline the date of construction, 1 7 3 8. The architecture and layout of the house are conventional — a central hall with two rooms flanking it, four bedrooms upstairs and small windows throughout.

In the autumn of 1778, General Washington made the Brinckerhoff house his headquarters and occupied a parlor-bedroom at the rear of the west side of the house. An apocryphal anecdote relates that Washington, queried by his host about military affairs, asked in reply if the gentleman could keep a secret. When assured that he could, Washington replied, "So can I."[124]

HENDRICK KIP HOUSE, FISHKILL, NEW YORK

The Kip House is associated with Baron von Steuben, the Prussian volunteer who joined Washington at Valley Forge. During the war the Kip House served for a short period of time as von Steuben's headquarters and it is more than likely that General Washington visited.

The Kip House, a one-story stone dwelling dating to 1753, has been restored and described in the literature of architectural history in New York as one of the best surviving Dutch stone farmhouses in the Hudson Valley.

PENNSYLVANIA HOSPITAL, PHILADELPHIA, PENNSYLVANIA

The original Pennsylvania Hospital, a three-story brick edifice known as Pine Building East, has remained in continuous service to the community since 1755. George Washington's diary entry for September 26, 1774, reads, "went to hospital," presumably for inspection, or perhaps to visit.[125] Pine Building East is currently utilized as an administrative and office complex of the hospital.

JACOB MORRELL HOUSE, CHATHAM, NEW JERSEY

On August 27, 1781, on his way to his destiny at Yorktown, General Washington spent the night at the two-story home of Jacob Morrell. The building is currently an Italian restaurant, the interior of which has been totally redone although the exterior remains as in colonial days.

WISTAR HOUSE, PHILADELPHIA, PENNSYLVANIA

The Wistar House is a brick townhouse currently serving as office headquarters for the Episcopal Diocese of Pennsylvania. In the colonial period, it was a private home where, according to his diary note of June 16, 1787, Washington "drank tea at Dr. Shippen's with Mrs. Livingston's party."[126]

SAINT GEORGES METHODIST CHURCH, PHILADELPHIA, PENNSYLVANIA

Saint Georges, the oldest Methodist church in continuous use in the nation, was dedicated in 1769. When George Washington faced disaster at Valley Forge, he appealed to financier Robert Morris for $50,000 to feed and clothe the army. Morris raised the money, reportedly finding strength and inspiration after an all-night prayer vigil at Saint Georges. An adjoining Methodist Historical Center contains many church relics.

SOLITUDE, THE PHILADELPHIA ZOO, PHILADELPHIA, PENNSYLVANIA

John Penn, a grandson of Pennsylvania's founder, sailed from England in 1780 with plans to inspect a large property he had inherited in West Philadelphia. Finding the area to his liking, he remained to build "Solitude," a 2½-story Adams-style stucco house surrounded by acres of landscaped lawns and exquisite gardens reflecting Penn's desire for a retreat of quiet contemplation. The somewhat reclusive gentleman stayed in Philadelphia for only a few years, but the mansion remained in the Penn family for many years before it was purchased by the City of Philadelphia. The manor house is located on the grounds of the Philadelphia Zoo that uses it as office space. The original first floor parlor and library are preserved as original. The exquisitely detailed plaster ceiling was among the first in America and Penn's original Sheraton-style bookcase is on display in the library. Except for modern improvements such as plumbing, air-conditioning, and desktop computers, John Penn would surely recognize Solitude as the gracious mansion he built over 200 years ago — a home in which he entertained George Washington on June 1, 1787. Solitude is visible from paths in the zoo.

SUN INN, FAIRFIELD, CONNECTICUT

Sun Inn, a colonial "ordinary," hosted George Washington on at least two occasions during his New England travels, the last on October 16, 1789, during the presidential tour of New England. The two-story frame house, located on the Town Green, is owned by the Town of Fairfield.

YOUNGS HOUSE, OYSTER BAY, NEW YORK

President George Washington stayed at Mr. Youngs frame farmhouse during a tour of Long Island. He described it as "private and very neat and decent."[127]

Other Sites

LACHLAN MCINTOSH HOUSE, SAVANNAH, GEORGIA

During his southern tour in 1791, President Washington spent two days in Savannah, at the time a struggling metropolis of perhaps 1500 citizens. He was entertained lavishly, however, with dinners, balls and other functions. Only one landmark of his visit to Savannah remains, the home of his patriot-in-arms, General Lachlan McIntosh. The three-story plaster and brick house, saved from destruction by Historic Savannah, Inc., is currently used as a law office.

WASHINGTON HOUSE, CAMDEN, SOUTH CAROLINA

President Washington's last day in South Carolina was spent in Camden, an important shipping center and scene of two pitched battles during the Revolutionary War. He was entertained with a festive reception and formal dinner at the home of patriot merchant James Chesnut whose imposing frame residence is privately owned and open to the public only during seasonal historical tours.

BENJAMIN ALLSTON HOUSE, GEORGETOWN, SOUTH CAROLINA

On April 30, 1791, Benjamin Allston entertained President Washington in Allston's Adams-style, two-story brick house. The house is presently owned by Carolina First Bank which maintains it as a corporate conference facility. The grounds that overlook the Sampit River are open to the public.

OGLE HALL/ALUMNI HOUSE, ANNAPOLIS, MARYLAND

Ogle Hall, built between 1735 and 1739, was the residence of the Ogle family from 1747 to 1815. Visitors to the magnificent brick colonial included George Washington and the Marquis de Lafayette. The United States Naval Academy Alumni Association utilizes the house for social functions and administrative offices.

THE ESPY HOUSE, BEDFORD, PENNSYLVANIA

In 1794, the brand-new federal government was faced with open rebellion when dissident farmers in western Pennsylvania defied the imposition of a tax on whiskey. President Washington donned his old uniform and led a federal army west. At Bedford he reviewed the army in a demonstration of arms that left no doubt as to the strength, resolve, and determination of the government. He spent the evening at the home of David Espy, then returned to Philadelphia after leaving orders for his aide, General Henry "Light Horse Harry" Lee to handle the dissidents. However, the dramatic show of force, especially Washington's presence, had been enough for the malcontents — the rebellion was quickly quashed and its leaders arrested. The Espy House is part of Bedford's National Historic District.

FORREST-MARBURY HOUSE, WASHINGTON, DC

President George Washington and other federal commissioners met at Forrest-Marbury in 1791 to determine the boundaries of the proposed District of Columbia. The building is now part of an office complex.

CORNWALLIS'S GRAVE, AUGUSTA, GEORGIA

The burial vault and headstone of Washington's dog, Cornwallis, as described in the foreword, have, unfortunately, been lost to time. If, in fact, they ever existed.

End Notes

1. Richard Brookhiser. 1996. *Founding Father: Rediscovering George Washington.* New York: The New Press. 4.

2. Harry S. Truman. 1989. *Where the Buck Stops: The Personal and Private Writings of Harry S. Truman.* Margaret Truman, ed. New York: Warner Books. 99.

3. *Bartlett's Quotations.* 1950. Boston: Little, Brown. 281.

4. Philip Barbour, ed. 1986. *The Complete Works of Captain John Smith.* Four volumes. Chapel Hill: University of North Carolina Press for The Institute of Early American History and Culture, Williamsburg. 1:144.

5. John C. Fitzpatrick, ed. 1931–1944. *The Writings of George Washington.* Thirty-nine volumes. Washington, DC: United States George Washington Bicentennial Commission. 34:405–406.

6. Daniel J. Boorstin. 1958. *The Americans; The Colonial Experience.* New York: Random House. 107.

7. Robert Dinwiddie. 1957. *The Official Records of Robert Dinwiddie in the collections of the Virginia Historical Society.* Two volumes. Robert A. Brock, ed. Virginia Historical Society. 1:59:106–107.

8. Douglas Southall Freeman. 1948. *George Washington: A Biography.* Seven volumes. Volume 7 completed by J. A. Carroll and Mary Ashworth. New York: Scribner's. 1:268.

9. William S. Baker. 1894. *Early Sketches of George Washington.* Philadelphia: J. B. Lippincott. 47–55.

10. James Thomas Flexner. 1965. *George Washington.* Four volumes. Boston: Little, Brown. 1: 56.

11. David Humphreys. 1991. *Life of General Washington.* Rosemarie Zagarri, ed. Athens: University of Georgia Press. 9.

12. Fitzpatrick. 1:67.

13. Freeman. 1:334.

14. Flexner. 92.

15. Freeman. 1:424.

16. Fitzpatrick. 29:41–46.

17. Flexner. 125.

18. Fitzpatrick. 29:47, 48.

19. *Ibid.* 2:336, 337.

20. Flexner. 1:271.

21. Louis D. Rubin, Jr. 1984. *Virginia, a Bicentennial History.* New York: W. W. Norton. 54.

22. John Ferling. 1988. *The First of Men: A Life of George Washington.* Knoxville: University of Tennessee Press. 115.

23. Freeman. 3:452, 454.

24. *Ibid.* 3:56, 57.

25. Ferling. 151.

26. W. B. Allen, ed. 1988. *George Washington, a Collection.* Indianapolis: Liberty Classics. 73.

27. Robert Leckie. 1992. *George Washington's War.* New York: HarperCollins. 266.

28. Fitzpatrick. 6:29.

29. *Ibid.* 398.

30. Freeman. 3:189.

31. Ferling. 196.

32. Leckie. 365.

33. Stanley J. Idzerda, ed. 1977. *Lafayette in the Age of the American Revolution.* Five volumes. Ithaca: Cornell University Press. 2:11.

34. Flexner. 125.

35. Fitzpatrick. 18:392.

36. Ebenezer Stanton to Thomas Noyes, Feb. 10, 1780. Manuscript on file at Morristown National Historical Park Library.

37. Fitzpatrick. 26:222–227.

38. Freeman. 5:469–478.

39. 1989. *George Washington. Journey to the Presidency. April 16–30, 1789.* Commission on the Bicentennial of the United States Constitution. Washington, DC: US Government Printing Office. Reprinted by Mount Vernon Ladies' Association, 1990. Pp. 2, 4, 5.

40. Ferling. 384.

41. Donald Jackson and Dorothy Twohig, eds. 1976–1979. *The Diaries of George Washington.* Six volumes. Charlottesville: University Press of Virginia. 6:19–25.

42. Ferling. 394.

43. Jackson. 6:107–112.

44. Felix Gilbert. 1961. *To the Farewell Address: Ideas of Early American Foreign Policy.* Princeton: Princeton University Press. 121–133.

45. Allen. 470.

46. Ferling. 507.

47. Page Smith. 1962. *John Adams, Volume II.* New York: Doubleday. 1021.

48. National Park Service Brochure. George Washington Birthplace National Monument.

49. Jack D. Warren, Jr. 2000. Historic Kenmore Web Site: *www.kenmore.org.*

50. Helen Comstock. 1965. *The 100 Most Beautiful Rooms in America.* New York: Viking Press. 106–107.

51. Fitzpatrick. 33:174–175.

52. Allen. 192.

53. Letter to Dr. James Anderson, Dec. 24, 1798, in Fitzpatrick. 34:406.

54. Cranston Jones. 1962. *Homes of the American Presidents.* New York: Bonanza Books. 2.

55. Virginia Department of Conservation and Recreation mission statement.

56. "Alexandria." *Alexandria Convention and Visitor's Association Publication,* Summer, 1997.

57. Freeman. 1:4.

58. Merrill D. Peterson. 1970. *Thomas Jefferson and the New Nation.* New York: Oxford University Press. 251.

59. Flexner. 1:60.

60. Fort Ligonier Museum mission statement.

61. Ferling. 85.

62 Henry Wiencek. 1989. *Smithsonian Guide to Historic America: Virginia and the Capital Region.* New York: Stewart, Tabori and Chang. 191–192.

63. Freeman. 3:350–353.

64. Hugh Morrison. 1952. *Early American Architecture.* New York: Oxford University Press. 347.

65. William Byrd II, from *"Historie of the Dividing Line betwixt Virginia and North Carolina"* as quoted in *Contact,* publication of the Union Camp Corporation. 4.

66. *Ibid.*

67. Freeman. 3:93–95.

68. Wilton House Museum brochure.

69. Jackson. 6:100, 101.

70. Stewart Mitchell, ed. 1947. *New Letters of Abigail Adams, 1788–1801.* Boston: Houghton Mifflin Co. Letter to her sister, Mary Cranch, December 1, 1800.

71. As recounted by Frederick Saunders, President of Friends of the Blue Bell, unpublished manuscript.

End Notes

72. Independence National Historic Park, National Park Service Brochure.

73. *Ibid.*

74. Powel House brochure.

75. *St. Peter's Church, Past and Present*, pamphlet provided by Saint Peters.

76. Jackson. 3:285.

77. Belmont Mansion mission statement.

78. Bartrams Gardens mission statement.

79. Inscription on plaque on exterior of the Old State House.

80. National Park Service. Boston National Historical Park brochure.

81. Merle Sinclair and Anabel Douglas McArthur. 1957. *They Signed for Us.* New York: Duell, Sloan and Pearce. 31.

82. Eric Foner. 1976. *Tom Paine and Revolutionary America.* New York: Oxford University Press. 139.

83. J. Robert Mendte. *General Wayne Inn.* Originally printed in the *Main Line Chronicle* from a paper read before the Anthony Wayne Historical Society. Merion, PA.

84. Kim Keister. "History lesson." *Historic Preservation Magazine.* November/December, 1993.

85. Will of Mrs. Alice Degn, as quoted in Hope Lodge Brochure.

86. Historic Yellow Springs mission statement.

87. Historical Society of Quaker Hill and Pawling mission statement.

88. John Adams. 1962. *The Adams Papers: Diary and Autobiography of John Adams.* Cambridge: The Belknap Press. 2:99.

89. National Park Service. Colonial National Historical Park Brochure.

90. Fitzpatrick. 26:29.

91. "Accounts, G. Washington with the United States, commencing June 1775, and ending June 1783, comprehending a Space of 8 years." Reproduced in facsimile with annotations by John C. Fitzpatrick. 1917. Boston: Houghton Mifflin.

92. George Athan Billias, ed. 1964. *George Washington's Generals.* New York: William Morrow. 241.

93. Allen. 267.

94. Flexner. 2:524.

95. Letter to Gunning Redford, December 25, 1783.

96. Flexner. 3:228.

97. *Ibid.* 2-228.

98. Fitzpatrick. 31:195.

99. Jackson. 5:160.

100. Richard J. Webster. 1976. *Philadelphia Preserved.* Philadelphia: Temple University Press. 1950.

101. Peterson. 251.

102. Fitzpatrick. 30:435.

103. Flexner. 3:228.

104. Jackson. 5:461.

105. William G. McLoughlin. 1978. *Rhode Island (Rhode Island Code of Laws, 1647).* New York: W. W. Norton. 31, 32.

106. Fitzpatrick. 31:93n.

107. From Diary of John Quincy Adams as provided by John Brown House.

108. Tryon Palace brochure.

109. Leckie. 622.

110. Ferling. 513.

111. Daughters of the American Revolution Museum brochure.

112. Hall of Fame for Great Americans mission statement.

113. Henry Ford Museum brochure.

114. House of Presidents brochure.

115. Museum of American Presidents mission statement.

116. Virginia Historical Society mission statement.

117. *Webster's Ninth New Collegiate Dictionary.*

118. George Washington Masonic Memorial mission statement.

119. *Charleston Post and Courier*, Dec. 15, 1999.

120. Jackson. 2:133.

121. *Ibid*. 4:9.

122. Fitzpatrick. 31:250n.

123. Marvin Kitman. 1970. *George Washington's Expense Account*. New York: Simon and Schuster. 225.

124. Helen Wilkinson Reynolds. 1965. *Dutch Houses in the Hudson Valley before 1776*. New York: Dover Publishing Company. 333.

125. Jackson. 3: 280.

126. *Ibid*. 5: 169.

127. *Ibid*. 6: 65.

Bibliography

Abbot, W. W., and Dorothy Twohig, eds. 1981. *The Papers of George Washington*. Charlottesville: University Press of Virginia.

Adams, John. 1962. *The Adams Papers: Diary and Autobiography of John Adams*. Two volumes. Cambridge: The Belknap Press.

Aikman, Lonnelle. 1983. *Rider with Destiny*. McLean, Virginia: Link Press.

Alberts, Robert C. 1975. *A Charming Field for an Encounter*. Washington, DC: National Park Service.

Alden, John Richard. 1984. *George Washington: A Biography*. Baton Rouge: Louisiana State University Press.

Allen, W. B., ed. 1988. *George Washington, a Collection*. Indianapolis: Liberty Classics.

Anderson, Fred. 1984. *A People's Army: Massachusetts Soldiers and Society in the Seven Year's War*. Chapel Hill: University of North Carolina Press.

Bahne, Charles. 1993. *Complete Guide to Boston's Freedom Trail*. Cambridge: Newtowne Publishing.

Baker, Thomas E. 1981. *Another Such Victory*. Conshohocken: Eastern National.

Baker, William S. 1890. *Itinerary of General Washington from June 15, 1775 to December 23, 1783*. Philadelphia: J. P. Lippincott Co.

_____. 1894. *Early Sketches of George Washington*. Philadelphia: J. B. Lippincott.

Baldwin, Leland D. 1939. *Whiskey Rebels*. Pittsburgh: University of Pittsburgh Press.

Barbour, Philip, ed. 1986. *The Complete Works of Captain John Smith*. Four volumes. Chapel Hill: University of North Carolina Press for The Institute of Early American History and Culture: Williamsburg.

Bartlett's Quotations. 1950. Boston: Little, Brown.

Bartram, William. 1996. *Bartram's Travels and Other Writings*. Philadelphia: Library of America.

Beesley, Charles Norbury. 1906. *St. Michael's Church*. Charleston: Walker, Evans & Cogswell Co.

Beirne, Rosamond, and John H. Scarff. 1958. *William Buckland, 1734–1774: Architect of Virginia and Maryland*. Lorton: The Board of Regents of Gunston Hall and Hammond-Harwood House Association.

Billias, George Athan. 1964. *George Washington's Generals*. New York: William Morrow.

Bliven, Bruce, Jr. 1956. *Battle for Manhattan*. New York: Henry Holt.

——————. 1972. *Under the Guns: New York 1775–1776*. New York: Harper and Row.

Bobrick, Benson. 1997. *Angel in the Whirlwind*. New York: Simon and Schuster.

Boorstin, Daniel J. 1958. *The Americans; The Colonial Experience*. New York: Random House.

Boudinot, Elias. 1968. *Journal or Historical Recollections of American Events During the Revolutionary War. Copied from His Own Original Manuscript*. Philadelphia: Arno Press, Inc.

Britt, Judith S. 1984. *Nothing More Agreeable: Music in George Washington's Family*. Mount Vernon: Mount Vernon Ladies' Association.

Brookhiser, Richard. 1996. *Founding Father: Rediscovering George Washington*. New York: The New Press.

Brown, Stuart E., Jr. 1965. *The Story of Thomas 6th Lord Fairfax*. Berryville: Chesapeake Book Company.

Brown, William Mosely. 1952. *Washington, the Mason*. Richmond: Garrett and Massie, Inc.

Buchanan, John. 1997. *The Road to Guilford Courthouse*. New York: John Wiley and Sons, Inc.

Buhler, Kathryn C. 1957. *Mount Vernon Silver*. Mount Vernon: Mount Vernon Ladies' Association.

Busch, Noel F. 1974. *Winter Quarters*. New York: Liveright.

Callahan, North. 1958. *Henry Knox, General Washington's General*. New York: Rinehart & Co.

Canby, Henry Seidel. 1946. *The Brandywine*. Atglen: Schiffer Publishing, Ltd.

Cappon, Lester J., ed. 1976. *Atlas of Early American History: The Revolutionary Era, 1760–1790*. Princeton: Princeton University Press.

Carpenters' Company. 1876. *Carpenters' Hall and its Historic Memories*. Philadelphia: Carpenters' Company.

Chambers, S. Allen. 1982. *Discovering Historic America: New England*. New York: E. P. Dutton.

Bibliography

Chidsey, Donald Barr. 1959. *Valley Forge*. New York: Crown Publishers.

_____. 1966. *The Siege of Boston*. New York: Crown Publishers.

Claghorn, Charles Eugene, III. 1999. *Crossroads of Revolution: A Guide to George Washington's Travels and Campaigns in New Jersey*. Jack D. Warren, Jr., ed. Trenton: The Society of the Cincinnati in the State of New Jersey.

Clark, Harrison. 1995. *The Life of George Washington; From Youth to Yorktown*. Two volumes. Washington, DC: Regnery Publishing, Inc.

Colby, Jean Poindexter. 1975. *Lexington and Concord: What Really Happened*. New York: Heritage House.

Colonial Williamsburg Foundation. 1973. *The Williamsburg Collection of Antique Furnishings*. New York: Holt, Rinehart and Winston.

Commager, H. S., and R. B. Morris. 1958. *The Spirit of Seventy–Six*. New York: Bobbs-Merrill.

Comstock, Helen. 1965. *The 100 Most Beautiful Rooms in America*. New York: Viking Press.

Cresap, Bernarr, and Joseph Ord. 1987. *The History of the Cresaps*. Gallatin: Cresap Society.

Cromie, Alice. 1979. *Restored Towns and Historic Districts of America*. New York: E. P. Dutton.

Crowl, Mim. 1970. "Guess who slept here." *Wilmington, Delaware Evening Journal*, March 28.

Crowfut, Florence S. Marcy. 1937. *A Guide to the History and Historic Sites of Connecticut*. New Haven: Yale University Press.

Cunliffe, Marcus. 1958. *George Washington: Man and Monument*. Boston: Little, Brown.

DaCosta, Beverly. 1957. *An American Heritage Guide: Historic Houses of America*. New York: American Heritage Press.

Davis, Burke. 1970. *The Campaign that Won America*. New York: The Dial Press.

_____. 1975. *George Washington and the American Revolution*. New York: Random House.

De Forest, Elizabeth Kellam. 1982. *The Gardens and Grounds at Mount Vernon; How George Washington Planned and Planted Them*. Mount Vernon: Mount Vernon Ladies' Association.

Dempsey, Janet. 1987. *Washington's Last Cantonment: High Time for a Peace*. Monroe: Library Research Associates, Inc.

DePauw, Linda Grant. 1975. *Founding Mothers: Women in America in the Revolutionary Era*. Madison: Demco Miller.

Detweiler, Susan Gray, and Christine Meadows. 1982. *George Washington's Chinaware*. New York: Harry N. Abrams, Inc.

Diamant, Lincoln. 1989. *Chaining the Hudson*. New York: Carol Publishing Group.

Dinwiddie, Robert. 1957. *The Official Records of Robert Dinwiddie in the collections of the Virginia Historical Society*. Two volumes. Robert A. Brock, ed. Richmond: Virginia Historical Society.

Donald, Ellen. K., and Gretchen S. Sorin. 1980. *Gadsbys Tavern Museum: Historic Furnishing Plan*. Alexandria: The City of Alexandria.

Dorr, Benjamin. 1841. *A Historical Account of Christ Church, Philadelphia*. Philadelphia: Swords, Stanford and Co.

Drake, Samuel Adams. 1900. *The Historic Mansions and Highways Around Boston*. Boston: Little, Brown.

Dreyer, Glenn D. 1989. *Connecticut's Noble Trees*. Hartford: Memoirs of the Connecticut Botanical Society.

Dull, Jonathan. 1983. *Definitive Treaty, Signed at Paris, 3rd September, 1783*. Washington, DC: National Committee for the Bicentennial of the Treaty of Paris.

Dunaway, Wayland. 1969. *History of the James River and Kanawha Company*. New York: AMS Press.

Dupuy, R. Ernest, Gay Hammerman, and Grace P. Hayes. 1977. *The American Revolution*. New York: David McKay Company, Inc.

Dwyer, William M. 1983. *The Day is Ours! An Inside View at the Battles of Trenton and Princeton, November 1776–January 1777*. New York: Viking Press.

Eastman, John. 1983. *Who Lived Where*. New York: Facts on File Publications.

Eckert, Allen. 1989. *Wilderness Empire*. Boston: Little, Brown.

Edenfield, W. Vernon, and Stacia Gregory Norman. 1992. 3rd edition. *Kenmore*. Fredericksburg: Historic Kenmore.

Faris, John T. 1917. *Old Roads Out of Philadelphia*. Philadelphia: J. P. Lippincott Company.

Farrar, Emmie Ferguson, and Emilee Hines. 1971. *Old Virginia Houses Along the Fall Line*. New York: Hastings House.

Felder, Paula S. 1981. *George Washington's Relations and Relationships in Fredericksburg, Virginia*. Fredericksburg: Historic Publications of Fredericksburg.

_____. 1993. *Handbook of Historic Fredericksburg, Virginia*. Fredericksburg: Historic Publications of Fredericksburg.

Bibliography

Ferling, John E. 1988. *The First of Men: A Life of George Washington.* Knoxville: University of Tennessee Press.

Ferris, Robert G. 1977. *The Presidents: National Survey of Historic Sites and Buildings.* Washington, DC: National Park Service.

Fischer, David Hackett. 1994. *Paul Revere's Ride.* New York: Oxford University Press.

Fitzpatrick, John C. 1931–1944. *The Writings of George Washington.* Thirty-nine volumes. Washington, DC: United States George Washington Bicentennial Commission.

_____. 1982. *The Last Will and Testament of George Washington...to which is appended the last will and testament of Martha Washington.* Mount Vernon: The Mount Vernon Ladies' Association.

Fitzpatrick, John C., ed. 1925. *The Diaries of George Washington, 1748–1799.* Boston: Houghton Mifflin Co.

Fleming, Thomas J. 1963. *Beat the Last Drum.* New York: Saint Martin's Press.

_____. 1984. *First in Their Hearts: A Biography of George Washington.* New York: Walker and Company.

_____. 1997. *Liberty!* New York: Viking Press.

Flexner, James Thomas. 1965–1972. *George Washington.* Four volumes. Boston: Little, Brown.

_____. 1974. *Washington: The Indispensable Man.* Boston: Little, Brown.

_____. 1975. *The Traitor and the Spy.* Boston: Little, Brown.

Folsom, Merrill. 1967. *More Great American Mansions.* New York: Hastings House.

Foner, Eric. 1976. *Tom Paine and Revolutionary America.* New York: Oxford University Press.

Frear, Edward K. 1984. *Anarchy Trembles.* Bedford: Gazette Publishing Company.

Freeman, Douglas Southall. 1948–1957. *George Washington: A Biography.* Seven volumes; volume seven completed by J. A. Carroll and Mary Ashworth. New York: Scribner's.

_____. 1968. *Washington: An Abridgement in One Volume.* Richard Harwell, ed. New York: Scribner's.

Freidel, Frank. 1977. *Our Country's Presidents.* Washington, DC: National Geographic Society.

Freidel, Frank, and Lonnelle Aikman. 1998. *George Washington: Man and Monument.* Washington, DC: Washington National Monument Association.

Gallagher, John J. 1995. *The Battle of Brooklyn, 1776.* New York: Sarpedon.

Gallagher, Patricia, ed. 1992. *A Smithsonian Book of the Nation's Capital.* Washington, DC: Smithsonian Institution Press.

Garrett, Wilbur E. 1987. "George Washington's Patowmack Canal." *National Geographic* 171 (June:6): 716–753.

Gilbert, David T. 1995. *A Walker's Guide to Harpers Ferry, West Virginia.* Harpers Ferry: Harpers Ferry Historic Association.

Gilbert, Felix. 1961. *To the Farewell Address: Ideas of Early American Foreign Policy.* Princeton: Princeton University Press.

Goodwin, Reverend W. A. R. 1941. *The Record of Bruton Parish Church.* Richmond: The Dietz Press.

Greiss, Constance. 1995. *Morris-Jumel Mansion: A Documentary History.* Rocky Hill: Heritage Studies, Inc.

Guiness, Desmond. 1982. *Newport Preserved: Architecture of the 18th Century.* New York: Viking Press.

Gutek, Gerald, and Virginia Gutek. 1996. *Plantations and Outdoor Museums in America's Historic South.* Columbia: University of South Carolina Press.

Haas, Irvin. 1972. *America's Historic Inns and Taverns.* New York: Arco Publishing Co., Inc.

_____. 1987. *America's Historic Battlefields.* New York: Hippocrene Books.

Hamilton, Edward. 1962. *The French and Indian Wars.* New York: Doubleday.

Handler, Oscar, and Lilian Handler. 1982. *A Restless People. Americans in Rebellion, 1770–1787.* Garden City: Anchor Press/Doubleday.

Happel, Ralph. 1984. *Chatham: The Life of a House.* Philadelphia: Eastern National Publishing.

Hastings, Lynne Dakin. 1986. *A Guidebook to Hampton National Historic Site.* Towson: Historic Hampton, Inc.

Hatch, Charles E. 1979. *Popes Creek Plantation.* Washingtons Birthplace: Wakefield Memorial Association.

_____. 1980. *Colonial Yorktown's Main Street and Military Entrenchment.* Conshohocken: Eastern Acorn Press.

Hawke, David Freeman. 1966. *The Colonial Experience.* New York: Bobbs-Merrill.

_____. 1988. *Everyday Life in Early America.* New York: Harper and Row.

Henderson, Archibald. 1972. *Washington's Southern Tour, 1791.* N. p.

Bibliography

Henriques, Peter R. 1989. "An uneven friendship: The relationship between George Washington and George Mason." *The Virginia Magazine of History and Biography* 97 (2: April): 185–204.

Henry, Joseph D. 1960. *Historic Tryon Palace: First Permanent Capital of North Carolina, New Bern, N. C.* Charlotte: Amercraft.

Hirschfeld, Fritz. 1993. *George Washington and Slavery.* Columbia: University of Missouri Press.

Hogarth, Paul. 1976. *Walking Tours of Old Philadelphia.* Barre: Barre Publishing.

Hoover, Ruth, and Blair Seitz. 1989. *Pennsylvania's Historic Places.* Intercourse: Good Books.

Howard, Blair. 1995. *The Virginia Handbook.* Edison: Hunter Publishing.

Hume, Ivor Noel. 1963. *Here Lies Virginia.* New York: Alfred A. Knopf.

_____. 1966. *Another Part of the Field.* New York: Alfred A. Knopf.

Humphreys, David. 1991. *Life of General Washington.* Rosemarie Zagarri, ed. Athens: University of Georgia Press.

Hutton, Ann Hawkes. 1983. *Portrait of Patriotism: Washington Crossing the Delaware.* Radnor: Chilton Press.

Idzerda, Stanley J., ed. 1977. *Lafayette in the Age of the American Revolution.* Five volumes. Ithaca: Cornell University Press.

Irving, Washington. 1964. *George Washington: A Biography.* New York: DaCapo Press.

Jackson, Donald, and Dorothy Twohig, eds. 1976–1979. *The Diaries of George Washington.* Six volumes. Charlottesville: University Press of Virginia.

Jackson, John W. 1992. *Valley Forge: Pinnacle of Courage.* Gettysburg: Thomas Publishing.

James, Alfred P. 1959. *The Ohio Company: Its Inner History.* Pittsburgh: University of Pittsburgh Press.

James, Mrs. Thomas Potts. 1874. *The Memorial of Thomas Potts, Jr.* Cambridge: The Potts Family.

Jensen, Merrill. 1968. *The Founding of a Nation.* New York: Oxford University Press.

Johnson, Neil. 1992. *The Battle of Lexington and Concord.* New York: Four Winds Press.

Jones, Cranston. 1962. *Homes of the American Presidents.* New York: Bonanza Books.

Julien, Carl. 1948. *Beneath So Kind a Sky.* Columbia: University of South Carolina Press.

Karaim, Reed. 1996. "The fields where my mother lives." *Preservation Magazine* (July/August): 45–51.

Keller, Allan. 1971. *Colonial America, a Compact History.* New York: Hawthorn Books.

Kern, Ellyn R. 1982. *Where the American Presidents Lived.* Indianapolis: Cottontail Publications.

Ketchum, Richard. 1957. *An American Heritage Guide: Great Historic Places.* New York: American Heritage Press.

_____. 1973. *The Winter Soldiers.* Garden City: Doubleday.

_____. 1974. *The World of George Washington.* New York: American Heritage Publishing Company.

_____. 1997. *Saratoga: Turning Point of the Revolution.* New York: Henry Holt.

Kidder, G. E. Smith. 1981. *The Architecture of the United States.* Garden City: Doubleday.

Kimball, David. 1989. *Venerable Relic: The Story of the Liberty Bell.* Conshohocken: Eastern National.

Kimball, Fiske. 1922. *Domestic Architecture of the American Colonies and of the Early Republic.* New York: Scribner's.

Kinnard, Wade Tyree. 1994. *Wilton.* Richmond: National Society of the Colonial Dames of America in the Commonwealth of Virginia.

Kitman, Marvin. 1970. *George Washington's Expense Account.* New York: Simon and Schuster.

Knight, Erastus C. 1901. *New York in the Revolution.* Albany: Oliver A. Quayle.

Kochman, Rachel. 1990. *Presidents: Birthplaces, Homes and Burial Sites.* Osage: Osage Publications.

Kopperman, Paul E. 1977. *Braddock at the Monongahela.* Pittsburgh: University of Pittsburgh Press.

Kruh, Louis, and David Kruh. 1992. *Presidential Landmarks.* New York: Hippocrene Books.

Law, Charles Cecil. 1985. *Mount Vernon: A Handbook.* Mount Vernon: The Mount Vernon Ladies' Association.

Lawliss, Chuck. 1996. *The Early American Source Book.* New York: Crown Trade Paperbacks.

Lebovich, William L. 1984. *America's City Halls.* Washington, DC: The Preservation Press.

Leckie, Robert. 1992. *George Washington's War.* New York: HarperCollins.

Bibliography

Lesesne, Thomas Petigru. 1939. *Landmarks of Charleston*. Richmond: Garrett and Massie, Inc.

Levin, Phyllis Lee. 1970. *Great Historic Houses of America*. New York: Coward-McCann.

Lewis, John, with Dan Lacy. 1975. *The Birth of America*. New York: Grosset and Dunlap.

Lewis, Thomas A. 1993. *For King and Country: The Maturing of George Washington, 1748– 1760*. New York: HarperCollins.

Lindsley, James Elliott. 1874. *A Certain Splendid House*. Morristown: Washington Association of New Jersey.

Lipscomb, Terry W. 1993. *South Carolina in 1791: George Washington's Southern Tour*. Columbia: South Carolina Department of Archives and History.

Lorant, Stefan. 1964. *Pittsburgh, the Story of an American City*. New York: Doubleday.

Lord, Suzanne. 1977. *American Traveler's Treaasury: A Guide to the Nation's Heirlooms*. New York: William Morrow.

Lord, Priscilla Sawyer, and Virginia Clegg Gamage. 1972. *Marblehead: The Spirit of '76 Lives Here*. Philadelphia: Chilton Book Company.

MacDonald, William. 1987. *George Washington: A Brief Biography*. Mount Vernon: Mount Vernon Ladies' Association.

MacNiece, Jill. 1990. *A Guide to National Monuments and Historic Sites*. New York: Prentice-Hall.

Manders, Eric I. 1978. *The Battle of Long Island*. Philadelphia: Philip Freneau Press.

Martin, Lawrence, ed. 1932. *The George Washington Atlas*. Washington, DC: Library of Congress.

Martin, Joseph Plumb. 1962. *Private Yankee Doodle, A Narration of Some of the Adventures, Dangers and Sufferings of a Revolutionary Soldier*. George F. Scheer, ed. New York: Little, Brown.

Mayer, Henry. 1986. *A Son of Thunder: Patrick Henry*. New York: Franklin Watts.

McGuire, Thomas J. 1994. *The Surprise of Germantown*. Philadelphia: Cliveden of the National Trust.

McLoughlin, William G. 1978. *Rhode Island (Rhode Island Code of Laws, 1647)*. New York: W. W. Norton.

McPhillips, Martin. 1985. *The Battle of Trenton*. Morristown: Silver Burdett Co.

Meyers, Nancy D., and Christopher Benbow. 1995. *Cabins, Cottages and Mansions: Homes of Presidents of the United States.* Gettysburg: Thomas Publications.

Miers, Earl Schenck. 1971. *Crossroads of Freedom.* New Brunswick: Rutgers University Press.

Mintz, Max M. 1991. *The Generals of Saratoga.* New Haven: Yale University Press.

Mitchell, Stewart, ed. 1947. *New Letters of Abigail Adams.* Boston: Houghton Mifflin.

Montgomery, Thomas, ed. 1916. *Frontier Forts of Pennsylvania.* Two volumes. Harrisburg: William Stanley Ray, State Printer.

Morgan, Edmund Sears. 1981. *The Genius of George Washington.* New York: W. W. Norton.

Morgan, John G. 1975. *A Point in History: The Battle of Point Pleasant.* Charleston: *Charleston Gazette.* (Reprint of a series of articles that appeared in the *Charleston Gazette* in 1974.)

Morrissey, Brendan. 1994. *Boston 1775.* Mechanicsburg: Stackpole Books.

Morrison, Hugh. 1952. *Early American Architecture.* New York: Oxford University Press.

Morton, Richard L. 1960. *Colonial Virginia.* Two volumes. Chapel Hill: University of North Carolina Press.

Moss, Roger W. 1998. *Historic Houses of Philadelphia: A tour of the Region's Museum Homes.* Philadelphia: University of Pennsylvania Press.

Mozier, Jeanne. 1998. *Way Out in West Virginia.* Berkeley Springs: Travel Berkeley Springs, Inc.

Muir, Dorothy Troth. 1946. *Presence of a Lady.* Mount Vernon: Mount Vernon Ladies' Association.

Munson, James D. 1986. *Col. John Carlyle, Gent.* Fairfax Station: Northern Virginia Regional Park Authority.

Murfin, James V. 1989. *From the Riot and Tumult.* Harpers Ferry: Harpers Ferry Historic Association.

Murtagh, William J., [Keeper of the National Register]. *National Register of Historic Places.* Washington, DC: US Department of the Interior.

Muse, Vance. 1989. *Smithsonian Guide to Historic America.* New York: Stewart, Tabori and Chang.

National Park Service. 1962. *A Guide to Independence National Historical Park.* Washington, DC: National Park Service.

_____. 1990. *Congress Hall, Capitol of the United States, 1790–1800.* Washington, DC: National Park Service.

Bibliography

National Society of the Sons of the American Revolution. 1914. *Journey of General George Washington from Philadelphia to Cambridge, June 23–July 3, 1775*. Louisville: National Society of the Sons of the American Revolution.

Newton, Arvin. 1963. *Longfellow: His Life and Work*. Boston: Little, Brown.

Nicholson, Arnold. 1965. *American Houses in History*. New York: Viking Press.

Norton, Mary Beth. 1980. *Liberty's Daughters: The Revolutionary Experience of American Women, 1750–1780*. Boston: Little, Brown.

Nutting, Wallace. 1935. *Virginia Beautiful*. Garden City: Garden City Publishing Company.

O'Meara, Walter. 1975. *Guns at the Forks*. New York: Prentice-Hall.

O'Neal, William B. 1968. *Architecture in Virginia*. New York: Walker and Company.

Peterson, Merrill D. 1970. *Thomas Jefferson and the New Nation*. New York: Oxford University Press.

Platt, John David Ronalds. 1973. *The City Tavern: Independence National Historical Park*. Denver: National Park Service.

Pollamine, Barbara. 1993. *Great and Capitol Changes: An Account of the Valley Forge Encampment*. Gettysburg: Thomas Publishing.

Powell, Allen. 1989. *Fort Cumberland*. Parsons: McClain Printing Co.

Powell, J. M. 1993. *Bring Out Your Dead*. Philadelphia: University of Pennsylvania Press.

Radoff, Morris L. 1972. *The State House at Annapolis*. Annapolis: Archives, Maryland Hall of Records.

Randall, William Sterne. 1997. *George Washington: A Life*. New York: Henry Holt.

Reed, John F. 1965. *Campaign to Valley Forge*. Philadelphia: University of Pennsylvania Press.

Reeds, Chester Albert. 1927. *Natural Bridge of Virginia and its Environs*. Lynchburg: Brown-Morrison Co., Inc.

Reynolds, Helen Wilkinson. 1965. *Dutch Houses in the Hudson Valley before 1776*. New York: Dover Publishing Company.

Riley, Edward M. 1990. *Starting America: The Story of Independence Hall*. Gettysburg: Thomas Publications.

Roberts, Allen E. 1976. *George Washington: Master Mason*. Richmond: McCoy Publishing Company.

Roberts, Bruce. 1990. *Plantation Homes of the James River*. Chapel Hill: University of North Carolina Press.

Roberts, Bruce, with text by Frances Griffin. 1986. *Old Salem in Pictures.* Charlotte: McNally and Loftin.

Rossiter, Clinton. 1985. "Our two greatest presidents." *A Sense of History.* New York: American Heritage Press, Inc.

Rouse, Parke, Jr., and Susan T. Burtch. 1980. *Berkeley Plantation and Hundred.* Williamsburg: Williamsburg Publishing Company.

Rubin, Louis D., Jr. 1984. *Virginia, a Bicentennial History.* New York: W. W. Norton.

Rutland, Robert Allen. 1961. *Reluctant Statesman.* Williamsburg: Colonial Willliamsburg Foundation.

Ruttenber, E. M., and L. H. Clark. 1881. *History of Orange County, New York 1683–1881.* Newburgh: Journal Printing House and Book-binding.

St. Amand, Sue. 1996. *St. John's: A Pictorial History.* Richmond: St. John's.

Sale, Edith Tunis. 1927. *Interiors of Virginia Houses of Colonial Times.* Richmond: William Byrd Press.

Seitz, Ruth Hoover, and Blair Seitz. 1989. *Pennsylvania's Historic Places.* Intercourse: Good Books.

Sibert, Jacquelyn S., managing ed. 1993. *The Presidents.* Funk and Wagnall's Special Edition. Indianapolis: Curtis Publishing.

Simpson, Bland. 1990. *The Great Dismal.* Chapel Hill: University of North Carolina Press.

Simpson, Pamela. 1982. *So Beautiful an Arch: Images of the Natural Bridge, 1787–1890.* Lexington: Washington and Lee Press.

Sinclair, Merle, and Anabel Douglas McArthur. 1957. *They Signed for Us.* New York: Duell, Sloan and Pearce.

Sipes, C. Hale. 1971. *Fort Ligonier and its Times.* New York: Arno Press.

Smith, Barbara Clark. 1998. *Boston and the American Revolution.* Washington, DC: National Park Service.

Smith, Jane Oldershansan. 1980. *One Day Trips through History.* McLean: EPM Publications.

Smith, Page. 1962. *John Adams.* Two volumes. New York: Doubleday.

Smith, Rex Alan. 1985. *The Carving of Mount Rushmore.* New York: Abbeville Press.

Smith, Richard Norton. 1993. *Patriarch: George Washington and the New American Nation.* Boston: Houghton Mifflin.

Smith, William Francis, and T. Michael Miller. 1989. *A Seaport Saga: Portrait of Old Alexandria, Virginia.* Norfolk/Virginia Beach: The Donning Company.

Bibliography

Spencer, Eve. 1993. *A Flag for Our Country*. Austin: Raintree Steck-Vaughan.

Stein, Jeff. 1997. "George Washington's sister slept here." *Historic Traveler* (May): 44–49.

Stillman, Gordon P. 1996. *100 Years in New York, the Story of the First Century of the National Society of Colonial Dames in the State of New York*. New York: National Society of Colonial Dames.

Stokesbury, James L. 1991. *A Short History of the American Revolution*. New York: William Morrow.

Stoney, Samuel Gaillard. 1964. *Plantations of the Carolina Low Country*. Charleston: Carolina Art Association.

Stotz, Charles Morse. 1970. *The Model of Fort Pitt*. Pittsburgh: The Allegheny Conference on Community Development.

Terkel, Susan Neiburg. 1993. *Colonial American Medicine*. New York: Franklin Watts.

Thane, Elswyth. 1963. *Potomac Squire*. New York: Duell, Sloan and Pearce.

_____. 1968. *Mount Vernon Family*. New York: Crowell-Collier Press.

Torres-Reyes, Ricardo. 1971. *1779–80 Encampment: A Study of Medical Services*. Washington, DC: National Park Service.

Truman, Harry S. 1989. *Where the Buck Stops: The Personal and Private Writings of Harry S. Truman*. Margaret Truman, ed. New York: Warner Books.

United States Capitol Historical Society. 1991. *We, the People: The Story of the United States Capitol*. Washington, DC: United States Capitol Historical Society.

Vila, Bob. 1993. *Guide to Historic Homes of the South*. New York: William Morrow.

Wall, Charles Cecil. 1988. *George Washington, Citizen-Soldier*. Mount Vernon: Mount Vernon Ladies' Association.

Wallace, Paul A. W. 1962. "Historic Hope Lodge." *Pennsylvania Magazine of History and Biography* 86 (April): 115–142.

Waller, George. 1966. *Saratoga, Saga of an Impious Era*. Englewood Cliffs: Prentice-Hall.

Warren, Jack D., Jr. 1999. "The childhood of George Washington." *Northern Neck of Virginia Historical Magazine* (December): 5785–5809.

_____. 2000. *The Presidency of George Washington*. Mount Vernon: The Mount Vernon Ladies' Association.

Washington, George. 1893. *Journal of Colonel George Washington commanding a detachment of Virginia Troops Sent by Robert Dinwiddie, Lieutenant-Governor of Virginia.* Edited, with notes by J. M. Toner, MD. Albany: Joel Munsell's Sons.

_____. 1925. *The Diaries of George Washington.* Four volumes. New York: Houghton Mifflin.

Webster, Richard J. 1976. *Philadelphia Preserved.* Philadelphia: Temple University Press.

Weigley, Russell F., ed. 1982. *Philadelphia, a 300-year History.* New York: W. W. Norton.

Whiffen, Marcus. 1984. *The Eighteenth-Century Houses of Williamsburg: A Study of Architecture and Building in the Colonial Capital of Virginia.* Williamsburg: Williamsburg Architectural Studies.

White House Historical Association. 1991. *The White House: An Historic Guide.* Washington, DC: The White House Historical Society.

Wickwire, Franklin, and Mary Wickwire. 1970. *Cornwallis: The American Adventure.* Boston: Houghton-Mifflin.

Wiencek, Henry. 1989. *Smithsonian Guide to Historic America: Virginia and the Capital Region.* New York: Stewart, Tabori and Chang.

Wiener, Frederick Bernays. 1991. "Washington and his mother." *American History Illustrated* 26 (July/August): 44–47.

Williams, Dorothy Hunt. 1975. *Historic Virginia Gardens: Preservations by the Garden Club of Virginia.* Charlottesville: University of Virginia Press.

Wills, Garry. 1984. *Cincinnatus: George Washington and the Enlightenment.* New York: Doubleday.

_____. 1994. *Certain Trumpets.* New York: Simon and Schuster.

Wood, W. J. 1990. *Battles of the Revolutionary War, 1775–1781.* Chapel Hill: Algonquin Books.

Wright, Louis B. 1957. *The Cultural Life of the American Colonies.* New York: Harper and Row.

Yetter, George Humphrey. 1988. *Williamsburg Before and After: The Rebirth of Virginia's Colonial Capital.* Williamsburg: Colonial Williamsburg Foundation Press.

Young, Joanne B. 1981. *Shirley Plantation: A Personal Adventure for Ten Generations.* Charles City: Shirley Plantation.

Index

433

Index